Studies in Economic Reform and Social Justice

LAND-VALUE TAXATION AROUND THE WORLD

Third Edition

T0340132

Also by Robert V. Andelson:

Imputed Rights
Critics of Henry George (ed.)
Commons Without Tragedy (ed.)
From Wasteland to Promised Land (with J. M. Dawsey)
Henry George and the Reconstruction of Capitalism
Land-Value Taxation Around the World, 2d. edition (ed.)

Studies in Economic Reform and Social Justice

LAND-VALUE

TAXATION
AROUND
THE WORLD

Third Edition

REPORTS ON CURRENT AND HISTORICAL
EFFORTS TO APPLY THE PRINCIPLE OF
COLLECTING THE COMMUNITY-CREATED VALUE
OF LAND FOR COMMUNITY BENEFIT

Edited by
Robert V. Andelson

Foreword by
Warren J. Samuels

Blackwell Publishers, Inc.
350 Main Street
Malden, MA 02148 USA

Blackwell Publishers, Ltd.
108 Cowley Road
Oxford OX4 1JF
United Kingdom

Library of Congress Cataloging-in-Publication Data

Land-value taxation around the world / edited by Robert V.
Andelson; foreword by Warren J. Samuels.—3rd ed.
        p. cm.
    "Reports on current and historical efforts to apply the principle
of collecting the community-created value of land for community
benefit."
    Includes bibliographical references and index.
    ISBN 0-631-22613-3 (case : alk. paper) — ISBN 0-631-22614-1
(pbk. : alk. paper)
    1. Land value taxation. I. Andelson, Robert V., 1931–

HJ4165 .L365 2000
336.22—dc21

                                                        00-051880

ISBN 0-631-22613-3
ISBN 0-631-22614-1 (P)
ISSN 0002-9246

To Barbara Sobrielo and Jose Mernane
devoted fellow laborers in the vineyard

Contents

Foreword—*Warren J. Samuels* ix

Preface and Acknowledgements—*Robert V. Andelson* xiii

Introduction—*Robert V. Andelson* xix

PART ONE	**THE ANCIENT AND MEDIEVAL WORLD**	

Chapter 1   Mesopotamia and Classical Antiquity—*Michael Hudson* 3

Chapter 2   European Feudalism from its Emergence through Its Decline—*Kenneth Jupp* 27

PART TWO	**THE AMERICAS**	

Chapter 3   Argentina—*Fernando Scornik Gerstein* 49

Chapter 4   Canada—*Garry B. Nixon* 65

Chapter 5   Chile—*John Strasma* 85

Chapter 6   Colombia—*Fernanda Furtado* 97

Chapter 7   Jamaica and Other Caribbean States— *John M. Copes and Walter Rybeck* 111

Chapter 8   Mexico—*Manuel Perló Cohen* 129

Chapter 9   The United States—*Walter Rybeck* 137

PART THREE	**EUROPE**	

Chapter 10   Denmark—*Ole Lefmann and Karsten K. Larsen* 185

Chapter 11   Estonia—*Aivar Tomson* 205

Chapter 12   Finland—*Pekka Virtanen* 211

Chapter 13   Germany—*Jürgen G. Backhaus* 221

Chapter 14   Great Britain—*Owen Connellan and Nathaniel Lichfield* 239

Chapter 15   Hungary—*Balázs Kónya* 259

PART FOUR   AFRICA

Chapter 16   Nations of Eastern Africa—*Rexford A. Ahene* 273
Chapter 17   Republic of South Africa—
                          Godfrey R. A. Dunkley 299

PART FIVE   ASIA

Chapter 18   Abu Dhabi—*Robert V. Andelson* 315
Chapter 19   Republic of China (Taiwan)—*Alven H. S. Lam*. . . . 327
Chapter 20   Hong Kong and Singapore—*Sock-Yong Phang* . . . 337
Chapter 21   Japan—*Y. Yamasaki and Robert V. Andelson* 353
Chapter 22   Kiao-chau—*V. G. Peterson and Tseng Hsiao* 365
Chapter 23   Republic of Korea (South Korea)—*Tai-Il Lee*. 371
Chapter 24   Papua New Guinea—*H. J. Manning and
                          Ciaran O'Faircheallaigh* 385

PART SIX   THE ANTIPODES

Chapter 25   Australia—*Geoffrey A. Forster*. 399
Chapter 26   New Zealand—*Robert D. Keall* 417

Contributors 439
Index 451

Foreword

THE TREATMENT OF the institution of land ownership is one of the underground chapters in the history of economic thought. The theory of rent—rent in the Ricardian sense—is much more conspicuous but is by no means fully comprehended. The theory and practice of land taxation, especially of unimproved land, is extremely controversial, yet derives from one of the oldest established theories in economics, that of Ricardian rent.

The ownership of land has historically conveyed not only social and economic power but also political power; the term "landlords" is instructive. Government has often, albeit to varying degrees and in varying ways, been controlled by the owners of real property. Such has been an institutional remnant of feudal and post-feudal societies in Europe and comparably in other continents. The distribution of property, largely in the form of land, with which the modern economy commenced, the lasting vestige of earlier social forms, has channeled the organization, operation and performance of capitalist and other modern economic systems. And, not surprisingly, the control of government by landed interests and classes has influenced not only the form which modern law—e.g., business law—has taken but also taxation, especially of land. Moreover, inasmuch as land has been so economically, socially and politically important, land ownership has a transcendental if not sacral status in the minds of both landowning and non-landowning people, one frequent consequence of which is common attitudes adverse to land taxation.

David Ricardo and others developed the theory of rent in the early nineteenth century. For some time before, it had been understood by sophisticated writers that the high price/rent of land does not cause the high price of food, but the high price of food, driven by growing population and the correlative demand for food, generated the high price/rent of land. Ricardo's theory helped ground and systematize that understanding.

For Ricardo, first, rent was the return to the owner of a factor of production, land, in permanent inelastic supply; changes in the price of land generally could not increase the aggregate supply of land, and each piece of land was nonreproducible.

Second, Ricardo argued that, as between lands of differential fertility and differential location, the latter in relation to markets, rent is differential in amount. The owners of more fertile land and better situated land receive higher rent per unit of land. Ricardo explicated the phenomenon of differential fertility in terms of increasing costs, along both intensive and extensive margins. As increasing demand for food, driven by population growth, led to increasing food prices and resort to more costly levels of production on both individual pieces of land (intensive margin) and less fertile pieces of land (extensive margin), the resulting rent to levels of production and pieces of land undertaken at lower unit cost, would both increase and be differential in amounts.

Technically speaking, therefore, rent in the Ricardian sense was the sum of the supramarginal returns. The questions then were, what drove the level of rent and who would get it, and why/how.

The level of rent (and thereby its capitalization in the value of land) was driven by the demand for food, which was in turn driven by the growth of population, i.e., of society. In other words, given the return to the landowners' investment in clearing and farming the land, which took the form of implicit interest and profit, rent was due to a source having nothing directly to do with the efforts of the landowners. Rent was, in this context, an unearned increment. Furthermore, rent was, generally speaking, a residual derivative of levels of production under increasing costs of production on both intensive and extensive margins. This being the case, how the rent was distributed would have no effect on the level of rent.

The foregoing has to do with Ricardian rent, the sum of the supramarginal returns. Rent as paid to landowners includes, it should be clear, Ricardian rent plus interest and profit on investment and enterprise.

Ricardian rent as the sum of supramarginal returns can be distributed in different ways as a matter of custom and institutions, including law. Different systems of land tenure, renters' rights, tithes, feudal dues, and taxation serve to distribute Ricardian rent to different established claimants. Actual payments designated "rent" are rarely, if ever, equal to and exhaustive of Ricardian rent, even aside from implicit interest and profit.

The understandings (1) that Ricardian rent was residual, and therefore taxation would have minimal if any disincentive effects, and (2) that Ricardian rent was generated by the growth of society, and therefore not directly related to the efforts and enterprise of landowners, led to the conclusion that such rent was both unearned and a proper subject of taxation. The conclusion applied in principle to both unimproved land and to the land component of improved land. This is the conclusion derived from Ricardo's theory of rent and advanced by Henry George as the so-called "single tax."

Needless to say, the attempt to levy or to increase any tax is unpopular with the owners of the object of taxation. This has been particularly and acutely the case with landowners confronted with Georgist efforts to tax land values (the capitalization of rent). Such taxation was seen to be an attack on the institution of private property in general and landed property in particular. It was seen by some as a "taking" of the productivity of the land belonging to the landowner. It was construed by others as a challenge to the institution of land markets understood as a lottery, a mode of betting on the results of future population growth.

The history of economic thought has been to no small degree a history of struggle over the institutional bases of the distributions of income and wealth. The history of the reception and treatment of Ricardian and Georgist ideas on rent and the taxation of land values has been a part of these developments. Economists, on the one hand seeking a safe and secure status in the pantheon of intellectual disciplines, and on the other, notably in England, often employed by universities and worshipping in churches which received no small amount of their income in the form of rent (and tithes), often if not typically reacted with disdain if not horror to Georgist tax-policy proposals. Yet the aforementioned conclusion as to the suitability of land taxation follows as a matter of logic from a well-established corpus of theory, one which is not only well-established but has no substantial competitor in the explication of the origin and nature of rent.

Establishing the suitability of land values for taxation nonetheless requires an additional normative premise if such taxation is to be pursued. Thomas Robert Malthus, another original theorist of rent, added to the theory of rent a premise postulating the desirability of maintaining a ruling landed aristocracy and on that basis supported the Corn Laws which restricted the importation of food into England, thereby keeping rents high. Ricardo himself interpreted the Corn Laws from the perspective of the interests of workers and employers, thereby using the theory of rent to oppose the Corn Laws. Taxing land values on the basis of the theory of rent rejects all claims for protecting rental interests against the ideas that rent is due to the growth of society and is a residual largely immune from disincentive effect, and affirms the impropriety of unearned income while seeking to minimize the disincentive effects of taxes on earned income. The Ricardo-George analysis is compelling: the increase in land values *is* due to the growth of society and *is* a fit object for taxation.

The taxation of land value has been undertaken around the world on both Georgist and non-Georgist grounds. At the very least, land is a ready target of taxation, if only because it is immobile and taxation can be correlated with land registry.

This work edited by Robert V. Andelson does several things: It surveys the systems of land-value taxation around the world. It indicates the enormous variety of land-value tax systems to be found. And it indicates the variety of problems which emerge in instrumenting and administering such taxes, problems which are due to (1) the nature of the tax, (2) the institutions and cultures in which the tax is levied, and (3) the level of economic growth of the economy in which it is levied. In all cases, the equity and financial case for land-value taxation must be juxtaposed to other considerations, however compelling the logic of Ricardian rent theory, and it is very compelling indeed.

This book is heartily recommended for anyone interested in understanding the present-day status of land-value taxation.

Warren J. Samuels
East Lansing, Michigan
November 1997

Preface and Acknowledgements to the Third Edition

THIS BOOK IS the maiden volume of the American Journal of Economics and Sociology Monograph Series. As such, it represents the first fruit of a long-range venture undertaken in cooperation with Blackwell Publishers, a venture that is anticipated to become a source of credit to both parties. Needless to say, I find it immensely gratifying that such a rare distinction has been accorded a book of which it is my privilege to be editor.

Readers will no doubt wonder why a third edition of *Land-Value Taxation Around the World* was brought out only three years after the second—especially in view of the forty-two year interval before the second edition followed the first. Several reasons entered into this decision:

1. New research (undertaken by scholars sponsored by the Lincoln Institute of Land Policy) convinced me that Colombia, Mexico, and Great Britain, three countries that had not been covered in the second edition, had experienced significant land-value taxation through "betterment levies" of one sort or another, i.e., efforts to recoup values created by public works or public structuring of development opportunities. I had deliberately omitted Great Britain from the second edition because the chapter devoted to it in the first edition was primarily an account, not of actual experience with land-value taxation, but of unsuccessful efforts to get it implemented. While that chapter did touch on some betterment levies instituted by the Labour Government in the late 1940s and early 1950s, they were of brief duration, and did not strike me as being very relevant. Since the time of that account, Britain's experience with such levies has been quite extensive, and is worth recording as a cautionary tale, if nothing more. The authors of the new studies to which I have alluded have adapted them for inclusion in the present work.

2. In the second edition, Estonia and Nicaragua were dealt with, not in individual chapters, but as passages in the Introduction. This

time, the Estonian situation had developed to a point where I considered it deserving of a short chapter.

The case of Nicaragua is quite different. The agricultural land tax enacted there in June of 1996 was repealed in March of 1999 by an almost unanimous vote of the National Assembly, with the major factions in agreement that it placed too great a burden on small farmers. This conclusion is quite likely accurate, since, even though extremely modest in the aggregate, the tax bore heavily on owners of useable but less desirable acreage that happened to be located in relatively fertile and settled regions. In point of fact, it was a land tax but not a land value tax except in the broadest sense of the term, because, instead of being based on the actual market value per acre of each holding, it was based upon the division of the country unto zones within which all tillable acreage was arbitrarily assumed to be of the same value. A Managua resident, Paul A. Martin, comments that the repeal came at a time when the government was on the upswing with new taxes on productive activities as dictated by the IMF-World Bank restructuring plan, imposed as a condition for further debt maintenance. In a recent letter to me, he writes: "Like many poor countries today, Nicaragua largely ignores rents as a public revenue source. A very small portion of land rent is collected in urban property tax. The Free Trade Zone laws create artificial tax-free conditions which allow private landowners to collect land rent at a maximum, while wages are paid at the competitive minimum."

3. When the second edition appeared, it contained news that legislation providing for land-value taxation in Greater Cape Town had been adopted and would be implemented beginning in July of 1998. This exercise of local option has since been abandoned in the face of a uniform system to be imposed by the Central Government upon the whole nation, a system that will also force the abandonment of land-value taxation in the majority of South African cities, where it has been operating successfully for many decades

It should not be assumed that the present edition differs from the second one only in terms of the items enumerated above. Actually, but two chapters (one of them devoted to ancient times) have escaped revision altogether, and many, including the editor's

Introduction, have been updated and/or otherwise altered quite substantially.

On February 28, 1998, an unsigned article, datelined Tallinn, appeared in *The Economist*. It spoke slightingly of Henry George, the ideological godfather of modern land-value taxation, as a "nineteenth century economic crank," and "probably the only tax theorist in history whose beliefs have become an object of cult devotion." It also stated that "other countries are following Estonia down the Georgist path. Slovenia has a land tax already, and Latvia and the Czech Republic are both planning one." But the anonymous author hastened to add that none of the countries mentioned "are embracing George with unequivocal enthusiasm."

Wishing to make this book as complete as possible (although it does not pretend to be exhaustive), I asked Walt Rybeck, a veteran investigative journalist, to follow up the claims about Slovenia, Latvia, and the Czech Republic. The minister of finance of Slovenia, which supposedly already had adopted a land tax, told him that he saw no prospect there for either a pure or a modified one for the foreseeable future. Latvian officials reported that in their country the debate is about how, not whether, to tax buildings. The situation in the Czech Republic was less clear, but, judging from what the director of the property tax department of the Finance Ministry told Rybeck, not even a two-rate property tax was being considered there. So much for the factual accuracy of *The Economist*'s correspondent, who presumed to belittle the great American thinker and his following! One might have expected better of such a highly regarded journal.

As I have said, this book does not pretend to be exhaustive. Had it been possible to make it so, the result would have so overloaded it with encyclopedic trivia as to interfere with its usefulness for the purpose for which it was intended. For example, in 1974, George E. Lent published an article[1] listing Greece and Iraq among the nations with special taxes on unimproved land, and Ecuador, Paraguay, Peru, Senegal, Switzerland, and Turkey among the nations with higher urban tax rates on land than on improvements. While in the context of his study it was entirely appropriate for Lent to list these nations, I did not include them in this survey because I was either unable to obtain relevant current information about them, or had reason to suspect that the magnitudes involved were too insignificant to warrant the effort that might have been required to get it.

* * *

My introduction to the second edition included the following passage, which is equally applicable here:

> I have been painfully conscious of the fact that editorial responsibility has . . . fallen solely upon me, whereas the [first] edition had the benefit of a Board of Editors consisting of four of the most eminent authorities in the field (Harry Gunnison Brown, Harold S. Buttenheim, Philip H. Cornick, and Glenn E. Hoover), as well as of the inestimable services of the Robert Schalkenbach Foundation's late executive secretary, V. G. Peterson (Violetta G. Graham). It is my hope that readers will bear this fact in mind as they encounter, as I am sure they will, defects that have escaped my notice.
>
> More than a score of authors have contributed to this volume. As might therefore be expected, its chapters exhibit considerable variety. Some concentrate narrowly upon the bare facts of property tax policy and legislation, often with statistics but little evaluative comment. Others delve into historical background, illuminate relevant cultural and political factors, and express personal opinions with abandon. To the extent that I have felt it necessary, I have not hesitated to invoke my editorial prerogative to enforce a measure of consistency as to style and content. Yet, insofar as possible in my judgment, I have allowed each author to approach his topic in his own way.
>
> As in the [first] edition, the work of all contributors has been compensated only by the satisfaction derived from involvement in a worthy project. To quote what was stated there, "they deserve the gratitude of all who believe in the just distribution of man's heritage."

It may be noted that toward the end of the first paragraph of the above extract, I alluded to my expectation that readers would encounter errors that had escaped my notice. Pat Aller and Walt Rybeck were among those who not only encountered but also directed my attention to such errors, some of which were corrected in later printings and others in this later edition. I thank them. It also gives me pleasure to acknowledge help from Michael

Hudson, Fred Harrison, Cathleen Johnson, Bryan Kavanagh, Paul Martin, Erika McEntarfer, and Walt Rybeck, who provided invaluable research assistance; from Martim Smolka, Pekka Virtanen, and Joan Youngman, who put me in touch with new contributors; from Alan Blackwood, Beverly Childress, Ken Easterday, Rodney Jordan, Tom Petee, and Roy Washburn, who compensated for the primitive level of my computer expertise; from Polly Cleveland, who oversaw the transcription of corrections and additions to the master disk, as well as the updating of the Index; and to Nic Tideman, who provided unfailing support whenever needed out of his discretionary fund as president of the Robert Schalkenbach Foundation. I wish to express my gratitude for the exemplary patience and understanding of the series editor, Larry Moss. Finally, to the many others whose names should doubtless be included in this roster but were inadvertently omitted, I offer both sincere thanks and abject apologies.

R.V.A.
Auburn, Alabama
May, 2000

Note

1. George E. Lent, "The Urban Property Tax in Developing Countries," *Finanzarchiv* 33 (1974), pp. 70–72.

Introduction

BY ROBERT V. ANDELSON, EDITOR

I

Scope and Definitions

THE PREFACE TO the first edition of *Land-Value Taxation Around the World* (1955) opened with a descriptive statement that was repeated in the Introduction to the second (1997), and is equally applicable here: "*This book deals with the efforts made by various peoples to take for public purposes their geographically and socially produced land values.*"

Taking land values for public purposes is an object of which the American political economist and social philosopher, Henry George (1839–1897), is universally acknowledged to have been the most famous, eloquent, and thoroughgoing exponent. In his best-known work, *Progress and Poverty* (1879), and in numerous other books, articles, and speeches, he called for the public capture of nearly all land value (i.e., economic rent), and the proportionate abolition of taxes on the products of private labor and capital.

Advocates of land-value taxation range from those at one extreme, who view it as the sovereign path to social justice, to those at the other, who see it merely as one of several useful fiscal tools to garner local revenue and/or stimulate desirable development. Between these two extremes—whole-hog "single-taxers" and limited land-value taxers—may be located a diverse spectrum of opinion including those who regard themselves as Georgist in a general sense, but who do not view "singleness" as precluding certain other levies such as users' charges to supplement the public appropriation of land values. However, even "Georgists of the looser observance" would agree that land-value taxes should be set-off against taxes on the rewards of productive effort instead of being simply piled on top of them. Any land-value taxer unwilling to accept that proviso would not be a Georgist but, at most, a "fellow-traveler."

Land-value taxation is understood in all three editions to encompass more than a literal construction of the term would indicate, for the public capture of "geographically and socially produced land values" sometimes takes other forms with respect to method. Since "land" in economics is a synonym for Nature, severance taxes[1] on extractive resources may (under certain circumstances and either singly or in combination) be an appropriate mechanism for such capture. Where land is publicly held, its rent may flow directly into public coffers without passing in the form of taxes through the hands of private owners. Some attention will be paid to both of these alternative approaches in this volume, but the primary focus will be on land-value taxation in the narrower sense, i.e., on site-value rating.

Severance taxes of one type or another are so widespread that anything like a full survey of them would enlarge this work unduly. They are, however, treated to some extent in several chapters, most notably with respect to oil in the chapter on Abu Dhabi, with respect to timber in the chapter on Finland, and with respect to a variety of natural resources in the chapter on Canada.

Public ownership of land in an overall framework of capitalism is a distinctive characteristic of Hong Kong and Singapore, and leasehold rent a major segment of their public revenue. This is described in detail in the chapter by Professor Phang.

Obviously, some economic rent is appropriated by public authority in all countries through other means—most notably income, estate, and "capital gains" taxes. But (with a few exceptions such as South Korea's differential levy on "capital gains") in most such cases it is lumped together with other returns in such a way as to defy separate identification, and hence cannot be dealt with in these pages. One should note, however, that land tends to enjoy so many special tax advantages that there is reason to believe that the land-based portion of public revenue from these sources is much smaller than might otherwise be supposed.

Efforts to capture land values for the public through legislation not specifically designated for that purpose have generally proven ineffectual in the long run. The United States income tax is a case in point. The Sixteenth Amendment, having removed the constitutional roadblock to a direct federal tax not apportioned among states by population, freed Congress to define taxable income any way it chose. Congress might have limited taxable income to realized land rents, or possibly even to the annual rental value of land. Instead, however, the Revenue Act of 1916 merely *included* land rent as part of taxable income. Prominent Georgists, led by Rep. William Warren Bailey of Pennsylvania, were instrumental in fashioning the tax in such a way that, for a number of years, it bore lightly on earnings and heavily on land rent and other monopoly profits.[2] But, over the past half-century, the rent component of the federal income tax has steadily and drastically declined, making the tax increasingly a burden on the work and enterprise of the median citizen.

II

A Personal Standpoint

IN THE PREFACE and Acknowledgments, I mentioned that some contributors "express personal opinions with abandon." Yet, the fact that the chapters constituting the chief body of the text are intended to consist chiefly of factual reporting has tended to impose a degree of constraint upon their authors with respect to the temptation to make their overall standpoints explicit. That is doubtless as it should be, but in this Editorial Introduction, I have not felt so constrained. If any readers of the second edition may have harbored doubts about my being a Georgist, such doubts should be fully dispelled here. I offer no apologies for being a Georgist.

To be a Georgist, however, does not mean subscribing to the notion that everything that emanated from Henry George's pen must blindly be accepted as infallible Holy Writ, or that no aspect of his system is open to question. Contrary to what some people mistakenly believe, Georgism is not a cult. It may inspire deep loyalty and fervor, yet it maintains no establishment for the determination or preservation of orthodoxy, and its most ardent adherents are quick to point out their disagreements with the master— whether as to terminology, interest theory, monetary policy, or whatever. To be a Georgist is simply to believe that, in the main, on the most vital points, more than any other political economist or social ethicist, Henry George had it right.

* * *

It is not my wish to plague my readers with the minute terminological distinctions that preoccupy some Georgist colleagues, but certain definitions cannot be avoided here: Unless otherwise specified, the term "rent" throughout this book should be understood as used in classical economic theory, i.e., as signifying the imputed periodic—typically annual—value of land (exclusive of improvements, expenses of cultivation and maintenance, and costs of management) as determined by the market, regardless of whether or not that value is realized in payments. It should not be understood in the broader contemporary theoretical sense, which applies it to all monopoly returns, land-based or otherwise. In some British Commonwealth countries, the meaning as used here is conveyed by the noun "rental," but this definition of "rental" is not included in the unabridged Oxford English Dictionary, or in any other dictionary of which I am aware; hence, to sometimes speak of "rental value" as a synonym for rent is not to be guilty of redundancy. Occasionally, we shall employ the locution, "land rent," which is technically redundant; we do so merely to provide recurring emphasis as a reminder of what is meant.

Were a site's rent to be socially appropriated in full for the foreseeable future, its capital or selling value would be extinguished, but the site would continue to bear non-speculative rent since its ability to do so is in no way affected by whether that rent be appropriated by society, on the one hand, or by a private owner, on the other. It is perhaps for this reason that some enthusiasts for terminological nicety insist that a distinction be made between rent and land value. George, however, frequently used the terms interchangeably, and to depart from his example at this stage would be both tedious and futile.

For the most part, the terms "land value" and "site value" are also used interchangeably in this book, although in economics "land" embraces the whole of Nature, including some motile phenomena such as wildlife, whereas "site" denotes a fixed location.

A comment is in order about the word "taxation" as applied to land values, for a land-value tax is not, properly speaking, a tax at all. A tax, strictly understood, is a levy imposed without respect to benefits received. A land-value tax, however, is what Walter Rybeck has aptly termed a "super user charge,"[3]—a payment for a very fundamental benefit indeed, namely, the exclusive use and disposition of a site or natural resource at the expense of the rest of the community. If this were not a new edition of a book with the phrase "land-value taxation" already in its title, my inclination would be to jettison the term in favor of one more descriptively accurate, such as, for example, "public charges upon land values," which happens to be the title of a study about which I shall have something to say a bit later. In Australia and New Zealand, the current tendency is partially to supplant land-value taxation at the local level with user charges for various amenities, evidently because of failure to appreciate that a land-value tax is itself the most basic user charge of all. If sufficient rent is publicly collected, no additional user charges should be necessary for site or neighborhood-specific benefits, for the value of such benefits will be reflected in the rent.

III

A Biblical Analogue[4]

INASMUCH AS this volume is essentially intended as a factual survey, the reader may be perplexed to find in it anything that might conceivably be construed as an appeal to revelation. Its topic, land-value taxation, may appear on the surface to be prosaic and mundane. Yet land-value taxation has not only a profoundly moral aspect (which I shall briefly discuss a little later), but also a Biblical forerunner or analogue in a plan of social justice that finds partial, if often much attenuated, application in the arrangements that this book describes. For land-value taxation, while certainly supportable on purely fiscal grounds, is, above all, a means of achieving social justice.

There is unintended symbolism in the convergence in time of this millennial edition of *Land-Value Taxation Around the World* and the movement that calls itself "Jubilee 2000." The Old Testament institution from which the latter takes its name was one feature of the plan to which I have alluded. But while forgiveness of Third World debt, as called for by Jubilee 2000 and endorsed by contemporary religious leaders from Pope John Paul II and Archbishop Desmond Tutu to the Reverends Billy Graham and Pat Robertson, may or may not be justified, depending on the circumstances, it has little or nothing to do with the authentic Jubilee concept of debt forgiveness as set forth in the twenty-fifth chapter of Leviticus. That concept was based on equity rather than on mere compassion for the poor, and was integrally related to a regime of land tenure and public revenue designed to create and maintain equal access to natural and community-created opportunity.

The object of the Biblical Jubilee was not to impede the discharge of legitimate contractual obligations. It was to assure that illegitimate ones would not occur. It was to assure that "the land [could] not be sold forever,"[5] and that, hence, long-range monopoly and the permanent division of society into hereditary "haves" and "have nots" could not arise. For under its provisions, no-one could permanently alienate the patrimony of later generations.

The royal "Clean Slate" proclamations of ancient Babylonia (described by Michael Hudson in chapter 1) have obvious affinities to the Jubilee provisions in Leviticus; quite possibly, both drew upon a common, earlier tradition. Each called for the periodic restoration of land which had been pledged as security and forfeited for unpaid debt. But the latter was part and parcel of a coordinated structure designed to secure to each family and generation within the Hebrew commonwealth the equal right to the use of the land, of which God was recognized as the sole absolute owner.

In the Book of Numbers one finds a description of how a census of the Hebrew tribes and families was taken on the plains of Moab before they entered into the Promised Land. Every tribe (except for Levi, for which other provision was made), and, within each tribe, each family, was to receive its proportionate share, depending on its size.[6] To ensure fairness, the final apportionment was to be by lot.[7]

As recounted in the eighteenth and nineteenth chapters of the Book of Joshua, the actual distribution of land in keeping with these stipulations was concluded at Shiloh. According to Josephus, the territory was not divided into shares of equal size, but rather into shares of equal agricultural *value*.[8] But Talmudic commentary held that value was determined by location (distance from Jerusalem) as well as by fertility.[9]

I have mentioned that the tribe of Levi did not share in the equal division of the land. This is because it was set apart for priestly functions. Since the early Hebrew polity was theocratic, these functions embraced the carrying out of what we would consider governmental duties as well as ceremonial ones.[10] To bring the Levites' ministrations within the reach of all the people, they were given official residences and surrounding acreage in forty-eight cities,[11] but that was only a small fraction of what they would have received had they been born into any other tribe. The tithe, one tenth of the produce of the land occupied by the eleven other tribes, was instituted partly as an indemnity to the Levites for the equal share which they did not receive in the division,[12] and partly as payment for their public service. Thus it was, in point of fact, a land-value tax, and operated as a mechanism for effectuating the substance of equal rights to land, alongside of and compatible with unequal physical division of the land itself.

As land reformers in modern times discovered, it is one thing to devise a one-time apportionment that is fair, and quite another to keep it that way. That is why the Mosaic Law established the Jubilee Year. At the end of every forty-nine years, any alienated lands—those given away, sold, or lost from unpaid debts—would be restored to the original families. (Temporary possessors were to be compensated for any unexhausted improvements they had made.[13]) Thus the value as collateral of landed property diminished as each Jubilee Year approached, and with it, the possibility of forfeiture because of loans that could not be repaid. Concentrated ownership and the partition of society into landed and landless classes, was thereby prevented from creeping into the system. The Jubilee effectively took the profit out of mere landholding as such, leaving no incentive for speculation.

There is no chapter in this book devoted to the Mosaic land system because many scholars hold that it was never fully implemented.[14] If their opinion is correct, that in no way invalidates the statutes' wisdom and justice, but merely demonstrates that the nation that had been privileged to receive them was not exempt from all-too-human arrogance and folly—a judgment recorded in its own sacred writ: "They have rejected the law of the Lord, and have not kept his statutes."[15]

It is certainly not my intention to suggest that the Mosaic plan could be used as an exact blueprint in a society that has moved past the pastoral or agricultural stage. But the public appropriation of economic rent, whether through an annual tax on land values, through a system of leasehold, through a tax on the abstraction of resources from nature, or through some combination of these, can, if sufficiently robust, accomplish the same objectives for our time.

IV

The Moral Case for Land-Value Taxation

THE MORAL CASE for land-value taxation is clear enough. It represents an indemnity to the rest of society for the privilege of monopolizing something the owner did nothing to create, and the market worth of which is a social, not an individual, product. Such a levy is, as George put it, "the taking by the community, for the use of the community, of that value which is the creation of the community."[16]

Under a Georgist regime, everybody would pay society for the use of land, according to its market value. Those who own land would pay directly. Those who do not, would pay indirectly via their landlords, who would keep a small percentage of the payment as an agency or collection fee. The proceeds would be used for purposes of general benefit in lieu of taxes on labor and capital. This contrasts with most present systems, in which people who don't own land pay *twice*—first to the landlord, for the privilege of using the land, and second, to the government for public services. (Of course, I am using the term "landlord" in the literal sense; if the same individual happens to own the building in which one lives or conducts a business, one's payment for the use of it, as distinguished from the land under it, is actually interest on capital, and would not be subject to social appropriation under Georgism.)

Heavy imposts upon land, even if offset by reductions in income and/or other taxes, will be decried as confiscatory by some parties on the excuse that the land was purchased in good faith under the protection of the laws existent at the time. But this assertion (which could apply equally to almost any change in the tax structure that might have an adverse effect upon anyone) rests upon the assumption that every transaction is entitled in perpetuity to the same legal protections as those under which it was entered into—an assumption that, if valid, would render all reform, or, for that matter, nearly any kind of legislated change, impossible. Whenever public authority does *anything* that constitutes a policy departure, someone's expectations are bound to be negatively affected, yet nobody contends that all present policies should therefore be carved in stone. Why then should policies that affect landowners be any different? People have the right to speculate in land just as in pork bellies or Picassos, but regardless of what they put their money into, society is under no obligation to ensure that their speculation be risk free. Practical wisdom, of course, dictates that changes insofar as possible be phased in gradually enough to enable people to make necessary adjustments, and this applies to the taxation of land values as it does to other matters.

At this juncture, it may be apposite to mention a point much emphasized by William S. Vickrey, the 1996 Nobel laureate in economics who died three days after learning that he had been chosen to receive the prize: The cost of public infrastructure may be defrayed at little or no expense to the general community merely by tapping the increase in land values generated by that infrastructure.[17] This seems only fair. (In hardship cases, the increased tax obligation could be permitted to accrue and its payment postponed until time of sale, transfer or death—or until the arrearage reduced the market price to zero, which would trigger forfeiture of title to the public.) It is the rationale behind the several forms of "betterment levy" that have been used with varying results in Great Britain, Colombia, and elsewhere, but may also be used to justify a straightforward land-value tax, which is more transparent, less complicated to administer, less subject to influence by special interests, and has no distorting impact on the market.

As the late P. I. Prentice (longtime vice-president of TIME, Inc.) never tired of emphasizing, the general property tax is really two separate taxes, opposite to each other both in terms of moral justification (or the lack of it) and in terms of economic impact. The tax on land values is the recapture by the community of a social product; the tax on improvements is a toll laid by the community on individual efforts and their fruit. The tax on land values cannot be shifted from the owner to the user; the tax on improvements is routinely so shifted. The tax on land values stimulates improvements and productive use; the tax on improvements discourages them. And the list could go on.

To the extent that the rent of land is *not* appropriated for social purposes, the fruits of private effort, initiative, and productive savings are almost certain to be so appropriated. The burden of proof lies with one who would contend for the moral superiority of the latter.

V

Economic and Fiscal Considerations

THE REMAINING ARGUMENTS for land-value taxation have to do with economic efficiency, on the one hand, and such fiscal considerations as ease of administration, and revenue stability and adequacy, on the other.

The first of these may be stated simply: If a sufficient percentage of a parcel's economic rent must be paid annually to the community regardless of how or whether the land is being used, its owner will have a compelling incentive to put that land to its optimum use or to sell it to someone who will, instead of holding it for speculation or (as is common in some Latin American countries, for example) merely for reasons of prestige. By "squeezing the speculative water" out of land prices, the policy makes land more readily available to those who could not otherwise afford it, and the purchase price is less apt to absorb funds needed for development, or to weigh the buyer down with a ponderous load of debt. Critics with a superficial understanding of the principle imagine that it would force all land into use and lead to overdevelopment. They fail to consider that economic rent reflects potential for optimum not maximum use, and that some land bears little or no economic rent. Instead of overdevelopment, there would emerge a more compact and rational pattern of development, with a wholesome reduction in the number of vacant and underused lots in urban centers, and a countryside not eroded by suburban sprawl. This compact pattern of development would cut the cost of public services. Insofar as the public capture of economic rent permitted the abolition or reduction of taxes on the returns to labor and capital, that much income would be freed up to raise living standards and/or for productive capital investment. Thus it may be seen that the impact of a substantial land-value tax is not (as is often claimed) merely neutral in the sense of causing no distortions in the economy at large, but actually positive, a conclusion set forth and demonstrated in detail by Nicolaus Tideman.[18]

The last set of arguments is fiscal in nature—i.e., they focus on social appropriation of land rent, not in its larger aspects, but merely as a source of public revenue.

Administration of any property tax is largely a matter of assessment. Unless assessment is both accurate and up-to-date, the successful operation of land-value taxation is severely compromised. Where sales are infrequent or there are no other parcels with similar characteristics in a vicinity, the valuation of a site may present difficulties, yet sophisticated techniques have been developed to deal even with situations such as these. Computers, aerial cadastral mapping, and other technological innovations make for greater uniformity of treatment, rendering the process less susceptible to personal and political pressure.[19]

In many jurisdictions, land and improvements are assessed separately although they may be taxed at the same rate. Where all real property is assessed at the same rate on the basis of land alone, the procedure is manifestly easier than where improvements must be included. Classification, exemptions, and differential rates introduce complications, but they are not insuperable.

Assuming a representative form of government in which official records are readily available for scrutiny, and provision is made for appeal at open hearings, a public revenue system based heavily on land-value taxation is as nearly corruption-proof as any public revenue system can be. This is not only because of the oft-mentioned fact that land cannot be moved or hidden, making illegal avoidance of a tax on it well-nigh impossible, but also because if such a tax accounts for a large enough proportion of people's public revenue obligation, their attention will be so focused on it that each property owner will habitually examine the rolls to compare his or her assessments with those of others. Under such circumstances, favoritism is practically impossible to conceal, and therefore unlikely to be attempted.

Land-value taxation has long been recognized as an unusually stable source of public revenue. In fact, the Georgist single tax on land has been criticized for being *too* stable, i.e., so inflexible as to be incapable of adjustment to changing fiscal needs. That is because it takes the total rent, less a small percentage which the owner is allowed to keep as an agency or collection fee. But the Georgist contention has always been that the single tax is far more than just a fiscal measure, and that its positive effects upon the economy would render many government operations (e.g., welfare) superfluous.

Of course, there is no source of public revenue that is wholly unaffected by the vicissitudes of the general economy. It is patent that a collapse in land values that precipitates or accompanies recession will constrict a tax base that depends upon them. But a land-value tax of sufficient magnitude, introduced incrementally, will forestall recession by providing a perpetual non-inflationary stimulus to the economy in terms of production and purchasing power alike. Land prices will fall as the incentive for speculation disappears. Yet even if a site's speculative value plunged to zero, so long as it still had use value, it would continue to yield rent. In fact (as demonstrated in Australia and elsewhere), the stimulus might well eventually raise its use value to a level higher than its former speculative value. Far from shrinking, public revenue would increase along with the increase in productive activity.

According to the standard wisdom, a *sine qua non* for a system of public revenue is that it be broadly based. It is argued that if revenue is drawn from many and varied sources, it is less likely to be seriously affected should any of them dwindle. It is argued, moreover, that the more widely the burden is spread among the various interests, the more lightly it will weigh upon any one of them.

This is all very well as far as it goes, but other considerations are also relevant: The more numerous and varied the sources, the more complex must be the system, and hence the more elaborate, expensive, and inquisitorial the collection apparatus and process. Sometimes the argument that public revenue must be broadly based is couched in terms of equity. Thus the sales tax is defended because "it spreads the burden more evenly to all consumers of public services."[20] But equity does not necessarily call for widespread distribution of the burden where the distribution of benefits is not similarly widespread; in fact, many would maintain the contrary. At best, one might concede it to be desirable that public revenue be broadly based, *all other things being equal*. Yet I trust that I have shown that, in the case of the land-value tax, all other things are not equal.

What is probably the most uncompromising and also the most theoretically elegant assertion of the adequacy of land value as a tax base was advanced by Thomas G. Shearman. It was his contention that it is logically impossible for the average annual cost of necessary government ever to be greater than the average annual value of its land:

> How can any government be necessary, which costs more than the privilege of living under it is worth? And what is the cost of the privilege of living in any particular place, except the ground rent of that place? ... Any pretended taxation which takes more from the people than this is extortion, not genuine taxation.[21]

The less local the jurisdiction, the more attenuated Shearman's argument becomes, so that the case for financing national defense, for instance, out of rent is not so clear and unequivocal as is the case for thereby financing services such as local law enforcement. Yet the advantage of being located in a free country with secure borders might conceivably confer rent even upon a site that had little else to recommend it.

Shearman believed that, after legitimate expenses of government at all levels had been defrayed by rent, an annual surplus of about thirty-five percent would remain (which he, contrary to George, advocated leaving wholly in the hands of the landholder). There are commentators who think it probable that, when Shearman made his calculations around the turn of the nineteenth century, he was not far off the mark.

Despite the force of Shearman's *a priori* reasoning, one frequently encounters the assertion that, although his estimate may have been accurate enough in his time, land rent would not be sufficient to meet the warranted costs of government today. One's opinion as to the warranted costs of government will, of course, depend in large measure upon one's opinion as to the legitimate functions of government. But suppose, for purposes of discussion, that we were to concede that the "rent fund" would fall short of the amount needed to maintain government that was as modest and frugal as it could be without becoming inadequate to fulfill essential functions. Would that be an argument against using it as far as it would go? In actuality, while we have no reliable contemporary estimate of the total quantity of rent, we do know that assessment figures are notoriously and often ludicrously low, and that, even when realized as income, rent is often concealed by being classified statistically under other headings. In view of this, when one deducts corporate welfare and other forms of privilege from the costs of government, it is not unreasonable to believe that Shearman's view of the sufficiency of rent might be well within the bounds of sober conjecture even now, at the dawning of the twenty-first century.

No fiscal instrument, however enlightened or potentially far reaching, operates in a vacuum, and land-value taxation is no exception. For example, in Hungary, Austria, and Weimar Germany, the runaway inflation that followed World War I undercut the nascent legislated programs for land-value taxation before they ever really had a chance to prove themselves, and paved the way for the ascendancy of totalitarian rule that crushed them altogether. Apt indeed is Will and Dorothy Lissner's admonition that "economic and social advances are dependent upon monetary stability."[22]

VI

The Empirical Record

BECAUSE THE DEGREE of land-value taxation in operation is usually too slight to provide definitive data that clearly outweigh other factors, there is a paucity of hard empirical evidence for its success in practice. Yet the evidence that does exist is consistent, and its cumulative weight, if not entirely conclusive, is, at the very least, impressive.

In 1955, when the first edition of this book came out, land-value taxation seemed to be advancing steadily if not dramatically: it was spreading at the local level in Australia and New Zealand, and its extension in Denmark was backed by all three parties that made up the coalition government. By 1997, the year of the second edition, serious reversals had occurred in New Zealand and Denmark, the nations where it had seemed most firmly entrenched, and there is now a definite possibility that what little remains of it in Denmark is about to be discarded. Although nowhere actually rescinded in Australia, it had been minimized there by growing reliance on users' charges. The "single-tax colony" of Fairhope, Alabama, had given up all pretense of assessing land at full market value. That year, the system's brightest prospects for extension seemed to be in South Africa, although they have since been dashed.

Meanwhile, public capture of economic rent had become a major feature of several countries on the Pacific Rim, and is being adopted ever more widely on the municipal level in the state of Pennsylvania. Now that Scotland has its own parliament, land reform is high on its agenda, and efforts are being made to point that reform in the direction of land-value taxation. The idea has also gained strong support among several of Russia's most prominent political leaders, and been endorsed without dissent by the Union of Russian Cities at a conference representing eighty of that nation's largest metropolitan jurisdictions.[23]

True, the system has in some few cases been abolished, but never because it was a failure. In Denmark, the explicitly Georgist Justice Party was voted out of Parliament and the advance of land-value taxation halted, but this happened at a time of unprecedented prosperity and for political reasons that had nothing to do with land-value taxation as such. In New Zealand, it was done away with in the three largest cities where it was in place, but this came in the wake of major jurisdictional reconfiguration, and was never submitted to the voters for approval. In various smaller municipalities, where the public had an opportunity to vote on whether to reject or to retain it, the overwhelming decision was to retain.

Hence, to those who share George's vision, retrogression is not unalloyed by gains. Yet it must be stressed that these gains are slender, tentative, and by no means secure. In point of fact, many of the "success stories" hailed and endlessly repeated in Georgist literature have been quite exaggerated. The implementation of land-value taxation has really been extremely modest, and its impact, where genuine, all too often blunted by countervailing policies, usually at other levels of government. The accounts set forth in the ensuing pages may have the effect of "throwing a wet blanket" on some cherished Georgist illusions. But better sober realism than naive complacency.

* * *

Public Charges Upon Land Values, subtitled "A Study of the Effects of Local Government Rating Systems upon the Social and Economic Development of the Australian States," was first published in 1945 by the Land Values Research Group, Melbourne. Updated in 1960, it remains the most compelling single brief for land-value taxation's practical efficacy. Primarily the work of the late A. R. Hutchinson, it compared the three Australian states with a substantial amount of land-value taxation with the three with little or none. It did so in terms, not merely of the usual criterion—number of building permits issued annually, but also of a wide range of indicators including agricultural development, development of manufacturing industries, volume of retail sales, value of improvements, average wages, population gain through immigration from other states, etc., finding a definite positive correlation between all of these and the extent to which land-value taxation was in effect! Unfortunately, a change in the government's method of gathering and classifying statistics made it impossible to further update all these findings, but a study by Hutchinson eighteen years later[24] confirmed the same pattern for those indicators for which data was then still available.

In South Africa, land-value taxation is almost wholly urban. In some Caribbean states, it is wholly rural. These differences seem to reflect purely political considerations, as there is no logical reason why it cannot work equally in both contexts, as has been amply demonstrated in Australia and elsewhere.

Western Canada offers a prime example of the truth that a property tax based solely upon land values cannot succeed unless a sufficient percentage of the land rent is collected. If the tax rate is set too low or the land is grossly underassessed, exemption of improvements only serves to help inflate land values and encourage speculation.

I have alluded to the fact that in Hong Kong and Singapore, where, in the first instance, all land and in the second instance, most land is public, rent flows directly to the state through leases instead of being paid by owners in the form of taxes. George had considered this approach and found it acceptable enough on moral grounds, but regarded the use of the tax method as more efficient administratively, and preferable where private ownership of land is well entrenched. This was not the case in the states in question, where the leasehold method seems to work quite well. Russia, which is not burdened with a vested landed interest, might be well-advised to follow the same path, instead of creating such a vested interest by privatizing land.

At the same time, it should be borne in mind that public ownership of land is no guarantee that its rent will be captured by the public. Even where land is publicly held, there may be vested interests with special rights to land use, and these interests will employ all the means at their command to resist full payment for such rights. In the US, some salient examples of such special rights (or, more accurately, privileges) are absurdly low grazing fees on federal land, rights to federal water at a fraction of market value, rights to monopolize bands or channels on the broadcast spectrum for little or no charge, etc., etc. Then there is the tragically ironic case of Israel, where ninety-three percent of the land is public, yet provides less than one percent of government income at all levels (through the Israel Land Administration). Although the seven percent of the land that is privately owned is mostly of much greater unit value, the value of the remaining ninety-three percent is estimated to be about half the total, which is scarcely the negligible portion that the rent collected from it would suggest. Meanwhile, the public staggers under the weight of heavy taxes on productive activity (especially personal income and value added taxes) that could be substantially reduced if a reasonable percentage of the value of public land were captured.[25]

* * *

Denmark and New Zealand have been cited as nations where land-value taxation, although long established, has recently received its greatest setbacks. In Denmark, this resulted for a time in the fragmentation and disarray of its proponents. In New Zealand, by contrast, its proponents saw the setbacks as a challenge to creatively rethink their program. The chapter by R. D. Keall discusses this development at length, but a few words of summary and comment seem appropriate here.

By 1982, ninety percent of all New Zealand municipalities had opted for land-value taxation, which supplied about two thirds of local revenue. Its importance was never actually so great as might be supposed from this figure, since local authorities in New Zealand are responsible only for certain amenities and not (as in the US) for such essential services as police and education.[26] Nevertheless, it seemed to be moving forward on its own momentum, and was so firmly established as to be taken for granted. Hence, despite continued educational efforts, membership in the New Zealand Land Value Rating Association fell away to almost nothing. When, at the decade's end, the deviously contrived reversions to capital value rating instigated by the minister for local government took place in Dunedin, Christchurch, and Wellington, legal measures were adroitly instituted to assure their permanence. Although efforts at reversion were roundly rejected by the electorate whenever it was permitted to register its opinion at the polls, the leadership of what remained of the Association decided that the time was ripe for a fresh approach that would push for a more comprehensive application of the concept of public capture of rent in lieu of taxing labor and capital.

Accordingly, "Resource Rentals for Revenue" (RRR) became the new slogan, betokening the progressive substitution for taxes on income, production, and consumption, not merely by site-value rating in the narrow sense, but also by rents for natural monopolies, and for publicly owned natural resources and publicly funded infrastructure. It was believed that the convergence of several factors, including a new system of proportional representation and widespread resentment of the privatization of infrastructure built with public funds, presented an unusual opportunity for the promotion of this program in New Zealand; concurrently, the program was commended to the rest of the world as a more thoroughgoing and exciting alternative to merely shifting local taxes off of buildings and onto sites. Sufficient time has not yet elapsed to test Kiwi receptivity to this approach; one might be more sanguine about its chances if its knowledgeable advocates had greater material assets at their disposal and were not so few in number. But the effort to extend the public rent idea to its full logical purview is a project eminently worthy of emulation. It reflects a strain in the thought of Henry George himself that, however muted in his later years, never was repudiated by him. In the first half of the nineteenth century it was echoed by Judge Jackson H. Ralston, among others.[27]

VII

An Hypothesis and an Exhortation

WHEREVER LAND-VALUE taxation has a foothold, it is essential that the officials charged with its administration be educated as to its advantages, both technical and moral, that this education be ongoing, and, insofar as possible, extended to the general population. The absence or inadequacy of such education may be one reason why the system has been brought to the verge of extinction in Denmark, and weakened even in Taiwan, despite the fact that it is mandated in the Taiwanese Constitution, and played a major role in moving that nation from penury to prosperity in the third quarter of the twentieth century.

Even limited experiments in land-value taxation are cumulatively helpful in establishing an empirical record. As will be shown in the following chapters, the record thus far established has consistently been quite positive, even where the experiments have, for various extraneous reasons, been abandoned. I recognize that political realities frequently preclude bolder action, that opportunities must be taken advantage of when they present themselves, and that they are normally of such a nature as to be linked with other issues and to admit only of partial legislative attainment. For these reasons, I do not disparage the modest approaches recounted in the pages that follow.

Yet I cannot but venture to suggest that their very modesty may be one reason for the fact that land-value taxation now seems to be in retreat in so many places where it was established. Too mild an application of a beneficial program will produce benefits too mild to stimulate strong and enduring general support. Almost invariably in these instances, not enough land rent was socially appropriated to ensure that the system's good effects were clearly attributable to it, and could not be ascribed to other factors. A closely associated reason could be that the approaches were too mixed—either including other taxes that watered down its impact by penalizing production, or implemented by round-about methods such as the income tax, so structured that their explicit aim was not the capture of land value any more than of any other type of economic value. Such circumstances blur the moral imperative of land-value taxation, making it seem but one fiscal tool among many. Indeed, it has proponents who view it that way.

Only homeopathy maintains that remedies are very effective in minute doses. If the record of land-value taxation has been one of consistent but only moderate success, that is most likely because it has been administered only in greatly diluted form. Even the best medicine, if too diluted, may readily be overwhelmed by stronger counteragents. A stout enough course of the unadulterated Georgist "Remedy" might demonstrate that the claims made on its behalf are not really so extravagant, after all.

No doubt, fanatic enthusiasts for the "single tax," who see it, not as a regimen to build up the social body in increasing degrees to a state of health, but as a magical elixir to be swallowed at one gulp, have alienated potential sympathizers of more sober temperament. But the Georgist vision is not, as some of its adherents' rhetoric might lead one to conclude, inherently simplistic. Their veritably evangelical fervor, although it might superficially appear almost ludicrous in the context of advocating a tax, ought not be viewed with condescension or disdain. For the tax they advocate is a tax in name only, and its significance as a fiscal measure pales beside its significance as an engine of social justice.

Assuming careful and knowledgeable implementation, it commends itself to common sense much more than do competing approaches. By now, the bankruptcy of socialism should be evident to all. The market economics of the New Right, while a welcome enough corrective to collectivist schemes in many nations throughout the world, has largely proven a disappointment, as evidenced by the return to power of Center-Left parties, however chastened, in the United Kingdom, Germany, New Zealand, and elsewhere. Yet such parties' programs, if they may be called that, exhibit no clear, coherent structure. They are mere patch-works of compromise, stitched together without design apart from that of appealing to powerful voting blocs and other interest groups. Why should it be too much to hope for, that, after enduring failure upon failure and disillusionment upon disillusionment from Left and Right alike, the world will awaken to the realization that if it socializes that which is inherently social because produced by society—namely, the rent of land and natural resources, it may safely leave in private hands the wealth that individuals in their private capacity produce? If such a regime cannot be fully instituted overnight without too great a shock, that is scarcely a conclusive point against it. Let it be instituted, if need be, in stages that allow for adaptation and adjustment. Let it be instituted with due consideration for circumstances of time and place. Let it even be instituted with temporary modifications for special cases such as the ubiquitous "poor widow" whose conjectured plight is the subject of lachrymose ritual invocation by the adversaries of reform. But let it be instituted!

Although words attributed to Helen Keller laud Henry George's "splendid faith in the essential nobility of human nature,"[28] it is to his credit that his system of political economy rests on no such faith, but, rather on the mundane observation that "men seek to gratify their desires with the least exertion."[29] His language might at times ascend to rhapsody, yet his was an uncommonly practical approach—radical in the sense of attacking the preeminent social problem at its root, but basically conservative as to method.[30] It might be characterized as being, both literally and figuratively, "down to earth." This is by no means to depreciate the powerful moral, even spiritual, appeal of his position. But it is precisely the seamless union of that moral and spiritual appeal with an eminently reasonable plan of reform that doubtless accounts for the remarkable persistence of the movement that bears his name. When Henry George died, that name was a household word. But so was the name of Edward Bellamy, and so was the name of William Jennings Bryan. Bellamy's Nationalist Clubs, which once spanned America from coast to coast, disappeared without a trace in less than a decade. Bryan's banner of Free Silver was furled for good after the campaign of 1896. In due course, later panaceas were proclaimed. Multitudes hailed the Townsend Plan, and sang the praises of Technocracy. Where are they now? But followers of Henry George are active still. Their political advances may be rather few in number and of relatively slight degree. And yet they soldier on.

Like Plato's ideal city, the full Georgist paradigm has been realized nowhere on earth. Only in pale and evanescent glimmerings here and there may faint terrestrial traces of its lineaments be glimpsed. But it remains a steady vision in the heavens. It is not, as in the *Republic*, too sublime for human nature, necessitating a "second-best" substitute like the city of Plato's *Laws*, better adapted to man's frailty; rather, it is eminently applicable to the problematic human situation. It awaits only the day, be it soon or in the far distant future, when thoughtful citizens, finally recognizing the hollowness of the Left and the obtuseness of the Right, and the futility of all the unstable mixtures in between, their gaze directed by the Remnant to that supernal vision, are kindled by it to affirm with one mighty and united voice: "Let it be instituted! Let it be instituted *starting now*! To that end we dedicate ourselves."

Notes

1. A more precise term would be "net product taxes"—i.e., severance taxes on the market value of the resource at the point of extraction but excluding extraction costs.

2. W. Elliot Brownlee, "Wilson and Financing the Modern State: The Revenue Act of 1916," *Proceedings of the American Philosophical Society*, Vol. 129, No. 2 (1985), pp. 173-210.

3. Walter Rybeck, "The Property Tax as a Super User Charge," in C. Lowell Harriss, ed., *The Property Tax and Local Finance* (New York: Academy of Political Science, 1983). pp. 133-147.

4. This section of the text (**A Biblical Analogue**) is adapted, with modifications, from Robert V. Andelson and James M. Dawsey, *From Wasteland to Promised Land: Liberation Theology for a Post-Marxist World* (Maryknoll, NY/ London: Orbis Books/ Shepheard-Walwyn, 1992), pp. 83-85.

5. Lev. 25:23.

6. Num. 26:1-56.

7. Num. 34:16-29.

8. Josephus Antiquities v. 76-78.

9. Gemara. Baba Batra 122, A.

10. Deut. 17:8-13; 21:5; 25:26; 27:14; 31:9-13; 33:10. Lev. 10:11; 13; 14; 15. I Chron. 14:8-10.

11. Num. 35:1-5; 8. Josh. 14:4; 21. I Chron. 6:54-81.

12. Num. 18:21-24. Lev. 27:32,33. II Chron. 31:5, 6. Neh. 10:37; 12:44; 13:5,12.

13. Josephus, Antiq. III.12, 283, 284.

14. See George A. Buttrick, ed., *The Interpreter's Dictionary of the Bible* (New York Abingdon Press, 1962), II, 101-102; IV, 141-144. But cf. Archer Torrey, *The Land and Biblical Economics* (2nd ed.; New York: Henry George Institute, 1985), and Frederick Verinder, *Thy Neighbour's Landmark* (London: Land & Liberty Press, 1950), p. 56, f.n. 1.

15. Amos 2:4.

16. Henry George, *Progress and Poverty* (original ed., 1879; New York: Robert Schalkenbach Foundation, 1962), p. 421.

17. See, for example, William S. Vickrey, "The City as a Firm," in M. S. Feldstein and R. P. Inman, eds., *The Economics of Public Services* (London: Macmillan, 1977), pp. 334-345.

18. Nicolaus Tideman, "Taxing Land Is Better than Neutral: Land Taxes, Land Speculation and the Timing of Development," in Kenneth C. Wenzer, ed., *Land Value Taxation: The Equitable and Efficient Source of Public Finance* (Armonk, NY/London: M. E. Sharpe/Shepheard Walwyn, 1999).

19. Paul V. Corusy, "Improving the Administration of the Property Tax," in Harriss, op. cit., p. 94.

20. Jon Kidwell, guest columnist in the *Birmingham News* (Alabama), March 12, 2000, p. 3C.

21. Thomas G. Shearman, *Natural Taxation* (3rd ed.; New York: Doubleday & McClure, 1898), pp. 132–34.

22. In their Introduction to Michael Silagi, *Henry George and Europe* (Will and Dorothy Burnham Lissner, eds.; trans. from the German by Susan Faulkner; New York: Robert Schalkenbach Foundation, 2000), p. 3.

23. Fred Harrison, "80 Russian Cities Declare for Georgism," *Land and Liberty*, May–June, 1993, p. 3.

24. A. R. Hutchinson, *Natural Resources Rental in Australia* (Melbourne: Land Values Research Group, 1978).

25. This quotation was cited for many years in the annual brochure of the Henry George School of Social Science; its source is a letter written around 1930 by Miss Keller to the Robert Schalkenbach Foundation.

26. The same thing is true of Australia, South Africa, and numerous other countries. In the two-rate cities of Pennsylvania, public education is the function of school districts, which were not permitted until recently to levy two-rate taxes.

27. George, *Progress and Poverty,* p. 12.

28. See Joseph A. Schumpeter, *History of Economic Analysis* (ed., Elizabeth Boody Schumpeter; New York: Oxford University Press, 1954), p. 865.

29. Israel: Selected Issues and Statistical Appendix, *International Monetary Fund Staff Country Report No. 99*, May 1999, Table A29.

30. Jackson H. Ralston, *What's Wrong With Taxation?* (2nd ed.; San Diego: Ingram Institute, 1932), pp. 40–42; and *The Land Question* (Bayside, NY: The American Association for Scientific Taxation, 1945), pp. 40, 76–82.

PART ONE

THE ANCIENT AND MEDIEVAL WORLD

Chapter 1

Mesopotamia and Classical Antiquity

BY MICHAEL HUDSON*

NO HISTORY OF taxation over the course of antiquity has been written, to say nothing of a satisfactory general economic history. Little wonder, then, that many economists and even historians still think about the early evolution of fiscal policy in ways that reflect modern practices more than those of antiquity. The first task in studying fiscal evolution is thus to understand how ancient social structures differed from those of today.

Although economies varied widely and often idiosyncratically, a number of fiscal characteristics can be traced through the first 4000 years, that is, from 3000 BC to feudal Europe. To start with, the most archaic communities did not support themselves by levying taxes either on the land or on income. Rather, they set aside designated lands for their temples and palaces to produce an economic surplus or usufruct to support their public activities.

The agrarian character of ancient societies made it natural for the land to provide the basis for public revenue. Most people lived

*Michael Hudson, whose Ph.D. is from New York University, left a successful career as a Wall Street bond specialist to devote himself to historical and economic research. He has taught graduate courses in international economics at the New School for Social Research, has served as a senior economics consultant for such think tanks as the Hudson Institute, and has written ten and edited some 42 books on economic theory and history. Dr. Hudson is currently president of the Institute for the Study of Long-Term Economic Trends (ISLET), and co-chairman of the International Scholars Conference on Ancient Economics. He is co-editor (with Baruch Levine) of *Privatization in the Ancient Near East and Classical World* (1996) and *Urbanization; Land Use and Real Estate in the Ancient Near East* (1998), both under the auspices of the Peabody Museum of Archaelogy and Ethnology, Harvard University.

on the land, including urban residents who held rural land (and often urban gardens as well) to provide their basic food needs. But most families lived near subsistence levels, producing crops mainly for their own consumption and some marginal barter. Money was used only for commodities that passed through the market.

Before labor for hire emerged, the land's occupants had to provide most public services themselves rather than paying money or crop taxes to governments to do so. Adult male citizens contributed their labor directly for military service and other communal needs. Because military and corvée labor was supplied directly rather than through government hiring in the marketplace, fiscal needs were much less than would be the case today. To be sure, many armies were built up largely through the levy of tribute, as warfare often was made a paying proposition through raiding and looting, capturing and ransoming of war prisoners (sold as slaves if not redeemed by their families or native towns), or demanding extortionate tribute for not attacking targeted towns.

I

The Nine Principles of Ancient Fiscal Evolution

THE FOLLOWING NINE principles may be generalized as characterizing ancient fiscal evolution:

1. Defraying the costs of military organization—including public outlays on naval vessels, chariots, and other heavy equipment— made warfare the largest absorber of the economic surplus, and hence a primary force shaping antiquity's social development.

The most important public service through the ages has been the military draft. Its economic importance is attested by the fact that the term "class" originated as a Roman word denoting military rank first and foremost, and economic status by implication. Each rank of the armed forces was apportioned to the ability of its members to arm and train themselves at their own expense. Their ability to do so was assumed to be proportional to the size of their landholdings. In this respect the land defined class distinctions, from Solon's five classes of Athenian citizens through those defined by Rome's Servian constitution.

2. Non-military temple and palace activities likewise were not financed by taxing the population in money or crops. First documented in Sumer, lands were set aside to produce a usufruct (usually on a crop-sharing arrangement) for the support of temples and, in time, the palace. Also dedicated were herds of animals, as well as dependent labor—war widows and orphans, the blind, weak and infirm, and anyone else who could not make a go of things on the land.

So important was this principle of self-support for public institutions that civilization's earliest documented land rents were produced by Sumer's temples and palaces on lands set aside for this purpose. (In the Old Babylonian period, 1900–1600 BC, these "prebend" usufruct rents were privatized, bequeathed to heirs and sold as civilization's first documented rentier securities.) Indeed, the elaboration of public enterprise in the Early Bronze Age led to the innovations of cost accounting and other managerial techniques.

3. When taxes as our epoch knows them came to be imposed on society at large, they were levied primarily by conquering rulers as tribute or forced gifts—on a district-by-district basis, designating local officials to raise the money from the neighborhood or region for which they were responsible. These levies were deemed to reflect the lack of political freedom on the part of territories subject to such imposts—the kind of payment from which free cities and their surrounding rural districts were exempt.

In Kassite times (after 1600 BC), Babylonia's old cities had special markers attesting to their exemption from such tribute. A thousand years later, in classical antiquity, "direct and regular taxes on the property of citizens and especially their persons were usually avoided," observe Austin and Vidal-Naquet; "they were felt to be degrading." Tyrants resorted to them occasionally, but cities with republican-type constitutions abolished them as far as possible. By contrast there was no hesitation in taxing non-citizens. Thus metics (foreign workers) in Athens had to pay regularly a special tax, the *metoikion*, which was admittedly moderate, but which symbolized their inferior status as compared with citizens."[1]

Taxes of this type thus reflected the lack of free status for the taxed population.

4. Special levies such as the Greek *eisphora* were imposed in time of war. These emergency taxes had to be based on the ability to pay, and hence fell on the families with the largest visible wealth as landowners.

5. Responsibility for funding major civic spending programs likewise fell on the community's richest members. The best known examples are the Athenian *leiturgoi* ("liturgies"). These were not a general tax, but a special wealth tax falling on exceptionally rich families. Once designated, the payers competed to receive civic acclaim for the excellence of the dramatic choruses they funded, as well as for outfitting public gymnasia and naval triremes.

6. Specific sources of public revenue were earmarked for each category of activity. No comprehensive budgets were compiled for overall public revenue and spending. This fiscal compartmentalization applies from antiquity down through feudal Europe, and indeed to the very eve of modern times. Consolidated overall public budgets would have to await the epoch of parliamentary democracy and its more rationalized oversight of royal finances.

7. An important fiscal feature *not* found in antiquity was public debt. Early temples and palaces were creditors, not debtors. Rather than borrowing money in emergencies, ancient states appealed to their wealthiest families (as did Rome in the dark days of its war with Carthage), or simply confiscated their wealth. Only with the emergence of royal war debts in late feudal Europe were special excise duties and sales taxes levied, increasingly on a non-agrarian basis, to carry their interest charges.

8. Starting in Bronze Age Mesopotamia, the proliferation of agrarian debts tended to "crowd out" the ability of rulers to collect taxes or other fees. The problem was that creditors took the surplus crop (or the debtor's labor at harvest time) in payment for personal debts. These typically represented tax or fee arrears from earlier seasons of military destruction (when cultivators were called away from their lands to fight), drought, or crop failure.

The fact that debts typically were owed to public collectors within the palace bureaucracy created a tension between palace and creditor. Matters were resolved by rulers proclaiming Clean Slates. By canceling agrarian debts and restoring the *status quo ante*, they freed the land's usufruct for their own fiscal use.

9. Throughout antiquity there was a tendency for the wealthiest families, above all the landed aristocracy, to break free of fiscal obligations. This threw the tax burden onto the shoulders of the classes least able to bear them, culminating in a fiscal crisis that smothered further economic development.

In retrospect, the economic historian can see how the emergence of public debts in modern times reflects this weakening political ability to tax the rich, and specifically their financial wealth and real estate. In this respect the privatization of land and natural resources tends to create fiscal crises. Today, real estate from the United States to Russia is becoming effectively free of income taxation. Non-property taxes (sales taxes, social security and other wage levies) are taking the place of land's former role as society's basis for levying taxes and directly supporting public services. This shift in the fiscal burden represents the long dynamic of civilization's economic history.

Having established these nine principles of ancient fiscal policy, we are in a position to place them in their concrete historical context. For individually, ancient economies differed not only from their modern counterparts, but also from each other. What they shared in common was the second characteristic cited above: *Although the land supported the most important public institutions and services, this support did not take the form of general crop or money taxation of the citizenry.* Many translators of archaic economic texts accordingly avoid using the word "tax" to describe Bronze Age societies and those of classical antiquity. Probably the nearest equivalent of general taxation as our epoch knows it was the tribute extorted by imperial powers—a relatively late development.

II

In the Beginning

"IN THE BEGINNING"—that is, in Mesopotamia c. 3500–1200 BC, when written records first began to be compiled—societies did not find it natural to finance public activity by taxing privately held land and other wealth. The reason was simple: rent-yielding lands and large workshops were not yet privatized. Popular taxation could come into being only after the community's subsistence holdings and public rent-yielding estates were taken over in private hands.

This was no easy development, for archaic societies mistrusted private wealth accumulation. Instead of personal gain-seeking being viewed as the mainspring of progress, it was perceived to sow the seeds for economic polarization, and hence social discord and decay. Down through the epoch of Roman Stoicism and into Christianity, wealth was seen to make its possessors drunk with arrogance (duly punished by justice goddesses, from Sumerian Nanshe through Greek Nemesis), addicting them to seeking riches without limit in predatory ways. It was largely to avoid this form of economic egoism that social pressures led citizens to consume surpluses conspicuously in public feasts, gift-giving, funerals, and similar rites of passage. At least when expressed in these ways, personal grandiosity and egoism did not disenfranchise the community's weaker members. But that is what happened when the well-to-do began to charge interest on personal obligations and use their economic power to injure others, most notoriously by appropriating hitherto subsistence lands.

Sumerian and subsequent Babylonian communities avoided this problem of concentrating expensive production technologies in private hands by delegating such enterprise to their temples and palaces. Palace or temple workshops employing handicraft labor would have land and animals assigned to them to produce enough food and wool to yield their administrators a prebend income, and to feed the dependent labor such as the widows and orphans consigned to their workshops.

Other lands were designated to support soldiers in exchange for their military service. The laws of Hammurapi precluded these self-support lands from being privatized by being pledged and forfeited for debt arrears. This ruling guaranteed that the land would serve the public purpose of supporting fighting men rather than being used to enrich predatory creditors.

Because Mesopotamia's temples and palaces were endowed with sufficient land to support their own needs, they did not develop the practice of collecting a tithe or some other proportion of what citizens or subjects produced. It was the temples (and in time the palaces) that produced the first systematic economic surpluses, the first contractual formalities, weights and measures, and other basic elements of enterprise. The practice of generating formal economic rent as a stipulated payment or share of the crop likewise is first attested on Sumerian public lands in the third millennium BC. These rents, earmarked for the temple or palace proprietors, saved the community's families from having to turn over their own crops to support these institutions, their weaving and metal-working workshops and cult activities.

Account-keeping also was a public-sector phenomenon, reflecting the fiduciary character of public assets held in trust for society at large (at least nominally). Down through European feudal times each public institution kept its own set of accounts. Each category of public spending had its own earmarked source of revenue. No consolidated public budgets are found until relatively modern times. (Matters are further complicated by the fact that public accounts are found mixed together with the personal accounts of Mesopotamian rulers and their royal administrators acting on their own behalf.)

The contrast between public usufruct-yielding lands and family-held subsistence lands is reflected in the fact that no terms for "property" have been found even as late as the Middle Bronze Age (2000–1600 BC in Babylonia). The closest relation is "domain of the Lord," evidently the first land organized to produce a systematic usufruct or land rent. Rentier income thus seems to have originated in the public sector. Only after private individuals adopted public-sector modes of enterprise to produce regular surpluses of their own could taxes as such be levied. Indeed, it was the private appropriation of the land and large workshops that brought in its train a reciprocal liability for paying taxes.

The privatization process started with the ruler's family, warlords and other powerful men at the top of the emerging social pyramid. After 2300 BC, Sargon's heirs are found buying land from the families of subject communities (as documented, for instance, in the Stele of Manishtushu). As palace rule weakened, royal and public landholdings came to be privatized by palace subordinates, local head-men, creditors, and warlords. Land formerly used to support soldiers was charged a money-tax, which governments used to hire mercenaries.

III

Taxation as Military Tribute

IN THE GILGAMESH epic c. 2500 BC, the elders of Uruk (and then the fighting men) met to decide whether to resist the armies of Kish or to pay tribute. The soldiers voted to fight rather than pay. But in time, Sumer's cities could not resist extortionary demands for tribute from alien conquerors. Imperial rule under Sargon and his Akkadian regime obliged local communities to squeeze out a surplus for the dominant city. But the ability to collect tribute, gifts, and related payments depended on how strong the ruler was. As imperial rule weakened—and as local palaces weakened relative to landed aristocracies—the amount of tribute reflected the power of the leaders involved.

In the late Bronze Age (1600–1200 BC) Babylonia's oldest and most important cities had *kidinnu* stones outside their city gates proclaiming their tax exemption from tribute levied by the Kassite kings. To be free, thus meant to be tax-free. "They apparently had a legal status which differed in essential points from that of any other community," writes Leo Oppenheim. "In Babylonia, these cities were Nippur, Babylon, and Sippar; in Assyria, the old capital Assur and, later, Harran in Upper Mesopotamia. In principle, the inhabitants of these 'free cities' claimed with more or less success, depending on the political situation, freedom from *corvée* work, freedom from military service (or perhaps from certain types of military service . . .) as well as a tax exemption which we are not able to define in specific terms."[2]

Free and self-governing communities thus resisted the idea of the palace or other public institutions taxing society as a whole. They sought to tax outsiders, such as metics or subject territories. "The classical Greeks looked upon direct taxes as tyrannical and avoided them whenever possible," finds Finley.[3] It was a hallmark of free populations *not* to pay tribute, fees or taxes of this sort.

When imperial rulers taxed subject territories, they did so on a province-wide basis, leaving it to the subject localities to decide just how to raise the payment being demanded. This is found down through medieval European times, when Spain, for instance, taxed its Jewish ghettos, leaving it to the leading rabbis or other representatives to assign specific taxes. Likewise in the Persian empire, report Dandamaev and Lukonin, "The satrap, nomarchs, governors of cities, and rural headmen, were responsible for the collection of taxes"; in the most distant, rural provinces "the tribal leaders were answerable for this."[4]

The word "fiscal" derives from Persian "*fisc*," the basket used to collect money or goods from Persia's provinces. "In c. 519 BC, Darius established a new system of state taxes," described as follows: "The land was precisely measured in parasangs and classified according to crops cultivated or even according to the size of the harvest (Herod. VI, 42). All the satrapies were obliged to pay taxes in silver; these taxes had been strictly set for each province and established on the basis of cultivated land and its fertility, as calculated by the average harvest yield for several years in accordance with the cadastres for individual provinces. We have examples of such cadastral documents from (Persian-administered) Babylonia, which contain the number of fruit trees, the kinds of crops, and the extent of arable land."[5]

Inasmuch as Persians were the rulers, they were free in the most important civic sense of all, tax-free (from foreign imperial levies). But territories had to support Persian troops as they moved through, and it was customary to give gifts to the king when he visited. This customary obligation to support the royal entourage continued down through feudal Europe, and gave birth to the English expression "eating one out of house and home."

Uncultivated crop land, grazing land, and mines belonged to the public domain, e.g., as the Laurion silver mines belonged to the Athenian people (a tradition which continues down to modern Latin America, whose states retained subsoil rights). In the Graeco-Roman world, public sectors were deemed the proper owners of mines and various civic monopolies. The right to operate these mines was auctioned off or they were leased for a share in the output. At first the yield of the Laurion mines was distributed to the population at large as an economic dividend, but in the fifth century BC the Athenian *demos* voted to use this revenue to build the ships that defended the city-state and defeated the Persian navy.

IV

The Uniformity of Taxation and Economic Standardization

TO THE EXTENT that the fiscal system was standardized, it was on the basis of a male citizen's uniform "minimum" holdings in his community, or his class within the community.

However, an array of levies on non-agricultural professions is documented from the mid-third millennium BC onward. Sumerian and Babylonian professional workers had to pay assessments to royal collectors. Extortionate levies by the palace became one of the paramount "abuses" cited in Urukagina's "reform" text c. 2350 BC.

Such professional "licensing" payments evolved into formal taxes in classical antiquity, e.g., for various activities such as wine-making in the Persepolis Fortification tablets. These indirect taxes became increasingly important, including taxes on harbors and other commercial business. They ended up by not discriminating between citizens and non-citizens. "The city taxed economic activity in its various forms in different ways, without ever wondering whether it was thereby harming the interests of citizens or not," conclude Austin and Vidal-Naquet. The assumption was that wealthy families should pay the most. For self-governing cities such as Athens, "wealthier citizens had an obligation to spend their wealth for the public good."[6] They were assessed with liturgies, "(literally, services for the community), such as the trierarchy, in which the state supplied triremes [naval fighting vessels], while the trierarchs had to provide for their upkeep and commanding, or the *choregia*, in which the *choregoi* had to recruit, train and pay a chorus for the great dramatic presentations." But this principle has been inverted since late Roman imperial times. Today, the wealthiest families have managed to *avoid* paying taxes—all the more so if their wealth takes the form of land and other real estate.

A striking feature associated with these liturgies is the practice of *antidosis*. "If a man thought it more just that the liturgy assigned to him should be borne by another man," explains Andreades, "he could 'indicate' this man, being himself relieved of the liturgy if his declaration was found correct." If the person thus indicated refused to assume the liturgy, "he was under the obligation to exchange his property with that of the one who accused him. . . . In this way the state succeeded in devolving upon private individuals the disagreeable duty of deciding what citizens should be taxed and of adapting the liturgies to the constant changes in the distribution of wealth."[7]

Looking at the broad sweep from Solon's Athenian constitution through the Roman constitution attributed to Servius, as inequality among the landholdings of citizens widened, the wealthy at first were charged more. But over time, as wealthy landholders increased their political power and democracies evolved into oligarchies, landed wealth for the richest families managed to avoid taxation. The Romans imposed such heavy demands on local tax-collecting officials that many were reduced to bondage while the largest land owners went free, as Rostovtzeff has described so vividly. Having appropriated public and communal lands, the richest families caused a fiscal crisis that ended up stifling economic development.[8]

V

The Relationship Between Taxes, Private Debt, and Economic Clean Slates

AS THE PRIVATE sector moved from a subsistence basis to one yielding an economic surplus, societies became more specialized and rent-producing land passed into private hands. Landless men willing to work as mercenaries became an alternative to drafting citizens. Under these conditions, direct labor service duties were commuted for money payments. Taxes were monetized, including the Mesopotamian *ilku*, originally to support royal military spending. This obliged citizens to have ready money. If they did not have it, they often were obliged to borrow it. Alternatively, the tax collector acted as a virtual money lender and paid the obligation himself, thereby establishing a financial claim on the delinquent tax payer—a claim that rapidly accrued interest, and often became the first step leading to the loss of personal freedom and land-rights.

Although fiscal strains did not lead to public debt in antiquity, royal demands were the major factor pushing early populations into personal debt. Cultivators unable to raise the requisite levies typically ran into debt to the royal collectors or other creditors advancing the needed payments. These debts quickly mounted up at interest, ending all too often in the foreclosure of family holdings by tax gatherers and local magnates acting as creditors. Under such conditions of personal insolvency, the land passed into the hands of wealthy and powerful individuals (whose position, to be sure, tended to stem from their public and/or military office). Even royal lands designated for soldiers became privatized by absentee owners. Often the cultivators remained on the land, transformed into serf-like bondsmen.

It was to reverse such concentration of land and wealth within local communities that Mesopotamia's royal "Clean Slate" proclamations (Sumerian *amargi*, Akkadian *andurarum*, Babylonian *misharum*, and so forth) and the Biblical Jubilee Year of Leviticus ch. 25 were designed, not to mention Solon's *seisachtheia*. Such royal actions (and the central religious role they were given by Judaic religion, which took the initiative out of the hands of kings and elevated it to the sphere of Mosaic law) have a pedigree going back at least to third-millennium Sumer. These "restorations of economic order" canceled the overhang of debt arrears, and also reversed the land transfers and debt bondage that had occurred as a result of insolvency stemming from the inability of cultivators to pay their debts. By annulling these debts, along with the obligations owed in turn by the public collectors to the palace, these

Clean Slates restored the *status quo ante* (which was presumed to be equitable). This liberated bondsmen and restored widespread access to self-support for families on the land.

The longest and most famous such edict from Babylonia is the edict that Ammisaduqa proclaimed in 1646 BC to celebrate his first full year on the throne (about a century after Hammurapi inscribed his laws).[9] His edict annulled most of the agrarian debts that had been run up by cultivators since the last such edict was proclaimed in 1662 during the reign of his predecessor. Every loophole that creditors might use to circumvent the Clean Slate was closed. Bondservants had to be freed, and lands on which creditors had foreclosed were restored. This freed the land to be used for the purposes for which it was intended—to enable citizens to support themselves, especially Babylonia's fighting men.

Hammurapi's laws, inscribed a century earlier (c. 1763 BC), already had addressed the fiscal problem of creditors seizing the crops of debtors and refusing to pay the taxes due, claiming that the harvest belonged to them as debt service. Such confiscations left cultivators unable to pay the palace their stipulated sharecropping rent and other fees. To avoid this problem, paragraph 49 of Hammurapi's laws directed all crops or their revenues to be paid to the palace, by stipulating that the debtor and not the creditor should take the crops on the threshing floor, and then turn over the rents or fees to the palace first, paying the creditor only out of what was left over.

To prevent the privatization of cropland from sneaking in via the back door of usury, paragraph 41 of Hammurapi's laws blocked such land from being pledged as collateral for debt. This ruling stipulated that if a creditor foreclosed on a field, orchard, or house belonging to a soldier or feudatory as a result of a loan foreclosure, or even if he paid the full price for the land, the debtor/seller could take back the field and keep any loan proceeds that had been made. Paragraph 71 prohibited creditors from foreclosing on royal fief-land owing feudal obligations to the palace, evidently on the logic that such seizure would deprive the palace of its scheduled yield.

What made it relatively easy for Bronze Age rulers to cancel personal debts was the fact that most such debts were owed ultimately to the palace (and intermediately to the royal collectors). A major reason why such financial Clean Slates no longer sweep away society's debt overhead when it threatens to stifle economic development, is that since Roman times, debts no longer are owed mainly to the public sector, but to private creditors. Even governments have fallen into debt to these lenders.

Increasingly, the public sector farmed out its sources of revenue in exchange for stipulated payments.[10] Ever since—that is, for the past four thousand years—the fiscal problem has been a fight between the public rulers and creditors (including well-placed officials) over who should obtain the land's economic yield (that is, its rent): the public governing power, or private creditors.

By the first millennium BC, private money-lending was gaining momentum while royal power weakened in the face of the monied oligarchies emerging throughout the ancient world. Under Persian suzerainty, for instance, the province of Mesopotamia had to sell its agricultural surpluses to obtain the money to pay the Persian kings, most of whose levy of tributary taxes had to be paid in silver and (from India) gold, as described by Herodotus (III, 90–94). Monetization of these levies made Persian public finance the great nurturer of private capital concentration (e.g. the business house of Murashu).

In the fiscal tug-of-war extending from Hammurapi's Babylonian dynasty down through Rome, the creditors ended up winning in every case. They typically sealed their victory by unseating kings, although often creating a new despotism. This is the broad dynamic of the history of land taxation, and must form the basis of any modern discussion.

VI

How Public Debts Shifted Taxes Away from the Land

AS NOTED ABOVE, there were no public debts in antiquity. The survey of stratagems cited in the pseudo-Aristotelean *Oeconomica* (Book 2) describes how tyrants or others squeezed out money from citizens, sometimes with insincere promises to repay forced loans. The usual method was simply to confiscate money and property from the rich.

A turning point occurred in the course of Rome's war effort in the closing decade of the Second Punic War with Carthage at the end of the third century BC. The ostensibly patriotic contributions made by the rich during the war emergency were declared to have been a *de facto* loan. The confusion was settled by resort to one of the most fatal early examples of privatization: Rome turned over its rich *campagna* lands to the wealthy families who had contributed their jewelry and other monetary metals. The importance of this episode, described by Livy, is well stressed by Arnold Toynbee.[11] (It is symptomatic of the lack of modern interest in ancient economic practices that all of Livy's passages concerning this remarkable chain of developments are edited out of the disastrous Penguin translation of Livy, and thus are available in English only in the Loeb Classical Library.)

But public loans as such, leading to new taxes to pay regular, stipulated interest to creditors, were unknown until late feudal European times. They have developed only since the Crusades. Nearly all such debts have been run up in the process of waging war, most conspicuously the internecine warfare between the Norman conquerors of France and England over the course of some eight centuries, ending finally with the Napoleonic Wars in 1815.

The culmination of national war debts has been to capitalize their interest payments into new debt principal each year. Thus, not only has the major expenditure pushing nearly every country into debt traditionally been military, but war spending is now being rivaled and surpassed by interest charges on the public debt.

Europe's government debts first emerged as the personal obligations of kings. At first they were liable to be extinguished upon the monarch's death. They thus were not yet truly permanent public debts. General public budgets developed only with the emergence of parliamentary democracies. Borrowing in the name of the entire nation, through its elected representatives, not only served as a check on royal financial autonomy and adventurism; it also established public credit on a sounder basis from the creditor's standpoint. And it was these debts entered into by democracies that led to the management of national budgets as a comprehensive whole. The new national budgets used public revenues and expenditures ultimately as a means of monetary management. Today, public debts form the very basis of national monetary and credit systems.

The role of permanent public debts in diversifying the modes of taxation beyond land cannot be overestimated. At first, each new public debt had a specific tax created to defray the cost of paying its interest. (Adam Smith's *Wealth of Nations*, Bk. V, ch. iii, gives a precis of the special duties and taxes imposed to pay the interest on each new bond issue. See also John Sinclair's *History of the Public Revenue of the British Empire*, originally published in 1785.) The result was a proliferation of commercial and excise taxes, import duties, consumption duties such as the salt tax, and so forth. (An added reason facilitating such diversification was the economy's increasingly commercial and urbanized character.) With this development we enter the modern fiscal epoch.

The culmination of this long financial dynamic has been for creditors to end up with nearly all the land's rent yield. For as real estate purchases have come to be financed by mortgage credit as a normal state of affairs (rather than mortgaging the land only under emergency circumstances), the land's rental value has been absorbed increasingly by interest payments to bankers, insurance companies, and other creditors. This conversion of rent into interest has made it unavailable for the public sector to collect.

Today, despite the fact that real estate accounts for some two-thirds of the assets in the US economy, the real estate industry pays almost no income tax. It is virtually tax exempt, thanks to the special tax breaks which its growing economic power has enabled it to pry away from government. The long fiscal evolution since antiquity thus has ended up becoming the opposite of a system deriving most public revenue from the land.

Inasmuch as this volume is devoted to the topic of land-value taxation, it is appropriate to note that proposals for taxing land rent (or gains in land prices) hardly can be expected to make headway without first being able to solve the financial problem. If the land's rental value is pledged as interest to private mortgage lenders, it will not be available as the basis for public taxation.

The problem is that a major share of the savings of modern economies has been invested in loans to the real estate sector. The object is to secure the loan principal by real estate's collateral value, not to finance new industrial investment and innovation. In the US and other countries, about 70 percent of business loans take the form of mortgages that extract the rent on behalf of the economy's financial intermediaries (banks, money market funds, insurance companies, pension funds and so forth) for the ultimate asset-holders (mainly the wealthiest 10 percent of the population).

This state of affairs is the consequence of having grounded Anglo-American type banking systems on a combination of mercantile trade financing and mortgage banking to securitize land values, rather than on long-term industrial investment banking to capitalize direct investment in creating new means of production. In this respect, the fiscal problem is associated with a malstructuring of the banking and financial system. To collect more rent for the public sector as a real estate tax would leave depositors and policy holders without the former backing for their assets. This would create a savings and debt crisis if done suddenly. If done slowly, it would oblige the banking system to invest the economy's savings in new non-land capital formation. But as Rudyard Kipling would say, that is another story.

The lesson of ancient history is that Sumer, Assyria and its trade colonies, Babylonia, Nuzi, and the Biblical Jubilee Year laws all resolved the problem of land rent passing into the hands of creditors by annulling the land's debt when it grew top-heavy—at least every 30 years in Mesopotamia and its commercial periphery, and 50 years for the Jubilee Year of Leviticus 25. These cancellations of personal debts attached to the land and its cultivators restored the rent-producing capacity of these lands for the public sector to collect. They did not create a debt crisis, because there was no pubic debt to be annulled. They did not create a monetary crisis—a break in the chain of payments—because the debts had no counterpart in savings, but were merely arrears that had mounted up at interest.

Indeed, canceling agrarian personal debts restored the cultivators' ability to pay taxes and fees, and to serve in the armed forces as free land-tenured citizens. It was the corrosive usurious debt overhead that was wiped out.

VII

Summary

THE NINE BASIC features of ancient fiscal systems cited at the outset of this chapter may be highlighted by comparing them with to-day's state of affairs.

1. The military budget has relinquished its preeminent former role. Interest payments on the national debt now exceed military spending. One thus might say that the money freed from war budgets is now being consumed by interest charges on what be-gan as war debts.

Countries still draft soldiers in time of war, but for most indus-trial nations the epoch of major wars has passed. Governments now employ volunteer (mercenary) armies, as in later antiquity. But the distinguishing feature of ancient and feudal military or-ganization—the obligation of soldiers to arm themselves—is long gone in today's world of expensive, high-technology weaponry.

2. Today's public sectors are less self-financing than those of an-tiquity. Instead of deriving revenue from their own properties and enterprise, they tax the private sector. Indeed, since 1979 the world has accelerated the privatization of hitherto public assets and services, selling off public monopolies and other assets, and hiring private firms to supply services hitherto provided by public agencies.

These asset sales are occurring largely under debt pressures, but there also is a perception that public management has not well demonstrated its efficiency. Wasteful dissipation of resources has become associated more with the public sector than the private sector, especially since the collapse of the Soviet Union has re-vealed the worst excesses of public kleptocracy. Governments thus have not solved the problem that first led to the refinements of cost accounting: the need to control internal abuses, embez-zlement and self-dealing on the part of public officials, or simply bureaucratic incompetence.

One response has been to lease public assets to private operators, as classical Athens did with its silver mines. Hong Kong has leased its land with great success, but most nations are selling off their public assets outright.

In the late Roman empire, municipalities frequently invested the proceeds of such sales at interest, so as to obtain ongoing rentier funding. This is being done today with Social Security and medical insurance obligations, but in general the proceeds of public sell-offs are used to pay interest and amortization on outstanding public debts.

Governments have become dependent almost entirely on taxing private-sector incomes. The danger is that by taxing wealth at its source, in particular where the gains of enterprise are highest, governments may stifle the very industries that should be encouraged.

It is a unique contribution of modern tax theory to see the logic in raising taxes not simply from where the government can get money most quickly and conveniently, but to view the tax code as an economic system of disincentives and incentives to shape the marketplace by discouraging certain behavior (such as smoking or liquor consumption) or encouraging desired behavior by providing tax abatements for investment in areas where it otherwise might not be made.

3. Paying taxes no longer is viewed as a mark of unfreedom (although it may reflect the power of strongly centralized states). International law forbids the levy of special taxes on aliens or other targeted groups. National taxes are levied uniformly on citizens and foreigners alike. Indeed, the US government exempts offshore bondholders (including corporate shells resident in offshore banking and tax havens) from being subject to withholding taxes.

4. As in antiquity, special wartime taxes were levied in this century's two major World Wars, e.g., the excess profits tax and various surcharges. National income taxes also gained momentum largely as a war tax. But most special taxes are imposed to retire bond issues for specified projects, such as hotel taxes to retire baseball stadium bonds.

5. Responsibility for funding cultural undertakings is still largely honorific, but is done increasingly via charitable contributions and

not-for-profit foundations, not as a formal government obligation as in Athens. Such contributions are tax-exempt (and often result in *lowering* the donor's tax burden) rather than representing a *de facto* tax as in classical antiquity. On the other hand, schooling and education have become public functions in modern times.

6. Reversing the long trend toward integrated comprehensive budgets, many countries are now seeing a proliferation of "off the balance sheet" funding and potential liabilities such as deposit insurance, social security, health care, and various other federal guarantee and entitlement programs. Increasingly, pressure for comprehensive budgets comes not from democracies trying to limit public power, but from creditors (including international lenders) to use budgets as a tool of financial control and to impose monetary austerity.

7. Interest-bearing public debt continues to grow precipitously, at compound rates of interest. The buildup of interest payments has empowered the finance, insurance and real estate (FIRE) sector to translate its growing economic power into political power and shift taxes onto other sectors. The upshot is that the public debt's carrying charges fall on tax-payers other than real-estate owners and *rentiers*. Ironically, this debt derives in large part from untaxing these sectors.

A perverse tendency thus has arisen to levy taxes not on an "economic" basis—not to encourage new direct investment, employment or rising living standards while discouraging activities not deemed as socially desirable—but to tax profits and wages rather than "unearned" rents and monopoly incomes from zero-sum economic free rides. This uneconomic tax policy represents a shift away from optimum fiscal principles.

Unlike the case in antiquity, the rental income generated by real estate is not being consumed mainly in the form of luxury consumption, nor is it paid out in taxes. Rather, it is turned over to creditors as interest on their mortgage lending. The modern objective of lenders is only rarely to foreclose. Nominal ownership and management is left in the hands of the borrowers so as to extract the maximum amount of current income by leaving on-site management to property holders who have an equity interest in the gains they hope to realize.

Inasmuch as the payment of interest is deemed a tax-deductible business expense (rather than simply a way of leveraging or "gearing" one's equity investment), the indebting of real estate has left less money for the tax collector. Property taxes have declined as a proportion of public budgets (and national income) while interest charges have risen, creating a fiscal squeeze.

8. The struggle between governments and creditors for the land's economic surplus persists today. The more mortgage credit is attached to the land, the more rental revenue is converted into interest payments, and hence is unavailable for the tax collector.

In Bronze Age Mesopotamia this led rulers frequently to cancel the debts attached to the land. Many creditors were in fact tax collectors who paid the tax themselves, and collected heavy interest payments out of the land's crop yield (which creditors sought to take on the threshing floor). The royal Clean Slate proclamations "restored order" by freeing the land of debts and thereby enabling its cultivators once again to turn over their stipulated payments to the palace.

In today's world the land has become so heavily mortgaged that nearly all the growth in land-rent over the past half century has been taken by mortgage lenders as interest. Taxation of the land and other real estate has shrunk proportionally. Indeed, to raise the land tax too sharply (to say nothing of suddenly collecting the entire land rent for the public sector) would create a financial crisis, because the rental income cannot be paid both to the government *and* the creditors. Higher taxes would "crowd out" the creditor's mortgage claim, wiping out the savings that are the counterpart to these debts. This would injure the economy's financial viability. On the other hand, if the land's mortgage interest continues to expand, either the government or landlords will be squeezed yet further.

In recent decades, it is governments that have been squeezed throughout the world. In America, the real estate industry has obtained so many tax breaks that it has become virtually free of income taxation. What the government has relinquished has been taken by the real estate lenders. In this respect the un-taxing of real estate has become a major factor contributing to budget deficits today.[12] For without the ability to tax the land's rental income, governments must tax profits and wages, thereby adding to national cost structures. (A land tax does not add to costs, and does not discourage the "production" of more land.)

If public capture of economic rent were phased in gradually, interest on real estate debt would be replaced by tax payments. And as fewer savings were invested in mortgages, they would be lent to other sectors, establishing similar debt-claims there.

Restoring the land tax to its historic role as the major source of fiscal revenue would reduce the rental income free to be pledged to creditors. This would shift the flow of credit away from mortgage lending to either more directly productive uses (such as the financing of industry or other direct investment), or to consumer debt, the funding of corporate takeovers and so forth. To the extent that these loans found their counterpart in new direct investment and employment, the economy would benefit.

9. As in the late Roman Empire, today's wealthiest property holders have broken free of taxation by obtaining special tax breaks and exemptions. Whereas antiquity's special amendments to taxation were designed to raise money from the wealthiest families, today's amendments to the tax code typically take the form of loopholes favoring the rich, and *rentiers* in particular. Society's wealthiest members thus are breaking free of taxation once again, creating fiscal crises much as they did in every ancient economy.

The upshot is that government budgets (especially at the local level) are shifting away from property taxes to sales taxes and payroll taxes that fall mainly on the lower 90 percent of the population, not the upper 10 percent as in early antiquity.

Notes

1. M. M. Austin and P. Vidal-Naquet, *Economic and Social History of Ancient Greece: An Introduction* (Berkeley and Los Angeles: University of California Press, 1977), p. 121.

2. Leo A. Oppenheim, *Ancient Mesopotamia: Portrait of a Dead Civilization* (rev. ed.; Chicago: University of Chicago Press, 1977), pp. 120f.

3. Moses Finley, *Economy and Society in Ancient Greece* (London: Penguin Books, 1981), p. 90.

4. Muhammed A. Dandamayev and Vladimir G. Lukonin, *The Culture and Social Institutions of Ancient Iran* (Cambridge, England: Cambridge University Press, 1989), p. 190.

5. Ibid., p. 178.

6. Austin and Vidal-Naquet, op. cit., p. 122.

7. A. M. Andreades, *A History of Greek Public Finance* (Cambridge, MA: Harvard University Press, 1933), pp. 291f.

8. The broad dynamics are discussed by Michael Hudson, "Land Monopolization, Fiscal Crises and Clean Slate 'Jubilee' Proclamations in Antiquity," in Michael Hudson, G. C. Miller and Kris Feder, eds., *A Philosophy for a Fair Society* (London: Shepheard—Walwyn, 1994), and "Private landownership, debt, and fiscal crisis in the ancient Near East," in Robert Hunt and Antonio Gilman, eds., *Property: The Economic Context* (Waco, TX: Society for Economic Anthropology, 1997). See also Mikhail Rostovtzeff, *The Social and Economic History of the Roman Empire* (Oxford: Oxford University Press, 1926) for the Roman Empire, and Louis Brehier, *The Life and Death of Byzantium* (Amsterdam: North Holland Publishing Co., 1977) for Byzantine society.

9. For a translation of this edict, see J. J. Finkelstein, "The Edict of Ammisaduqa," in James B. Pritchard, ed., *The Ancient Near East: Vol. II: A New Anthology of Texts and Pictures* (Princeton: Princeton University Press, 1975), pp. 36–41.

10. On the dynamics of this privatization see Michael Hudson and Baruch A. Levine, eds., *Privatization in the Ancient Near East and Classical World* (Cambridge, MA., Peabody Museum of Archaeology and Ethnology, 1996).

11. Arnold Toynbee, *Hannibal's Legacy: The Hannibalic War's Effects on Roman Life* (London: Oxford University Press, 1965).

12. See Hudson, works cited.

Chapter 2

European Feudalism from its Emergence through its Decline

BY KENNETH JUPP*

AFTER THE COLLAPSE of the Roman Empire, the outstanding feature of Europe was the feudal system. Thenceforward until the late Middle Ages, land paid virtually all the costs of government in England, and indeed throughout most of Europe. The following account focuses primarily on England as a particular case of a system that obtained quite generally, although, of course, details varied from country to country and also within countries. The land in use was overwhelmingly agricultural. Europe took refuge in a feudal system in the face of increasing barbarian invasion. In England, following the Norman Conquest in the eleventh century, the continental feudal system was super-imposed on the existing Saxon tenure of land, which had already developed some of its characteristics.

Feudalism is now a term that carries connotations of privilege and oppression. It was indeed a system of unequal hereditary status. Yet it stood for a kind of justice, because no one was so high that his privileges were not conditional upon the discharge of obligations, and no one was so low that he was without certain rights. Although in practice it often fell short of this ideal, it was only when feudalism began to disintegrate, that privilege became wholly divorced from obligation, which simply disappeared. This

---

*Sir Kenneth Jupp holds an M.A. from Oxford University. After preparing for the Bar at Lincoln's Inn, he practiced as a barrister, being ultimately named Queen's Counsel, and later accepting appointment to the Bench. He served as a justice of the High Court for 15 years from 1975 until his retirement. Sir Kenneth was awarded the Military Cross for valor under enemy fire as an officer during World War II, and was knighted in 1975. He is author of "On the Wisdom of Mr. Bumble" (1992), *Economics—A Christian View* (1995), and *Stealing Our Land* (1997).

disintegration was inextricably tied to the increasing treatment of land (whether in town or country) as absolute private property free from obligation, and to the increasing dependence of government upon other sources of revenue. In systems based on Roman law, a landowner always had *dominium*. England differs from the continent of Europe in this, because under the English common law the Crown remains the sole ultimate owner of the land. The subject has freehold tenure (Lat. *tenêre*: "to hold") from the Crown.

It is tempting to regard this as a vestigial remnant of the early Teutonic and Celtic systems (including the clan systems of Scotland, Ireland, and Wales) in which ultimate ownership of all land was vested in the chief or king, not as his private property, but in his capacity as trustee for the tribe or nation. But title to English land derives from William's conquest, and probably took this form because of William's need to establish an armed guard over his conquered Saxon subjects, and at the same time to reward his followers in the venture.

I

The Legacy of Rome

THE ECONOMY OF the Roman republic was almost entirely agricultural. Its political history was dominated by the land, of which there was always a shortage. Hemmed in from access to the mouth of the Tiber and the coastal ports by the Etruscans in early days, then by the Latins, and finally by the Carthaginians, Rome was unable to trade independently, so that there was very little industry. Merchants, shopkeepers, and workmen in the city dealt mostly in imported goods. The urban dwellers were fed on cheap imported grain. The *ager publicus* (public land) could be rented from the state, but to the peasant proprietor who lacked capital, it was useless except for grazing. Military service was frequent. Bad harvests, enemy raids, and neglect of husbandry during absence on military service could put the peasant proprietor into debt. But his land tax remained unchanged. Had he been paying the true rental value on the land, the tax would have varied to reflect such vicissitudes, and he could have survived unscathed. Under harsh laws of debt, defaulters could be sold into slavery. The only escape was *nexum*—a personal pledge of service with the creditor until the debt was paid off.

A hundred and twenty years of war against Carthage vastly increased the ager publicus, but left it so devastated that the peasantry would not re-occupy it. New colonies were founded on land allotted to discharged soldiers. But the bulk of it was sold off to the rich patricians who had made fortunes from war and provincial administration. Moreover, the rich bought up the lands allotted to peasants who had subsequently failed through lack of capital. At the same time, the wars brought enormous numbers of prisoners who were sold by the government as slaves.

As Roman power spread in further conquests, Carthaginian slaves were joined by Spanish, Greek, Macedonian, and Syrian prisoners of war. Slavery sapped the vitality of Roman life. It allowed the capitalist to accumulate wealth without paying wages. It drove out free men from any form of work, urban or rural. Large areas of Italy, especially in the south, fell into ruin and became infested with malaria. Towns decayed. The unemployed crowded the city, and were sustained by state imports of grain, now available as tribute, which glutted the markets, fed the soldiers, and were from time to time distributed to the populace at cheap rates. The peasants were unable to sell their grain.

The establishment of the Principate and the rule of Augustus brought peace and prosperity, but no change in the basic class structure. The economic expansion which followed was enjoyed by a minority of the population. The lower classes continued to live near subsistence level.

A. The Later Roman Empire

With the decline of the Roman empire, barbarian attacks impoverished and depopulated the frontier provinces, and laid a burden of defense on the empire which overstrained the administrative machinery and its economic resources. The army doubled in size between the second and the fourth centuries, and the corrupt civil service expanded in proportion. By the sixth century, Christian bishops and clergy had become far more numerous than the civil 'service. The Senate, though numerically small was immensely rich, and its members and their families maintained an army of slaves and craftsmen to keep them in luxury. These unproductive classes were supported by the rents and taxes extorted from the peasantry. The idle urban poor were kept at bay with bread and circuses.

A high proportion of the land in the empire was owned by absentee landlords. Increasingly high taxation caused the abandonment of marginal land when landlords could no longer make a profit. Land of high quality continued to yield high rents, command high prices, and pay high taxes. The peasant freeholder lived a hand-to-mouth existence which made it impossible for him to accumulate any capital reserve. Faced by a sudden stroke of misfortune and the inexorable demands of the tax collector, the peasant had either to abandon his land and seek employment with a neighboring landowner, or borrow at exorbitant interest rates which made foreclosure ultimately inevitable. Malnutrition and disease took their toll. Barbarian invasions resulted in massacres, famines, and epidemics.

After taxes, and other exactions including, in many cases, rent, the peasantry had not enough left to rear sufficient children to counterbalance the high death rate. The sale of newborn infants was legislated against, and must have been common.[1]

> The paramount importance of agriculture in the economy of the Empire can scarcely be exaggerated. In taxes, it provided the bulk of the revenue of the state. The praetorian prefecture, which supplied all the major needs of the administration, relied entirely on a land tax, which was exclusively based on agricultural land, farm stock, and the rural population . . . By far the greatest part of the national income of the Roman empire was, so far as we can estimate, derived from agriculture.[2]

The land tax (*tributum*) had always been the mainstay of the Roman tax system. However "land tax" is something of a misnomer because it was not wholly based on land, and urban land was exempt. It was reorganized by Augustus, and later by Diocletian (284–305), but not applied uniformly throughout the empire. Diocletian's system as a whole was called *Capitatio*. The assessment was made on land, stock, and the rural population (slave and free). The urban population in almost all provinces was not included. The land was measured by the *iugum*—an area of land not unlike the English "hide" which varied in size to allow for differences between ploughland (in three classes), vineyards, lowland olive groves, and upland olive groves. Hence its name *iugatio*. The labor working the farm was counted for tax at one head (*caput*) per man, two per woman, and a fraction of a head per animal. It was collected in kind (*Annona*), probably to avoid the effects of inflation.

There were in addition some seven other imperial taxes at different times and in different parts of the empire. These included sales taxes, customs dues; "gifts" (in practice obligatory) of gold from senators and from cities; and a surtax on the landed estates of senators, which brought in little revenue. Constantine added a tax on merchants of all kinds.

II

The Development of Feudalism

IN THE LATER empire, a common resort of peasant freeholders driven to desperation was to seek refuge in the patronage of a powerful person. Sometimes villagers paid a regular bribe to the military commander of the province to station troops in their village to frighten off, or if necessary eject by force, the landlord's agent or the tax collector. If either of these sought legal redress, the case, because it involved soldiers, would be tried in the military court. The fifth century emperors legislated against this kind of patronage, from which somehow or other the patron became the owner of the land in return for his protection of the client. Here we see the germ of a practice which later on developed into the European feudal system. In the face of continuing barbarian invasions, the smaller landowners were driven to seek protection and maintenance from more powerful men in return for which they gave service and obedience. Two institutions grew up in the Frankish kingdom from as early as the seventh century: *commendatio*, by which a man, while remaining free, placed himself under some powerful lord for protection in return for service, and *beneficium*—land given him at little or no rent other than his service. He was then the lord's "vassal," increasingly on terms of military service on horseback. The bargain between them was struck by a ceremony of *homage* and *fealty*.

In Britain it was not until after the Norman Conquest that a full system of feudalism came into existence. Even then it differed from the Continental. In England,

> the doctrine of tenure is a doctrine of universal application in the land law. It was applied to the free tenures, to the unfree tenures, and to the relation of lessor and lessee for years . . . [This] is a purely English phenomenon. Other countries knew feudal tenure; but the law governing it was only applicable to noble or military tenures.[3]

A. The English Settlements

The Germanic tribes who succeeded the Romans in occupying Britain had one thing in common. They were regarded by the Romans as utter barbarians. They had not been affected by contact with Rome, as had the Franks, who had fought both for and against the Roman Emperors. Angles, Saxons, Jutes, and Frisians who settled in England were still imbued with the traditional freedom of primitive German society. They were loyal to their leader, but recognized no authority between the leader and themselves. Once settled in Britain, their leader was a king. The large number of kings gradually reduced to the Heptarchy of the sixth to eighth centuries: Mercia, Anglia, Kent, Wessex, and so on. The *Ceorl* (Churl) formed the basis of society. The ceorl was a free man. He cooperated with other free men in farming the land, and sharing the available woods, springs, marshes, rough ground, and fisheries. Any disputes between them were subject to adjudication only by or on behalf of the king. The ceorl was often a slave owner. His "family land" could not be alienated so as to by-pass expectant heirs. He was the independent master of a peasant household, whose position was protected by the king's law. He had no claim to nobility, but was subject to no lord below the king.[4]

Protected to a considerable extent from the rest of Europe by the sea, and never fully Romanized, the Saxons, and later the

Danes, and later still Danes and Saxons together, escaped the fate of subject peoples under the later Roman Empire. They were able to build up a society where the peasant farmers were considerably more free than were their continental counterparts. Their lands bore the expense of the king's household and government, and of frequent war taxes, but the burden was spread with some semblance of justice by being levied on a measure of land called, in most of the south, a *hide*.

In Wessex, this unit of land-division was sufficient to support a man and his household—*terra unius familiae*. It was differently measured in *sulungs* in Kent, and in *carrucages* in the Danelaw. The heaviest peace-time burden was the duty of supporting the king by contributions to a *feorm* (food-rent): the amount of provision needed to support the royal household for 24 hours, which was later collected in kind and then in money at the nearest royal farm. The second burden was the building and maintaining of bridges and fortresses (*brycg bot*, and *byrh bot*), and service in the *fyrd* (the military array of the kingdom) when called upon. There were also dues payable to the church. Above all and distinct from these peacetime burdens was the war tax called *danegeld*. It too was based on hidage.

There is no trace of nobility amongst these invading tribes, except the nobility of the kingly family. But round the king were gathered his *gesiths*—companions who were supported by grants of newly conquered or unoccupied land. There was a class distinction between gesiths and ceorls in terms of the *wergild*—the price of a man payable in case of manslaughter. The *gesithcund man's* wergild was 1,200 shillings, as against the 200 shilling wergild of the ceorl. By the seventh century, grants were being given to the king's companions, not of land, but of the rents and services deriving from it which were properly due the king. As this custom grew, there were soon men of higher class who were lords over large number of small villages. The duty to repair bridges easily passed into a duty to repair the buildings of the new lord's farmstead. Hence, the "Manor" which features so much in the Domesday Book. It was basically the big house, or farm at which dues were paid.

Subsequently, the idea grew that the landlord needed written evidence of his rights, and this by Alfred's time (871–899) had become familiar as "book"—viz., charter—, land. It stands distinguished from *folc-land*, which may mean common land (ager publicus), or more probably ordinary land, that is to say, land held under common law.

Thus the Normans, after the Conquest, found a system of land tenure which, in part at least, was not unlike the feudal system which covered continental Europe. The classes which had by then evolved were: *Thegn* (or Thane), *Geneat*, *Cottar*, *Gebur*, and *Slave*. The status of Thegn, meaning "one who serves another," varied widely, but by the time of the conquest a class of hereditary thegns had emerged who, bound to the king in military service, can be equated to the later barons as holders of extensive lands scattered over the country. The *Geneat* was a retainer, usually mounted, whose services were those befitting a free man—escorting, guarding, running errands, and at harvest time, working in the fields. The *Cottar* was a peasant occupying a cottage usually as an out-servant.

The *Gebur* was the lowest class of tenant farmer. At the risk of oversimplifying, we may say that he fell within the generic category of serf, that is, a person bound to, bought, sold, and inherited with the land, yet possessed of certain hereditary rights in it, and not being the personal property of his lord. He seems to have held a "yardland" (a quarter of a hide), which was the typical villein tenement of the Middle Ages. Its acreage would vary, as did the acreage of his hide, in different districts, but 30 acres might be a reasonable guess as to its average size. For this, he had to perform a very heavy burden of services, and pay some money and some rents in kind. Into this class sank "innumerable men of free descent, cultivating on unalterable terms family lands which they and their ancestors had been compelled to surrender into the hands of a lord in return for relief from present necessities and in the hope of future security."[5] Into it likewise rose innumerable slaves. We have already noted the existence of the *Slave* in Saxon England. Although the Domesday Book in 1086 records slaves as still forming nine percent of the population, they were becoming absorbed into the large gebur class, and by the 12th century ceased to exist as a separate body.

It would seem as if the term, "villein," which in Domesday is used simply to signify villager, gradually came to take on the meaning of "gebur" and eventually to supplant it. The villein, half-slave as he was in some respects,

> held lands of his own which he tilled on those days of the year when his lord had no claim upon him or his oxen. And he had his share in the use and profit of the village meadow, the village pasture, and the village woodland and waste, where the swine and geese were turned loose . . . There was for him no "equality before the law." . . . But he had double protection against ill-usage. First, the lord and bailiff found it in their interest to receive from him willing rather than unwilling work and to give him no motive to run away. For he could not be easily replaced (like the overworked slave in old Rome). And secondly, he had the security of village tradition, legally expressed in "the custom of the manor," and enforced in the Manor Court.[6]

In the Danelaw, in the north and east of England, there was an extensive free peasantry individually enjoying personal independence. This was particularly the case in East Anglia and even more so in Lincolnshire. In the region known as the territory of the Five Boroughs (Lincoln, Nottingham, Derby, Leicester, and Stamford), "a free population established long before the reign of William I continued in possession of its ancient rights and liberties throughout the whole of the Middle Ages."[7] Here there was a body referred to in Domesday as "sokemen." The Danelaw sokeman, though bound to his lord by the tie of homage and such payments and services as resulted by custom therefrom, had his own recognized place in the courts; could alienate his land or any portion of it by gift, sale, or exchange; paid his taxes directly to the king or the sheriff; and, above all, was free of the villein's duty of working two or more days a week on his lord's land. He might be expected to help out by supplying labor at those seasons when work was heaviest, but this detracted neither from his dignity nor from his independence.[8]

B. The Norman Conquest

The Normans were Vikings from Scandinavia who had ravaged the coastal areas of Britain and France, and settled in Northern France in (traditionally) the year 911. They there adopted the ex-Roman civilization, and sallied out to conquests in the Mediterranean. The Norman William conquered England. He began his reign in the hope of associating Frenchmen and Englishmen in his government on equal terms. But it was not to be. After two harshly-crushed Saxon revolts, by the end of his reign, "all directive power within the English state had passed into alien hands. With less than half a dozen exceptions, every lay lord whose possessions entitled him to political influence was a foreigner."[9]

William regarded the whole of England as his by conquest, whence the doctrine of present day English law that all land is owned by the Crown, and that the highest estate a man may have is a tenancy in fee simple. The Conqueror distributed the land to his followers as a reward for their services, in "manors" scattered all over the country. They held these manors upon condition of rendering the king service in person, or in kind, or in money. Most of the head tenants and some of the under tenants held on condition of knight service, later commuted into a money payment in lieu of service called *scutage*. Indeed, nearly all the feudal dues were before long commuted into money. Scutage ought to have been made into a regular rent, rising to match the increasingly rapid decline in the value of money. But the kings were never able to achieve this. Beneath this overlay of those who held directly from the king, later called "barons," the Saxon undertenants continued to a large extent to cultivate the land on the same conditions as before the conquest.

William inherited a financial system which brought him the income from royal lands, the revenues from justice, and his dues as overlord. The Saxon method of collecting danegeld assessed on hidage of land continued until the 13th century. The judicial system of local courts, which was the great virtue of the Saxon state, continued (surprisingly) on Saxon lines even though the names changed from thegn to count or baron, until royal courts began to take over later in the twelfth century. Nevertheless, the Saxon population felt the Conquest as a terrible disaster. The new forests reserved for the king's hunting and the cruel new forest laws governing them were certainly disastrous. But historians vacillate still between regarding the conquest as the destruction of a fine civilization, or as clearing the ground for a cosmopolitan culture of which Anglo-Saxon England gave no promise.[10]

Both systems, the Saxon and the feudal with its overlay of Norman masters, recognized the basic necessity of land, without which a family must starve. Land everywhere was held in return for payment in service—military, civil, or personal—or in money. Even the "unfree tenure" of the lowest classes was protected by custom, and when money payment became more common the royal courts extended their protection to the unfree as "copyholders"—that is to say, on the basis of the copy of their customary rights to be found in the Rolls of the Manor. The basis of contribution to the revenue of the Crown was the land which provided the subject with the means with which to pay. His position and status in society was determined by the land he possessed.

III

The Decay of Feudalism

THE REIGN OF Richard I (1189–1199) brought about a subtle change which was the seed-bed for shifting the Crown's revenues from the land to the personal wealth (or poverty) of the people. Richard was an absentee ruler, spending in England only six months of his ten year reign. His wars in France and the crusade to recover Jerusalem made him a popular king. But his financial demands on the country weakened the realm and left his unpopular youngest brother, John, who succeeded him, in an impossible position.

The Saladin Tithe to support the crusade, and Richard's huge ransom after he was captured by the Duke of Austria, had been raised by a levy on the goods and chattels of the whole people of the realm. In 1225 (ten years after Magna Carta), these precedents were used when the archbishops, bishops, abbots, priors, earls, barons, knights, free men, and *all people of the realm* (italics added), in return for a renewal of the Great Charter, along with its clauses concerning the harsh forest laws (now extracted and made into a "Charter of the Forests"), granted to the king a fifteenth of their movables. This was an entirely non-feudal tax, quite unrelated to the land a man held. It was a wealth tax levied entirely on movables, and not on land. Needless to say, "the people of the realm" had had no say in it. By the end of the century, it had become a regular system of taxation known as the "fifteenths and tenths." By that time too, inflation of around 50 percent had made scutage valueless, and it was no longer collected, although it was not abolished until 1660.

The Charter of the Forests was the relaxation of the very harsh forest laws of the Norman kings which resulted in imprisonment or death for many a poacher of deer. But it also provides the background to a cheerful life led by merry and carefree men consorting there, and giving rise to ballads, folklore, and romance. In 1230, the sheriff of Yorkshire was accountable for 32s. 6d. of the chattels of "Robin Hood, *fugitivus.*" Was this the famous outlaw?—or was he the dispossessed Earl of Huntingdon?—or was he a Saxon holding out against the Normans, as *Ivanhoe* represents him? It may be simply a myth. But it represents forever the delight in imagining war waged on the proud abbots and rich knights, to make them give back to the poor something of the goods which they had in truth stolen from them. "All my bones shall say, Lord, who is like unto thee, which delivereth the poor and needy from him that spoileth him." (Psalm 35, and elsewhere in the Psalms and the Prophets: for example, Ps. 10, Is. 3:14, Is. 5:8, Mic. 2:2, and Jesus himself in Mt. 23:14.)

Following the Norman Conquest, but not necessarily because of it, there had been a considerable rise in trade, national and international. Monks from the various orders in Europe had flocked to England to set up religious houses. There was a boom in the building of castles, abbeys, and priories. The wool trade with the continent flourished. The crusades brought luxury goods from the more cultured kingdoms of the East. The upper classes took on more and more expensive life styles. The use of money became widespread, including paper money in the shape of what we would nowadays call letters of credit. These were available from Jews who had come to England following the Conquest, and who were able to retain contacts with their relatives and friends on the continent, which made the transfer of coin or gold unnecessary.

The scale of this expansion can best be inferred from the *Scaccarium Aaronis* which had to be set up to deal with the estate of Aaron of Lincoln on his death in 1185. He was found to number amongst his debtors, beside the English king, the King of Scotland, the Archbishop of Canterbury, and several bishops, abbots, and earls. He had provided the capital for the building of nine Cistercian Houses, and the Abbeys of Peterborough and St. Albans. Aaron was exceptional, but a similar though less wealthy Jewish financier was to be found in nearly every city of England. The Jew's house, the castle, and the priory were often the only stone buildings among the wooden houses of the city.

The Jews were expelled in 1290 after appalling persecution, and did not begin to return until Stuart times. Edward I and the kings who followed him were now able to borrow from their rich city merchants, who, paying no rent to the Crown for their lands, were in a position to lend the king at interest what their rural forefathers had had to pay him as legal and customary dues. They were able to do this because the feudal taxes "fell only upon the landed interests." The urban population, whose wealth and importance was steadily increasing, were not comprehended in this scheme of finance.[11]

The phrase "landed interests" points to the trouble. The word "land" is used to mean the country as opposed to the town. The land which had disappeared under buildings was forgotten, although it was much more valuable than country land, and yielded increasingly high ground-rent. To get at this wealth, the king had to exercise his feudal right to tallage (an arbitrary tax levied on towns and demesne lands of the Crown), and he sold and re-sold charters, and amended or renewed charters granting the towns jurisdiction over their affairs. The towns paid up, but did very well out of it. Their land was the most valuable. Urban sites at that time possessed an important feature over and above those which render them relatively more valuable than rural ones today: They were generally enclosed by fortified walls which provided a measure of security to the inhabitants. Had the rental of this land been appropriated for the common weal, we might look back upon those centuries as a golden age.

These and many other developments caused the breakdown of the ancient system of land tenure. Change began within half a century of the Conquest, when the kings used mercenary soldiers in preference to their feudal knights and levies, and later employed professional judges and administrators. Over a long period of time, the courts gradually removed the prohibitions of law on the alienation of land, so that much of it became available for speculation. Greed overtook all classes. Foreign wars brought in booty which temporarily enriched the lower classes. When the booty was exhausted, discharged soldiers became a menace as vagrants. Peasant proprietors were only too ready to remove their neighbor's landmark when his body lay in a foreign field. Outbreaks of disease, the Black Death (1348) in particular, left land vacant, inviting enclosure by neighbors. The internal Wars of the Roses (1455-85) unsettled the land tenure of the contending noble families and put more discharged soldiers onto the highways. Medieval England ended when the House of Tudor took over after the Battle of Bosworth Field in 1485.

A. England in Tudor Times

High inflation, and greedy speculation in land, which necessarily gave rise to great wealth standing in stark contrast with great poverty, were features of Tudor England. There was much controversy between the radical Protestant and the conservative Catholic factions, usually expressed in the somewhat fierce rhetorical language of the age.

Sir Thomas More in his *Utopia* (1516) had outlined in the form of a Platonic dialogue the ideal state in which wealth was shared as Plato suggested in the *Republic*. More wrote of the sheep-breeding ecclesiastical landlords: "Sheep have become so great devourers and so wild that they eat up and swallow down the very men themselves. They consume, destroy, and devour whole fields, houses, and cities." He noted the "great dearth of victualles" in a time of rising prices. These economic changes—now accepted as a test of growing prosperity—were at the time looked upon as an unmitigated evil. More ultimately lost his head, although not as an English Protestant. He wrote chiefly in Latin.

Hugh Latimer's seven Lenten sermons before Edward VI in 1549, were in ripe colloquial English. They contain stinging indictments of the rich, and vigorous pleas in defense of the poor. He had already been accused of sedition to Henry VIII and was now accused of treason.[12] He railed against judges taking bribes. He pointed to the sins of landlords' extortionate rents, and to the impoverishment of the English yeomen class from which he himself had come. He publicized the oppression of poor widows by their rapacious overlords. He ridiculed a certain Bishop of Winchester to whom "the Bishop of Rome sent a Cardinal's hatte. He should have had a Tyburne tippet, a halpeny halter, and all such proud prelates." Latimer died eventually at the stake.

Enclosures had been going on for a long time. But only in the reigns of Henry VII and Henry VIII did Parliament pass Enclosure Acts attempting to put a stop to "the pulling down of towns," "the waste of houses," and the decay of husbandry. These attempts were so ineffective that Cardinal Wolsey appointed 17 commissions to inquire what towns and hamlets, houses and buildings had been destroyed since the passing of the first such Act; and what additions had been made to existing parks.[13]

The Inquiry of 1517 showed that in Bedfordshire, Leicestershire, and Warwickshire, the chances of eviction were about even for tenants on both lay and ecclesiastical estates . . . In Leicestershire, the enclosure carried out by the abbey of Leicester (notably Baggrave and Ingardsby) prompted the violent attack of Thomas Rous: "It is a den of thieves and murderers. The profit of the enclosures the monks enjoy . . . but the blood of those slain and mutilated there cries every year to God for vengeance."[14]

These developments produced a floating population of vagabonds who lived on the roads and "slept in haylofts, sheep-cotes, or on doorsteps, spreading terror in the country and disease in the towns."[15]

A little later, Poor Relief was introduced for the deserving poor, while at the same time for the rogues it was whipping, and in the last resort, if they continued in their roguery, death for felony.[16] Poor relief was administered by parish officials employed by the landed interests. It was often accompanied by harsh treatment. It was always meager, and came increasingly to be accompanied with conditions so humiliating that many who needed it were ashamed to resort to it.

From the Tudor period onwards, efforts to raise taxes had continued using various expedients, but nearly always on the basis of movable wealth, except for poll taxes, which were a sorry failure, on one occasion (1381) touching off a peasant uprising. When in 1787 the customs and the "hated excise" (a foreign importation during the Commonwealth) were consolidated, they controlled no less than 3,000 dutiable articles.

B. The Peasants' Wars in Germany

De Tocqueville, in his famous treatise, *L'Ancien Régime*, explains why Feudal Rights had become more odious to the people of France than anywhere else.

> The revolution did not break out in those countries where the better preservation of those institutions made their annoyance and their harshness most felt by the people, but on the contrary in those countries where they were felt the least; so that the yoke appeared most intolerable just in those places where it was most light.

The conditions which led to the French revolution are well known, and need no further comment. But de Tocqueville points out that "in no part of Germany was serfdom completely abolished, and in the greater part of Germany the people were actually *ascripti glebae*, as in the Middle Ages. Almost all the soldiers who (in the 18th century) formed the armies of Frederick II and of Maria Theresa were veritable serfs."[17]

There were frequent uprisings, especially in western Germany, toward the end of the fifteenth century. The growing money economy and debased coinage had put pressure on the landlords, who in turn exacted increased labor services and dues from the peasants, and encroached upon the common lands. The Reformation, by encouraging free speech and Bible-reading, enabled Protestant peasants to use scriptural texts to support their claims to emancipation. The policies of Charles V when he became emperor in 1519 encouraged belief that he would be their protector against their oppressors. In 1525, the Peasants' War broke out. Spreading from the Black Forest to the Rhine valley, the Tyrol and Austria, the movement was joined by some of the townsmen revolting against the town aristocracies. Luther, who recognized the justice of the peasants' grievances but not their right to armed rebellion, eventually sided vigorously with the authorities, who after defeating the French at Pavia, had troops enough to put down the inadequately armed peasants—which they did with appalling cruelty.

A gradual decline in serfdom followed in the areas affected, but this was probably due not to the revolt, but to economic progress of industry in western Germany, particularly along the Rhine. The old conditions continued in the eastern and northern parts where there had been no revolt. In the area dominated by the Junker agricultural estates, serfdom was not abolished until 1807.

C. England after the Restoration

The moribund remains of feudalism were swept away by Parliament in 1660 by the Statute of Tenures, and the land law systematized by the Property Acts of 1925, with the result that practically all tenure of land became *socage* tenure. It was the least encumbered of all the tenures with obsolete and burdensome features, reminiscent of an older day, when land-holding involved public rights and duties as well as private rights of ownership. It was because it fit better with the newer ideas, which regarded land-holding simply as a form of property, that it finally superseded all the other free tenures.[18] But after 1660, Parliament was supreme. The great landowners sat in the Lords, and the Commons consisted of landowners elected only by persons with a land owning qualification. In the following century, Parliament reversed the policy of the early Tudors, who legislated against enclosures, and passed private Acts *allowing* enclosure in the name of "improvement." An estimate was given to the Select Committee on Enclosures in 1844 that there were some 1,700 private Enclosure Acts before 1800, and some 2,000 between 1800 and 1844. By this means, according to the General Report of the

Board of Agriculture on Enclosures of that year, 4,187,056 acres were enclosed between the time of Queen Anne and 1805.[19] There were in addition many enclosures without Act of Parliament, and some of the Acts merely legalized engrossments which had already occurred, and were patently illegal when they were perpetrated.

IV

Conclusion

FEUDALISM HAD ITS faults, but it had its virtues also. In the US, paragon of so-called "capitalism" in the enlightened times in which we live, *Tax Freedom Day* in 2000 fell on the third of May. Assuming his taxes at all levels to be concentrated at the beginning instead of being spread throughout the year, that was the average date that an American could start working for himself instead of for the government.[20] Of course, conditions under feudalism were not uniform, but taken as a whole, the number of days annually that the feudal tiller of the soil was obliged to work on his lord's demesne was certainly no greater, and may well have been considerably fewer, than the 123 that an American is obliged to work for Uncle Sam and his state and local uncles.[21] For his labor, the medieval peasant received, in addition to protection, a cottage with garden and field, and access to the village commons. On top of his labor, a gebur paid ten pence to his lord at Michaelmas, 23 bushels of barley, and two hens at Martinmas, and either a young sheep or two pence at Easter. But his lord would have set him up for life with livestock, implements of husbandry, and basic household furnishings.

Notes

1. A. H. M. Jones, *The Later Roman Empire, 284 to 602* (Oxford: Basil Blackwell, 1973), Vol. 2, pp. 1025–1068.

2. Ibid., Vol. 2, p. 729.

3. William Holdsworth, *Historical Introduction to the Land Law* (Oxford: Clarendon, 1927), pp. 21f.

4. Frank Stenton, *Anglo-Saxon England* (3rd ed.; Oxford: Clarendon, 1971), pp. 277f.

5. Ibid., p. 475.

6. G. M. Trevelyan, *History of England* (3rd ed.; London: Longmans Green, 1945), p. 147.

7. Stenton, *The Free Peasantry of the Northern Danelaw* (Oxford: Clarendon, 1969), p. 1.

8. Ibid.

9. Stenton, *Anglo-Saxon England*, p. 680.

10. Ibid. p. 286.

11. Austin Lane Poole, *Domesday Book to Magna Carta* (2nd ed.; Oxford: Clarendon, 1955), p. 418.

12. Hugh Latimer, *Seven Sermons Before Edward VI* (London: Constable, 1895), 3rd sermon, p. 82.

13. J. D. Mackie, *The Earlier Tudors, 1485–1558* (Oxford: Clarendon, 1952), p. 451.

14. Peter Ramsey, *Tudor Economic Problems* (London: Gollancz, 1972), pp. 27f.

15. J. B. Black, *The Reign of Elizabeth* (Oxford: Clarendon, 1959), p. 264.

16. Ibid.

17. Alexis de Tocqueville, *L'Ancien Régime* (1856; Oxford: Basil Blackwell, [1856] 1949), p. 27.

18. Holdsworth, op. cit., pp. 38 and 36.

19. Cited in J. L. and Barbara Hammond, *The Village Labourer* (4th ed.; London: Longmans Green, 1927), Vol. 1, p. 35.

20. Calculation by the Tax Foundation, Washington, DC.

21. The present writer is indebted to the editor for suggesting this comparison and providing the US statistics.

PART TWO

THE AMERICAS

Chapter 3

Argentina

BY FERNANDO SCORNIK GERSTEIN*

THE CONCEPT OF land-value taxation has a long history in Argentina. Some of the country's early national heroes came under the influence of Physiocracy and its theory of the *impôt unique*. Among them were General Manuel Belgrano, principal mover behind Argentina's Declaration of Independence, and Bernardino Rivadavia, its first president.

I

The Law of Emphyteusis[1]

THROUGH Rivadavia's initiative, the Law of Emphyteusis was passed by the General Constituent Congress held in Buenos Aires in 1826. It provided for the granting of long-term leaseholds of public land (which at that time constituted most of the country), with the expectation that land rent would thus become the chief and perhaps the only source of pubic revenue. The way for it had

*Fernando Scornik Gerstein received his law degree from the University of Buenos Aires. A specialist in agrarian and taxation law, he was legal advisor for ten years to the Argentinean Agrarian Cooperatives. Later he was appointed advisor on land taxation to the minister of economics, and, subsequently, to the minister of agriculture. In 1975, he chaired the Special Commission on Land Taxation set up by the Ministry of Agriculture. During his years with the Ministry of Agriculture, he also served as visiting lecturer on agricultural law at his alma mater. In 1974–75, he was chairman of a political party, the Union of the Argentine People (UDELPA). Anticipating the military coup of 1976, Dr. Scornik moved to Spain a few months before it took place. There he pursued his legal career, and is now senior partner in the firm, Fernando Scornik Gerstein-Abogados, with offices in the Canary Islands and in London. He is the author of six books or monographs, including *The Basis of a Tax System on the Rent of Land* (1973), and *Poll Tax: The Tax That Sank a Government* (1996).

been paved in 1812 by a decree forbidding the sale of public lands.

As enacted, the law was not perfect in its administrative detail. Nevertheless, it established as a national policy necessary for the development of agriculture (then existing only in a very rudimentary form) the long-term leasing of public land instead of its sale. For this reason, the Law of Emphyteusis was certainly Argentina's most important step toward meaningful land reform. While the abuses inflicted by subsequent governments caused it eventually to be repealed under the stigma of "failure," the emphyteutic principle itself survived and has inspired reform-minded circles in Argentina since early in the 20th century.

The law provided for twenty-year leases. During the first ten years, the lessee would pay into the public treasury a rent or annual fee amounting to eight percent of the assessed value in the case of land used for cattle raising and four percent in the case of smaller parcels used for agriculture. The valuation was to be made by a jury of neighbors, and at the end of ten years, the Legislature was to determine the rents to be paid thereafter, according to new appraisals.

The principle underlying the government's action in passing this law is well expressed in the words of Dr. Ignacio Nuñéz, Rivadavia's diplomatic envoy to London at the time, who told the British government that "the spirit of the project is that publicly-owned lands should never be held in any way other than by leaseholds . . . The present taxes bear harmfully upon the people and hinder (the country's) development . . . The rent of land is the most solid and definite source of revenue on which the State must count." It was confidently believed, according to Nuñéz, that the public collection of land rent would make it possible to do away with tariffs and all other taxes.[2]

The statements of Julián S. de Agüero, Rivadavia's secretary of state and learned collaborator, serve further to illustrate the benefits which it was hoped the Law of Emphyteusis would bring. Agüero pointed out that the emphyteutic system was beneficial to producers since it enabled them to occupy land without having to purchase it, and, at the same time, gave them security of tenure.

"If the capital employed in the purchase of land is invested in the purchase of cattle, it will yield more profits," he said. "It is in the nation's interest . . . that the cultivated area increase, that the countryside be populated with the aid of foreign immigration, that various industries be organized and beautiful cities built. . . . If the State collects all the just rent that corresponds to each parcel, let there be no fear that anyone will apply for or monopolize a greater area than that which he can usefully exploit, for who would be willing to pay so much for land which he does not intend to utilize? Nobody!"[3]

The enactment of the law brought immediate results. Young men left the cities to devote themselves to rural occupations, and it seemed that Rivadavia's dream of creating a democracy on a solid foundation was about to be fulfilled.

The reversal of these promising developments must be viewed against the backdrop of the long and bitter conflict between the two great factions in the nascent republic—the *Unitarios* and the *Federales*. The Unitarios, of whom Rivadavia had been the dominant leader for more than a decade, were cosmopolitan idealists based in the city of Buenos Aires, who stood for centralized but liberal government reflecting advanced European ideas such as the emphyteutic principle. The Federales, a loose alliance of provincial *caudillos*, were rough-hewn populists, suspicious of centralization and foreign influence alike, who regarded the Unitarios as elitist visionaries, prone to sacrifice Argentine to British interests. Despite his enlightened sentiments, Rivadavia had an autocratic personality, and made little effort to build consensus. At a moment of crisis, after fewer than 16 months as president, he dramatically resigned, expecting to be implored to remain in office with increased authority. Instead, confidence in him had so declined that 48 of 50 legislators voted to accept his resignation.

The ensuing Federale regime (which soon gave way to some half dozen years of civil war and anarchy) took immediate opportunity to point out the shortcomings of the law—shortcomings which, in the year it had been operating, there had been no time to remove: the poor financial yield to the public treasury owing to the low appraisals made by the juries, and the fact that the system allowed too large an area to be placed under a single leasehold. (These defects time and experience would have remedied.) This laid the groundwork for changing the law, and in February 1828, it was amended to establish a uniform assessment for all lands and to fix the rents at the ridiculously low rate of two percent of the arbitrarily fixed value.

When, in 1835, General Juan Manuel de Rosas was made dictator, the fixed rent fell to practically nothing owing to the sharp devaluation of the currency,[4] and to the fact that Rosas was unwilling, in many cases, to collect it. Of course, under these circumstances, revenue from this source continued to fall short of the nation's requirements, and customs duties remained the main source of public income. The still unfinished era of landed privilege (under independence) had begun.

During the Rosas dictatorship, which lasted until 1852, large grants of land were made outright to many persons, mostly military men, and to Rosas himself, by his docile Legislature. All who opposed him were persecuted and their families despoiled of the lands they owned or held under lease from the government. Except for the warlords, who engaged in perpetual strife among themselves, the inland provinces became practically depopulated. In these regions, scarcely any foreigners dared to settle, and European immigration all but ceased.

The Emphyteutic Law, by this time robbed of most of its beneficial qualities, was repealed in 1857. All the emphyteutic leaseholders were recognized as the legal owners of the public land they had leased, and the domination of the country by a landed oligarchy was consolidated.

In the years that followed, fabulous amounts of public land were sold at nominal prices, and by 1921 it was estimated that the nation had given up forever "28,000,000 hectares of its best lands, that is, an area larger than that of several European nations combined,"[5] without the population being thereby increased to any great extent. The reason for these purchases was the anticipated price rise that would come through the expected construction of railways and the resumption of European immigration. As these expectations materialized, the landowners of Argentina suddenly found themselves so wealthy that in Paris they became as famous as the Russian aristocrats for their extravagances.

The Argentine *pampas*, or great plains, occupying an enormous area about the size of Texas, to the north, west, and south of Buenos Aires, comprises some of the richest soil on earth, ideal for intensive cultivation of a variety of crops. Yet "outside Buenos Aires and other scattered cities and towns, Argentina is an almost empty country. The reason is that a very few powerful families monopolize most of the land in enormous *estancias* (landed estates) and are satisfied to use it inadequately, usually for extensive livestock grazing. With but small investment per hectare, they can accumulate enormous wealth."[6]

For more than half a century following its repeal, the Law of Emphyteusis was virtually forgotten, and only mentioned briefly in school books as a sample of Rivadavia's idealism. Only after 1917, with the publication of *La Obra Económica de Bernardino Rivadavia* (Bernardino Rivadavia's Economic Work), by the Uruguayan historian, Andrés Lamas, did it become again a focus of public attention.

II
The Early Twentieth Century

IN THE FIRST decades of the 20th century, a new movement for land reform through changes in the incidence of taxation began in Argentina. It reflected considerable single-tax agitation in Spain, resulting from the publication in Barcelona in 1893 of a Spanish translation of Henry George's *Progress and Poverty*. (The translation was done by Magin Puig, under the supervision of Carlos Federico Adams y Michelena, a California lawyer who was a personal friend of George.)[7]

Before proceeding, however, it might be well to mention Silvio Gesell (1862–1930), whose unorthodox monetary theories were highly regarded by Lord Keynes,[8] and influenced Social Credit and the Townsend Plan. He was a German merchant who lived part of his life in Argentina, and began his economic writings there in the last decade of the 19th century. His main work, *The Natural Economic Order* (Vol. I ,1906; Vol. II, 1911) proposed, together with a plan to reduce the money rate of interest, a land reform in some ways similar to that of George, to whose memory (along with that of Moses and Spartacus) the book was dedicated. Although Gesell's monetary views had considerable impact in Argentina, some of them finding actual embodiment in government policy, his views on land were unacceptable to the dominant interests. They were more radical than those of George in that he advocated confiscating and nationalizing land instead of simply taxing its value, but less radical in that they also advocated compensation.

The fate of Gesell's land reform ideas was typical in these decades. In 1912, President Roque Saenz Peña, who in the same year introduced free, secret, and obligatory manhood suffrage to Argentina, sent to Parliament a bill providing for the taxation of "the progressive unearned increment in land values," but, despite its prestigious sponsorship, it was not even considered. However, a number of organizations were formed to promote reform along the lines urged by George, and a few excursions into politics were eventually made with moderate success.

Of these, the most noteworthy was the Partido Liberal Georgista, formed in 1921 by Carlos Villalobos-Domínguez and several other professors from various universities. Its platform demanded first a tax on the annual rental value of land which would, by gradual stages, absorb the full rental value. When this point had been reached, land would have no selling price, and it was proposed that private titles would then be abolished. Land thereafter was to be offered for lease at public auction and lifetime tenures were to be granted to the highest bidders on the basis of annual rent. All tariffs and all national, provincial, and municipal taxes were to be lowered gradually, and eventually wiped out. As can be seen, the principle bears a resemblance to the Rivadavian idea, and it won the enthusiastic support of the tenant farmers (the majority of Argentine farmers being tenants) and their sons. In the municipal elections held in the district of Pringles in the Province of Buenos Aires in 1923, the Partido Liberal Georgista offered candidates for six then-vacant seats, two of whom were elected. Despite this modest but promising success, however, the party withered away, owing to lack of efficient central leadership after the withdrawal, for personal reasons, of Villalobos-Domínguez.[9]

Parallel to this, under the government of the middle-class Radical Civic Union (1916–1930), other projects were attempted at the national and provincial levels. A number of efforts were made under Radical leadership in the Parliament to introduce a nationwide land-value tax to replace certain taxes on consumption, but to no avail.

In 1920, the Socialist Party included in its program a proposal to tax land values while exempting improvements. It was able to get land valued separately from improvements in the Federal Capital and in the national territories. In 1923, the mayor of the City of Buenos Aires, Carlos S. Noël, and his secretary of finance, Emilio Ravignani, both from the Radical Civic Union, succeeded (with strong Socialist Party backing) in passing a local by-law in Buenos Aires providing for a tax on land values to meet the costs of such public services as street lighting and cleaning, but after being falsely attacked as "unconstitutional," the law was repealed later the same year. According to Saúl P. Martinez, all these initiatives followed the economic ideas of the president, Hipólito Irigoyen.[10]

Military intervention overthrew the Radical government of Irigoyen in 1930, placing the Conservative Party in office. Although this period of Conservative rule was marked by economic growth and civil liberties were generally respected, electoral fraud was rampant and political and economic power were concentrated in the landowning classes.

However, in the province of Córdoba, laws were passed providing for separate valuation of land and improvements, with land values taxed progressively and improvements exempted from taxation. Objections were raised to the rate of progression, and the Supreme Court ruled unconstitutional any tax in excess of 30 pesos per 1,000 pesos of assessed land value, but the other provisions remained more or less in place. In 1938 (after the Radicals had long been replaced at the national level), the province of Entre Ríos, which had a Radical governor, passed legislation similar to that of Córdoba.

Finally, in 1940 a new Law for Land Development (Ley de Colonización) was approved by the Parliament, together with the "Enmienda Palacios," an amendment introduced by the Socialist

senator, Alfredo L. Palacios, authorizing the use again of the emphyteusis as a means of developing public land.

III

The Perón Era

ALL THIS CAME to an end with the military coup in 1943. It was led
by authoritarian officers, among them the dynamic Col. Juan Do-
mingo Perón, who built up a strong popular following as labor
secretary, assuming in 1945 (through free elections) the presidency himself. At first, the coup was welcomed by many who expected it to bring authentic social reform and put an end to the
fraud at the polls. Even two leading Georgists, Dr. Antonio Manuel
Molinari and Mauricio Birabent, embraced Perón and played a
significant supporting role in the first stages of his political career.
Among other things, they provided economic and technical
backing to an influential Perónist newspaper, *Democracia*, and
did much to rally support for Perón among agricultural workers.[11]

As was bound to happen, the honeymoon was brief. After being
elected president, Perón (who had imbibed fascist notions while a
military attaché, in Mussolini's Italy) moved swiftly to consolidate
his power by turning the General Confederation of Labor into an
engine of personal authority, stifling the press, and persecuting
the opposition parties. He instituted a sharply protectionist and
inflationist program that, after three or four bonanza years,
brought the economy to a state of virtual collapse. But, at the same
time, Perón pushed forward laws recognizing social rights for the
workers, giving the right to vote to women, and some other progressive measures. In all these policies, he was aided by his char-
ismatic second wife, "Evita." Although a populist with no love for
the agrarian oligarchy, Perón contented himself with reducing its
income and humiliating it in petty ways instead of effectively sepa-
rating it from its power base in the land.

Needless to say, Perón's erstwhile Georgist allies were given
short shrift when they protested his authoritarian measures. Molinari was appointed early on to a high-sounding agrarian post, but
resigned when he found that it carried no real authority.[12] Yet, al-

though nothing like land-value taxation was undertaken by Perón, he imposed a key policy that favored tenants over landed interests (which had always been hostile to him): He froze both urban and rural rents. With rapid inflation going on, this freeze gave tenants a major advantage and, being a principal cause of income transfer to workers, at least partly explains Perón's extraordinary and lasting appeal among them. He nationalized exports (which were mainly agricultural), forcing their producers to accept prices well below the market. While this affected both landowners and tenant farmers, the former were squeezed between low prices and low rents, whereas for the latter, the low rents constituted a benefit that outweighed the adverse impact of the low prices.

Eventually, in 1955, the miserable state of the once-prosperous economy, combined (after the popular Evita's death from cancer in 1952) with Perón's recklessness in courting open conflict with the Catholic Church, led the navy and part of the army to turn against him in revolt. He resigned, fled to Paraguay, and landed finally in Spain. Toward the end of his regime, Molinari and Birabent made a futile last attempt (through his vice-president, Rear Admiral Alberto Teisaire) to persuade him to undertake a genuine land reform.[13]

IV

The Last Decades

IN THE 1960s and 1970s, Birabent and the Social Agrarian Party (which he headed after the death of its founder, Dr. Bernardino Horne) worked to achieve meaningful land and tax reform. Although this party had some local success at the polls, it failed to gain any important political influence in the country as a whole, and quickly disappeared.

A significant option for stability and social justice lay with the Union of Argentine People (UDELPA), a party led by one of the military officers who overthrew Perón. General Pedro Eugenio Aramburu had served as provisional president from 1955–58, during which time he ended press censorship and restored the liberal Constitution of 1853. But his provisional government had suffered from internal contradictions, and even more seriously from the fact that the outlawed Justicialist Party continued to enjoy wide popular support. After his presidency, a succession of civilian and military governments, none of which managed to undo the economic damage wrought by Perón (and even worsened it), eventuated in the dictatorship of General Juan Onganía, strongly supported by the Catholic Church. Aramburu, who had been introduced to Georgist thought by Dr. Hector Raúl Sandler, a UDELPA representative in the Chamber of Deputies, prepared to challenge Onganía and seek to become president again, this time with land-value taxation as his goal.[14] But he was kidnapped and murdered by an extreme left-wing group, the Montoneros. It is still far from clear who was really behind the Montoneros.

Sandler assumed the leadership of UDELPA and returned to the Parliament in 1973, but the general's death put an end to the party's chances of becoming a major force, although Sandler continues to be a well-known spokesman for land-value-taxation. The Instituto de Capacitation Económica (Institute for Economic Teaching), which he founded and directs, is now the main organization that coordinates Georgist efforts in Argentina.

Alongside the political turbulence of the 1960s and 1970s, other voices arose in favor of land and tax reform, mainly from Academe and the agrarian cooperatives. On the scholars' side, a notable voice was that of the late Professor Dino Jarach, an Italian lawyer teaching in Argentina, who stressed placing the burden of taxation on the potential or "imputed" rent of land rather than on its actual return, as a way of stimulating production in the stagnant agrarian sector. At the request of Walter Kugler, secretary of state for agriculture under the presidency of Arturo Ilia of the Radical Civic Union (UCR), he produced a report recommending this policy, but, despite the backing of many experts, nothing came of it at the time.

Due mainly to the protectionist "pro-industrial" policies of Perón, Argentina had fallen from being one of the richest nations on earth to one that approached third-world levels. These policies continued long after his ouster until 1989, when they were swept away by Carlos Saúl Menem, who had gained the presidency, ironically enough, under the banner of the Justicialist Party, the party of Perónism. The idea of maintaining protected industries had become firmly rooted in the country, even though proven a complete failure. At the expense of its agricultural production and potential, Argentina built a protected industrial complex incapable of competing in world markets; the whole nation was thus impoverished. But a remarkable consequence of industrial protection was that the traditional rural oligarchy that had ruled the country for most of its history lost power and influence. In the 1970s, a national debate about the taxation of land occurred both in the media and among scholars, something that would have been unthinkable were it not for that decline in power.[15] The dominance of the landed rural oligarchs had given way to that of a new conservative class consisting chiefly of the owners of protected industries.

The fact is that the concept of taxing the imputed rent of agrarian land gained support even in the leading parties—the Radicals and the Justicialists or Perónists. To extract the most from the agrarian sector to benefit the protected industries was within the accepted framework of the ruling orthodoxy in those days. Few people realized and fewer still dared to point out that although private appropriation of agrarian rent may present a problem for the equitable distribution of wealth, for a predominately urban nation such as Argentina, private appropriation of urban rent presents an infinitely greater one.

During Onganía's dictatorship, a reform was instituted in connection with agrarian taxation. In 1969, Law No. 18.033 (ITAEA) was promulgated creating an "emergency tax" of 1.6 percent on the value of rural land, excluding buildings and other improvements. The goal of this quite modest measure was to increase agricultural production by discouraging the under-use of rural land. It was fiercely resisted by the remains of the agrarian oligarchy, which retained enough clout with the military to help to get Onganía removed from office.[16] He was succeeded consecutively by two other generals, the latter of whom, Alejandro Lanusse, arranged for the return of the exiled Perón. While this was being negotiated, a Perón stand-in, Hector Cámpora, was elected president and sent to the Parliament a bill to tax rural land heavily on its imputed rent rather than merely on its actual returns, so as to discourage under-use. It was passed during the interim régime that was briefly in place after he resigned so that Perón could run. Despite the fact that Perón was now 77 years of age and obviously ailing, he was returned to the Casa Rosada by a substantial margin, in the hope that his unquestionable popular support and leadership would lift the country out of the spiral of decline in which it was submerged. It is highly doubtful that this would have happened in any case, but Perón died of a heart attack barely a year after his return. His last wife, "Isabelita," who had been his running mate, was invested with the presidential sash upon his demise. But, faced with a country convulsed by left and right-wing terror, she was ill-equipped for the responsibility and came under questionable influence, which elicited another seizure of power by the military. Argentina then entered one of the darkest periods of its history, characterized by extreme right-wing repression, organized and directed by the government. Sandler, who had earlier risked his life to expose, on the floor of the Chamber of Deputies, the murder of political prisoners by the army, was obliged to become a refugee in Mexico when his house was blown up by a notorious "death squad." Thousands were killed or disappeared during this time of terror and outrage.

Under the Lanusse government, the present writer had produced for the Ministry of Agriculture a report on ITAEA, advocating that it be replaced by a two percent tax on the capital value of all land in the nation, with corresponding reduction of taxes on production.[17] His views were well known to Carlos Emery, who became minister after the Cámpora presidency, and who in 1974 appointed him chairman of a Special Land Taxation Committee in the Ministry, charged with implementing the new law. But, needless to say, with the rightist military takeover, all ideas of tax reform were abandoned, and the Special Committee was dissolved.

Eventually, the military government led the nation into the disastrous Falklands War with Britain, thus precipitating its own downfall, Since then, Argentina has witnessed the return to constitutional democracy and latterly the rejection of protectionism, accompanied by an unaccustomed thrust toward privatization and deregulation.

In 1983, Dr. Raúl Alfonsín was elected president on the UCR ticket. Although a decade earlier he had been exposed to a two-hour briefing by the present author on the importance of freeing up the economy through shifting taxes off of production and onto land, he initially appointed an old-fashioned economic team imbued with the protectionist and inflationist notions of the Perón era. After several months, the country was in turmoil and its economy in a tailspin. Faced with both internal and international pressure, Alfonsín replaced his economic advisers with a more liberal and modern team.

In 1986, the secretary of agriculture, Lucio Recca, promoted a new legal project to tax the imputed rent of agricultural land as an advance payment against income tax that would be due even if there were no taxable income. But Perónist opposition prevented its adoption. The focus during the Alfonsín period, as before, was almost entirely on agricultural land, leaving aside the very important problem of urban rent. On October 5, 1988, the national director of highways, Saúl P. Martínez, gave two public speeches advocating the taxation of both urban and rural land rent with corresponding reduction of taxes on labor and capital; the following day, President Alfonsín requested his resignation.

Fierce opposition by the Perónists and the trade unions controlled by them doomed the efforts of the Alfonsín administration to liberalize the economy, which was devastated by two rounds of hyperinflation in five years. The turmoil was so great that Alfonsín cut short his mandate and in 1989 transferred power to a new democratically-elected chief executive, the Justicialist candidate, Carlos Saúl Menem, who also had the backing of several other parties.

Once in office, Dr. Menem almost immediately departed from the policies associated with Perónism, and pushed forward a strong program of free trade and privatization of state-owned companies. Inflation was controlled at the price of linking the peso to the dollar, an approach that has been maintained up to the present, but which poses dangerous long-range challenges.

Needless to say, Menem's drastic abandonment of the historic principles of his party alienated large segments of the labor movement, and antagonized many Perónists. Nevertheless, he managed to put through a sweeping revision of the Constitution of 1853, and win reelection in 1995. Toward the end of his second term in office, a law providing for the taxation of the imputed rent of rural land was finally approved. Despite the low rate of the tax (0.5 to 1 percent), it faced fierce opposition from organized rural interests.

The land issue is not at present in the forefront of political action. Most certainly, the problem of urban land is totally ignored. Yet Hector Sandler, now a senior member of the Faculty of Law at the University of Buenos Aires, together with such respected figures as António César Copello (former under secretary of agriculture), Saúl P. Martínez (former national director of highways), and Dr. Juan María Marchionatto (a distinguished jurist), have attracted a coterie of brilliant scholars who have caught the Georgist vision. We may expect that it will surface as a dynamic political force at some point in the future.

Notes

1. Emphyteusis: "Under Roman civil law, a kind of perpetual lease of real estate upon condition of taking care of and paying taxes upon the estate; ground rent." (*Webster's New Twentieth Century Dictionary of the English Language.* Unabridged.)

2. *Noticias Históricas, Políticas y Estadísticas de las Provincias Unidas del Río de la Plata* (London, 1825), pp. 294–96.

3. Diario de Sesiones del Congreso General Constituyente de las Provincias Unidas del Río de la Plata, No. 132.

4. The peso dropped from 100 cents to five cents in value.

5. The primary source of this quotation is not indicated in Carlos Villalobos- Domínguez's chapter on Argentina in the original (1955) edition of *Land-Value Taxation Around the World,* from which it has been taken.

6. James L. Busey, *Latin American Political Guide* (20th Edition; Manitou Springs, CO: Juniper Editions, 1995), p. 50.

7. "Noticias de Henry George en España e Implantación del Movimiento Georgista—Don Antonio Albertin e Impuesto Unico," by Ana María Martins Uris, in the introduction to *Henry George, Progreso y Miseria* (Madrid: Instituto de Estudios Agrarios, Pesqueros y Alimentarios; Madrid, 1986), xliii–xciv.

8. John Maynard Keynes, *The General Theory of Employment, Interest, and Money* (Cambridge, England: Macmillan/Cambridge University Press, 1973), pp. 353–57.

9. The preceding text has been excerpted, with minor changes, from Villalobos-Domínguez's chapter on Argentina in the original (1955) edition of *Land-Value Taxation Around the World.,* op. cit.

10. "El pensamiento económico de Hipólito Irigoyen." Conference paper by Saúl P. Martinez at the "Instituto Irigoyeniano" in October 1995.

11. Dr. Molinari was a senior figure of the Georgist movement in Argentina until his death in 1990. His most important book was *El drama de la tierra en Argentina* (Buenos Aires: Editorial Claridad, 1994).

12. Mauricio Birabent, who was a close friend of the present writer, confided to him that his friendship with Eva Perón enabled him to recoup some of the money he had invested in Democracia. She granted him a monopoly of the newspaper's advertising for a certain period on condition that he promise to sell the paper for one peso to whoever Perón chose. In a published letter to FICHAS, dated October 27, 1965, he said that he was obliged to sell the paper to the ALEA Group, organized by "Miranda, Maroglio, Cuadrado and nazi and nationalist groups," for 50,000 pesos, from which 10,000 pesos was deducted as a commission.

13. According to Birabent, Molinari approached Teisaire, proposing a radical land reform for Perón's consideration. When the proposal was presented to Perón, he dismissed it with the remark that it was too late, that it was "too big an idea for him now."

14. In a meeting with Students Union leaders from the University of Buenos Aires held at the house of the author, Aramburu spoke clearly in favor of reform based on a land-value tax.

15. In those days, the author participated in several television debates concerning taxation of the imputed rent of land.

16. In a private meeting with the author in 1975, Onganía cited this as an important reason for his ouster.

17. Fernando Scornik Gerstein, *Bases para un Régimen Impositivo sobre la Renta del Suelo* (Buenos Aires: Dirección General de Economía y Sociología Rural. Ministerio de Agricultura y Ganaderia. 12 de Mayo de 1973).

Chapter 4

Canada

By Garry B. Nixon*

"LAND" IS A concept that is as much misunderstood in Canada as anywhere else in the industrialized world. Even economists often fail to point out that land includes all natural resources and that its return is called rent, not profit. "Canada collects perhaps five percent of the rent of its land," stated Mary Rawson, Vancouver town planner.[1] The various levels of government in Canada, be they national, provincial, or municipal, do collect land tax, but almost inadvertently.

I

Property Tax

THE PROPERTY TAX in Canada is usually levied by the municipality, but in more remote areas, by the provinces, or in the territories by the national government. As if to reflect the general confusion of land with capital (evidenced even by some economists) the property tax falls on improvements as well as land.[2]

"The four western provinces have, throughout their history, adopted site value assessment (i.e., excluding improvements) to a greater or lesser degree, though, and contrary to inherited misinformation in the Canadian tax literature, at no point did they ever fully implement this system."[3] Property tax in the four western

*Garry B. Nixon, a graduate of the University of British Columbia, has been a cinema owner, a private and public school teacher, a community newspaper publisher, and dean of arts and commerce at Columbia College, Vancouver. Since 1978, he has headed G. B. Nixon & Associates, a tax consulting firm with offices in Vancouver, BC, and in Cork, Ireland. He is co-author of *The 1200 Days—a Shattered Dream* (1978), a study of British Columbia's New Democratic government of the early 1970s.

provinces originally fell more heavily, even at times exclusively, on land.[4] But by the 1900s, this was no longer the case in British Columbia,[5] then Manitoba,[6] and Saskatchewan,[7] and finally Alberta[8] where exemptions for improvements were largely abolished and the improvements taxed the same as land. There have always been exemptions for farm improvements, partially in BC and Manitoba, and completely in Saskatchewan and Alberta.[9]

By the early twentieth century, land-value taxation was widespread in the four western provinces, which had been settled largely by homesteaders. Herbert T. Owens advances four reasons for this: First, "the power of the land-value tax, by exempting improvements, to encourage capital investment"; second, "the eagerness of residents to force a contribution from absentee landowners in proportion to the progress of the communities from which they benefited;" third, "the principle of 'equality of opportunity' inherent in the tax," which "appealed strongly to the instincts of the hardy pioneers;" and fourth, "the understandable desire to keep the improvements they made themselves out of the reach of taxation."[10]

The period between 1901 and 1906 was marked by a 260 percent increase in population in these provinces, with still greater augmentation of production, and massive spending on public buildings and infrastructure. Land values appreciated tremendously, especially in the urban areas. All of this might have translated into lasting prosperity if the land had been taxed sufficiently to discourage speculation, but it was not. Because it was not, the exemption of improvements, whether whole or partial, merely helped to fuel the mania for speculation, which inflated land prices to artificial heights that could not be sustained. The rate of the land tax never exceeded two percent until after the speculative boom collapsed with the cessation of European immigration. At that point, it became common for municipalities, many of which had incurred heavy indebtedness to fund lavish expenditure, to eliminate or reduce the exemption of improvements in order to recoup revenue lost because of shrinking land prices and tax delinquency.

During the boom years, some over-enthusiastic single-taxers held up Western Canada as a model of their system in action. After

the crash and subsequent depression, they were left looking foolish. Of course, it never was an example of anything remotely like
the single-tax or even of land-value taxation in any thoroughgoing
sense, but merely of the full or partial exemption of improvements
from local property taxation. The fault, in Owen's trenchant
words, "was not that land values were taxed as much as they were,
but that land values were not taxed enough."[11]

As well as losing revenue, Canadian cities have lost much of
their cohesion through development. Nowhere is this clearer than
when one compares two adjoining suburbs in Greater Vancouver.
New Westminster is a compact, well developed city. Its first century of development saw it tax improvements lightly and at times
not at all. As they were lightly taxed, there were more improvements in relationship to the land, contributing to a highly developed sense of community. In contrast, the neighboring municipality of Surrey, largely developed after tax exemptions for
improvements were abolished, is a sprawling eyesore reminiscent
of Los Angeles. As buildings are taxed, there are fewer of them in
relation to the land, large tracts of which are held for speculation,
causing spiraling costs of municipal servicings. The resulting urban sprawl causes the suburb to have little cohesiveness and almost none of the sense of community which New Westminster
has enjoyed for years. Indeed, one of the reasons for Vancouver's
relatively compact downtown area can be traced to a policy implemented by its eight-time mayor, L. D. "Single Tax" Taylor, of
exempting buildings completely from taxation in the crucial years
of its post-fire development in 1910–1918. In spite of his opponents' dilution of his policy, Vancouver taxed buildings less severely than land up to 1980, which further reinforced the pattern
of compact development.

It cannot be overemphasized that land values assessed are often
not the current ones, but up to as much as forty years out of date.
Naturally when attempts have been made (as in Vancouver, Winnipeg, and Toronto) to correct this,[12] the land owners (who show
a marked disinclination to share their new found gains) band together and lobby for the status quo, or as near to it as can be allowed.[13] Property taxes are disliked out of all proportion to the
effect they actually have on the population.[14] As city councilors are

often in a similar land-owning position as the complainants, they have been partially successful in curbing taxes by using devices such as capping the rate of increase each year in assessments, no matter how great the actual increase in value has been. Thus, even in Vancouver, which was thought to have achieved market assessments, the assessments on the more affluent west side will be at times less than sixty percent of the properties' real value; in the less prosperous east side they will be commonly over ninety percent. The landowners' success has led to a shift to higher taxation on commercial properties in Vancouver, having the effect that they are now being taxed up to four times the rate of their non-commercial counterparts.[15] Far from earning the distinction of having a property tax that taxes land more than improvements, Canada now has reversed it to the extreme that less than thirty percent[16] of all property tax is on land, capturing only a small part of the rent.

To gain an appreciation of the hugeness of the uncollected rent involved, it should be understood that in the years 1980–92 land prices in BC rose twelve fold, with certain suburbs of Vancouver and Victoria experiencing a twenty-three fold increase. In that twelve year period, the cost of living rose by less than fifty percent. In comparison, during the years 1966–96 it was not unusual for a house on the west side of Vancouver to have risen fifty fold at a time when there was less than a five fold rise in overall prices, caused in part by these very same land price increases. This is a transfer of wealth to a privileged few on the scale of Margaret Thatcher's privatizations[17] in Great Britain, causing costly urban sprawl and societal fabric erosion. Another result is that a new would-be home owner is now unable to afford land near the city center, if indeed he is able to afford land at all. It has been noticed that, for the first time in Canada's history, large numbers of young people find it impossible to buy land—with the inevitable consequence of a two class society. It should also be noted that most of this gain in land escapes any tax whatsoever. A taxpayer is entitled to a complete exemption of Canadian income tax on land that is used as a principal residence, and, until recently, a $100,000 exemption for land that is not. Commercial land used as an integral part of a Canadian business usually qualified for a $500,000 exemption.

Throughout the world, the public has a vague notion that not all gain from natural resources may convincingly be attributed to the application of entrepreneurial skill or effort; however, neither politicians nor academics are willing to shed much light on this matter. Canada, for example, has had conflicts arise between levels of government where the rent question has been inadvertently brought to the fore. Discord has occurred in matters pertaining to oil, natural gas, forests, mining, coal, hydro power, Indian land claims, the railways, and immigration—to name just a few.

II

Oil

CANADA IS A country blessed with enormous conventional and especially unconventional petroleum resources. The Athabaska Tar Sands in north-central Alberta form a bitumen of sand and oil that when properly treated can yield nearly half as much as the earth's known conventional petroleum resources.[18] Substantial amounts of oil and gas were discovered in the western provinces (mainly in Alberta) in the years immediately after World War II. As the governments had no experience regarding this new-found windfall, they were content to tax it lightly. At no time did Alberta's revenue from oil and gas equal twenty percent of its wholesale value. Frequently it was less than fifteen percent.[19] Substantial profits and even more substantial portions of the rent went to the oil companies even when the oil sold at under $2 a barrel. When the problems in the Middle East caused the price to jump to $7 in 1973, and ten years later to $24, huge increases in rents suddenly became available. Not only available, but also highly visible.[20] The public at large, though, could see that costs had hardly risen at all, while the price had increased ten-fold.

Canadian intergovernmental conflict made the rent issue even more pronounced. The oil was in the lightly populated western areas, while the population, and consequently the political representatives, were mainly in the central provinces of Ontario and

Quebec. These two provinces, ironically, import a great deal of their oil from other countries while an equal or greater amount of the west's oil is exported to the US.

Oil was supposed to be a provincial responsibility, and, if left to its own devices, the major oil producing province, Alberta, was willing to give the oil companies a generous share of the increased value in the oil it exported. In return, it demanded that the price in Alberta remain low. Needless to say, this wasteful overselling of resources at subsidized prices takes away from the next generation's inheritance. But, through sheer numbers, central Canada, not Alberta, determined the federal government's policies.

A second look at the Canadian Constitutional hat, and a rabbit of increased federal powers was pulled out; Prime Minister Trudeau imposed his "solution." Alberta would be allowed a slight increase in rent,[21] as would oil companies. The federal government would be given the lion's share of the increased rent via a huge oil export tax equaling two-thirds the selling price of the oil, the proceeds of which would subsidize the oil imports of the more populated central Canada, and the four small eastern maritime provinces.

The oil companies (almost all US based) were largely unaffected by the rent-collecting efforts of Alberta, or, indeed, the Middle Eastern governments. They had obtained a ruling from a relatively junior Internal Revenue Service official that any oil price increase would not be deemed a price increase[22] but a rise in foreign taxes which could, dollar for dollar, reduce their US taxes—even taxes on US-produced oil.[23] This keeping of resource prices below market level was popular with the public as well as with many economists. The claim was made that the consumers (i.e. those voting in the politician's constituency) should be protected against huge price increases on vital goods—such as oil or other forms of energy. In reality, of course, the government caused these low prices by not charging the full rent it could obtain on the open market. Instead, it traded this forgone rent for other government taxes, usually unprogressive, frequently cost-ineffective and always unfair. The government then employed these revenues to subsidize the energy user in direct proportion to how much he used, during a time when conservation was supposedly politically correct.

III

Natural Gas

THE RENTS FROM natural gas—usually found when oil is nearby, were treated even more cavalierly. Although it did not always follow the Middle Eastern habit of burning gas in the open air above the well, Canada did treat it most strangely. The Canadian government proclaimed natural gas to be far less polluting than oil (let alone coal), but instead of charging the oil and coal companies a tax to compensate for their pollution, it sold natural gas far below the energy equivalent price of oil. For instance, the price of natural gas in Alberta was 42.5 percent and 55.5 percent of the energy equivalent price of oil in 1992 and 1993 respectively. In a three year period (1972–75), BC, which was by no means the largest Canadian producer of natural gas, lost over $1 billion by selling natural gas below its energy equivalent oil price. This scheme from a socialist government that prided itself on collecting large natural gas rents by forcing the gas transmission companies to sell the gas as it came out of the pipeline to a government owned company, the BC Gas Corporation, then a moment later, sell it at an enhanced price to the consumer, was dubbed "sixty second socialism." The government did collect rent, but not nearly the amount lost by not selling it at the energy equivalent price.[24] The successor, non-socialist government abolished this new company, thereby transferring the rents to the gas producers and consumers.

IV

Forests

RENT OF FOREST lands was brought into Canadian focus when US competition asked for trade sanctions on lumber from Canada. The US producers claimed they had to bid for lumber-cutting rights in the US but that producers in Canada did not. Instead, in Canada where the government owns over ninety percent of the forest land, the US saw Canada give logging rights mainly to a few large corporations and then collect royalties in the form of stumpage fees.[25] These stumpage fees were considerably lower than the bidding amounts paid by the American counterparts, and US producers had little problem convincing their government of their case. Canadian provinces promised to raise their stumpage rates, and in the largest lumber producing province (BC) they did, capturing, according to an ex-BC resource minister,[26] up to 25 percent of the rent[27] but set it aside for a special fund for forest renewal. Recently however, the BC government, having made a wildly optimistic pre-election over-estimate of resources, was forced to raid its special forest renewal fund for $500 million. It stated that this might become an annual event, leading to speculation that collecting resource revenue might be one solution to the government's debit crisis. When the stumpage increase still did not bring the Canadians closer to the US bidding fee the Americans paid, the US government acted. In the mid 1990s, it gave the Canadians a choice of increasing their stumpage fees or facing a quota. Strangely enough, all governments (except Quebec) chose the quota structure, foregoing the increased rental revenue, and passed on the benefits to the exporting quota holders.

V

Mining

NUMEROUS SURVEYS[28] HAVE shown that Canadian government expenditures, in providing infrastructure to new mines in the form of roads, railways, subsidized energy, free water, sewers, schools, and hospitals (particularly relevant in view of illness caused by the mines) almost always exceed, according to a former Manitoba mines minister, the mere ten percent[29] of the resource rents the government collects. (These immense expenditures do not begin to pay for correcting all of the environmental and health damage caused by mining.) An anomaly to this was the huge potash rent situation in Saskatchewan in the 1970s, like the lumber rent situation, brought to light by an intergovernmental conflict. Once more there were complaints from the US, but this time not because the price was too low as with lumber, but too high. The American importers claimed the Canadian exporters were colluding to set high prices, which the latter were able to do as most of the world's potash was in the province. This led to the provincial government nationalizing all the province's potash production in the 1970s.[30] The Americans succumbed to the new arrangement, reasoning that a monopoly cannot possibly collude with itself, and rents well in excess of the usual ten percent began flowing to the province.

The succeeding Conservative government in the 1980s, following the Thatcherite model in theory and in practice, disposed of the potash mines at bargain basement prices and used these dollars and several billion others to invest in various losing business ventures.

VI

Coal

A FURTHER EXAMPLE of government ineptness with the issue of resource rents was BC's dealing with its coal mines. After helping to set up the infrastructure for a huge open pit coal mine in the south-east of the province, the same BC government proceeded a few years later (presumably for the sake of job creation) to grant an even greater infrastructure subsidy to start up another huge open coal mine field in the north-east. The two mines began competing with each other, driving down the price paid (and consequently the rent collected). The province consequently lost hundreds of millions of dollars of resource rent revenues as a result of these maneuvers.[31]

VII

Hydro Power

NOT ONE, BUT two international disputes have highlighted the question of hydro-electric rent in Canada. In the mid-1960s, Canada found itself with an economic windfall from its Columbia River. In the US International Rivers Treaty of 1911, Canada was added as "window dressing." The reason for the treaty in the first place was to force Mexico to give up the Rio Grande's potential, under the principle that the country with the headwaters gets the floodwaters. Its framers were remiss in that they failed to notice that the headwaters of the Columbia River begin in Canada. Forty years after the treaty was signed, after threats to divert the Columbia's floodwaters from even reaching the US, the Canadians were offered substantial cash for flood control projects and half the newly located power. (The power was very cheap to produce, as most of the needed turbines already existed as a result of several US New Deal projects.) The resource-owning BC provincial government of the day, however, decided it would sell the next thirty years' worth of this power *in advance.* As it was a few years before the 1970s' crises and the subsequent substantial rise in energy prices, the province lost out on billions of revenue dollars.[32]

Before the decade was out, the same situation occurred on Canada's east coast. The province of Newfoundland wished to develop its massive Churchill Falls project in its Labrador territory, wanting to sell the power to New York State. Unfortunately, the transmission lines had to go through the neighboring province of Quebec. Consequently, a deal was concluded in 1969 to sell the power to Quebec for a sixty-five year period, beginning in 1976 at an initial set price to be lowered in twenty-five years, and *lowered again* in another fifteen. As the deal was negotiated long before the huge energy price increases, Canada's poorest province was to lose outright from the beginning. Indeed, in 1994, Newfoundland collected only $70 million, while Quebec siphoned off eleven times that figure. Newfoundland's premier now predicts that within a few years, the province's share will not even cover the costs involved and will have to be subsidized by taxing some of Canada's poorest citizens. This conflict has also, for the first time, brought the matter of Hydro Quebec resource rent into focus.

The entire hydro question is a highly emotional one in Quebec province. Before 1962, the mainly US privately-held hydro companies paid virtually no rent to the province. That year the provincial Liberal government under the direction of its resources minister, René Levesque (later Quebec's first separatist premier), nationalized these power companies, using the slogan: "Masters of our own house." Some thirty-five years later, it is now being pointed out that if the almost sacrosanct Hydro Quebec (the government agency) only shows a profit of less than $375 million annually after taking into account its Labrador fees, it must be experiencing a $400 million loss on all its other ventures. In other words, it not only obtains no rent, it loses money and loses it prodigiously. Prices deliberately set below market, a huge bureaucracy, and massive ineptness on politically based projects may be cited as obvious reasons for these losses.[33]

In contrast to its earlier policies, the BC provincial government in the early 1980s began to charge its state-owned hydro monopoly a rent for its water. The rent soon reached $269 million, and at this time is now over $300 million annually. The utility also pays school property taxes of $180 million a year plus annual dividends to the government of $125 million. This dividend, at least partly based on its resource costs, was forecast to rise to $214 million by 1997.

VIII

Indian Land Claims

THE PRESENT "POLITICALLY correct" clamor for native Indian land claim settlements has also brought the rent issue into focus. A proposed "settlement" with the few thousand Nisga'a in northwestern BC raises such questions. Having lost their case in the courts,[34] the Nisga'a leaders, on behalf of their five thousand band members, prevailed upon the federal and provincial governments. In 1996, they were offered a new level of self government, $190 million in cash, 7,700 square miles of land, and mining, fishing, hunting, and timber rights on such land—a settlement some experts estimate to be worth over one billion dollars.[35] Other Indian tribes,[36] comprising five percent of the population and which lay claim to 125 percent of the province, are now awaiting their negotiations, as are Aboriginals in other provinces.[37] The federal government has recently turned over half of its territorial land (one third of the land in Canada) to fewer than 38,000 Eskimos and Metis, together with an open-ended commitment to finance their self government.

Further intergovernmental squabbles yet again brought into focus land rent being given to a few. In the late 1980s, BC native In-

dians laid claim to South Moresby Island, one of the Queen Char-
lotte Islands. The federal government gave way, as did its BC
counterpart, and created a national park on most of this land. Then
the BC government paid Doman Industries over $30 million in
compensation for a timber cutting license that could not be hon-
ored—an agreement which had not cost Doman a penny in the
first place.

IX

The Railroads

RAILROADS PLAY A special role in the history of land taxation in Canada. It was the besottment of the Canadian government with railways in the late 19th century that caused it to highly subsidize no
less than three railways across a country with the second largest
land mass in the world. Thus Canada had more miles of railway
per capita than had any other nation. Canadian Pacific (CPR), the
first to build railroads, was given a huge cash subsidy, $25 million
dollars ($1 billion today), numerous tax exemptions, freedom
from any government interference in setting fares, and above all
twenty-five million acres of land. Of the railways in North America,
it was the only one that did not always have to take alternate sections on either side of the tracks. Rather, it was allowed to pass
over poorer lands and choose instead large tracts of valuable land,
such as prime farm areas in southern and northwestern Alberta.[38]
This maneuver represented a transfer of resource rents to an elite
on a scale not seen since the Enclosures in 18th and 19th century
Britain.

In addition, the railway was given vast tracts of what turned out
to be prime urban land for its yards. Now that it has forsaken much
of its original purpose of providing train service (the sole reason
for it being granted land), it has re-zoned or is in the process of rezoning most of this land and selling or leasing it at many times its
present rail-yard value.[39]

Government will continue to throw away opportunities to collect vast amounts of rent,[40] as was the case in Vancouver's north-
side of False Creek. Much of this prime site (next to the city's

downtown) was given to the CPR. In 1973, the railway applied to Vancouver City Council to re-zone from industrial to commercial and residential use. Overnight the increase in land value would have been $100 million. A motion was put to City Council to only allow this re-zoning if the City was paid half the gain, but the motion failed 6–5 when left-wing alderman and later BC cabinet minister Darlene Marzari surprisingly voted against it. A decade later, the False Creek CPR-owned land was traded for prime provincial government commercial land in the heart of Vancouver, then used in part for the highly successful 1986 World's Expo Fair. After the fair, the government decided to sell the entire 300 acre site, but to only one buyer. Advised by a company that hired an assessor later to work for the winning bidder, Hong Kong billionaire Li Ka-shing, an arrangement was made that rivaled the Indians' "sale" of Manhattan Island to the Dutch. Mr. Li managed to purchase this land at 320 million, which many considered well below market value, and negotiated a fifteen-year mortgage with suspended payments for ten years and *no accrued interest*.[41]

X

Immigration

IN THE YEARS when Canadian railways began, the pre-empting of continental US farm land was being completed.[42] For the next quarter century after 1890, new immigrants turned northward to Canadian lands. For the first time in history, more immigrants came to Canada than left.[43]

Subsequent waves of immigrants arrived on Canadian shores after World War II. Most recently, the Canadian government has sought out Asians to immigrate and then has bowed to their demands for extended family entries. With the world's most generous refugee admission policies,[44] large numbers of East Indian, Philippine, Southeast Asian, and particularly Chinese immigrants have entered Canada in the last two decades, predominantly settling in Toronto, Montreal, and especially Vancouver.

As many of the immigrants are wealthy (escaping the 1997 Mainland China take-over of Hong Kong), land prices, mainly in

Vancouver, have shot up. This in turn is causing considerable re-sentment toward the newer immigrants, not the least of which comes from the previous generation of Asian immigrants, high-lighting the land rent situation.

XI

Other Rents—Uncollected

VARIOUS TYPES OF land in Canada such as airwaves,[45] fishing, graz-ing,[46] and water[47] escape any tax whatsoever.[48] Airwave broad-casting rights are even liberally handed out by the government's Canadian Radio-Television and Telecommunications Commission in return for promises of on-air Canadian content quotas which are rarely enforced.[49] Fishermen pay the most nominal of fees for the exclusive license to fish (these privileges can then be sold at a profit of thousands of dollars). A consequence of this is that the huge fish stocks on the east and now west coasts, are approaching extinction. As in the US, grazing and water rights are given for amounts that can hardly justify the word fee. Indeed, the 1980s and 1990s have witnessed unseemly bidding by provincial gov-ernments in the giving away of rents allegedly to save or create jobs.[50]

With the low or non-existent specific rent taxes, it is left to the income and corporate taxes to recoup some of this rent for the public. Yet it is only in the past quarter century that Canada has taxed the rent segment of "capital gains" at all, and even today large parts of it remain exempt.[51]

XII

Tax Expenditures

WITH THE EVER increasing exemptions and qualifications to various taxes, some economists as well as a few civil servants have begun to use the term "tax expenditures" to describe lost government revenue caused by various loopholes. Although the term tax ex-penditure may not always be valid (as the government's right to tax the item in question might be dubious), if applied to all types of government activity that confer privilege, and the amounts involved actually calculated, it might throw greater light on the economic effects on government. But this may well be an unrealized expectation. Judging by past experience, a more likely prediction is that Canadians will not be more than vaguely aware of the concept of rent, let alone make serious efforts substantially to tax it.

Notes

1. Mary Rawson at the 18th International Conference on Land-Value Taxation and Free Trade, Vancouver, 1986.

2. In the eastern province of Nova Scotia, farm land is not taxed at all; only the improvements are.

3. F. K. Peddle, *Cities and Greed* (Ottawa: Canadian Research Committee On Taxation, 1994), p. 36.

4. Herbert T. Owens, *Land Value Taxation in Canada Local Government* (Montreal: Henry George Foundation of Canada, 1953), p. 61.

5. British Columbia, from 1874 allowed municipalities to exempt improvements entirely and nineteen years later granted a minimum 50 percent exemption. Thirty-nine municipal governments exempted improvements completely, 22 granted exemption anywhere from 75 percent down to the 50 percent minimum. By 1952, the minimum exemption had been removed and 35 municipal governments had exempted improvements less than 50 percent, 54 gave a 50 percent exemption, 13 gave more than 50 percent, and two minor entities exempted the full 100 percent. In the late 1960s, the province began a school property tax on all land and improvements equally for administrative convenience. All municipalities, save these two entities, followed suit for bureaucratic convenience. (Such was the total lack of power of those who knew about land economics and such was the general economic ignorance of the public who did not, that this change was barely noted, let alone objected to.) Presently there is a 50 percent exemption on improvements for those on farms, otherwise there are no exemptions.

6. By 1913, Manitoba saw all but four municipal governments (one of which was the capital city of Winnipeg) tax land and improvements equally. By 1952, all municipalities were following Winnipeg's example and exempted improvements 33 percent. To date all exemptions are abolished except for some farm improvements.

7. Saskatchewan, from 1911 required a minimum 40 percent exemption for improvements and by 1914 its cities were giving exemptions of 55 to 85 percent. A quarter of its smaller municipalities granted more than the 40 percent exemption, but by 1952, all municipalities were at the 40 percent exemption, save the capital of Regina, which remained at the 70 percent rate. Today all improvements are taxed except on farm buildings.

8. Alberta, even as a territory in 1897, allowed exemption of improvements from taxation. This practice continued when Alberta became a province in 1905, and in 1912 required that all but five of the 206 local governments grant this exemption in full. The other five granted exemption from 20 to 75 percent. Revisions were made in the intervening years to reduce this exemption, and in 1951–52 the province forced all seven cities to exempt just 40 percent of improvements while all other municipal entities granted no exemptions whatsoever. Today the government allows a 25 percent exemption on improvements, but this is being phased out as in BC, with the implementation of the new provincial education property tax.

9. However, in 1972 farm land in BC was so lightly taxed that the Socialist premier of the day stated to his advisor, the renowned Georgist, Mason Gaffney, that "as (farm tax) was so low, they might as well abolish it." Perhaps unsurprisingly, Dr. Gaffney's advice to the government was rarely followed.

10. Herbert T. Owens, "Canada," in H. G. Brown et al, eds., *Land-Value Taxation Around the World* (1st edition; New York: Robert Schalkenbach Foundation, 1955), p. 69.

11. Ibid., p. 76.

12. "Assessment reform . . . often accomplished indirectly what tax policy fails to do directly. For example, the 1992 re-assessment in the regional municipality of Ottawa-Carleton for taxation year 1993 resulted in a shift of the building-land ratio for inner-city Ottawa from 60/40 to 40/60. The re-assessment itself, therefore, scooped up a lot of the economic rent previously missed, especially on vacant and under-utilized properties." Francis K. Peddle, Canadian land economist, in a letter to the author, November 28,1996.

13. See Owens, *Land Value Taxation in Canada Local Government*, p.73: ". . . Many times the property tax was not even collected. Real estate interests were well represented in city councils and municipalities showed undue tenderness toward delinquent speculators."

14. This is probably due to the fact that they are usually paid once, or at most, twice a year and are highly visible. The same tax payers will uncomplainingly hand over ten times as much in income tax that is deducted at source and is never seen.

15. Canada has yet to surpass Ireland which in 1977 abolished all taxes on residential, but not commercial, properties. However, Canada may yet be moving more toward the Emerald Isle's example. The BC Liberal party, which led in the popular vote in 1996, has called for the abolition of property taxes for educational purposes.

16. Peddle, op. cit., p. 33. Not only can a tax on improvements discourage making them, it can cause them to disappear altogether. A wrinkle in the Canadian Income Tax Act allows sellers to avoid taking

back into income the amounts they have claimed for depreciation (on assets that have increased in value!) by simply destroying the improvement (as a further tax bonus, claim the remaining value of the building as an expense) and by selling the now vacant land.

17. This "privatization" was really a sale of government owned assets, specifically land, at fire sale prices to the well connected.

18. David Crabbe and Richard MacBride, *The World Energy Book* (London: Kogon Page, 1978), pp., 22 and 279.

19. Canadian Petroleum Production Statistics (Calgary: Canadian Petroleum Institute, 1995), pp. C 1-13; Karen Trett and Tad Cook, *Finances of the Nation* (Toronto: Toronto Canadian Tax Foundation, 1995), pp. 17–23.

20. Oil did drop to $20 a barrel in 1992 and to $18.71 in 1993, but the Iraqi conflict caused it to rise to over $22 in 1996.

21. Even this sanctioned increase was enough to drive Alberta oil revenues to over $2 billion Canadian a year, but never more than 20 percent of oil proceeds. An accrued $12 billion surplus was set aside for the Alberta Heritage Fund for future generations. This fund proved largely fictional as the Alberta government of the 1980's and early 1990's accumulated a government debt in excess of this. Other oil producing provinces collected similar percentage amounts, but made no pretense of having a heritage fund.

22. John Blair, *The Control of Oil* (New York: Random House, 1976) pp. 268–272.

23. This credit against domestic profits was stopped by the Reagan Tax Reform in 1986. Except innocuously enough, as the Act states, ". . . for any company incorporated in Barttlesville, Oklahoma on July 11, 1917." Readers may be left to guess where and when Phillips Petroleum came into existence.

24. L. J. Kavic and G. B. Nixon, *1200 Days–A Shattered Dream* (Vancouver: Kaen Publishers, 1978), pp. 104–110.

25. Ken Drushka, *Stumped* (Vancouver: Douglas and McIntyre, 1985), pp. 91–114.

26. Bob Williams in private conversation with the author.

27. As the forestry resource was so undervalued, little attempt was made to replenish it and consequently harvesting amounts were reduced. It remains to be seen whether the new talk of renewing forests through improved sivilculture and "sustainable" development will lead to anything more than just talk.

28. For example, the exhaustive report prepared for the Manitoba government in the mid-1970s by the ex-Quebec and federal cabinet minister (and former head of the Montreal Board of Trade) Eric Kierens.

29. Wilson Parasiuk in private conversation with the author.

30. The hapless Quebec government similarly nationalized the mining of a major mineral within its boundaries. Unfortunately, the environment

and health costs by now had been realized, for this mineral at least—their Asbestos Company was to run up deficits in the hundreds of millions of dollars.

31. The habitual ignoring of the rent question by government officials can even be contagious. During the rule of BC's Socialist government in the 1970s, the resources minister let it be known that he favored development of yet another of the provinces' huge coal mines: the southwestern Hat Creek fields. He stated they could fuel generators at below the cost of some of the province's hydro projects. Quite apart from the environment costs of acid rain and post-mining restorations, the resources minister (who was a Georgist!!!) forgot to factor in the cost of resource rent to be paid to government.

32. Not that the US government captured all the rent, but several businesses moved to Washington State due to its now extremely low power costs.

33. The province directly west of Quebec has had government owned electrical generators for over seventy years. Ontario Hydro however, has squandered much of that province's hydro rent on subsidizing nuclear power (with even more subsidies to be required for future decontamination and waste that has a half life of thousands of years).

34. Three justices said they had claim to the land. Three said they did not, and one said they didn't even have the right to be in court without the province's permission.

35. According to Robin Richardson, a Victoria financial consultant.

36. Problems are now coming to light over just who is an Indian. In the Vancouver suburb of Coquitlam, a group many times larger than the original local Indian contingent is claiming entitlement rights.

37. Few Georgists and even fewer liberals seem to find fault with the concept of Indian land claims. It has been left to the conservatives to point out that it is being proposed to give less than four percent of the population a portion of natural resources many times what their numbers warrant, on the grounds of race. That race claims that this land was once "theirs" (a claim that could also be made by the descendants of those they pre-empted).

38. The E&N Railway, later part of the CPR, was given ownership, including the seldom-granted rights to the forest, on Vancouver Island. These highly valuable lands were traded to BC's largest forest company, MacMillan Bloedel, for a substantial minority share of its stock. Despite the fact that the lands were given to obtain a passenger rail service on the island, no one has suggested the contract be enforced and the land be turned back to the government when passenger rail service on the island shuts down in 1997.

39. The other two major railways, Canadian National and Grand Trunk Pacific, ineptly lost money, were bailed out and taken over by the federal

government early this century. The government is presently selling off (at low prices) much of these assets to put toward general revenue. However, the government permitted the successful CPR to gain doubly from its passengers—once when they paid their fares, and then again when they bought land, pushing the price upwards.

40. Railways continue to receive preferential treatment. The left wing BC government recently forced municipalities to cut railway land taxes by $7.5 million. Not only did the railway give nothing in return, one of them charged the provincial government heavily for letting the new light rapid transit use the much under-utilized Vancouver tracks. The same legislation also severely limited what BC municipalities "can assess property taxes on utilities such as BC Tel, cable firms, pipelines, and BC Hydro." *BC Report*, October 7, 1996.

41. Former Vancouver Mayor and soon to be Socialist Premier Mike Harcourt stumbled upon the key to urban land prices when he said, "Li's bid was richer but Li's densities (of buildings) would be . . . much higher." The *Vancouver Sun*, March 29, 1987. Apparently unbeknownst to Harcourt, this statement confirms what every developer already knew, to wit, when density is allowed to rise, land values immediately follow.

42. Even the most fanatical Malthusian would have to concede that this did not mean the US could not support more people, merely that all the good "free or cheap land" had been taken. Those tempted by Malthusian teachings would do well to realize that if all the people in the US were to live in the density of those in Harlem, the entire country's population would almost fit in New York's five boroughs!

43. Strangely enough, although Americans and almost all Europeans were welcome to Canada's new lands, certain Canadians were not. One million French Canadians, prompted by Quebec's near-feudal land-holding laws, emigrated from that province during the thirty-five years prior to World War I. Unfortunately, once the English speaking emigrants formed a majority in any area, rights the former Quebecers thought were guaranteed them in all of Canada, (i. e. to speak French as an official language and to have Catholic French education) were denied. Thus, when a million French Canadians realized they could not save their language or religious schooling, they emigrated just across the border to New England, consequently increasing land prices in the US, not Canada.

44. According to Charles Campbell, former vice chairman of the Canadian Immigration Appeal Board.

45. Although three western provinces have captured some of the rent via a government owned telephone monopoly, two provinces are in the process of privatizing this.

46. The power of the privileged can be seen in US Interior Secretary Babbitt's attempt to raise public land grazing fees, currently set at 1910 prices. The utter hypocrisy of the "conservatives" was witnessed in their

fanatical opposition to his proposal. Free market bidding was apparently no longer a public good.

47. The almost freely granted US water licenses in desert areas (originally meant for the small farmer of 160 acres, but now the preserve of the large agri-businesses) is the most notorious example. But in Canada, water giveaways in more sparsely populated rural areas are substantial, especially considering the amount of water used in mining and pulp and paper production. Here the water is not only used, but abused: most of this polluted water is never treated.

48. "Other examples of types of land which escape most taxes are airport landing slots, tradable licenses, and any situation where there is a co-opting of a time-slot and thus monopolization of a natural resource." Peddle, in the letter cited.

49. Canada's policy differs from the US where certain airwaves are put up for bid. Recently however, President Clinton agreed to exempt radio and TV licenses from bidding, thereby costing the US treasury over $70 billion.

50. Apparently no one in power (and few academics) consider that these rents, if collected, might be spent on producing non-subsidized items, creating longer lasting jobs.

51. There are exemptions of 25 percent from income tax, plus provincial oil tax credits, low rates for family trusts, the aforementioned principal residence exemption, and a $500,000 exemption on the capital gains from the sale of a small Canadian corporation (including any and all real estate used in the business).

Chapter 5

Chile

BY JOHN STRASMA*

LAND TENURE IN rural Chile has gone through two major changes in thirty years, emerging as largely a modern commercial farming structure noted for an exceptional growth rate based in part on high-quality counter-seasonal fruit exports to the Northern Hemisphere. For a century, ending in the early 1960s, Chilean agriculture was characterized by a mixture of large haciendas owned and managed by traditional families, and a large number of small production units (under five ha.[1]) farmed by persons who also served as day laborers for the nearby haciendas.

In 1963, under a conservative businessman, President Alessandri, the government sold off several huge state-owned farms (such as those bequeathed a century before as patrimony for hospitals to serve the poor) to extension agents and other professionals, in parcels of 50 to 150 ha.. Previously, the state farms were leased for five years at a time to well-connected oligarchs in the capital city, who hired managers but invested little or no capital in improvements. Derided as a "land reform in a flower pot," this breakthrough showed that land tenure could be changed, with positive results. Simultaneously, a forward-looking bishop authorized

*John Strasma, Ph.D., Harvard University, has been professor of agriculture and applied economics at the University of Wisconsin-Madison since 1972, and is currently also director of its Center for Development (a training program in economics for civil servants from around the world). He works closely with the Land Tenure Center at the University of Wisconsin. He taught economics at the University of Chile from 1960 to 1972, except for periods on the staff of the Fiscal and Financial Branch of the United Nations Secretariat, as advisor to the Peruvian Ministry of Economy and Finance, and as a guest scholar at the Brookings Institution. Dr. Strasma's books include *Agricultural Land Taxation in Developing Countries* (1987), *Market-Based Land Redistribution in the New South Africa* (1993), and *Resolving Land Conflicts in Nicaragua* (1996).

young Christian Democrat technocrats to experiment with transferring church-owned farms to their workers. The results of these experiments fed into the design of a massive land reform under Christian Democrat President Eduardo Frei Montalvo (1964–1970). Basically, owners were allowed to retain up to 80 ha. (200 acres) of irrigated Maipo River Valley land or the agronomic equivalent in other lands, but holdings in excess of that could be expropriated, with compensation in the form of long-term bonds with indexing to compensate at least in part for Chile's inflation.

Frei's reform affected about half of the farms large enough to be eligible, involving perhaps 20 percent of all the agricultural land. Before and after studies, by the University of Chile and the University of Wisconsin Land Tenure Center, showed that the reformers had followed Frei's instructions to seize first the most underutilized farms but not touch the best-managed farms in each valley. A sample survey found that on average, from 1965 to 1970, output rose well over benchmark levels on both the land that was expropriated and transferred, and on the land that was not expropriated.[2] This result surprised both advocates and enemies of land reform. Actually, it merely confirmed that on average the functionaries had followed orders to seize first the land which produced the least under former management, while leaving the best farm operators alone.

In 1970, Senator Salvador Allende, backed by an uneasy coalition of five groups with a greater or lesser degree of leftist orientation, was elected president by a plurality of the voters, narrowly defeating Former President Alessandri. Allende's government attempted to expropriate most of the remaining large farms, but hard data on output effects were non-existent because his cabinet also tried to nationalize wholesale trade, freezing prices to favor consumers. Farmers and land reform beneficiaries alike sold their output in a thriving black market.

In 1973, General Augusto Pinochet led a military coup in which President Allende died. Pinochet governed as an authoritarian ruler for the next 15 years before agreeing to a plebescite. Voters chose to return to democracy, and Chile is now into its third post-Pinochet presidential term, under a center-left coalition government.

Under Pinochet, land was returned to the former owners if they had not accepted compensation. Where the legal formalities were completed and compensation paid, many land reform beneficiaries were allowed to keep the land they had received. However, most beneficiaries and traditional landowners alike were soon forced into bankruptcy by a combination of tight money, high interest rates, and low demand for farm products because of a deep recession caused by Pinochet's conservative economic policies. The buyers at foreclosure auctions were mostly urban businessmen, who eagerly embraced market incentives, and especially the potential market for counter-seasonal fruits to be sold in the US and other Northern Hemisphere markets.

The result of Chile's tumultuous land policy experiments is thus the product of a mild land reform followed by a radical land reform, followed by a market-induced shakeout, tending to produce a rural sector now dominated by modern entrepreneurs. Typical farms are now more likely to be 40 ha. (100 acres) than 400 ha. (1000 acres), and they are likely to be well-managed, but relying still on a lot of seasonal laborers who live nearby.

I

Land Taxes in Chile

THE CHILEAN REAL estate tax is conceptually defined as a tax determined by the assessed value of both land and improvements. The rate varies from 1.2 percent to 2 percent of assessed value, depending on the date of the most recent property appraisal. The real estate tax in Chile is levied by the central government, but most of the revenues go to the municipalities, urban and rural alike. A formula redistributes the revenue somewhat, favoring communities with less real estate value per person. The basic rate is two percent. A 30 percent surcharge is added to the tax on vacant lots, on commercial and industrial properties, and to residential properties assessed at US $29,200 or more. However, underassessment and exemptions greatly reduce this rate in practice.

Chile has some 466,000 agricultural properties and 2,299,000 urban or other non-agricultural properties. The average tax bill for agricultural properties is estimated to be US $291/year, about equal to 13 percent of per capita Gross National Product (GNP), and for urban properties it is about US $234, or 10 percent of GNP/capita in the cities.[3]

Youngman's study, published in 1994, estimated the assessment ratios at 25 percent (agricultural) and 45 percent (non-agricultural).[4] The reappraisals of non-agricultural land since 1995 may have changed the non-agricultural ratio somewhat, but the reappraisal of agricultural land was postponed indefinitely. If assessments were up-to-date, the taxes due would be about four times as much (agricultural) or almost twice as much (non-agricultural). Even so, in 1997 real estate tax revenues came to US $543 million, about 4 percent of total tax income. They are entirely earmarked to municipal government use, producing about half of all resources at that level.

II

Exemptions

PROPERTIES OWNED AND used by the Chilean government, international organizations and foreign governments, schools, churches, cemeteries, hospitals, and similar non-profit and charitable organizations are exempt, as are properties used for sports activities and agricultural property in an approved forestry management plan.[5]

According to the Chilean *Servicio de Impuestos Internos* (SII), property tax exemption applies to agricultural real estate with 1998 assessed values of less than US $3,533 and the owner's residence on the land. Also exempt are residences with assessed values of less than US $19,039 in areas where non-agricultural land has been reappraised, and residences of less than US $12,111 in areas where it has not.[6]

III

Assessment

HISTORICALLY, THE CHILEAN tax is famous because the 1961–63 reassessment of agricultural land values was one of the very first to be carried out massively, based on the productive potential of the land, with the aid of the then-new techniques of aerial photo-interpretation.[7] That work was funded by the Organization of American States, with monies contributed by other governments in the hemisphere for relief and reconstruction following a destructive earthquake in 1960, and by the US Agency for International Development. The reassessment made the Chilean tax the best-managed of the time, to the credit of both the Chilean government and these international organizations.

The law states that agricultural and non-agricultural real estate are each to be reassessed at least every ten years, but not more often than every five years. In fact, however, the SII reports no reassessment for agricultural properties, and it may be assumed that there has been none since 1980. However, the most recent reappraisal process for non-agricultural real estate began in mid-1995. By 1998, non-agricultural properties had been reappraised in 330 of the 341 commune districts of Chile.[8] The apparently indefinite postponement in the one case, and the delay in the other, may be attributed to complex bargaining among political parties in order to produce a broad-based government after the military dictatorship that ruled from 1973 to 1987.

Chile's chronic inflation, well over 100 years old, is largely offset by automatic valuation adjustments every six months, based on the Consumer Price Index. However, the ratio of assessed values to market values for specific properties does not reflect major changes in location values since the last reassessment.

The Chilean tax is based on a mass valuation technique derived from unit prices applied to property type, adjusted for estimated quality. The unit prices are drawn from the real estate market. Every year, the SII makes approximately 250,000 changes in the real estate register, in response to the latest data on new properties or expansions of existing ones, subdivisions of land, and changes of property ownership.[9]

IV

Unit Value Methodology

A FISCAL VALUATION methodology is applied by the Internal Revenue Service to every one of the 2,700,000 parcels, both urban and rural. For farm land, soil quality, availability of irrigation water, and distance to a market city are major factors. One of the basic principles of land-value taxation is present in that most productive improvements such as barns, fences, irrigation canals, and plantations are exempt for ten years. In the cities, the value of the site and of the improvements is calculated separately and then summed. Unit values are derived from market prices, with considerable input from local interest groups as to relative prices by location.[10]

A. Agricultural Land

Agricultural land is classified into land quality types typical of each zone, with unit values based on the potential profitability of each soil type and microclimate, adjusted for distance and quality of the road to the nearest market center. No discount is made if actual use is less than optimum, so this land value aspect of the tax encourages full utilization. A reference table of land values is based on actual market transactions in the prime agricultural area, and on a separate table for the southernmost region, where the climate is quite different. A separate table is then applied to adapt the reference values to each local municipality.

Improvements such as irrigation canals, erosion protection, plantations, etc., if financed by the owner, will be left out of the land value for ten years, but the exemption vanishes if the property is transferred. It is unclear, however, whether there is any mechanism in place to oblige the owner to even report making such improvements in the first place, until the next revaluation. Owners were last required to update descriptions of properties in 1988 (non-agricultural) and 1992 (agricultural). One cannot say how effectively the Tax Service is able to verify the honesty of these declarations. In the original 1960s' reassessment, air photos were studied carefully and field visits were actually made to resolve doubts as to whether land was irrigated or not, the age and value of plantations, etc.

In that original reassessment, owners also failed to declare all of their lands and buildings. Some 60,000 "holes" in the matrix of land declared were clarified with field visits, and bills were sent out for three years' worth of land taxes for the omitted property. This alone reportedly recovered the entire cost of the reassessment.[11]

B. Non-Agricultural Real Estate

All urban land is assigned to a specific "Similar Characteristics Zone" within a municipality. The zones reflect location, utilities and transport available, etc. Again, unit prices based on current market values are established for each zone.

Buildings are valued similarly. The Internal Revenue Service had 185 staff assigned to property tax administration, of whom 125 had university degrees in engineering, architecture, agriculture or the like.

Standardized exterior and interior materials, characteristics and quality grades are assigned unit values per square meter of construction, based on current building costs in the capital city, Santiago.[12] Cost differences outside the capital are reflected in adjustment coefficients for groups of municipalities with similar characteristics. Every building is depreciated at a constant yearly rate on its base value, for each type of construction. However, cumulative depreciation never reduces a building's tax value by more than 25 percent, no matter how old it is.

Special characteristics, like relative lot locations within blocks, odd shapes, or topography may be allowed for in individual properties.

V

Liability and Collection

THE REAL ESTATE tax is an annual tax, payable in four installments, one at the end of April, June, September, and November, respectively. (The last two are automatically adjusted for inflation, as measured by the Consumer Price Index.) Internal Revenue Service (SII) mails tax bills twice a year to the property address as recorded with the Service; the bill includes detachable receipts to be completed by the bank at which payment is made. For vacant lots, agricultural properties, and any other cases for which there is no mail address on file, the bills are delivered to the municipality where the property is located. Any taxpayer may ask the local office of the Treasury for a print-out of tax liabilities related to a property, and use that as a bill.

The Tax Code states that any person with responsibility for a property is liable for payment of the tax without further notice. This includes owners, occupants, lessees, etc.. However, no study has been made to identify the extent to which persons other than owners actually pay the tax. In theory, it enables the Treasury to collect taxes even when a property is involved in litigation among various parties. It is unclear how often, if ever, the Treasury takes advantage of its legal power to settle such conflicts by seizing the property itself for non-payment of taxes.

VI

Appeals of Assessed Values

TAXPAYERS MAY ONLY appeal the assessed values to correct errors in classification or description, or to seek relief if a natural disaster affects the property. They may not appeal the unit values for land and buildings, nor the values that result from multiplying areas by unit values. There is no provision to argue that the assessment exceeds actual market value, thus eliminating one of the biggest costs and headaches for property taxation elsewhere.

Each time unit values are reassessed, the proposed new tables of unit values are put on display at local municipal and Treasury offices, and are published in the official Gazette (*Diario Official*). Appeals proposing changes must be filed within 60 days of their publication, and are dealt with at various levels, ending in the Supreme Court if necessary.

Whatever unit values are thus finally determined, are applied to all properties of those characteristics. One may thus hypothesize that the Chilean tax is less regressive than real estate taxes in many countries, including the United States, in which wealthy or assertive property owners aggressively seek reduced assessments for *their* properties, while middle and lower-income owners do not. Because the real estate tax assessments also serve for gift and inheritance tax purposes, as well as the value added tax on newly-built properties, this ban on individual appeals probably reduces the regressivity of the entire tax structure as well.

In this writer's opinion, the Chilean Unit Value method is more equitable and more efficient than efforts to approximate the actual market value of each property. Because it reduces appeals to matters quickly settled administratively, the Chilean method also cuts costs and reduces the regressivity produced by appeals pursued in other countries by the wealthier owners.

The centralized management is also less vulnerable to local political pressure than local assessment based on perceived market values would be. But in this writer's view, the virtual elimination of individual appeals based only on a vague desire to pay less taxes, probably deserves much of the credit for the fact that the cost of administering the entire property tax was estimated at only 2.2 percent for 1991.[13]

VII

Enforcement

CHILEAN LAW ACCEPTS the *in rem* approach, and by the early 1960s enforcement was similar in theory to the best practices in the United States.[14] The Treasury Service, which is part of the central government, has the power to seize and auction properties, but has not always used it. Thus, collection was only 73 percent for 1989.[15] An Amnesty Law was passed in 1990, and about US $29

million in taxes due for prior years was collected, for a total of
$202 million in 1991.

The property tax, like all Chilean taxes, may be paid at any bank,
regardless of the location of the property or the address of the
owner. The banks do not charge for the service, but are allowed a
"float" of three days before they transfer taxes collected to the
state's account in the State Bank. The Data Processing Center of
the Treasury Service reconciles taxes paid with taxpayer liabilities
generated in the tax billing process.

To discourage tardiness, and to ensure equity vis-a-vis those
who pay on time, the taxable value is increased by the difference
between the due date and the date of actual payment, and interest
is charged at 18 percent a year on the adjusted tax due.

VIII

Redistributive Formulas

PERHAPS PARTLY IN frustration over their inability to update relative
prices, the Chilean authorities have developed unusually complex
arrangements to redistribute real estate tax revenues among municipalities. In general, 40 percent of revenues is allocated to the
municipalities in which the properties are located, while 60 percent is redistributed. However, local governments have no power
to raise or lower the rate to suit local priorities. A recent World
Bank country study of Chile's Subnational Government Finance[16]
was highly critical of the formula.

IX

Taxation of Mineral Deposits

CHILE HAS A significant metallic mining industry. However, there is
little tradition of taxing the ore in the ground. Rather, like other
Latin American nations, Chile deems resources below the ground
to be property of all the people, represented by their government.
Private mining companies negotiate for mining concessions,
which enable them to build and operate mines in exchange for
royalties, profits taxes, or a partnership share for the government.

Typical arrangements for large mines are for profits taxes higher than those applying to manufacturers or commerce, often with a minimum annual tax even when metal prices fall. And small miners usually pay only token severance taxes.

X
Summary and Conclusions

CHILE HISTORICALLY WAS one of the best countries in the design and implementation of an annual tax on land and improvements. Site value plays a major role in determining assessed values, and farm land is assessed according to its productive potential, even if the owner or tenant fails to realize that potential.

Total real estate revenues were US $543 million in 1997, about four percent of all Chilean taxes. Their average for the decade of the 1990s was approximately US $400 million. Regular reassessment of both agricultural and non-agricultural land (as required by law but not enforced) would generate considerable increase in revenue, which could be used to reduce taxes on productive investment and activity.

Notes

1. Hectares are the normal area measuring units for land in the metric system. One ha. is 10,000 square meters, or approximately 2.5 acres.

2. John Strasma, in Arthur P. Becker, ed., *Land and Building Taxes* (Madison, WI: University of Wisconsin Press, 1969).

3. Joan Youngman, "Chile," in Joan M. Youngman and Jane H. Malme, eds., *An International Survey of Taxes on Land and Buildings*. A study sponsored by the Lincoln Institute of Land Policy, Organization for Economic Co-operation and Development, and the International Association of Assessing Officers; (Boston: Kluwer Law and Taxation Publishers, 1994), p. 106.

4. Ibid.

5. Ibid., p. 107.

6. Website of the Servicio de Impuestos Internos (SSI), the Chilean equivalent of the US Internal Revenue Service; 3rd updated version [March 2000]. The figures have been converted from 1998 Chilean pesos to US dollars, using the exchange rate of January 1999.

7. Luis Vera, *Land and Resource Inventories: The Chilean Case* (Washington, DC: Organization of American States, 1964).

8. SSI website, op. cit.

9. Ibid.

10. Strasma, op. cit.

11. Ibid.

12. Indeed, base values for commercial and other buildings in the most expensive areas of Metropolitan Santiago and certain coastal areas of the central region are increased by 10 percent, apparently to reflect the higher standard of building quality that would be appropriate in such high-value locations in addition to the pure site values in prime locations.

13. Youngman, op. cit., p. 108.

14. Chilean politicians do not always resist the temptation to try to wield political clout for personal benefit. The author's favorite memory of research in Chile is from a day in 1963 when he was collecting data in a tax office, and overheard an employee tell a powerful senator how an *in rem* tax works: "No, Senador, the listing of your house in the paper to be sold for nonpayment of taxes next month is not a lack of respect toward you or your position. It's just that the *house* failed to pay its taxes on time. Just as soon as the *house* pays its taxes, it will be taken from the list."

15. David Vetter, *Chile: Subnational Government Finance* (Washington, DC: World Bank Country Studies, 1993).

Chapter 6

Colombia

BY FERNANDA FURTADO*

THE COLOMBIAN EXPERIENCE with the principle of collecting the community-created value of land for community benefit is significant in the context of Latin American land-value taxation because of the nation's long tradition of effective use of the *Contribución de Valorización* (CV), a valorization or assessment surcharge imposed on properties that benefit from land value increments originating from public works.

This charge has usually been understood as the main form in which the principle of value capture has been embedded in the legal framework of most Latin American countries. These countries other than Colombia have had charges similar to its CV, many of which were introduced in legislation since the 1930s and 1940s. Nevertheless, outside Colombia the implementation of the instrument has generally been very sparse and controversial, in keeping with the familiar Latin American practice of "the law that does not rule"—i.e., legislation that is on the books but not enforced. In this setting, the Colombian CV is recognized as exceptional, because, albeit subject to shortcomings that eventually led to its retreat in

*Fernanda Furtado holds a Ph.D. in urban planning from the University of São Paulo, and is also an architect. She is currently a fellow and faculty member of the Lincoln Institute of Land Policy, and has served as a research assistant in the Institute for Research on Urban and Regional Planning of the Federal University of Rio de Janiero. Dr. Furtado is the author of two published papers and an article, and co-author of a book chapter—all dealing with land-value capture and related issues in Latin America.

The author acknowledges the support of the Lincoln Institute of Land Policy which made possible the carrying out of field research in Bogotá between 1995 and 1998 and the completion of her doctoral dissertation on the subject. Special thanks are due to Martim O. Smolka for fertile discussions on the Colombian experience.

the 1980s, it was effective for many decades after its first introduction in the 1920s, and had a fundamental role in financing the modernization and servicing of Colombian cities throughout the country.

Besides its paradigmatic role in the use of the CV, the case of Colombia is now of great relevance because of the recent (1997) enactment in national legislation of the *Participación en Plusvalías* (PP), a new instrument guided by the value capture principle. The PP is explicitly based on the right of the community to participate in land value increments created by community effort, including in its scope not merely increments arising from public works but also those arising from land use norms and regulations defined by the public sector in the urban planning process.

The importance of this new initiative does not stem from its originality in the Latin American region. The basic idea for the new Colombian instrument may be traced in the legislation of many other countries, ranging from traditional law precepts (as in the expropriation law in Venezuela in the 1940s) to more recent initiatives (as in the attempts since the 1970s to regulate the selling of development rights in Brazil). However, those efforts were always subject to stiff political resistance related to a weak internalization of the principle that land value increments originated by the community are unearned and undeserved by private owners in their capacity as such.[1] As a consequence, the associated instruments were usually not implemented, or at best they were used in pragmatic ways in which the link with the ethics of value capture was loosened.[2]

The promising nature of the Colombian PP comes, in truth, from the legacy of accumulated experience with the CV. It is on the current stage in technical, human, political and institutional development in this sphere that Colombia can build an effective use of the new instrument, opening the way to a wider understanding of the value capture principle in Latin America in the coming years.

I

The Experience with the
Contribución de Valorización

THE LEGAL FOUNDATION for the Colombian CV goes back to 1921, when a levy designed to recover the costs of local public works that brought benefits to certain properties was introduced in legislation at the national level. Over the decades this legislation was amended and complemented by several other laws and decrees, adapting and in times changing the scope of the instrument. This legal evolution in the use of the instrument may be divided into four periods: introduction, expansion and consolidation, peak, and retreat. In each of these periods, some bench marks indicate the uniqueness of the Colombian case in Latin America and set the bases for the development of the new Participación en Plusvalías.

A. Introduction

In the first period, it is important to recognize the motivations for the introduction of the instrument in Colombia as contrasted to other Latin American countries, and also to know how its use came about. From the 1920s, and through the 1930s with the Great Depression, there was a steep rise in urban growth in the region, and with that, an increase in the demand for public investments in the more important cities. It happened that the financing of public works through external capital secured or collateralized by the national government, such as eventually occurred in other countries of Latin America, was hindered in Colombia. Because of international political problems as well as economic reasons,[3] Colombia lost ground in its bidding for external financing, and some of the urban public services for which foreign concessions were not renewed at the turn of the century, were assumed by local business groups.

The combination of the relatively strong local operational capacity that was then developed, with the shortage of foreign capital, contributed to making the new instrument the most and possibly the only available resource adequate to face the challenge of providing the necessary urban infrastructure expansion. Spurred by these specific factors, the legal framework passed through a series of adaptations, in order to better define procedures for implementing the instrument and obviating some of its limitations. Examples are the enlargement of its scope to any public work of local interest, the inclusion of an extra charge of ten percent to cover administrative costs, and the permission by the National Government for its use at the municipal level.

As for the ambiguities that are frequently associated with customary weakness in the application of such instruments in Latin American countries,[4] this first period witnessed the development in Colombia of a practice for overcoming such ambiguities as were recognized as being at least partially inherent in the letter of the law. The strong need to apply the instrument guided the practice of adjusting the interpretation of legal precepts to facilitate its use. For instance, the instrument, although legally defined as a tax (i.e., technically irrespective of public services), was implemented as a charge—a practice that was, in fact, more in keeping with its moral justification.

B. Expansion and Consolidation

As a consequence of the adaptations just summarized, the use of the instrument entered into its second phase. This began in 1943 with the enactment of Law 1 of that year, which established a new role for the levy by stating important criteria and procedures that favored the expansion of its use by local governments. The key feature of this legislation was that it authorized the municipalities to exercise considerable freedom in the various steps involved in putting the instrument into practice. These steps, ranging from the types of projects to be financed by the levy to the management of resources collected, were to be locally defined by the municipal councils.

This local autonomy contributed to the consolidation of the levy by encouraging local political pacts respecting both the approval and the concrete implementation of local regulation. Besides, it led to the creation of local assessment agencies that were fundamental to the development of human resources and to the improvement of technical support necessary to the success of the various procedures involved in the collection of such levies.

The new legislation was not, in itself, framed in such a way as to preclude ambiguities in its interpretation; on the contrary, some of its precepts introduced further complications. For example, the law clearly abolished the previous limitation of the amount collected to the costs of the public investment, yet the connection of the levy with land value increments was loosely defined. This critical point with respect to the potential role of the instrument was also to be defined by each local government. Consequently, the levy acquired distinctive characteristics in each city.

The interpretation of the law in the city of Medellín, which by its intensive use of the instrument over the decades became a model for the other Colombian cities, well illustrates the wide range of possibilities. There, a series of regulations over the years, consolidated in the Municipal Fiscal Code in 1962, established two different levies to be used in two distinct situations: the first, the *Contribución de Valorización*, a charge for financing works undertaken by the municipal government, and limited to the costs of the public work plus administrative costs; the second, the *Impuesto de Valorización*, a tax to recover three fourths of the land value increments generated by public works constructed in Medellín by agencies at the national or departmental level without the participation of the municipal government.[5]

Interpreting the law in this ingenious yet perfectly plausible fashion gave Medellín a decisive lead in the collection of revenue through the use of the CV approach. The same vigor did not extend to other major cities, so that until the middle of the decade of the '60s the nationwide collection of revenue from the CV was still modest in relation to its potential. In 1966 it reached the nationwide total of fifteen percent of aggregate municipal taxes collected, and about two thirds of this was collected in Bogotá and Medellín, Colombia's largest and, at the time, second largest cities, respectively. Even in Bogotá, the utilization of the system was still quite limited, for it was not considered a priority program of the local government. In fact, official figures show that collection from CV in that year was nearly six times larger in Medellín than in Bogotá.[6]

C. Peak

The expansion and consolidation of the use of the CV instrument reached their peak with the approval of Legislative Decree 1604 in 1966, converted to national statute in Law 48 of 1968, which not only consolidated all previous legislation on the matter, but extended the application of the CV to all kinds of public works and to all levels of government. At the same time, the law eliminated the possibility of alternative interpretations, for example, the one developed in Medellín.

It did so by defining the CV as an instrument for the purpose of recovering the costs of public works, and these costs became the basic criterion to be used for calculating the charge. The principle of received benefits was maintained solely as an individual upper limit for the amount to be paid by each landowner. This more narrow scope made it easier to overcome important technical and political difficulties that had hampered more widespread use of the instrument. On one side, the cost-recovery clause facilitated the necessary procedures and calculation for the application of the instrument; on the other side, the upper limit clause protected private landowners' interests, in the worst cost-benefit situation of costs higher than valorization.

Although the new law interrupted any attempt to enlarge general understanding and use of the instrument from a mere cost-recovery mechanism to a true device for the public capture of land value, it had the advantage of functioning as an incentive to encourage acceptance of the idea that land value increment resulting from urban development benefits is the natural source from which to pay for them. It did so especially by helping those who would otherwise be likely to reject it, to realize that public works and services in an infrastructure-scarce locale tend to generate valorization in excess of what it costs to provide them. As a consequence, benefits would accrue to landowners in two ways—by their use of the infrastructure, and by their ability to appropriate some of the net increase created by it in the value of their property.

The impact of the new law was tremendous. With its passage, the CV became and for at least a decade remained the favored instrument for financing public works investments, especially in relation to enabling the construction of the transportation grid. In Bogotá, projects financed by the CV more that tripled between 1966 and 1967, maintaining a high plateau during the following years. The investments realized in the seven-year period between 1967 and 1973 in that city were five times greater than during the previous seven years.[7]

Success in implementing of the CV, however, was measured only in terms of the amount collected, other eventual outcomes from its use being relegated to a secondary plane, if not ignored altogether. Moreover, the establishment of a firmer basis for its continued development was not seriously taken into consideration. Thus, after a period when it was at its zenith, a series of problems in the application of the CV began to emerge and to proliferate.

D. Retreat

The administration of the CV in Colombia was managed by valorization departments, which also maintained capitalization (rotation) funds for the financing of public works through the CV. These funds were constituted by income generated by the CV or derived from CV-related sources, such as the municipal shares in the works, subsidies from the National Government, financial credits, etc. In the mid-1970s, inflation, heavy expenses in connection with expropriation (condemnation) procedures, major cost overruns, and administrative inefficiency all combined to deplete the capitalization funds. This resulted in weakening the credibility and autonomy of the valorization departments that managed the funds, and (what is especially germane to this discussion) loss of confidence in the CV as a fiscal instrument. These difficulties reflect in large measure the problems generated by its standardization, which vitiated local autonomy in the establishment of political agreements. According to official data, the collection of the CV among all of the municipalities underwent a decline of almost one quarter during the decade of the 1970s, and its percentage of total municipal current revenue was reduced by approximately half.[8]

However, one must consider this first phase of the "retreat" period in relative terms, for it reflected primarily the cases of Bogotá and Medellín. For instance, in Cali, which competes with Medellín for the designation of Colombia's second largest city, the CV accounted for thirty percent of municipal tax revenues at the beginning of the 1980s. Overall, its collection was still, in 1980, very important relative to other municipally-generated incomes, totaling something like half of property taxes, which constitute one of the major sources of local tax revenue, especially in small and medium cities where taxes on services are less important.

Between 1980 and 1990, the retreat entered into a second phase during which the instrument's low political attractiveness and low generation of funds fed upon each other in a vicious circle that spread throughout Colombia. By the decade's end, the collection from CV represented in national terms (comprising 900 municipalities) only around one sixth of the total property tax revenues, declining from the plateau of fifteen percent of the municipally-generated tax revenues in 1980 to around five percent in 1990, with a real decline of about twenty-seven percent.[9] In Bogotá and Medellín, revenues from CV accounted for less than one tenth of property taxes in 1990.

Because, in Law 48 of 1968, the instrument was limited to fiscal goals, unintended and perverse outcomes with respect to urban planning, social welfare and redistribution eventually occurred. Especially unfortunate was the reinforcement of an urban pattern of social-spatial segregation, stemming from the tendency to favor use of CV in areas where payment capacity was greater. This tended to force removal and exclusion from such areas of users (owners or otherwise) who lacked such capacity.[10]

The many technical, institutional and political difficulties associated with its use eventually brought about a virtual standstill in the financing of public works through the CV, and led to concerted efforts, at the end of the 1980s, to develop a new and more comprehensive framework for urban land policy in Colombia.

II

The New Instrument

THE NEW INSTRUMENT, Participación en Plusvalías (PP), mandated in Law 388 of 1997, concretizes the precept of the new Colombian Political Constitution adopted in 1991 that "public entities will participate in the plusvalía generated by their urbanistic action." ("Plusvalía" may be defined as an increase in land value resulting from governmental, and particularly municipal, activity.) According to this national law, each municipality must develop a master plan for urban development, and the PP is defined as one important instrument to balance costs and benefits arising from the development process.

The major concerns that arose in the course of the use of CV are addressed in the design of the new instrument. In keeping with the idea of integrating urban land and fiscal policies, the PP is tailored to capture land value increments generated not only through public works but also and mainly through administrative decisions related to urban land uses. The PP is to be considered in three situations that must be part of the municipal master plan: the designation of rural and suburban land for urban uses, changes in zoning to more profitable uses, and allowance for additional development rights.

Social welfare and re-distributive concerns are also present in the design of the new instrument. Revenues collected through it are not, as in the case of CV, to merely recover the costs of directly associated local public works, but to help finance public works of general interest—especially urban infrastructure in areas of incomplete development, and the purchase of land for social programs.

With these orientations, the PP implies a substantial extension of the principle of collecting social value as it was traditionally understood in Colombia. This extension, of course, is subject to political resistance both from powerful landowners and developers and from many homeowners, who view their residences as a source of personal savings. To deal with this problem, some of the instrument's characteristics are clearly intended to enhance its acceptability and weaken anticipated arguments against its use.

The first of these characteristics is that land value increments to be captured are fixed between thirty and fifty percent of the valorization. The underlining idea is that the instrument constitutes a provision for the sharing of plusvalías between private owners and the public. A second important idea is that although the plusvalía effect is calculated when the master plan is approved, the effective charging of the PP depends on the landowner's participation, inasmuch as the payment is only required when there is a positive initiative on the part of the landowner, such as by selling the property, changing its use, or requesting a building license. Related to both ideas is the possibility, stated by law, of alternative ways of paying for the plusvalías, including "in kind" payments with a portion of the land affected or other properties in the same urban area.

Another key element to facilitate its operation is the local autonomy conferred by the legislation. Law 388 states general rules and provisions to the use of the PP, but each municipality is responsible for defining the specific circumstances and ways in which the instrument is to be applied.

Despite these important statutory provisions that tend to guide political agreements on the best use of the instrument for each local situation, there are still fundamental open issues to be discussed and resolved in connection with its implementation. Examples of issues in debate are the ambiguities involved in the definition of which base value to consider in the assessment of the PP. For instance, in areas where previous land use norms authorize development rights that have not yet been fully exercised with respect to some of the properties, it is not clear whether the base value of these land parcels should be calculated according to their highest and best use or to their actual use. If the new master plan or its revision defines additional development rights for this area, the plusvalías (consisting of the difference between the new and the previous value) would be higher in the case of choosing the actual use of these parcels to calculate the base value. However, in this case affected landowners may claim that they have acquired the previous development rights, be it by having bought the land with these potential values already capitalized in land prices or just for having made a long-term investment on these lands. On the other hand, if the highest and best use is chosen as the parameter for the base value, this could have perverse outcomes such as encouraging land retention for speculative reasons, which, ironically, is recognized as one of the major problems to be redressed by the application of the PP.

To resolve this and several other political and procedural issues of how to assess affected land, the experience with the CV can be of great help. Some of the lessons of this experience may already be recognized within the scope and design of the new instrument, but it is in the process of implementing the PP that the legacy of the CV can make a real difference.

III

Summary and Conclusions

THE COLOMBIAN EXPERIENCE, and Latin American experience in general, shows that to evolve from the general formulation of a new value capture instrument to its effective use is not an easy process.[11] In the first place, a great range of factors must be considered in the instrument's design. However, that is not alone sufficient to guarantee its successful implementation. Technical, institutional, political and cultural factors can hinder or even stop the process.

The lessons of the Colombian experience with the Contribución de Valorización are cited in the literature as worthy of serious attention by other Latin American countries, due to Colombia's success in overcoming some of the usual impediments in the region to the implementation of such instruments. Furthermore, it must be noted that the Colombian practice has left a legacy that, besides being useful to other countries, may now be of great help to Colombia itself in the process of effectuating the Participación en Plusvalías. The main points of this legacy are:

First, the long-standing use of the CV solidified a fiscal culture, that is, popular acceptance of the concept of participating in the costs of the urban development process as well as in its benefits.

This is a very sensitive issue in Latin American countries. Many of the incentives to strengthen the property tax in the region, such as those promoted by multilateral agencies, were obstructed because of failure to take into careful consideration the need for this prerequisite. The established fiscal culture may certainly be accurately regarded by Colombia as advantageous to the positive understanding of the new instrument by the people.

Second, human and technical resources were developed in the field of land and real estate with the continuous operation of the CV. Colombia is a pioneer in Latin America in offering a career in land and real estate assessing to prospective public officials. This is an essential ingredient for dealing with issues involved in the functioning of urban land markets, and is a much needed requirement for the fiscal and urban planning public departments all over Latin America. From this viewpoint, Colombia is now well prepared to face the procedural and technical challenges posed by the new instrument.

Finally, the effective use of the CV was made possible by overcoming serious ambiguities that existed in the legislation or that arose in the implementation process. The Colombian case offers strong evidence that this is a *sine qua non* condition if such value capture instruments are to work effectively in Latin America. Without it, no matter how much care is taken in the theoretical design of the instrument and the approval of the necessary laws and norms, all such effort may be in vain.

To Colombia, the achievements in this process constitute important precedents to be considered in the construction of political pacts that can accommodate the diverse interests and motivations involved in the operation of local urban land markets.

Notes

1. In Latin America, land has historically been an important source of wealth and political power, and for the majority of the population is still the major source of family savings. Acceptance of the idea of private appropriation of land-value increments in the urban development process, far from being confined to powerful landowners, is spread over society. The lack of social housing and adequate social security programs contributed to the dissemination of this attitude to people of medium and even low incomes.

2. As, for instance, in the use of market prices in expropriation processes associated with public works. In some cases, those (highest and best use) prices include even the expected valorization to be capitalized when the public work is completed. Evidences of this practice in overcoming obstructions to the completion of the related works may be found in many countries in the region.

3. An important political motive was resentment of the United States, going back to its role in the independence of Panama, prior to 1903 a Colombian department. Of the economic reasons, the most important were those flowing from the crisis of 1929, which strongly affected the price of coffee, the basis of Colombia's export economy.

4. As, for instance, in the comprehensive evaluation conducted by Jorge Macon and José, Merino Manon for the International Development Bank, *Financing urban and rural development through Betterment Levies: the Latin American experience* (New York: Praeger Publishers/IDB, 1977).

5. This municipal norm is understood as having introduced the term, "Contribución de Valorización." Analyses of the case of Medellín are undertaken by Rafael Mora Rubio in *Régimen de Valorización Municipal y Renovación Urbana* (Bogotà: Editorial ABC, 1966) and Francisco Dario Bustamante Ledesma in *Manual de la Contribución de Valorización* (Medellin: Teoria del Color, 1996).

6. Carolina Barco de Botero, "The Valorization Tax in Colombia as Applied at the Municipal Level." Department of City and Regional Planning, Harvard University, 1975. Mimeo.

7. William A. Doebele, "Valorization Charges as a Method for Financing Urban Public Works: the example of Bogota, Colombia." (World Bank Staff Working Paper 254, March 1977).

8. Fernando Ortega Garzon, *Examen acerca de la Contribución de Valorización en Colombia* (Departamento Nacional de Planeación, Informe de Asesoria, 1993).

9. Samuel Jaramillo, "La Contribución de Valorización y la Participación en Plusvalías" (Essay presented to the Lincoln Institute, 1997).

10. For an evaluation of these trends in the use of the instrument in Latin American countries, see Guillermo Geisse and Francisco Sabatini, "Urban Land-Markets Studies in Latin America," in Matthew Cullen and Sharon Woolery, eds. *World Congress on Land Policy, 1980.* (Lexington, MA/Toronto: Lexington Books-D.C. Heath, 1982), pp. 149–176.

11. This process is analyzed in the author's doctoral dissertation, "Land Value Recapture in Latin America: debilities in implementation, ambiguities in interpretation." (Faculty of Architecture and Urbanism, University of Sao Paulo, Brazil, 1999).

Downtown Bogotá reflecting the improvements financed by the Contribución de Valorización.

A typical scene in Latin America showing poor families living in poverty. This particular picture was taken by the author on the outskirts of Lima, Peru.

Chapter 7

Jamaica and Other Caribbean States

BY JOHN M. COPES* AND WALTER RYBECK**

I

Jamaica

JAMAICA, THE THIRD largest island in the West Indies, was seized by England from Spain in 1655 and, after more than three centuries as a British colony, became an independent member of the British

---

*John M. Copes was a life fellow of the Australian Institute of Valuers and Economists, and was for several years editor of its journal, *The Valuer*, during which time he also lectured on valuation to post-graduate students in the town planning department of the University of Sydney. He served as commissioner of valuations in Jamaica from 1957 to 1962, as UN adviser on land valuation and taxation in the Caribbean from 1963 to 1973, and as one of the three members of Australian Valuation Board of Review until his retirement. He is author of the chapter, "Reckoning with Imperfections in the Land Market," in Daniel Holland, ed., *The Assessment of Land Value* (TRED 5, 1969), and co-author of *Land Valuation and Compensation in Australia* (2nd ed., 1978). Mr. Copes died some two months after completing his chapter for the second edition of *Land-Value Taxation Around the World*. It has been updated for this volume by Walter Rybeck.

**Walter Rybeck, since 1983 director of the Center for Public Dialogue, is a graduate of Antioch College in economics and political science. Following a career in journalism that culminated in a six-year stint as Washington, DC, bureau chief for the Cox newspaper chain, he became assistant director of the National Commission on Urban Problems (a presidentially-appointed body popularly known as the "Douglas Commission" after its chairman, Senator Paul H. Douglas), and then spent nine years as editorial director of the Urban Institute. He served as special assistant on housing and urban affairs to two congressmen, Henry S. Reuss of Milwaukee from 1978–80, and William J. Coyne of Pittsburgh from 1980–83. Mr. Rybeck is author of numerous monographs, congressional reports, book chapters, and journal articles, and produced and directed a documentary film, "A Tale of Five Cities: Tax Revolt Pennsylvania-Style" (1984).

Commonwealth of Nations in 1962. It is a parliamentary democracy, with a prime minister as head of government. The nation is divided into 13 parishes for purposes of local administration. Its population, upwards of two and a half million, is primarily of African extraction (its Arawak Indians having died out under Spanish rule), with lesser European, Chinese, and East Indian strains. Its official language is English, with a purported literacy rate of 98 percent, but Jamaican Creole is also spoken. A slight majority of the inhabitants is Protestant.

Rising from the coastal plain is a mountainous core that covers four-fifths of the island. The Blue Mountains in the east (where an extremely expensive variety of coffee is grown) soar to a peak of 7,402 feet above sea level. The island's climate is semi-tropical; yearlong rainfall keeps it green; heat and humidity are tempered by soft breezes.

Bauxite exists over the western two-thirds of the island, and has been mined by US and Canadian companies since 1952. In the 1960s, Jamaica was the world's largest exporter of bauxite, and it remains a major one. The government acquired 50 percent ownership of the companies' Jamaican holdings in 1976.

In the years following British seizure, sugar cane became the chief crop grown on the coastal plains. Numerous slaves were brought in from Africa to work the sugar plantations, which occupied lands granted under Cromwell, and extended from the coast into the lower slopes. The mountains remained mostly unoccupied until the slaves (approximately 311,000 in number) were emancipated in 1838. Over the ensuing decades, freed slaves progressively "squatted" on unutilized mountain lands, defining the boundaries of their respective plots with plants recognized as "boundary plants." Access to the plots was mainly by series of tracks.

Captain William Bligh (the notorious martinet of HMS *Bounty*) had brought in breadfruit from Tahiti. With this, together with mangoes, bananas, corn, root crops, pigs, and poultry, the former slaves became basically self-sustaining. For cash, they took their produce on donkeys to the nearest markets.

A. The Introduction of Land-Value Taxation
in Jamaica

The move toward land-value taxation (LVT) in Jamaica commenced in 1943 (19 years before independence) with the appointment of a Commission of Inquiry chaired by the Hon. Simon Bloomberg. Its charge was to examine, with particular reference to their effect upon parochial revenue, the incidence, assessment, and collection of real property taxes under the existing system based on the combined capital value of land and buildings, to determine whether that system should be retained or replaced by another. As a result of its investigations, the Commission recommended that the existing system be replaced by one that made unimproved land value the sole basis for the taxation of real property, whether urban, suburban, or rural. This recommendation was endorsed by the Mission of the International Bank for Reconstruction and Development in a report, "The Economic Development of Jamaica" (1952).

In 1949 and 1951, attempts were made to implement the Commission's recommendation, but Jamaica had no large scale maps delineating the various parcels of land. It was thought at the time that a full scale legal cadastre was a fundamental requirement, so the program was shelved.

When the Norman Manley administration took office in 1955 (still before full independence), one of the matters to which it gave priority was the suspended program of assessing unimproved land value. The government sought technical assistance from the United Nations. The UN approached the Australian government, since Australia has had wide experience in the public capture of unimproved land values since early in this century both at the federal and state levels as taxes, and at the local level as rates. Following a preliminary report by J. F. N. Murray in 1957, John Copes (one of the two authors of this chapter) was appointed commissioner of valuations.

The Land Valuation Law was passed by the Jamaican Parliament, and proclaimed on January 18, 1957. The rationale for advocating the new law was set forth by Mr. Manley in Parliament during the debate on the bill:

Mr. Speaker, what is the reason for advocating taxation on the unimproved value of land? The present system (taxation of land and buildings) is a tax not upon land, but on man's efforts put into land. It is a tax on labor—and the consequence is that it implies that there is no tax upon those who do nothing with land, and more tax on those who do more and more with land.

Speaking on windfall increases in land values arising from public works, Mr. Manley said:

The (new) method of taxation has another overriding and fundamental justification, and it is this: In effect, the tax increases with the value which the community as a whole has put into the land—therefore it is only fair that if there should be any increase in taxes, it should fall where the increase in value occurs—not from the labor of man on the land, but from the value put into the land by the community.

Also included in his remarks was the argument that "the new system will tend to discourage the withholding of land from use, and to encourage the putting of land to use."[1]

Prior to the change of the tax base from improved capital values to the unimproved capital value of land, the tax on real estate was known simply as "property tax," and this designation continues to be used even though the base is no longer the same.

B. Definitions in the Land-Valuation Law

A statement by Lord Dunedin with respect to the New South Wales Valuation of Land Act (1916) is equally applicable to Jamaica's Land Valuation Law:

What the Act requires is really quite simple. Here is a plot of land; assume that there is nothing on it in the way of improvement; what would it fetch in the market? It will be observed that the value is not what has been sometimes designated by the expression "prairie value." The land must be taken as it exists at the date of valuation.[2]

The land "as it exists" may have been cleared of timber and vegetable growth, or earth works such as excavation, filling, draining, and the like, carried out at some time long past. These "invisible" improvements are said to have merged with the land,

and for the purpose of the valuation law are not to be regarded as improvements.

It is not proposed here to include verbatim the various definitions from the Jamaican Land Valuation Law, but rather to briefly state a few points pertinent to it. These points are as follows:

1. The test of value is the market value of the fee simple of the land.

2. When it comes to the unimproved value of a property on which improvements exist, the law requires the assumption that the improvements have not been made.

3. Improvements are defined to mean those physical additions or alterations which have the effect of increasing the value of the land. The exception to this is that those "invisible" improvements described above shall not be regarded as improvements.

4. Since the definition of land in the Jamaican Valuation Law is not exclusive of mineral deposits, it follows that the unimproved capital value of the land would include such deposits. However, the bauxite companies and the government reached an agreement that in lieu of taxing the capital value of the bauxite deposits, public revenue from bauxite would be raised on a royalty/income tax basis. Because bauxite is exported from Jamaica either as bauxite or alumina for processing elsewhere, taxable profits are not earned in Jamaica. The agreement was for the payment of a royalty plus a notional income tax on each ton of bauxite mined. As a result of these agreements, the lands owned by the bauxite companies are valued for the purposes of the Land Valuation Law on the basis of their surface use, which for the most part would probably have been agricultural.

C. Hardship Cases

The zoning of land for specific uses will often adversely affect the owners of land within a given zone who are utilizing their land in legal ways that do not conform to the uses contemplated by the zoning. The Jamaican Land Taxation (Relief) Law makes provision for such nonconforming users by providing for the issuance of Relief Certificates under circumstances of hardship. Thus a person living in his own residence on land zoned for commercial use, for example, may be relieved of the higher taxation resulting from the valuation of the land for commercial use. The Certificate for Relief remains valid until a new Valuation Roll is issued; the person to whom it is granted dies; or the land to which it relates (or any part thereof) is sold, exchanged, given away, leased, licensed, or otherwise disposed of on terms whereby the land (or part thereof) may be used for any purpose other than the purpose for which it was being used at the time when the application for the relief certificate was made.

D. Resources Needed for the Valuation Project

To undertake a valuation program such as that envisaged by the Jamaican Land Valuation Law, certain basic resources are required. Needless to say, a nucleus of competent professional staff is one of these. With such a corps, a subordinate staff with various levels of responsibility can be trained.

Another essential is an adequate cadastre. As mentioned earlier, it was at first believed that this had to be a "legal" cadastre, where under a system of title registration, the owner and the dimensions of his holding are guaranteed by the registrar. A cadastre of this nature presented technical obstacles of such severity that the entire project was at first abandoned. It was later decided that the Law's purposes would be served by a "fiscal" cadastre, where the commissioner records on the Valuation Roll the name of the person he believes to be the owner and the dimensions of his holding, without guaranteeing the accuracy of the information. This necessitates a large scale map upon which is delineated the presumptive boundaries of each parcel, identifiable by a numerical map reference system. The map is a ready means of locating and identifying the parcel on the ground.

Jamaica did not possess such a map, so the country was mapped and valued as the staff "rolled" over the territory. Large base maps were established by aerial photography. Recognizable features such as rivers, roads, tracks, and contours provided basic information. Each map was divided into six grids, and a numerical reference system developed as shown in the following example:

Map number	001
Grid	1
Enclosure	001
Parcel	001

Thus, for a given parcel: 0011001001.

An "enclosure" is an area of land definable on the map by physical features and enclosing a number of "parcels" of land. The parcels were discovered by compass and chain survey, often with the assistance of existing plans or descriptions.

Near the beginning of this chapter, reference was made to the squatter occupation of the mountain country. The occupied sites were of very low value, and negligible from the standpoint of potential public revenue. The exercise of identifying these parcels was time-consuming, but yielded benefits other than revenue. For the owner, the Notice of Valuation served, in effect, as a Certificate of Title. For the government, the maps and records provided useful statistical information in development planning.

Computers have become almost indispensable in the preparation and publishing of the Valuation Roll. The use of the numerical mapping system provides the means for ready access to the details on the Roll. The use of mass valuation techniques and computerized valuation calculations has relatively wide application, and the data can be retained in the computer memory, easily available in dealing with objections or for revision at revaluation time.

E. Tax Rates and Revenues

Valuation of all land, urban and rural, was completed in all 13 parishes of the country in 1977. Commissioner Norma E. Dixon of the Inland Revenue Department in Kingston provided the following information about the tax in late 1999, just before the start of the 21st century:

The tax is administered both at the national and local level. However, a single national tax rate is used throughout Jamaica. As shown below, the tax rates increase as does the value of the land, to incorporate what is believed to be an "ability to pay" element. In 1999, when the prevailing exchange rate was 40 Jamaican dollars (Ja$s) for one US dollar, the rate schedule was as follows (all figures in Jamaican dollars):

Table 1

RATE SCHEDULE				
Schedule of Rates			Example of $1,2000,000 Plot of Land	
Land Tax Rate	Unimproved Land Value		Tax Bill	Running Total of Value
Flat sum of $50		$20,000 or less	$ 50 on first $ 20,000	$ 20,000
.001 %	Per dollar of next $	30,000	$ 30 on next $ 30,000	$ 50,000
.003 %	" next $	50,000	$ 150 on next $ 50,000	$ 100,000
.0075%	" next $	400,000	$3,000 on next $400,000	$ 500,000
.015 %	" next $	500,000	$7,000 on next $500,000	$1,000,000
.020 %	" next $1,500,000		$4,000 on remaining $200,000	$1,200,000
.025 %	" next $2,550,000			
.030 %	Per dollar of remainder		$14,730 TOTAL TAX	

To translate this example from Jamaican to US dollars, Ja$1.2 million (the value of the plot) equals US$30,000 and the Ja$14,730 tax on it equals US$368. The effective rate is 1.2 percent. One may also see that for a Ja$500,000 plot (US$12,500) the tax would be Ja$3,230 ($50+$30+$150+$3,000) or $US81. Its effective tax rate would be 0.65 percent. For an even cheaper plot worth only Ja$100,000 (US$2,500), the tax would be Ja$230 (US$6), for an effective tax rate of 0.25 percent. While the rates drop considerably for owners of cheaper pieces of land, even the top rates recover only a small portion of the socially-created site values in each parish of the country.

The total revenue from the land tax for the financial year ending in March 1999 was Ja$512,865,125. This accounted for approximately 1.1% of the total taxes collected in Jamaica. Both the income tax and the sales tax, by comparison, raise billions in revenue. Land tax revenue is devoted primarily for solid waste management and municipal lighting. "The public's attitude toward the tax," Commissioner Dixon reported, "is in keeping with their overall negative attitude toward taxation." She said she knew of no serious efforts either to expand or to abolish it.

An elected member of the St. Ann Parish Council said he believed it would be "political suicide" for any office holder to suggest a return to taxing housing or any improvements on the land. However, he expressed disappointment with the "ridiculously low" level of the land tax for three reasons: One, local officials must still go "hat in hand" to the central government to fund most of their facilities and services, hampering the ability of a parish to improve its management. Two, anticipated effects of the land tax—discouragement to keeping vacant and underdeveloped properties out of use, and the promotion of development within cities rather than on farmland—do not come into play. Three, the consequent reliance on a high national income tax discourages commercial growth and fosters a large underground economy, turning workers away from readily-taxed wages in commerce and industry to small crafts, the income from which is easily hidden.

II

Concluding Comments about Valuation Methodology

JAMAICA PROVIDES AN instructive example for an administration planning to move to a property tax system based exclusively on unimproved land values. The initial program of establishing the Valuation Roll was delayed for a number of years following 1963 due to political changes. Such delays can be avoided by arriving at political concurrence at the start. Extensive use of the computer greatly facilitates the completion of the initial Roll of Values and its regular revision as required by law; however, no mechanical device can substitute for a sufficient number of professionally qualified valuers to supervise the work of locally trained subordinate staff.

It is desirable that the Roll be revalued triennially or even biennially. In time of inflation with increasing speculative land values, the number of objections is likely to be considerably less if the revaluations are carried out routinely on a frequent, incremental basis, because increases will not be so large each time. If revaluations occur as far apart as every five years or more, the increases are apt to come as a shock, eliciting an avalanche of appeals that swamp the staff. When there is regular revaluation no less often than two or three years, the operation of the system becomes more proficient and less politically hazardous, as land owners find fewer reasons to lodge objections.

III

Barbados

BARBADOS, THE MOST easterly of the Caribbean islands, was first occupied by the British in 1627, and was a slave economy until 1834. It remained a colony until 1966, when it became an independent member of the Commonwealth of Nations, with a parliamentary form of government. Its inhabitants, largely of African descent, number close to 270,000 on an island 21 miles long and 14 miles wide. Its population density of about 900 to the square mile is among the highest in the world. Natural resources are scanty.

In the late 1960s, tourism became the leading industry, supplanting sugar production, which now accounts for only one percent of gross national product. Rum is a major export. Barbados became a tax haven in 1977. It freed foreign companies from income tax, assured banking confidentiality, and offered other economic incentives. As a result, approximately 200 foreign and domestic industries were started. Financial services now generate the second largest earnings for the country.

Until mid-twentieth century, when the English practice of rating according to the combined annual value of land and improvements was adopted, church wardens had collected property taxes for poor relief, etc., under what is known as the "vestry system." In 1969, Barbados introduced the Land Valuation Act, its purpose being to prepare a Roll of Values preparatory to a shift to site-value rating. As in Jamaica, it was necessary to train staff and to prepare a cadastral map. The Valuation Roll was completed in 1973 and the Land Tax Act enacted the same year, indicating a serious attempt to implement a property tax based purely on land values.

However, in 1975 the law was changed to include improved values in the tax base. On improved properties, the tax rate is imposed on the combined value of the land and structure. Properties that are highly improved bear increasingly heavy tax burdens, so the incentive for making optimal improvements that is inherent in the land-value tax approach is absent. An exception is that completely idle land bears a higher tax rate than improved parcels, as shown in the following table:

Table 2

TAX RATES ON VACANT LAND AND IMPROVED PROPERTIES (1999) (Value in Barbados Dollars (2 Bar$ = 1 US$ in 1999))				
Land Use Categories	Up to $2000,000 Rated at	$200,000 to $500,000 Rated at	Over $500,000 Rated at	Assessed at
Vacant Land	.08 %	.08 %	.08 %	75 % of value
Agricultural Land	.08 %	.08 %	.08 %	50 % of value
Improved—Residential	.02 %	.07 %	1.2 %	75 % of value
Improved—Nonresidential	.07 %	.07 %	.07 %	75 % of value

B. O. Kinch, the Barbados commissioner of land tax, provided the following 1999 information: Taxpayer bills show the separate assessed value of land and improvements. Revaluations are required every three years. The tax is administered nationally. Revenues, which amounted to Bar$55 million, go into a "consolidated fund" mainly for the support of roads and schools. The property tax revenue represents a substantial 26 percent of the total tax revenue of Bar$209,036,000. (A few years ago, before an aggressive collection program was undertaken, it accounted for only five or six percent.) Public lands generally are not taxed unless they are leased, in which case the tenant is treated like the owner and taxed accordingly. Commissioner Kinch said that 70 percent of the 1999 property taxes were actually collected, a major improvement after years of widespread nonpayment.

IV

Belize[3]

BELIZE IS A sliver of a country on the east coast of Central America, hemmed in by Mexico to the north and Guatemala to the west.

Before gaining independence in 1981, it was the colony of British Honduras, and remains a member of the British Commonwealth. Within its 8,867 square miles live approximately 200,000 people of mixed ancestry—Maya and Carib Indians, European settlers (primarily British and Spanish), East Indians, and African slaves. They boast an unusually high literacy rate of 92 percent.

The early settlers were attracted by the logwood, from which was extracted dyes used by the Lancashire cotton industry. Mahogany trade became the most important source of income until the 20th century when mahogany forests were depleted. Sugar, citrus fruits, and lobster and other seafood then became major exports. Tourists visit Mayan ruins, take jungle safaris, and explore a long barrier reef. After Hurricane Hattie crushed Belize City in 1970, the capital was moved to higher ground at a site named Belmopan. Yet Belize City still has 30 percent of the country's population, and remains a major commercial center.

Since the early 1990s, international business has become the nation's growth "industry." Belize transformed itself into a free trade zone with no customs duties on imports and exports, no license fees, no quotas, and low shipping rates. According to the authors of *Tax Havens of the World*, these incentives attracted more than 3,500 international firms by the end of the decade.[4] Dividends of export zone firms are exempted by law "in perpetuity" from taxation. No capital gains or income withholding taxes are imposed on any business. To deter illegitimate businesses from capitalizing on these advantages, Belize imposes heavy fines and imprisonment for money laundering.

Despite its high literacy rate, and the abundance of international business, living standards in Belize are low, attributable in large measure to exploitative land tenure arrangements. The British colonial government recognized claims of early explorer-settlers who had seized huge tracts. After Emancipation in the 1830s, official policy priced land that was not already in private hands beyond the reach of former slaves, leaving them no alternative to working as laborers at subsistence wages. Land ownership remains highly concentrated, much of it in the hands of absentees. In rural areas, there are thousands of tiny one-acre, five-acre, and ten-acre plots in contrast to the large holdings of thousands of acres each where well over half the land suitable for agriculture is not under cultivation.

To bolster the economy and ease poverty, two United Nations reports in the 1960s urged adoption of a two percent land-value tax. This likely would have been too modest to alter the country's land tenure pattern. Yet the reports focused public attention on the land problem, which became one of the rallying points of the independence movement. The first prime minister, George Price, won enactment in 1982 of a national tax on the capital value of land exclusive of improvements.

Landholder opposition almost completely overturned this approach in Belize's cities. As a result, in urban areas improved properties are taxed on the annual rental value of both land and buildings, according to Chief Valuer Armin Cansino of the Belize Land Department. Cities have discretion to set their own tax rates. As of 1999, one city had a low 4 percent rate; Belize City used the maximum allowable 12 percent, and the other half-dozen communities adopted rates of 6 to 8 percent. In the case of vacant urban land, these rates were applied to the assessed market value of the site.

Rural areas retain the pure land value tax, completely exempting buildings or other improvements. Unfortunately, the very low tax rate throughout the 1990s of 1 percent of assessed market value—only half the feeble rate recommended by the UN—was not potent enough to break up oversized holdings or to help stimulate agricultural production.

Mr. Cansino completed the required three-year revaluation of rural lands in 1999. Municipalities have their own assessors, assisted when necessary by the national Land Department, who must revalue properties every five years. He said that the 1999 estimates showed the combined urban and rural property taxes accounting for between five and six percent of Belize's total tax revenue. At that time he knew of no efforts either to expand the rural tax rate or to win adoption of the rural system in the cities.

V

Montserrat

THIS 38-SQUARE-MILE East Caribbean island, despite devastating eruptions of the Soufriere Hills volcano in 1995 and 1997, survives and continues to have a limited land-value tax as part of its fiscal system.

A British colony since 1783, Montserrat is internally self-governing. Its inhabitants, of mostly African extraction with some Irish admixture, numbered close to 13,000, but two thirds of them fled the island after the catastrophic eruption in June of 1997. Some began to return in 1998. The capital was moved to Salem after Plymouth was almost totally destroyed by the volcanic activity. Unemployment was high. Many people, schools, and churches were housed in makeshift structures. A great deal of fertile land was buried under ash. Tourism suffered too; vacation homes were wiped out, and cruise ships failed to stop at the country's new thirty million dollar seaport. Attempts to revive the economy focused on fresh produce and light industry. Food exports include melons and other fruit, hot peppers, and live plants. Major manufactured items are electrical equipment, polyethylene bags, fiberglass, Sea Island cotton and knitwear. Montserrat also tries to exploit its role as a tax haven by offering light or no taxes on certain international business operations and on agricultural income.

Since the 1960s, the property tax system has imposed lower tax rates on buildings than on the unimproved land value of each parcel. This apparently has had salutary effects:

> Several large tracts of land which hitherto had been regarded as wasteland and in respect of which little or no real estate taxes had ever been paid in the past, have been forced into economic production by way of agriculture or other meaningful development. In many cases, landowners, realizing that it was no longer advantageous to hold land until such time as a substantial capital gain could be obtained, because of the punitive land tax were forced to dispose of part of their holdings. This disposition often resulted in a general upsurge in the overall economy and served to effectuate the general distribution of land wealth.[5]

After volcanic explosions rendered so much formerly inhabited and productive land unusable and dangerous, Montserrat designated parts of the island as "safe" and "unsafe" zones. The property tax administration, aided by a computerized system, simply took all properties in the unsafe zone off the tax rolls. Within the safe zone, properties were still valued according to their market value as of the last previous valuation—almost two decades earlier in 1980. Mr. Haycene Ryan, comptroller in land revenue with the Inland Revenue Department, explained that attempts to hire a valuation officer had not yet succeeded by late 1999, and that the department had to rely on help from an occasional visiting valuer on loan from the United Kingdom.

The tax rates in 1999, based on an ordinance of the previous year, were as follows:

Table 3

ZONING CLASS	TAX RATE ON LAND	TAX RATE ON BUILDINGS
Agricultural	1.00 %	zero
Residential	1.65 %	0.3 %
Commercial	2.00 %	0.6 %

As a further incentive for commercial buildings, those constructed from 1998 through year 2002 are to be taxed at half the stated rate, or .3 percent, for their first five years, while the land tax remains the same 2 percent. In short, the land-value tax is almost seven times higher than the tax on the improvements for owners who take advantage of this partial abatement on new structures.

An indication of Montserrat's combined volcanic and economic crisis is seen in the pattern of revenues derived from the property tax. In 1997, the revenue was $924,048 in East Caribbean dollars (US $341,898). In 1998, revenue fell to EC $490,792 (US $181,593). A partial recovery could be seen in the approximate EC $500,000 (US $185,000) collected in the first nine months of 1999, or about EC $667,000 (US $247,000) on an annual basis. In 1998, the property tax revenue accounted for 4 percent of the total of all direct taxes on the island.

A study of the property tax system, due to be released in early 2000, was directed at anomalies in the outdated assessments and related issues. Mr. Ryan said that one possible outcome of the study would be a considerable increase in the land valuations, along with at least a temporary decrease in the land tax rates to make the new tax bills more palatable and affordable.

Volcanic activity, although not entirely halted, was more subdued. An announcement that the safe zone might be extended a mile became one of the more optimistic news items on the verge of the 21st century for Montserrat citizens because of the extreme scarcity of usable land there.

VI

An Excursus about Tax Havens[6]

TAX HAVENS GET a bad press, linked frequently with stories of income tax evasion, money laundering, and other nefarious or suspicious activities. This publicity obscures the more relevant fact that substantial numbers of reputable individuals and firms from the United States and elsewhere run legitimate businesses and make honest investments under the flags of Barbados, Belize, Montserrat, and other Caribbean basin locations. Why do they do so?

A better question might be this: Given an opportunity to safely triple one's earnings (for example), why would anybody with enough wealth to afford the lawyers and accountants to tell him how to move his savings or commerce to these tax havens without running into legal trouble at home not do so?

True, many Americans and people of other nations never consider this option. One reason is inertia. Another is that many believe philosophically that taxes are the price for living in a free and civilized society. They have a surprisingly high tolerance for taxes—even taxes that leave their families and the general economy worse off.

Yet there is a breaking point beyond which individuals and businesses devote increasing time and effort to tax avoidance. Tax havens flourish by providing escape hatches for them—places where they can protect assets already earned, and avoid large tax bites on future production. The late economist and New York City official, Philip Finkelstein, once said: "Taxing anything that can move is one sure bet that it's going to move."

Tax administrators and others bemoan the drain of tax revenues and the loss of enterprise captured by the tax havens. They appear not to understand that the anti-enterprise taxes which they propose, promote, or accept without protest are what spurs the flight of capital, financial services, corporate headquarters and even people to the sunny business climate of these little states.

In this context, a virtue of a land-value tax is that, if it were imposed rigorously enough, it would permit a substantial decrease of taxes on production. Uptaxing the land, which can't move, and downtaxing the labor and capital that can move, could halt or even reverse the outflow of assets, firms, and people. Greater application of this mechanism could enable almost any jurisdiction that so desired to become a tax haven.

Notes

1. *The Gleaner* (Kingston), Nov., 1956.

2. Lord Dunedin in Tooheys v. Valuer General NSW (1925). New South Wales Local Government Law Reports, vol. 7, p. 18.

3. The pre-1982 portion of this section is adapted from Fred Harrison's paper, "Fiscal Policy and the Economic Development of Belize with Special Reference to the Tax on Land Values," presented at the Fifteenth International Conference on Land-Value Taxation and Free Trade, Utrecht, July 24-31, 1982.

4. Walter H. and Dorothy B. Diamond, *Tax Havens of the World* (New York: Matthew Bender, 1999).

5. Caribbean Community Secretariat, "Taxation of Land and Buildings in Montserrat," a paper presented to the Conference on Property Tax Administration, held at Bassetierre, St. Kitts, Nov. 10–11, 1980.

6. This section of the chapter is solely the work of Walter Rybeck.

Chapter 8

Mexico

BY MANUEL PERLÓ COHEN*

MEXICO IS A federal republic, consisting of thirty one states and one federal district. There are three levels of government: federal, state, and municipal. Each state is sovereign in the conduct of its internal affairs as provided by its own constitution, and is divided into territorial units called *municipios*, of which there are 2,426 throughout the country. The municipal level of government is responsible, according to Article 115 of the Federal Constitution, for the administration of its treasury, which embraces all the revenues that come from its own goods, taxes, fees, and other revenues approved by the state legislature. Municipalities also get monies from both federal and state revenue-sharing.

Paragraph "a" of the aforementioned article provides that each municipality collect taxes on real estate, as approved by its state legislature. Of these, the main taxes are property tax, sales tax, value-capture tax (*impuesto a la plusvalía*) and location tax (*impuesto de radicación*); however, the first two are important both in terms of revenue collection and geographical extent, while the other two are not significant sources of income and only few states include them in their fiscal codes.[1] Most municipalities use

*Manuel Perló Cohen, who earned his Ph.D. at the University of California-Berkeley, is a tenured researcher at the Institute of Social Investigation, National Autonomous University of Mexico. His most recent books and articles, all in Spanish, include *The Porfirian Paradigm: The History of the Drainage of the Valley of Mexico* (1999), "New Global Methods of Land Development and Their Expression in Mexico" (1999), *Recent Developments in the Mexican Real Estate Market* (2000), and "Strengthening Institutions Through Property Tax Reform: The Case of Mexicali" (2000). Dr. Perló is a faculty associate of the Lincoln Institute of Land Policy, and a member of the United Nations Scientific and Technical Committee for the International Decade for Natural Disaster Reduction.

the combined value of land and improvements as their property tax base—i.e., the method known in some countries as "composite rating," or "flat rating." The only exception is the municipalities of the states of Baja California and Baja California Sur, where a property tax based solely on land-values is in operation.

Before 1983, the municipalities left state governments in control of their treasuries. However, in that year, a constitutional amendment was introduced to give the municipal governments more powers to organize their own finances. Since then, important changes have occurred in relation to local finances and the administration of taxes levied on real estate property. The first years were difficult. For reasons cited in the next section, revenues coming from real estate taxes fell off dramatically, as did local revenues in general. Municipalities relied basically on state and federal revenue-sharing. That situation improved during the 1990s, when a large number of municipalities were able to raise their own funds, particularly those stemming from real estate, which have become a very important source of total revenue. Other local governments, however, were not as successful, and encountered enormous difficulties in attempting to reform their cadastre systems, update values, improve collection methods, and persuade citizens to accept tax increases.[2]

The present chapter documents the experience of a successful property tax reform that was carried out during that decade in Mexicali, a city of nearly 527,000 inhabitants, which is the capital of the border state of Baja California.[3] This is a very interesting and unique case within the national context because Mexicali was the first municipality in the country to apply a land-value tax—an example that later spread to other cities in Baja California and then into the neighboring state of Baja California Sur.

I

Implementing Land-Value Taxation in Mexicali

AS MENTIONED EARLIER, accomplishing property tax reform did not always seem to be an easy task in Mexicali or anywhere in Mexico. Since 1983, the local level of government has been responsible for setting up and collecting property taxes, although state authorities kept certain responsibilities. However, property tax revenues, and local revenues in general, experienced a severe drop caused by a combination of high inflation rates, economic recession, lack of political interest, and reduced administrative competence of local governments, which preferred to rely on revenue-sharing sources. The drop in property tax revenues began prior to the 1983 reform, and they remained at the same level for some four years after it had been instituted.

Figure 1

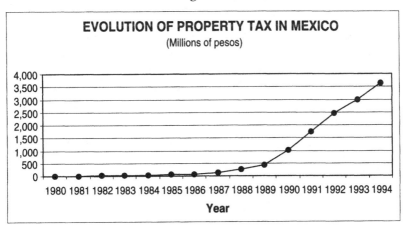

In the early 1990s, a clear improvement in the nation's macro-economic performance made conditions more favorable for change, although political and technical factors reduced the incentives for many state and local governments to embark on fiscal reform. Nevertheless, the federal administration of Carlos Salinas de Gortari (1989–1994) launched a program to improve local finances, basically through a cadastre modernization program lead by BANOBRAS (Banco Nacional de Obras y Servicios), a public development bank. The results have been noticeable in terms of property tax revenues (Figure 1).

Even before this program and other national policies began to exert an influence on local and state administrations, Mexicali took the lead in property tax reform. Starting in 1989, the newly elected mayor, Milton Castellanos Gout, saw the importance of having strong local finances, and he wanted to raise revenues at the beginning of his term.[4] He hired a private consulting firm to update cadastral values. The main consultant, Sergio Flores Peña, a graduate in city and regional planning from the University of California at Berkeley, was a convinced believer in the fairness, equity and efficiency of land-value taxation, and convinced the mayor to change from a mixed land-and-building-value tax base to a land-value system, and also to design a mathematical model to calculate land values.

Rather than being attracted by theoretical or ideological beliefs about the advantages of a land value tax, Castellanos was simply convinced that it would be the easiest and fastest way to raise revenues. He organized a Municipal Cadastral Committee, which included appraisers as well as representatives from real estate owners' organizations, professional organizations, and the general public, to which he proposed new cadastral values relying on the results of the mathematical model. After an intense process of bargaining with the committee, the mayor was able to convince its members to approve new cadastral values and to accept his fiscal reform. The state legislature passed his bill, and the new budget was approved.

The results were spectacular in two ways: first, the new tax raised revenues quickly (see Figure 2); and second, there was not a single legal or political objection from taxpayers. The increase from annual real estate taxes and taxes on property sales, together by far the most important source of local revenues, allowed the mayor to launch an important public works program. In the next fiscal year, however, fearing opposition to further tax increases, he refrained from pursuing land valuation updates and abandoned the mathematical model that was originally created for that purpose.

Opposition to updating land values came from both the Municipal Cadastral Committee and the government officials in charge of the cadastre and valuation office, who lacked the technical capability to manipulate the model and feared that their power and control might be weakened by the participation of the private consulting firm. From that moment on, the mathematical model was abandoned and land values where defined by a process of negotiation and bargaining between local authorities, elected representatives and the committee. However, land values remained the sole real estate property tax base.

At the same time, the Castellanos administration embarked on a cadastre modernization program with financial resources from the federal government. However, since the mayor saw that his main objective of raising revenues had been achieved, the efforts to modernize the cadastral system became a secondary priority that was not as successful.

II

Evolution of the Fiscal Reform in Mexicali

IN SUBSEQUENT ADMINISTRATIONS, the policy towards tax revenues and cadastre modernization varied. The next mayor, Francisco Pérez Tejeda (1992–1995), was a member of the same political party, Partido Revolucionario Institucional (PRI). He experienced a drop in property tax revenue during his first year in office, and taxes increased only at the end of his administration. While he abandoned the cadastre modernization program, the land value taxation system continued.

The next administration was led by Eugenio Elourdy (1995–1998), a member of the Partido de Acción Nacional (PAN). He was the first opposition party leader in Mexicali, although a member of PAN had governed at the state level from 1989 to 1994. During Elourdy's term, land values were updated, property tax revenues grew steadily and cadastre modernization was vigorously resumed. The current administration, headed by Victor Hermosillo (1999–2001), is continuing with cadastre reform.

Figure 2

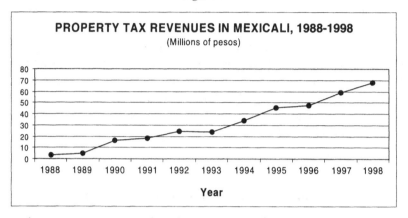

There is no question that the process of fiscal reform has stimulated property tax revenues as the fastest and most important financial source for the city government. Currently, property tax revenues account for more than 50 percent of local municipal revenues. This puts Mexicali way above the nation-wide averages at the local, state, and federal levels (in 1995: local, 15.3 percent; state, 8.4 percent; federal, 10.3 percent) for the relative share of property tax revenues to total revenues. Local government officials in charge of the cadastre and valuation systems are well prepared with technical expertise and an awareness of the need to conduct permanent reform within the system. Mexicali's example has already been replicated in the rest of the state of Baja California and in the neighboring state of Baja California Sur.

III

Assessment and Conclusions

THE MEXICALI CASE offers some important lessons. First, the property tax plays a central role in strengthening local governments, not only for raising sufficient revenues for urban development but also for providing government officials with the skills to organize the tax system in a way that can be sound, legitimate, and transparent.

Second, property tax reform requires vision, leadership and, most of all, political will and commitment from the executive. However, successful reform to raise taxes also depends on a sound technical base and the acceptance of the public.

Third, the land value tax proved to be extremely helpful in achieving successful reform at an early stage. It is clear that the initial rationale for adopting land value taxation had more to do with a pragmatic approach than with theoretical positions or debates over different schools of thought. However, this should not prevent government officials, consultants, scholars and the general public from thoroughly analyzing the diverse consequences of this approach in terms of economic efficiency, equity and administrative management. Flores Peña, who introduced Mayor Castellanos to the concept, was committed to it in both theory and practice. Castellanos, whose only interest in it was pragmatic, advanced it energetically only insofar as it served his immediate purposes. The next mayor, Pérez Tejada, completely abandoned the development of an important tool for improving its efficiency, but that effort was revived and forcefully pursued by his successors, Elourdy and Hermosillo.

Although a land value tax has proven to be successful in the case of Mexicali, it should not be viewed as a panacea for all situations. It is important to recognize that the tax per se can be of little help without other measures that have to be considered as part of property tax reform, such as cadastre modernization, clear policies on tax rates, and public participation.

Finally, cases of property tax reform around the world should not be viewed in black-and-white terms as unqualified successes or failures, but rather as experiments that combine successes and flaws, as well as steps both forward and back. Mexicali is such an experiment. It should be viewed, not as a perfect example of property tax reform, but as a work in progress, from which much may be learned. Among other things, it demonstrates that genuine progress can take place in a field where one is often tempted to think that little can be accomplished.

Notes

1. José Antonio Zarzosa Escobedo, "Importancia de la modernización cadastral," *Federalismo y Desarollo-BANOBRAS*. Vol. 10, April–June 1997.

2. Gerardo Dávila Jiménez and Ismael López Padilla, "Evolución y perspectivas de la modernización cadastral en México 1987–2000," *Federalismo y Desarollo-BANOBRAS*. Vol. 10, April–June 1997.

3. Instituto Nacional de Estadistica Geográfica e Informática, Gobierno del Estado de Baja California, Anuario Estadístico del Estado de Baja California. (Mexico City, 1997).

4. Milton Castellanos Gout, *Historia de un esfuerzo communitario.* (Mexicali, 1993).

Chapter 9

United States

BY WALTER RYBECK*

THE UNITED STATES has always had a measure of land-value taxation. After independence, major reliance on land taxes for public revenue lay at the very core of the nation's economic development. As will be shown later, this had a tremendous and positive impact on the character of American society.

Before the twentieth century, state and local governments began turning increasingly to non-land taxes for added revenues. After the Civil War era, economists, officials, and citizens generally

*Walter Rybeck, since 1983 director of the Center for Public Dialogue, is a graduate of Antioch College in economics and political science. Following a career in journalism that culminated in a six-year stint as Washington, DC, bureau chief for the Cox newspaper chain, he became assistant director of the National Commission on Urban Problems (a presidentially-appointed body popularly known as the "Douglas Commission" after its chairman, Senator Paul H. Douglas), and then spent nine years as editorial director of the Urban Institute. He served as special assistant on housing and urban affairs to two congressmen, Henry S. Reuss of Milwaukee from 1978–80, and William J. Coyne of Pittsburgh from 1980–83. Mr. Rybeck is author of numerous monographs, congressional reports, book chapters, and journal articles, and produced and directed a documentary film, "A Tale of Five Cities: Tax Revolt Pennsylvania-Style" (1984).

Acknowledgment: The author of the USA chapter is indebted to many researchers, past and present. He owes special thanks to Gerard T. Keffer, chief, Taxation Branch, Census of Governments, US Bureau of the Census, for help in unearthing historical and current data. The information on Hawaii was supplied in large part by Raymond T. Higa, Real Property Assessment Division, City and County of Honolulu. That on Alaska was supplied in large part by Larry Myers, Department of Revenue; Chuck Logsdon, petroleum economist, Department of Natural Resources; Kathleen White, director, Permanent Fund; Joan Cahill, communications assistant, Permanent Fund; Gene Dusek, director, Anchorage Office of Management and Budget; and Penny Herndon, Anchorage Tax Assessor's Office. Mason Gaffney, Gale W. Rowe, Mike Curtis, and Dian Arnold also shared invaluable information, but conclusions drawn are wholly the author's responsibility.

seemed overcome by amnesia about the importance of land and land taxation.[1] Families of wealth and corporations, on the contrary, far from losing sight of the land, accelerated their ownership of the nation's natural resources and prime urban sites. The originally low-budget federal government, meanwhile, grew to overshadow the state-local sector, funding itself with taxes on production and income.

Land-value taxation-USA, on the cusp of the millennium, is a story of the struggle to recall and apply overlooked lessons from the nation's formative years to ease the mammoth socio-economic pathologies generated in large part by the detrimental tax policies of later eras.

A sketch of early land policy and how it was radically altered sets the stage for the movement to untax labor and capital. Some historical perspective throws light on the significance of the specific examples of land-value taxation that will be detailed later.

I

Land Access and Land Duties

THE EARLY STAGES of nation-building were characterized by severe hardships for settlers, an almost complete absence of government benevolence to ease adversity, and minimal public amenities. Despite this, Americans developed an optimistic "can-do" spirit and built the most dynamic society the world had seen. These attitudes and deeds stemmed in considerable measure from several factors related to land.

Land hunger was one of the driving forces that drew people to America. To immigrants, land meant *opportunity*. (Shamefully, whites deprived native Americans and African slaves of land and other basic rights. This drastic departure from democratic ideals led to war and left scars that long civil rights struggles have not yet healed; it should be kept in mind as otherwise commendable features of the nation's socio-economic climate are recalled.)

With plenty of land for farming, housing, or trade, and with neither landlords nor oppressive government to expropriate earnings, how a family prospered depended on its abilities and prudence—so the *work ethic* flourished. Exploitation did not disappear, but land gave victims a way out. Abundant free or cheap land encouraged *geographic mobility* and *mobility of status*. Those in poverty, and they were numerous, were buoyed up by constant evidence of people pulling themselves up by their own bootstraps.

Easy access to land supported *free market capitalism*. This was in sharp contrast to the Latin American experience, where a few conquistadors quickly took dominion over vast territory and reduced the mass of society to peons, suppressing initiative and enterprise.

The inclination to amass land was no Latin peculiarity; some of America's most distinguished leaders, George Washington among them, were avid land speculators. The growth of vast estates, however, was thwarted by the US *local* tax system. "Local" is stressed because the federal sector in that era financed its almost unbelievably low budgets largely from customs duties.

Cities, counties, and states, the major governmental players, raised public funds almost exclusively from property taxes which, at first, were predominantly *taxes on land values*. These taxes imposed a financial drain on people "stuck" with large unused land holdings. To avoid tax bills, many owners sold off excess holdings. This, added to already large supplies of available land, took away what makes land grabbing and speculation so profitable and seductive—the reality or the impression of land scarcity.[2]

The US was blessed not only with rich and ample land, but also with political philosophers, such as Jefferson, Paine, and Madison, who were able to link the popular notion of political equality with the more radical idea of universal access to land. They sowed the idea of distributing the public domain in parcels suited for family farming, instead of in huge grants to favored individuals; they kept "landed possessions" from becoming a constitutional qualification for voting or election to Congress; Jefferson and Paine even proposed hefty taxes on large land holdings.

The land tax helped sustain *grass roots democracy*. Holders of land recognized a duty to repay their fellow citizens for the privileges such land conveyed. Real property proved to be a suitable and adequate base for financing local government, enabling cities to remain true centers of power, even in the 20th century when the federal government towered over them.

The Homestead Act was not a case of sharing land *values* via taxation, but of sharing the land itself to provide jobs and family welfare. This act signed by President Lincoln enabled families to get 160 acres of free public domain land. By building a home and working the land for five years, they acquired title. An estimated 300 million acres were distributed in this way.[3]

II

Land Taxes via Property Taxes

THE EXTENSIVE USE of land taxation—not via pure land value taxes, as previously noted—is documented below. There is not now and never has been one US property tax. State laws differ. Counties, cities, townships, and special districts within states use different assessing practices and tax rates. Thus the facts and figures presented here obscure wide variations among 68,000-plus jurisdictions with authority to levy property taxes—39,028 general purpose governments (50 states and 38,978 counties, municipalities and townships), 14,422 school districts, and 14,951 special districts.

- From the 1700s on, the property tax has been the major fiscal resource of American local governments.[4]
- Until the 20th century, the property tax was virtually the sole support of state as well as local government. Early on, considering the humble homes and shops, it is fair to say that it was derived primarily from land values.
- At the end of the 20th century, real estate, with land representing at least 40 percent of its value, remains the single most important source of local tax revenue.[5]
- The growth of property tax revenues from $94 million in 1860 to almost $200 billion in 1993 is phenomenal, especially in light of continuous efforts to besmirch and denigrate this tax. E. R. A. Seligman wrote in 1905, ". . . the general property tax as actually administered is beyond all doubt one of the worst taxes in the civilized world."[6] J. P. Jensen countered in 1931,

"Though almost universally criticized as being unsound in principle and impossible in practice, it has been, and continues to be, the backbone of both state and local tax systems and almost the sole source of local revenue."[7]

- Property tax revenues collected nationwide from the land portion also have soared, from 1.6 billion to $70 billion in the last half century.

Table 1

PROPERTY TAX COLLECTIONS BY ALL UNITS OF GOVERNMENT, 1860-1993, AND ESTIMATED PORTION FROM LAND VALUES ALONE, 1946-1993 (amounts in billions of dollars)				
Year and Era	Total Property Tax Collected (1)	Personal Property Tax (2) (3)		Estimated Tax Paid from Land Values (4)
1860 Pre-Civil War	$ 0.094	% -	$ -	$ -
1913 World War I	1.3	-	-	-
1927 Post-war boom	4.7	-	-	-
1934 Depression	4.1	-	-	-
1946 Post-World War II	5.0	18	.9	1.6
1963 Kennedy killed	20.1	15	3.0	6.8
1976 Carter elected	57.0	12	6.8	20.5
1982 Reagan Years	81.9	10	8.2	29.5
1993 Latest date	188.5	7	13.2	70.1

Notes:
  a. Column 1 × Column 2 = Column 3; Column 1 - Column 3 × 40% = Column 4.
  b. Declining percentage of personal property tax based on Census reports.
  c. Land as two-fifths of real estate tax based on mid-range of estimates by Allen D. Manvel
  (National Commission on Urban Problems) and Gerard T. Keffer (Census of Governments).

Table 1 shows government revenues from property and land alone. Table 2 presents the market value of that property and land, showing land values doubling again and again, with an almost 900 percent increase from 1956 through 1991.

Table 2

TOTAL ASSESSED VALUE OF PROPERTY, REAL ESTATE AND LAND, 1956–1991			
Year	All Property Total Gros Assessed Value	Gross Assessed Real Esatate (Land plus Buildings)	Assessed Value of Land Alone
1956	$ 300 Billion	$ 697 Billion	$ 269 Billion
1966	1.261 Trillion	1.261 Trillion	523 Brillion
1983	3.000 Trillion	2.515 Trillion	1.200 Trillion
1991	7.000 Trillion	6.044 Trillion	2.400 Trillion

Sources: Allen D. Manvel, "Trends in the Value of Real Estate and Land, 1956 to 1966," Three Land Research Studies, National Commission on Urban Problems, Washington, 1968; data for 1983 and 1991 from Census of Government reports.

III

Financing Local Public Works

AMERICA USED TO recapture publicly-created land values in another important way. To finance public works—or infrastructure, to use the term now in vogue—states and localities employed *benefit assessment districts.*

When a neighborhood petitioned for paved streets, sidewalks, water and sewer extensions, street lights or other amenities, a city or county designated a district embracing all benefiting properties. Project costs were divided among properties according to each owner's "front footage." The length of lot lines facing a street provided a rough equivalency to the relative land values of the affected properties served by or adjacent to the facility.

A small number of benefit districts of this type remain, but most "special assessment districts" now in existence depart from the original design. Their taxes fall on total property value rather than on front foot or land value. The fully-developed properties pay more.[8] Such districts give a free ride to holders of vacant land or blighted properties.

Because funding the nation's infrastructure has become a major political problem, merits of the old-style assessment district bear underscoring:

- Tapping expected land value increases from public works is a viable option. At their peak in the 1920s, benefit districts financed one-fifth of the budgets of many large cities.[9]
- Citizens found the approach fair. Those receiving benefits bore the cost; others, who did not benefit, were not expected to pay.
- Orderly urban growth was fostered. (Chaotic growth accelerated when localities began charging builders "impact fees" to fund streets and other public facilities serving their projects; local governments often abdicated to developers control over where infrastructure was to be extended.)
- Benefit districts tend to be democratic and efficient. Projects go forward only if affected owners approve. Waste is minimized because those who must pay take pains to confirm that facilities will be worth their cost.

This is not to say that all infrastructure should be financed through benefit districts. When beneficiaries of public facilities are widely dispersed, a land-value tax administered by regular political jurisdictions better mirrors which properties gain and which do not.

IV

A Changed America

AMERICA'S HEAVY RELIANCE on the taxation of land values reveals a nation that, during its first half century, was more in line with what land-value tax proponents urge than is generally realized. By 1902, states still raised over half of their taxes from property, or about one-quarter from land values; in the same year, all local governments combined raised 89 percent of their revenue from property taxes, or between 35 and 50 percent from land-value taxation; as late as 1922, counties in half the states obtained over 95 percent of their revenue from property. This set the stage for an explosive growth of new cities and the nation's unprecedented rise in living standards.

The Industrial Revolution and prodigious concentrations of wealth began to materially alter the American landscape in the mid-1800s. Power shifted from rural to urban, from local to national, from small to large business. Farming as an economic factor and as a way of life gave way to urban dominance. Mechanization permitted rapid exploitation of resources and people, including cheap labor imported from Europe and Asia. City slums festered. Poverty and joblessness increased. Periodic bank failures and panics, as national depressions were called, wiped out the savings, farms, and businesses of multitudes. The frontier—the traditional escape hatch for the exploited and the ambitious poor—was declared all but gone by the 1890s.[10]

This is not to say, of course, that there is no more federal land for homesteading. One may still stake a claim, but the available acreage is apt to be located in one of the more inhospitable regions of Alaska or in the Mojave desert. (In the early 1930s, the editor's uncle actually did stake a claim in the Mojave desert, on which decades of backbreaking toil yielded him nothing but a handful of industrial grade diamonds and a few Mexican fire opals.)

The Civil War fueled the rise of central government. Federal power was needed to prevent the Union from breaking up, to force states to give up slavery, and to execute the war. Federal power was also championed to curtail the rise of monopolies. To underwrite its expanding role, the federal establishment turned primarily to taxes on personal and business incomes.

State governments meanwhile reduced their reliance on property taxes. Partly this stemmed from a theory that local governments should use property taxes; state governments, sales taxes; and the federal government, income taxes (distinctions long since ignored). It also reflected the power of landed interests in state legislatures. At any rate, land values began accounting for a diminishing share of revenues collected for pubic purposes.

Historical data do not go back as far as one would wish, but Tables 3 and 4 illustrate how the trends that have been discussed continued throughout the 20th century. Since 1902, state reliance on the property tax dropped from 53 to only two percent, and cities' reliance dropped from 87 to 53 percent.

As late as 1927, federal revenues of $3.4 billion were about half of the $6.1 billion of state and local taxes (property plus nonproperty). By 1993, the federal government's annual tax take of $712.9 billion far surpassed the $592.9 billion taken by all state and local governments combined.

Henry George entered the public arena during the turbulent transitional period of the late 19th century. His *Progress and Poverty*[11] addressed industrial depressions and unequal distribution of wealth and privilege. His compassion for the underprivileged and the clarity of his analyses attracted a fervent following, but his native country was slow to accept his prescriptions. He saw virtually no shifting of taxes off production and onto land values during his lifetime. Looking back, some of the reasons are readily apparent:

The Yankee optimism discussed earlier led Americans to view the evils George portrayed as momentary rather than systemic. The great technical advances of his era made it easy to accept Andrew Carnegie's notion that society was on an uphill, not a downhill course. Those who worried about the economy tended to blame labor or management or put their faith in socialist (later Keynesian) views that government controls and gimmicks could correct market failures.

Citizens and politicians today are keenly aware of the social ills George delineated, but most Americans do not yet share his insights into their causes or cures. Despite this lag, as succeeding sections show, George's ideas are being put into practice in scattered parts of the US.

Pittsburgh's skyline. Photo by M. G. Ellis.

Incline view of Pittsburgh from Mt. Washington. Photo by Jeff Greenberg.

Table 3

TOTAL TAX REVENUES AND PROPERTY TAX REVENUES IN STATE AND LOCAL GOVERNMENTS, 1902–1992 (in billions of dollars)			
States	Local Tax Revenue	Revenue from Property Tax	Property Tax as Percent of Total Taxes
1902	$ .156	$ .082	% 52.6
1922	.947	.348	36.7
1927	1.608	.370	23.0
1940	3.313	.260	7.8
1980	137.075	2.891	2.1
1992	329.296	6.689	2.0
Counties			
1902	-	-	* 91.1
1922	-	-	* 92.1
1942	.920	.893	97.1
1980	18.813	14.300	76.0
1992	54.926	40.808	74.3
Cities			
1902	-	-	* 86.7
1912	-	-	* 77.5
1922	-	-	* 82.8
1942	2.314	1.999	86.4
1980	31.256	16.859	53.9
1992	75.486	39.706	52.6
All Local Governments Beneath State Level Including Special Assessment Districts			
1902	.704	.624	88.6
1922	3.069	2.973	96.9
1942	4.625	4.273	92.4
1980	86.387	65.607	75.9
1992	227.099	171.723	75.6
Source: Census of Governments. Starred data, estimated by Jensen, op. cit.			

Table 4

AMOUNTS AND PERCENTAGES OF RELIANCE BY VARIOUS LEVELS OF GOVERNMENT ON PROPERTY AND NON-PROPERTY TAXES, 1927–1993 (amounts in billions of dollars)				
Federal	Non-Property Tax Revenues $	%	Property Tax Revenues $	%
1927	3.364	100.0	0	0
1993	712.912	100.0	0	0
State				
1927	1.238	77.0	.370	23.0
1993	346.160	97.8	7.796	2.2
Local				
1927	.119	2.7	4.36	97.3
1993	58.232	24.4	180.738	75.6
All				
1927	4.721	50.0	4.730	50.0
1993	1,117.304	85.6	188.535	14.4

Source: Historical Statistics on Governmental Finances and Employment, 1982 Census of Governments, Vol. 6, No. 4, January 1985. US Bureau of the Census research.

V

Single Tax Enclaves

IDEALISTS EAGER TO correct society's flaws, following an American utopian tradition, formed new communities to put their ideas to the test. Most such experiments failed, including many land tax enclaves. One prospered and was often cited as validation of Georgist concepts, but now appears to be a shell of its former self. One other land tax enclave still adheres fairly closely to its original guiding principles.

Before focusing on specific single tax enclaves, their common features should be understood. First, a corporation or trusteeship purchases tracts of land. People wanting to reside there do not buy lots but *lease* them from these bodies at rents subject to annual readjustment. Real estate within the colony remains under jurisdiction of the local county which assesses and taxes each property in the enclave as it does all other property—on the combined value of buildings and land. The corporation pays these conventional taxes.

Residents, as per their leases, repay the corporation an annual charge supposedly based solely on each parcel's land value. Improvements built on the land belong to the lessees; they may use, rent, or sell them.

Among land tax enclaves that fell by the wayside were *Tahanto* (founded 1909), *Shakerton* (1921), and *Trapelo* (1927), all in Massachusetts, and *Halidon* (1921) in Maine. All were created by Fiske Warren of Boston. A trustee of Trapelo said that people were attracted more to the pleasant surroundings and the subsidies Warren provided than to single tax features. The land rent formulas—devised to cover not only the lessees' real estate taxes but also portions of their income and estate taxes, with adjustments for inflation—were so technical that few understood them, leading to their abandonment after Warren's death.[12]

Free Acres, serving about 100 leaseholders, also had a generous benefactor, Bolton Hall of New York. He gave 60 acres in central New Jersey to the Free Acres Association. A sense of responsibility to the community and its mission did not materialize. Leaseholders eventually privatized growing land values, and the fees began to reflect building values. Differences between owning land outside Free Acres and leasing it inside evaporated.

A. Fairhope

In 1894, E. B. Gaston and James Bellangee of Iowa and a few others from around the country, all fervid anti-monopolists, bought farmland on a high bluff overlooking Mobile Bay in Alabama, and established Fairhope. The colony began as a socialist as well as a single tax community. While the socialist aspects faded rapidly, land tax aspects held on for generations.

Within a decade, the original 132 acres expanded to 4,000, greatly aided by gifts from Joseph Fels, the soap manufacturer.

Census figures chart the population growth—from 25 to 590 by 1910, to 853 by 1920, to 1,873 by 1940, and to 3,359 by 1950.

The story is complex, starting with an odd land pattern. The colony, lacking funds for orderly expansion, bought what scattered nearby parcels it could afford. Meanwhile, farmers who had long been there, former socialists who did not see eye-to-eye on Gaston's land rent arrangements, and others attracted to the fastest-growing community in Baldwin County, all held parcels that were not under leasehold. The result was a kind of checkerboard with colony and non-colony lands interspersed.

Land rents from lease holders not only enabled the governing Fairhope Single Tax Corporation (FSTC) to pay the county and state taxes on personal and real property; the rents also brought in a surplus for community facilities. Before there were roads or rail links, the colony built a pier so boats could transport people and supplies from Mobile. Fairhope paved all its streets long before this was common practice. It built the county's first water works. It built a public library and school. It set aside park lands including beautiful beach frontage along the Bay.

Governance is a further complexity. The FSTC did not seek to govern the people living and working on non-colony lands, hence a separate municipality of Fairhope was incorporated in 1908. The FSTC gradually deeded its public facilities to the city—the streets in 1911, the parks and beach front in 1930 (with the stipulation they remain as parks), the pier in 1931, the library in 1963. Some FSTC officers wear two hats, serving as city officers as well.

Some 1996 numbers: Fairhope *area* population is about 17,000; Fairhope city about 10,000; FSTC *leaseholders* about 1,700 (counting four family members per leasehold, about 6,800 *people*). Some 20 percent of city residents are colony lessees; their land comprises 16 percent of the city's total. Another third of colony lessees reside outside the city. About 150 FSTC *members* vote and set colony corporation policy.

Unlike other land tax enclaves that were overwhelmingly residential, Fairhope attracted a full spectrum of land uses. People raised crops, chickens, and livestock, grew orchards, cut pine lumber or found employment in fishing and crabbing. Commerce, starting with an ice house, creamery and blacksmith shop, expanded to auto dealers, retail stores, and shopping centers. Assembly plants, printers, and many other producers entered the picture. In short, Fairhope became a genuine city.

By 1946, a visiting planner described Fairhope as a city "where civic officials have no financial worries and the citizens pay no taxes." He said it "gives impetus to the earnest hope of people all over America that they can enjoy the advantages of living in a modern and prosperous community and still retain in full the fruits of their labors."[13]

In 1979, an economic analysis firm listed a city in each of ten states—Fairhope, Alabama, among them—as affording the best life for retirees in the US. Winning characteristics included low living costs, good climate, recreational facilities, low taxes, opportunities for part-time work, available housing and proximity to medical services and shopping.[14]

Prior accounts of Fairhope presented evidence that its unique land tenure program was a major factor in the community's fine development. But another complication must be mentioned. While still calling itself a single tax colony, Fairhope has not functioned as a land tax community since the 1980s.

As air conditioning made hot Fairhope more livable, booms in the late 1940s and 1960s bid up prices of non-colony land, giving speculators handsome gains. Some leaseholders looked with envy on those "killings" and fought in the courts and the Alabama legislature to liquidate the Single Tax Corporation. After years of contention, it was finally certified that the FSTC's charter and its land rent provisions were legal.

A further schism developed among those favoring the colony's existence. A small group argued for better land assessments as the basis for charges to lessees.[15] A dominant group rejected these ideas as "purist" and out of tune with Alabama's tax system which makes the corporation pay high local taxes on Fairhope's large commercial structures. Gale W. Rowe, secretary of the FSTC since 1980, said the elected officers contend that redistributing taxes on a land-only basis among all lessees would cause farmers and homesteaders to carry burdens of big businesses. With this rationale, the FSTC essentially accepts county assessments for each property on the value of *land and buildings combined* as the equivalent of the land rent owed by the leaseholder.[16]

Each year, Fairhope still invites someone to teach a course in economics with attention to Henry George. Completing the course is a prerequisite for those applying for FSTC membership. Also, in 1996 Fairhope was beginning a strategic planning exercise, reviewing its problems, trends, assets, and potentialities to chart a course for the next century. A FSTC election in 2000 resulted in the ouster of the long-dominant faction, and its replacement by officers committed to returning the colony to its land-rent roots. How successful they will be remains to be seen.

B. The Ardens

The Ardens, formed by the three adjacent communities of Arden, Ardentown, and Ardencroft, remain the most nearly Georgist of the original single tax colonies. They are what Americans call "bedroom communities"—places from which people commute to work and to shop. The Ardens occupy some 300 acres of rolling wooded land north of Wilmington, Delaware.

Arden was founded as a living Georgist laboratory in 1900 by sculptor, businessman and Shakespearean actor Frank Stephens and by architect Will Price with a loan from Joseph Fels of Fels Naphtha Soap fame and fortune, all of Philadelphia. More people than it could accommodate wanted to live there. Ardentown was added in 1922 with financing from Fiske Warren of Boston. Ardencroft, adjoining the other two villages, was added in 1950.

According to Donald Stephens, son of Frank, Arden's land rent policy was not an end in itself but "the essential foundation" on which real democracy could be built.[17] Various innovations related to this theme:

- Town planning. Arden Forest, a large village green and pathways are set aside for recreation and esthetics. Road and lot lines follow contours of hills rather than uniform geometric patterns. An array of public facilities, unusual for a small community, include an outdoor theater, clubhouse, community center, archives, library, and day care center.

- Governance. Each of the three communities has its own un-paid, annually elected officials and committee chairs, includ-ing the head of the all-important assessment committee. Ex-ecutive power is vested in the standing committees. The chair of the Town Assembly has no executive power, but runs quarterly town meetings where community decisions are reached.
- Culture. Drama, music, and handicrafts have been promoted from the start. Poets, artisans, and writers who found the set-ting congenial gave the Ardens a certain celebrity status in the Wilmington-Philadelphia-New York region. A popular dinner theater attracts visitors.[18]
- Community life. Residents may join Arden Club where folk dances, dinners, and other events foster neighborliness. Un-like utopian communities that pre-selected adherents of one philosophy, the Ardens have always been deliberately open to people of all political creeds, races, religions, and national origins.
- Leases. Nominally leases run for 99 years, but are renewable; in effect, they are perpetual leases. Leases are transferable. As a measure of Arden's attractiveness, leases sold in the 1990s brought prices close to or somewhat higher than sale prices of similar properties in nearby communities.
- Land rent and finances. The Town Assemblies collect from all lessees a charge based primarily on land values, totaling $319,000. From this, the town pays $53,000 in New Castle County real estate taxes and $145,000 in school district real estate taxes. The remainder is used for maintaining and oper-ating town facilities and for services such as garbage collec-tion. The Ardens receive $10,000 in state aid for road repairs, unrelated to land rent since the money comes from Dela-ware's income tax. Leaseholders also pay a water fee based on how much they use. (All figures are for the 1996 tax year.)

The Ardens, forming a single block of land, are fortunate not to have the mix of colony and non-colony properties or the mix of governing and tax systems that prove vexing for Fairhope. The Ardens share the common problem among all intentional communities of keeping its original goals alive. Mike Curtis, director of the Philadelphia Henry George School and a resident of Arden, has seen that even the fundamental issue of defining rent becomes a matter of contention; understandably so. Arden citizens are educated and working in the "outside world" where economists confuse land with capital and pay scant attention to how land values are created or to the ethical issues arising therefrom. To have persisted for a century under this handicap without losing sight of the founders' dreams has been no mean feat.

VI

Flood Control in Ohio

ENGINEER ARTHUR E. Morgan, later renowned as first head of the Tennessee Valley Authority, was called on to prevent a recurrence of the catastrophic 1913 floods along the Great Miami, Little Miami, and Mad Rivers that took hundreds of lives and destroyed thousands of properties in Dayton and southwest Ohio. He designed a flood control system that has withstood the test of time, and an equally exceptional species of land-value tax to pay for it.

Assessing the flood damage to each property, Morgan reasoned, would approximate the land value benefit that would accrue to the owner as a result of preventing future flooding. In one of the largest and most complex appraisals carried out in America, some 77,000 parcels along 110 miles of river valley were individually assessed within two years. Only one percent of the owners challenged their assessments; in only two dozen cases did the courts modify the damage/benefit amounts assigned by the appraisers. Morgan welcomed a court test of this scheme, and when the Ohio Supreme Court confirmed its legality, its legal status was ironclad.[19]

The original assessments, interestingly, calculated total benefits to properties exceeding $100 million, more than three times the cost of the flood protection project. Such a cost-benefit ratio lends weight to the proposition that, in many cases, infrastructure can be self-supporting, generating its own land value revenue source.[20] In the Miami Conservancy, assessments were reduced to avoid excess collections. The taxes paid financed the construction and operation of extensive dams and levies, and the moving of two towns above the flood plain. Far from imposing a hardship, the unique tax system hastened the rapid restoration and economic burgeoning of the Dayton region.

VII

Irrigation in California

USING LAND VALUES to finance irrigation in California occurred before it was assumed that large regional public works had to be funded by federal or state governments. Now that non-beneficiaries are commonly taxed to provide facilities used by others, it is timely to focus on this alternative course.

The setting: The Gold Rush, continental railroads, and Americans' enduring land hunger brought torrents of settlers West. Farmlands adjacent to streams were soon cornered.

Pressure to bring water to fertile but arid lands mounted. A common practice was to construct irrigation facilities and charge farmers according to how much water they consumed. At first, this seemed a variation of the benefit districts discussed earlier, but California's legacy of mammoth landholdings dating back to grants from the Spanish Crown added a different dimension.

C. C. Wright, author of the 1887 statute defining California irrigation districts, detected a flaw in water fees as the prime revenue source. He saw that wealthy owners of grand estates, unlike small farmers, could afford to make minimal use of their lands. Using little or no irrigated water, they could avoid sharing the cost of dams and canals, yet enjoy seeing the value of their haciendas rise as a result of projects.

The Wright Act therefore called for funding from taxes on *all* property in an irrigation district. The law was amended in 1909 to permit, and again in 1917 to require, that these taxes fall on *land values only*, not on crops, orchards, vineyards, buildings, or other improvements. Farmlands situated where they could not benefit from irrigation were exempted. Town sites, on the other hand, were taxed on the premise that their value was enhanced by the higher productivity of surrounding farms. Districts became multipurpose, providing electric power, recreation, and reclamation as well as water.

Some five million dry acres turned green under this land tax approach, which one analyst called "an extraordinarily potent engine for the creation of wealth."[21] Huge ranches were rapidly cut up and sold in smaller tracts, paving the way for some of the most productive and intensive farming operations in the nation. In 1958, the then Republican Leader of the US Senate, William F. Knowland of California, described the Wright Act as "more important to the growth of California than the discovery of gold. It taxes people into instead of out of business."[22]

Christian Science Monitor correspondent Harlan Trott described the specific accomplishments of two adjoining districts, Modesto and Turlock: they built their multi-purpose project without a cent of state or federal aid. Their Don Pedro Dam was the world's highest when built in 1922. The electric power generated as a byproduct was distributed at cheaper rates than those of nearby private utilities. Irrigation water was provided free of charge.[23]

Those puzzled by the slow progress of land tax reforms should not overlook how big landlords, bankers, and private utilities fought mercilessly to undermine the Wright Act. When their votes failed to overturn it, they took their opposition all the way to the US Supreme Court where they called the act "Communism and confiscation under guise of law." The high court disagreed, holding that the act "does not deprive the landowners of any property without due process of law."[24]

The enemies did not give up. During the 1930s Depression, Californians who had made excessive loans on land in the districts were unable to meet their payments. Mortgage bankers holding these loans urged Congress to pass arcane bankruptcy laws to rescue them in a way that erased the obligation to pay the district land taxes. When this was ruled unconstitutional, the law was amended and case after case finally led to a Supreme Court ruling supporting the original genius of the districts. J. Rupert Mason, who documented these episodes, said "perhaps no other law in any State has been more often attacked in the courts."[25]

In the post-World War II era, rapid urban and rural growth again made water scarcity a top California priority. Local and state leaders, instead of turning to the Wright Act, persuaded the federal and state governments to cough up billions for the Central Valley and Feather River irrigation projects, respectively. This approach has given American public works projects the bad name of "pork barrel," with politicians voting to please each other's constituents. It taxes the many for the profit of a relative few, without the local attention and care induced when beneficiaries pick up the tab.

The hundred or so California irrigation districts still functioning suffer somewhat from their own success. Free water led to waste of this precious resource, so water tolls were added.[26] As fees for electricity paid off debts and met revenue needs, land value rates were greatly reduced. This encouraged a return to some of the very conditions the districts originally remedied—absentee ownership, land speculation, and over-sized holdings.

VIII

Solving a Housing Crisis

THE PROPERTY TAX in its earlier incarnation was, as already noted, largely a land-value tax. Gradually it became mainly a tax on improvements. Economists who pay attention to the property tax (a small minority, unfortunately) tend to agree that the virtues of a tax on land values are contradicted by, if not negated by, a high tax on structures. They regard building taxes as a disincentive to construction and maintenance.

This insight came into play in New York City after World War I. The city faced an acute housing shortage. Rents were high and rising. Crime and unrest were erupting in squalid slums. Home-building activity, forced to a halt during the war, instead of resuming remained at a standstill. Industry spokesmen blamed the crisis on shortages of investment capital and excessive labor costs.[27]

Conditions, in short, were not unlike those in large cities across America and elsewhere eighty years later. With one interesting exception: New York at the start of this episode was relying on the law of supply and demand to resolve these troubles; currently, housing problems are addressed with an array of controls, restrictions, subsidies, and charities, that, despite small successes, rarely succeed in stopping or reversing the downward trend.

The state legislature sensed that high taxes on buildings were a serious impediment. In 1920, it passed enabling legislation and a year later the city enacted an ordinance to exempt taxes on new buildings used exclusively for dwellings, or on new buildings of four or more stories used only for dwellings above ground floor.[28] A building's tax freeze would continue for ten years. The good part of the property tax remained: *land beneath exempted buildings would continue to be taxed.*

Serious revenue losses were feared. Supporters argued that buildings were not being erected in the absence of an exemption, so the city could not be worse off by untaxing them. They correctly predicted that restored neighborhoods and public improvements would generate higher land assessments.

A building boom commenced two months after the 1921 ordinance passed. The building frenzy increased in volume year after year until the ordinance was phased out in 1926.

Exemptions on the thousands of apartments, single-family, and duplex homes built in that short five-year period amounted to almost a billion dollars. This understates the total tax savings to builders and owners because the exemptions lasted a full decade after construction.

No awesome police powers or public expenditures were involved in this program. A rather moderate tax change made housing an attractive investment. It resuscitated the home-building industry, ended the shortage of dwelling units, alleviated civic panic, and boosted municipal revenues.

Unfortunately, lessons from this achievement were soon lost sight of. The exemption, enacted as emergency legislation, was rescinded. It was not incorporated in permanent housing legislation then being fashioned for two reasons. First, when the housing crisis ended, real estate spokesmen contended that government should stop interfering with the free market. Since the building tax exemption was a market correction, not an interference, that was a self-serving argument for slumlords and land speculators to make. Second, the exemption did not bring down rents for middle and low-income tenants as had been hoped. With hindsight it seems likely that if the exemption had been continued and applied to all housing, old and new, benefits soon would have reached poorer residents as the housing desires of higher-income families were satisfied or stabilized.

Nevertheless, impatient housing specialists and officials, trying to bypass the market rather than restore it to health, launched rent control and public housing programs. It is not necessary to join those who deny that these approaches produced any worthwhile results to observe that New York City was still plagued at the brink of the 21st century with homelessness, miserable slums, and shortages of decent dwellings for low-and middle-income people.

Some few urban experts, citizen groups, and *New York Times* editorials have periodically urged a return to the city's brief but happy romance in the 1920s with a just and practical tax reform. Nevertheless, interest groups that profit from the existing system have prevailed. The property tax in America's largest city, as elsewhere, weighs heavily against the creation and upkeep of housing. In the 1960s, as the next section spells out, elements of the New York plan reappeared, but without an emphasis on housing.

IX

Temporary Abatements

MAINSTREAM URBANOLOGISTS AND economists are less likely to attack land-value taxation today than to downplay it, insisting that property taxes have at most a minute impact on how cities and the private market behave. Nothing gives the lie to that view more than the widespread adoption during the 1960s of temporary property tax abatements as a tool for fighting urban decay.

If taxing buildings truly had no bad effects, why did the development community clamor for relief from this tax? Why did states and cities provide it? Why has lifting these tax burdens brought new life to many cities?

During the late 1950s and 1960s, many cities saw private building dry up except for heavily subsidized urban renewal projects. Then, for several decades, private investors came back into the picture. They erected millions of dollars worth of new buildings in New York City, Philadelphia, Boston, and many other cities—almost all of them under the umbrella of abatements. Laws excused developers from taxes on the *increased* value of their properties for anywhere from 10 to 30 years after construction. In only two years after offering a 15-year freeze on property taxes at the pre-development level, Birmingham, Alabama, attracted at least ten major new developments.

St. Louis grew magnificently with abatements for *commercial and industrial* development. Missouri State Senator Walt Mueller said, "We have a downtown area that would knock your eyes out." Yet large areas of blighted housing ring the heart of St. Louis. To induce renewal in all sectors of the city, Mueller has tried for years to persuade the legislature to let cities eliminate or reduce tax penalties on improvements of all types and ages.[29]

Scores of cities used state "enterprise zone" laws in the 1970s and 1980s to upgrade deteriorating urban areas. Localities were allowed, within these zones, to bypass or modify regulations or taxes that applied everywhere else, and to provide subsidies. Peoria, Illinois, created such a zone for its decrepit industrial area of old distilleries, abandoned machine shops and obsolete factories; employment there had fallen from 50,000 at the start of the century to just 2,000. Unique among enterprise zones, Peoria offered 10-year abatements on the value of new or repaired commercial or industrial buildings, with the proviso that owners' taxes on the land would rise as land values went up—comparable to New York City's housing program in the 1920s.

John L. Kelly, the Peoria businessman who spearheaded this approach, reported that in the three years after the start of the plan, compared with the prior three years, the dollar value of industrial-commercial building permits within the zone rose from eight to 21 percent of the city's total. Kelly said his plan was accepted because everybody "knew" the scheme would not work.

Once in operation, he said, "enormous building investments led to a consensus that this abatement of taxes on new construction is the best development program Peoria ever undertook."[30]

Abatements aimed at inducing new or rehab housing had much less success than the commercial abatements in Central Business Districts (CBDs). One explanation is that the CBD office building market has few players, mostly big operators with the savvy and financial incentives to make abatement deals, while the housing market has many players, mostly small-time operators who are reluctant to risk major projects and who tend to be wary of the "abatement game." Also, underlying causes of housing blight were not attended to; units lost to demolition or abandonment outnumbered the new housing that came on line with the lure of abatements.

On the plus side, abatements testified to the serious disincentives imposed by taxes on buildings. Under some plans, they also shifted more of the tax burden onto land values.

On the negative side are factors that reduced the popularity of abatements. Typically they do not apply across the board and are open to political favoritism. Enterprises in old buildings object to paying taxes that subsidize tax relief and new structures for their competitors. The temporary nature of abatements is also questioned: after a locality lifts the offending tax burden long enough to induce development, it reinstates the disincentive that discourages the next normal round of repair and renewal.

X

Reform by Obeying the Law

ROSSLYN, VIRGINIA, ACROSS the Potomac from Washington, DC, and Southfield, Michigan, bordering on Detroit and ten miles from its downtown area, are often cited as land-value tax success stories. These jurisdictions did in fact realize impressive development by increasing their public collection of land values. Some accounts, however, fail to clarify that they each accomplished this under cover of the conventional property tax.

As noted several times, the property tax evolved from a tax mainly on land values to one that falls mainly on improvements. An added point must be stressed. A majority of US assessors was consistently undervaluing land relative to improvements; and the more poorly land was utilized, the more they understated its market value. They magnified the injurious part of the tax and weakened the wholesome part despite laws mandating uniform appraisal of all properties.

A. Rosslyn

Across the Key Bridge from the classy Georgetown section of the nation's capital was an unappetizing hundred-acre tract of Arlington which, as this story begins, was filled with pawn shops, palm readers, slummy residences, lumber yards, cleaning plants, storage tanks, and warehouses.

Lyle C. Bryant, economist and behind-the-scenes guru of Arlington planning circles, brought together an advisory group that understood real estate market incentives, among them, Max Wehrly of the Urban Land Institute, Harold Buttenheim, planner and editor of *American City*, Treasury economist L. L. Ecker-Racz, land economist Homer Hoyt, and economist E. Howard Evans of the US Chamber of Commerce. Their activities led to a countywide reassessment by the state of Virginia with rigorous attention to the true market value of sites, regardless of their current use.

This 1950 reassessment led to a colossal rise in Rosslyn valuations. A 154-acre tract had its appraisal increased from $300 to $2,300 per acre. Valuation of a five-acre commercial tract increased sixty-five times from $3,000 to $196,000 an acre. The system survived such shocks for several reasons:

- All new assessment notices were mailed simultaneously; owners could see they were being treated alike.
- The assessment specialists read the market better than most owners. Arlington's new assessments ranked among the tops in quality in the nation.[31]
- Assessor Francis Austin acted less as a tax enforcer than as an educator, helping owners make more rational land use

decisions. For example, one owner threatened to take the assessor to court for valuing his 80 acres at $2,500 an acre; within weeks after Austin discussed the potential of his property, instead of suing, he sold his land at $5,250 an acre.

A recognized leader in real estate circles, Fred A. Gosnell, Sr., was named to head the reassessment board. Word got around that if owners insisted their property deserved a lower valuation, Gosnell would take out his checkbook with a flourish and ask, "Will you sell it for that?" The owners knew he was serious, and so they would back down.

Success of the first new enterprises under the revised tax regime gave a hint of Rosslyn, as a "gateway to Arlington," having the potential for becoming a prime office building, hotel, and upscale apartment district. And it did.

Another element was critical: annual revaluations. Many new developments peter out when rising site values make them attractive plums for speculators. Rosslyn land values increased rapidly, but so did assessments; this kept up the pressure for renewal and took the profit out of mere land holding.

One skyscraper after another appeared. Tenants within two decades included an array of federal agencies, major media, and *Fortune* 500 firms that employed tens of thousands. By 1975, land values had grown from $2 to $25 a square foot. Rosslyn was then returning $43 million a year to the county in exchange for $13 million in public expenditures, a net gain of $30 million. That was before a subway station put Rosslyn just minutes from downtown Washington, giving its apartments, offices, cafes, and shops—and its land values and tax revenues—another burst of growth.[32]

B. Southfield

In 1960, buildings in Southfield were assessed at 70 to 85 percent of value, land at five to 10 percent. S. James Clarkson ran for mayor to correct this defiance of the Michigan law that all taxable property be appraised at market value. Once in office, he had to battle his assessor (eventually replaced by Ted Gwartney who understood land economics), special interest groups, and the courts to carry out his campaign promise. The city stopped exaggerating the value of new construction and renovations relative to older structures, and appraised all land according to its highest and best use.

Soon, crossing from Detroit into Southfield was like going from night to day—from slums and neglect to an area bustling with construction and well-maintained homes.

Asked to explain this contrast, Mayor Clarkson credited "stretching the law as far as we can" to tax land more and buildings less. "That's why Southfield is developing, as you see it today—by taxing this monopoly, this God-given monopoly." He testified that Detroit taxed land values "next to nil," using property assessments from the Depression era when values were dropped to token amounts to avoid putting taxpayer-owners into default.

Clarkson was re-elected for four terms, each time winning on the issue of fair assessments. Taxes on average homeowners were immediately reduced 22 percent. The burden was shifted to holders of large empty parcels of strategically-located land, but they were not hurt by steeply higher taxes. As Gwartney explained, Southfield's desirable tax climate put their sites in such demand that they wound up making good profits on future sales or development.

Southfield benefited from good utilities, excellent highways and the outmigration of Detroit people, all of which boosted its land values. Assessment reform helped Southfield capitalize on these factors. The steady rise of its tax base by 20 percent a year showed that it was doing something right.[33]

C. Reform by Ignoring the Law

Two other cities deserve mention in the context of assessments. They taxed land values more and buildings less, not by obeying the law but by ignoring the law (which had also been consistently ignored previously but in the opposite direction). *Houston, Texas*, reaped benefits from this policy under J. J. Pastoriza, finance and tax commissioner, from 1912 through 1914.[34] In the 1920s in *San Diego, California*, Harris L. Moody, described by then-Mayor John L. Bacon as "a crackerjack assessor who really knew real estate values and was fair in every way," decided on his own to go as far as he could in shifting taxes off buildings and onto site values.[35] Both of these experiments were halted, to the detriment of local enterprise, when the courts, at the behest of special interests, found them in violation of uniformity laws.

D. Addendum

Assessment practices nationwide have improved markedly since the 1950s. Yet adhering rigorously to a market value standard for valuing land would still be a major step in the right direction in many regions. *Simply obeying the law* produced excellent results in Rosslyn and Southfield. How much more could they have achieved if their state legislatures had let them reduce or phase out taxes on buildings—as Bryant in Virginia and Clarkson in Michigan both requested?

When cities with two-rate taxes, discussed later, seriously under-assess land (as sometimes happens), do they collect more land values in name but less *in substance*, compared with a Rosslyn or Southfield? The question is not raised to put assessment reformers and differential rate reformers in rival camps. Rather, since each technique is a valid way of tapping land values and down-taxing enterprise, ideally, both should be used in tandem.

XI

Banking on Public Lands

A CENTURY AFTER America's frontier is said to have vanished, the US government remains the country's principal landowner in terms of area. Of the nation's 2.3 billion acres, about 30 percent is in federal hands. State and local governments and Indian reservations hold another seven percent.[36]

Holding a third of the nation in public domain would seem to reflect the noble concept expressed by Thomas Jefferson, "The earth is given as a common stock for men to labor and live on."[37] But do the people truly reap the value of these public lands?

To an extent they do. The 250 million who visit the national parks each year for recreation and inspiration obtain what might be called an *in-kind* distribution from their land. The general public receives a *public welfare* distribution broadly defined, as national forests, wildlife refuges and wilderness areas conserve scenic beauty, ecological balance and air and water quality. The people receive *monetary* distribution from their public land. This takes the form of *rents, fees,* and *royalties* collected for the Treasury from grazing lands, timber, minerals, and petroleum resources, including billions annually from the leasing of off-shore drilling rights. It also takes the form of sales of portions of the public domain itself.

The preceding points present a partial but extremely misleading view unless seen against the fraud, waste, and corruption that have formed the backdrop of public land management. Instead of enriching the general public, federal lands are not even self-sustaining financially under present pricing policies.[38] Federal agencies and politicians caved in to special interests who won mineral rights and use of public lands at ridiculously low fees.

Massive land grants were given to railways to promote the opening up of the West. This occurred but at an unanticipated cost. Rail owners got so enmeshed in speculative schemes with their land empires that they let the railroad system fall into a decline from which it never fully recovered.

Ranching, mining, corporate farming and timber moguls are so accustomed to federal giveaways that they look upon them not as a privilege, but as a right. They support a so-called "property rights movement" and the "sagebrush revolution" that aim to diminish public controls over federal lands and the collection of rents from them. They support the wholesale turning over of the public domain to private ownership. Justice seems to call for retaining and enlarging the public domain and for setting user fees close to true economic rent. Landowning interests have successfully blocked moves in this direction.

Not surprisingly, people unschooled in Georgist philosophy find it hard to imagine that the invisible broadcast spectrum is "land" in an economic sense. Yet radio frequencies and television channels are clearly part of nature, part of the pubic domain. Traditionally, segments of the ether have been assigned cost-free, another case of taking what belongs to everyone to enrich a privileged few. In the 1990s, however, the government began selling some air waves at auction, reaping surprisingly high sums. This falls short of annual rentals to keep pace with the growing value of a scarce resource, but it is an advance over past practices.

XII

Two-Rate Taxes

THE MOST SUCCESSFUL efforts to increase taxes on America's land values in the 20th century have been in the state of Pennsylvania where, by 2000, eighteen cities (and two other local jurisdictions) had adopted the *two-rate tax*.

General Results. Because these cities simultaneously used many means to improve their performance, careful observers properly hesitate to claim specific effects due to the tax reform alone. To resolve this difficulty, two sets of surveys were undertaken: one, comparing each city's own construction record before and after adopting the two-rate tax, and two, comparing each city during the same time periods with similar neighboring cities that retained the conventional property tax. For example, see Table 5.

One must preface the findings by stressing that two-rate cities are not models of perfection. They all wrestle with continuing social, economic, and political problems. The question is whether conditions in these cities are getting better or worse. The studies address that question.

The positive results borne out by many studies have been too consistent to be dismissed as coincidences. Following are among the significant changes detected time and again after adoption of the reform:

- Taxes on the majority of owner-occupied and rental homes were reduced.
- Construction and rehabilitation of residential and commercial buildings were stimulated.
- The serious escalation of housing prices and rents experienced by most US cities was averted in the two-rate cities as housing supplies expanded.

Table 5

City	Anual Average for 1977–1979	Anual Average for 1980–1982	Percent Change
\multicolumn{4}{c}{NEW BUILDING IN MCKEESPORT, CLAIRTON, AND DUQUENSE[a]}
\multicolumn{4}{c}{Dollar Value of Annual Building Permits[b]}
\multicolumn{4}{c}{Comparing Three-Year Periods Before and After 1980[c]}
McKeesport	$ 1,716,000	$ 2,370,191	+38
Clairton	$ 746,710	$ 539,564	−28
Duquesne	$ 1,053,315	$ 839,731	−20

Notes:
a. These neighboring cities on the Monongahela River look alike and are served by the same chamber of commerce. During the study years, a time of crisis in the steel-making region, all had huge vacant mills and high unemployment.
b. Each city issues permits for construction and records project costs.
c. McKeesport adopted the two-rate tax in 1980; the three-year periods before and after chart the economic trend following its introduction. The other cities did not use the two-rate tax at those times (both adopted it some years later).
Source: Derived from Steven B. Cord, *The Evidence for Land-Value Taxation* (Columbia, MD: Center for Study of Economics, 1987).

- Central business districts were revitalized as they attracted greater private investment.
- More efficient land use resulted as the city's idle lots and under-used buildings were put into productive use; this in turn reduced the pressure for costly and environmentally harmful urban sprawl.

A. How It Works

Not a pure land tax, the two-rate tax lets the property tax burden fall more heavily on land values, less on building values. The mechanism is simple. As in most American taxing jurisdictions, the assessor first appraises the separate market value of land and buildings for each taxable parcel. However, instead of applying one tax rate to the total of these two values, the local government imposes a higher rate on the land assessment and a lower rate on the building assessment.

Since the 1970s, many two-rate cities have taken advantage of the Local Economic Revitalization Tax Act (LERTA), Pennsylvania's abatement law. This program offers commercial and industrial properties a sliding scale benefit—90 percent of the value of new structures is tax exempt the first year, 80 percent the second, and so forth, until the exemption disappears. The underlying land remains fully taxable. Use of LERTA gives an added push to the tax relief aspect of the two-rate tax.

B. Graded or Gradual

Pittsburgh and Scranton pioneered this system in 1914. Over ten years they increased the rate differentials in small grades until the rate on land was double the rate of buildings. This is why it was called the graded tax.[39]

Introducing the system gradually makes it politically palatable. It does not rock the boat. Moving slowly delays potential benefits. However, if the full reform would arouse too much opposition from land speculators to gain acceptance, this foot-in-the-door feature has unquestionable merit.

C. The Golden Triangle

Pittsburgh thrived with its two-to-one land-building ratio. After World War II, despite the decline of its steel industry, Pittsburgh enjoyed a renaissance. Sixty new buildings and skyscrapers costing over $700 million shot up on former rail yards and warehouse areas. An area that had employed 4,000 gave jobs to 20,000 after the *privately financed* renewal. David Lawrence, mayor at the time, stressed the importance of the "stick"—the higher rate on land—saying it "discouraged hoarding of vacant land for speculation." His successor, Mayor Joseph M. Barr, emphasized the "carrot," saying "fine structures erected through private investment as part of the renewal program benefited by the lower tax rate on buildings."[40] The business district framed by two rivers, called the Golden Triangle, won nationwide acclaim when many other American cities were loosing their vitality.[41]

D. Others Follow Suit

The state legislature gave other cities the two-rate option in 1951. Harrisburg, the state capital, chose that path in 1975. Small industrial towns adopted the reform in the 1980s—McKeesport, New Castle, Duquesne, Washington, Aliquippa, Clairton, Oil City. Titusville in 1990 and Coatesville, DuBois, Hazleton, and Lock Haven joined the list in 1991. Allentown, a city over 100,000 whose council members several times voted to adopt the two-rate only to have their decision vetoed by the mayor, finally succeeded in 1996. It has been followed by Steelton and Ebensburg.

Uniontown adopted but then rejected the reform in 1992. Its story is a cautionary tale of how *not* to introduce a two-rate tax. The city of 12,000 had suffered dreadful decline, capped when a new shopping center opened just outside the city limits. Eighty percent of downtown sites were vacant. One retailer who bought a store for $200,000 felt lucky to sell it 15 years later for $50,000. Officials adopted the two-rate tax without first correcting the distorted 34-year-old assessments. They chose differential rates that hit the few remaining retailers hard. They presented no advance public information. When taxpayers got their tax bills, they were confused and very upset. City council immediately rescinded the reform.

E. The Two Rates

The differential land and building rates usually apply to municipal taxes only.[42] City owners also pay property taxes to the overlapping county and school district, both of which tax land and buildings *at the same rate*. After World War II, county and school budgets expanded rapidly; this greatly diluted the impact of the two-rate tax in Pittsburgh and Scranton.

The 1951 law erased ratio limits. A few cities retained the two-to-one ratio, but half a dozen opted for five-to-one. Under the leadership of Councilman (later, Congressman) William J. Coyne, Pittsburgh moved to three-to-one in 1979 and soon increased it to nearly six-to-one. Washington, 30 miles from Pittsburgh, in 1995 decided to tax land almost 11 times higher than building values. Aliquippa initiated its reform with a sixteen-to-one ratio.

Even with higher ratios, the differential is weakened by flat county and school rates. Pittsburgh's municipal ratio of six-to-one is reduced to two and a half-to-one when the total city, county, and school tax load is calculated. Some researchers, seeing this modest differential, conclude that the two-rate system cannot have an effect. The evidence from actual experience, however, justifies the contrary conclusion that the system must be quite potent if such small doses can induce beneficial results. Findings from a 1962 study by prominent economists, Table 6, underscores this point.

An obvious solution to the problem of overlapping taxing jurisdictions would be to let them, as well as cities, use differential rates. The legislature gave this option to selected school districts, but efforts to extend it to counties and all local governments have thus far been only partially successful. In 1998, Pennsylvania enacted a law (Act 108), extending the two-rate tax option to its nearly 1,000 boroughs. This culminated a five-year effort, exemplifying the tedious progress toward property tax modernization by dedicated land-value tax proponents. Their next step was to launch an equally difficult campaign to persuade borough managers to apply this device in their communities.

F. Revenues

Cities customarily estimate expected revenue from all other sources—sales taxes, income taxes, excises, licenses, fees, fines, state and federal grants—and then set property tax rates at a level needed to fund the rest of their annual budget.

Two-rate cities do the same thing. Various cities in various years have used the two-rate tax to produce more, less, or the same revenue. Many cities adopted the reform as a less painful way of *increasing* taxes. Some increased rate *levels* to reduce objectionable non-property taxes. Some increased rate *differentials* to produce the same revenue while enhancing their tax incentives. At one time, cities finding a need for less revenue kept the prior tax rate on land and reduced only the rate on buildings.

Table 6

GROWTH AND DECLINE IN RUST-BELT CITIES Pittsburgh and 14 other Midwest Cities[a] 1960-1979 compared with 1980-1989[b] AVERAGE ANNUAL VALUE OF BUILDING PERMITS (Values in Millions of Constant 1982 Dollars)			
City	1960–1979	1980–1989	Percent Change
Akron	$ 134.026	$ 87.907	–34.41
Allentown	$ 48.124	$ 28.801	–40.15
Buffalo	$ 93.749	$ 82.930	–11.54
Canton	$ 40.235	$ 24.251	–39.73
Cincinnati	$ 318.248	$ 231.561	–27.24
Cleveland	$ 329.511	$ 224.587	–31.84
Columbus[c]	$ 456.580	$ 527.026	+15.43
Dayton	$ 107.798	$ 92.249	–14.42
Detroit	$ 368.894	$ 277.783	–24.70
Erie	$ 48.353	$ 22.761	–52.93
Pittsburg	**$ 181.734**	**$ 309.727**	**+70.43**
Rochester	$ 118.726	$ 82.411	–30.59
Syracuse	$ 94.503	$ 53.673	–43.21
Toledo	$ 138.384	$ 93.495	–32.44
Youngstown	$ 33.688	$ 11.120	–66.99
Fifteen-City **Average:**	**$ 167.504**	**$ 143.352**	**–14.42**

Notes:

a. "Rust belt" was a term for northeastern cities whose heavy industries declined sharply after World War II. Of these comparable cities, only Pittsburgh used the two-rate tax. The data are for the cities proper and do not pertain to the much larger metropolitan areas surrounding them.

b. The year 1979, used as the dividing point for the before-and-after annual averages, was when Pittsburgh significantly increased its land taxes and lowered its building taxes.

c. Columbus, the only other city showing positive growth, annexed surrounding communities in the 1980s (March 1996 discussion, Rybeck and city planner); noteworthy because Oates-Schwab found that, unlike Pittsburgh, most cities in the sample witnessed greater suburban than in-city growth during that decade.

Source: Wallace E. Oates, Robert M. Schwab, Impact on Urban Land Taxation: The Pittsburgh Experience, University of Maryland, 1995; based on Table 3.

G. The Harrisburg Story

In 1981, Harrisburg, suffering blight and a sluggish economy, was cited by a federal agency as the second most distressed city in the nation. By 1994, it had reduced vacant boarded-up housing units from 4,200 to less than 500. Its business firms in that period grew from 1,908 to 4,329. An additional 4,700 new job positions had been filled. The market value of private real estate rose from $212 million to over $880 million. According to Mayor Stephen R. Reed, the two-rate tax played a central role in Harrisburg's resurgence. He also relates tax reform to farmland preservation, an issue of concern throughout America as well as to the region around Harrisburg. "Many states try to save farmland by buying development rights. That's expensive. Without spending a dime, we can achieve the same goal with a two-tier tax. Unused urban land is what pushes development into open spaces. This tax, by assuring better use of unused land in cities and suburbs, will discourage the gobbling up of farms."[43]

H. Hawaii

In Hawaii, a graded property tax was adopted by the State Legislature in 1963 in order to encourage the highest and best use of land throughout the state. From the outset, this legislation was known as the "Pittsburgh law" because the differential rates on land and buildings were similar to those used in Pittsburgh; however, in Pittsburgh they applied only to municipal, not to county and school district levies, whereas in Hawaii they applied to all jurisdictions.

Hawaii, more than any other state, suffers from an extremely high concentration of landownership—much of it in the hands of descendants of those missionaries who "came to do good and did well." In 1969, for example, twelve owners held 52 percent and 60 owners controlled 80 percent of the private lands of the state, a situation that limits the amount available for use and development. However, shortly after the passage of the legislation cited (Act 142), "there was a move on the part of the large landowners on Oahu to enter into development agreements with land developers transferring the development rights to the land to them, and also the tax burden. The Bishop estate, the largest private land owner in Hawaii, has transferred the development rights to practically all of its developable lands on Oahu to developers."[44]

The law was amended in 1969 to simplify administration and exclude older residences from the differential rates provision. Because property tax rates were always quite low in Hawaii, the graded system, while modestly successful, did not achieve the dramatic benefits hoped for by its proponents; for instance, it was unable significantly to stem the speculative rise in land prices caused by population growth.

At the time this modified system of site-value taxation was adopted, Hawaii was unusual because its tax structure was highly centralized, and its real property tax, state-imposed. But in 1978, the State Constitution was changed to transfer the authority to assess, impose, and collect real property taxes to the four counties. At present, land is taxed at a higher rate than improvements only in the counties of Hawaii and Kauai. This may be because public sentiment in Honolulu and Maui, the most developed counties, opposes a system that is perceived as likely to encourage further development. In the county of Honolulu, the differential rate now applies to improved residential properties alone, and *bears more lightly on land than on improvements*. On these parcels (where the land's average valuation is approximately 73 percent of the property's value) there is obviously no tax incentive to keep old houses in good condition or replace them with better ones.[45]

I. Postscript on Pittsburgh

Pittsburgh took its reform a step further in 1997 when it launched a BID or Business Improvement District in its 100-block downtown. Many older cities enacted BIDs as retailers and others agreed to an extra tax on themselves to pay for greater customer safety, better clean-up, and marketing to compete with suburban malls. Most based the tax on total property value. The Pittsburgh Partnership, however, decided to base its tax—of 11.5 mills—*on land value only*. Ms. Terry Lorince, the Partnership director, explained to the present writer: "If the fee were based on total value, those who already invested most in the city, the biggest high-rises, would pay a ton of money while those who have done little with their property would pay almost nothing. We agreed it was too skewed. Besides, we're used to a bifurcated property system. It just seemed a logical step in the same direction."

XIII

Exceptional Alaska

STARTING IN 1982, every man, woman, and child in Alaska began receiving cash dividends. Between then and 1999, the annual amount increased from $1,000 to $1,770; a family of four who had resided in the state all 18 years received a total of $66,190.

The way Alaska manages its oil and gas, not merely to provide these distributions, but to stimulate production and jobs, to support public services, and to provide for the future, offers a striking example of how citizens and industry alike can prosper by equitably distributing the value of their land resources.

Russia established fur trading posts in the region in the 1780s. In 1867, prodded by Secretary of State William H. Seward, the US bought Alaska from Russia for $7.2 million. It was dubbed "Seward's Folly" until gold was discovered in Nome in 1899 and later in Fairbanks. Fishing and lumbering became major enterprises. The territory became the forty-ninth state (the largest in the Union, twice the size of Texas) in 1959.

That same year vast oil fields were discovered in the frigid and almost inaccessible North Slope. While the TransAlaskan Pipeline was being built to market this oil, Alaskans devised a system to spur production and let the general public share in the benefits of their natural heritage: Oil and gas sites, almost entirely on public lands, are leased, not sold, to highest bidders. Winners make a one-time payment for rights to explore and produce for five years. Producers pay royalties and severance taxes from oil and gas they take out, corporate income tax on profits, and property taxes on production and transmission line lands. Anticipating that oil revenues would be more than enough to meet state needs, Alaska established a Permanent Fund (a 1976 vote put it in the constitution) to advance the welfare of the state and its citizens, currently and in the future.

Production in fact burgeoned, as did the economy. In 1980, three years after the pipeline opened, the state was able to abolish both its personal income tax and sales tax. Population, multiplied from 200,000 in 1960 to over 622,000 by 1999.

Translating the oil bonanza into public dollars, for fiscal year 1997 the state got $5 million from leases, $785 million from royalties, $250 million from the petroleum corporate tax, $925 million from the severance tax, and $60 million from the oil property tax. In the same year, these oil revenues financed 80 percent of the state's general fund. The remainder of state revenue came from the corporate (non-petroleum) graduated income tax with a maximum 9.4 percent rate, which brought in $227 million; taxes on fisheries and motor fuel, $38 million each; and minor amounts from licenses, fees, and other taxes.

Counties and cities in 1997 received $240 million from an oil property tax. Localities also benefit indirectly. In Anchorage, with 225,000 people, the largest city, the state picked up 38 percent of the city and school budgets. Property tax rates ranged from only .01 to .018 percent of market value (42 districts choose different service levels). The $286 million in property tax revenue paid 48 percent of city and school budgets. After state aid, the rest came from fees, business inventory taxes, and utility charges. Anchorage imposes no sales tax, but Fairbanks and some other localities do.

A quarter of Alaska's royalty revenue goes into the Permanent Fund, which is professionally invested. Through 1999, it had grown to over $27 billion and citizens had received $8.8 billion from its earnings.[46] The Permanent Fund Corporation staff estimated that 7,000 jobs a year stemmed from the dividend payments.

Petroleum economist Chuck Logsdon with the Department of Natural Resources made this statement to the author: "Private companies own the gas and oil they extract; the people get the land rent."

For two decades Alaska has offered a contrast to Appalachia and other resource-rich areas. By permitting mining and drilling companies to capture land rent plus profits, these states and nations deprive society of its share of nature's bounty, deny their governments adequate funds for public services, and leave nothing for future generations.

Oil prices, volatile at best, plunged sharply from over $30 a barrel to only $8 or $9 in 1998 and 1999. Oil production also declined. The consequent shortfall in oil revenues left the state with a budget deficit. Some officials urged reviving the state income and sales tax. Others called for dipping more deeply into the Permanent Fund to balance the budget. By early 2000, as oil prices began to climb steeply, no legislative action had been taken on such proposals.

Communications Assistant Joan Cahill with the Permanent Fund Corporation explained that oil revenues add to the Fund's *principal*. This is conservatively invested to generate *earnings*. These go, first, back to principal to offset inflation, second, to support state government, and third, to citizen shares, all according to formulas spelled out in laws.

Many citizens, especially new arrivals, got the impression that dividends were an entitlement and the sole purpose of the Permanent Fund. A public education program is needed to remind Alaskans that it was set up primarily for "a future rainy day" when oil runs dry, Ms. Cahill said.

How soon will Alaska's legislators—and lawmakers elsewhere—recognize that surface land, unlike oil or coal, need not be depleted? Rather, its value expands if cities and towns remain healthy. Further, recapturing this value induces production and job growth to keep communities healthy. A question this volume prompts is whether Alaska will be wise enough to consider converting its very low local property taxes into a robust state land-value tax for bolstering its Permanent Fund.

XIV

Conclusions

DUE IN LARGE part to more than a century of inattention to the role of land, help for reform comes from very few professional assessors, economists, tax administrators, or state and local officials. Politicians typically promise to reduce property taxes, without giving so much as a nod to their worthwhile recycling of community-created land values or to their reliability as revenue producers. A substantial share of the property tax billions currently collected (see Table 7) is derived from the land value portion and merits high praise. Unfortunately, the entire property tax, not just the tax on improvements, is constantly vilified.

Table 7

DISTRIBUTION OF PROPERTY TAX REVENUES TO JURISDICTIONS BY AMOUNTS AND PERCENTAGES, 1993 (amounts in billions of dollars)		
All	$ 189	% 100.0
School Districts	78	41.8
Counties	44	22.9
Cities	42	22.3
Townships	12	6.2
States	7	3.7
Special Districts	6	3.1
Source: Total and percentage estimates from Census of Governments.		

Although the two-rate tax in Pittsburgh and Scranton has enjoyed local editorial support, the press generally has ignored this issue.[47] Media silence handicaps those who are trying—in California, New York, New Hampshire, West Virginia, Missouri, Wisconsin, Minnesota, the District of Columbia, Maryland and elsewhere—to duplicate or improve upon the Pennsylvania experience.[48] Often greater barriers are the state constitutions and laws that must be changed to permit or mandate tax reform.

Despite these frustrations, a favorable word about the US political system is in order. Advances achieved via single tax enclaves, special assessment districts, assessment reforms, and the two-rate tax owe much to the intergovernmental division of powers. It is difficult to imagine that these reforms would have gained a toehold if they had relied on federal action—that is, if the Congress, the White House, and the special interests they represent had had to endorse them.

At the end of the 18th century, America's state and local governments embarked on a course of land taxation that served the people exceedingly well. Then they lost their way. It seems appropriate at the end of the 20th century that US land tax reformers were exerting much of their efforts on this same state-local level—to help the country find its way back.[49]

Notes

1. This amnesia is illustrated by the fact that, after an excellent but brief 1931 history of the property tax by Jens Jenson, no comprehensive treatment of the topic reappeared until Dick Netzer's work 35 years later.

2. Aaron M. Sakolski, *Land Tenure and Land Taxation in America* (New York: Schalkenbach, 1957), passim, presents a thorough discussion of US land policy from colonial times to the mid-20th century.

3. Ibid., pp. 136–147.

4. Dick Netzer, *Economics of the Property Tax* (Washington, DC: Brookings Institution, 1966), p. 3.

5. Ibid., pp. 2–3, 136–147. The "general" property tax was intended to cover tangible and intangible personal property as well, but these forms of wealth or claims on wealth proved difficult to trace and assess. Nine states eliminated personal property taxes altogether; many more narrowed its reach by exempting business inventories and household goods from the tax.

6. *Essays in Taxation* (5th edition, New York: Macmillan, 1905), p. 61.

7. Jens P. Jenson, *Property Taxation in the United States* (Chicago: University of Chicago Press, 1931), p. vii.

8. A notable exception is the Pittsburgh downtown improvement district discussed toward the end of this chapter.

9. George E. Lent, "Special Assessments (Land Betterment Taxes)," International Monetary Fund staff paper, Washington, DC, 1967.

10. Historical scholarship, which previously dwelt on the influence of key figures, was revolutionized in 1893 by Frederick Jackson Turner, who demonstrated how greatly the frontier shaped American democracy. Whereas Turner's followers focus on the loss of that frontier, land tax proponents argue that America (or any nation) could regain a potent force for freedom and economic opportunity if its land (its perpetual frontier, so to speak) were made economically accessible to all via a rational system of taxation.

11. (New York: Robert Schalkenbach Foundation, 1962), originally published 1879.

12. Francis G. Goodale, in *Land-Value Taxation Around the World* (1st ed.; New York: Schalkenbach, 1955), pp. 128–132.

13. James Cassels. "Fairhope—Hope of the Future," *March of Progress* magazine, January 1946, pp. 53–56.

14. Chase Econometrics Associates survey, *New York Times*, August 5, 1979, p. 24.

15. Colony officials originally set the annual lot rents. Later they adopted the Somers system (designed by a noted appraiser), a formula of frontage rates and depth factors based on relative location values. This was modified into a computer version that also took account of pedestrian and auto traffic. Next the colony relied on the land value portion of the county property assessments. In all cases, only a percentage of full rent was charged to lessees by the FSTC—sufficient to meet the annual budgets.

16. Baldwin County assesses and levies a tax on each parcel's land and buildings. The Single Tax Corporation pays this tax from rent it charges the leaseholder. The new 1993 formula to calculate "annual rent" is the sum of the county's improvement and land taxes, plus a flat administrative fee ($50 per parcel) and a small "demonstration fee" (two one-thousandths of assessed land value as of 1996, or $40 on a $20,000 lot). The so-called rent is thus almost identical with a conventional property tax, with the exception that the colony established a ceiling of six percent of the assessed land value on the rent any lessee is charged.

17. Brown et al, eds., *Land-Value Taxation Around the World* (1st ed., 1955), op. cit., p. 116.

18. See Henry Wiencek, "Laying Out the Idyllic Life in a Latter-day Arden," *Smithsonian* magazine, May 1991, pp. 124–142.

19. Arthur E. Morgan, *The Miami Conservancy District* (New York: McGraw-Hill, 1951), pp. 312–330.

20. See Walter Rybeck, "Property Tax as a Super User Charge," in C. Lowell Harris, ed., *Property Tax and Local Finance* (New York: Academy of Political Science, 1983), pp. 133–147.

21. Albert T. Henley, "The Evolution of Forms of Water Users Organizations in California," 45 *California Law Review*, 1957.

22. Quoted in Robert V. Andelson, "The Day They Froze San Diego's Skyline," speech to San Diego League of Women Voters, January 16, 1961.

23. Trott, "Doing It the Wright Way," *Frontier* magazine, August 1956, pp. 7–9.

24. 164 US 112.

25. "The California Irrigation Districts Case," *American Journal of Economics and Sociology*, April 1943, pp. 393–402.

26. It can be argued that water, as a category of "land," is the proper object of a public tax, and that a further fee to conserve water is simply an extension of this proper charge.

27. See *How Tax Exemption Broke the Housing Deadlock in New York City*, and *Tax Policies and Urban Renewal in New York City*, both by Citizens' Housing and Planning Council, New York City, 1960.

28. Exempt buildings had to be erected within two years of approval. They could qualify only up to maximum limits of $1,000 per room, $5,000 per family unit, and $15,000 per building.

29. "Success Story Number 8," W. Rybeck, ed., *From Poverty to Prosperity by 2000*, (Kensington, MD: Center for Public Dialogue, 1982), p. 59.

30. "Success Story Number 6," Ibid, p. 43.

31. The US Census of Governments rates local assessment systems according to a "coefficient of dispersion." This measures the variance of the official assessed values from actual sales prices as verified by market surveys.

32. See Lyle C. Bryant, Rosslyn: *A Case Study in Urban Renewal*, (New York: Schalkenbach Foundation, 1965); and Bryant, "Assessments and Their Effect on Land Use," in *Proceedings, American Society of Planning Officials*, Philadelphia, 1966.

33. *Hearings, National Commission on Urban Problems*, (Washington, DC: 1968) and W. Rybeck, Moderator, *Property Taxation, Housing and Urban Growth* (Washington, DC: Urban Institute, 1970), p. 48.

34. H. G. Brown et al, eds., op. cit., p. 134.

35. Andelson, op. cit. An example of Moody's system: He assessed a bank property in 1928 at $540,000 for the land and $240,000 for the building. Thirty-three years later, after San Diego's population had grown from 150,000 to 500,000, the supposedly legal assessed values for the same property were set at $262,000 for the land, and $522,000 for the building!

36. Gene Wunderlich, "Agricultural Landownership and the Real Property Tax," in Wunderlich, ed., *Land Ownership and Taxation in American Agriculture* (Boulder, CO, and Oxford, England: Westview Press, 1993), p. 4.

37. In a letter to the father of James Madison, October 28, 1785; p.2., Ford, ed., *Jefferson's Writings* (Federal edition; New York: Putnam's, 1904–05), Vol. VIII, p. 196.

38. Marion Clawson, *The Federal Lands Since 1956, Recent Trends in Use and Management* (Washington, DC, Resources for the Future, 1967); Clawson, *Uncle Sam's Acres* (New York: Dodd Mead, 1951); and Sakolski, op. cit.

39. Some localities call it a two-tier or split-rate tax. Others refer to it in a somewhat misleading manner as a land value, site value, or land tax, in which cases it must be understood that the word "modified" or "limited" should precede each of these terms.

40. *Hearings, National Commission on Urban Problems*, Vol. 1 (Washington, DC; Government Printing Office, 1967), p. 313.

41. Pittsburgh was the primary inspiration for launching the federal urban renewal program. Ironically, however, analysts who stressed the critical role of its two-rate incentives were ignored. Instead, the national

program instituted a system of buying out slumlords and other speculators while subsidizing developers. After some accomplishments and many scandals and disappointments, the program fell into disrepute.

42. Two recent exceptions are the Aliquippa School District and the Pittsburgh Improvement District.

43. Walter Rybeck, "Pennsylvania's Experiments in Property Tax Modernization," *NTA Forum, National Tax Association*, No. 7, Spring 1991.

44. John Hulten, "Hawaii's Modified Property Tax Assessment Law," *Assessor's Journal*, Vol. 5, No. 3 (October 1970), p. 11.

45. Data supplied by Raymond T. Higa, Real Property Assessment Division, City and County of Honolulu.

46. Throughout this book, whenever the word "billion" is used, it should be understood in the American and French sense (a thousand million) rather than the British and German sense (a million million).

47. This silent treatment of constructive reform of the property tax by the national media is puzzling. In the late 1970s, when California enacted a destructive change called Proposition 13 (which set limits on assessment increases, regardless of market values, and which set rate ceilings that forced greater reliance on non-property revenue sources), the press made this "tax revolt" front page news, setting in motion a mindless anti-tax furor from which the nation had not recovered two decades later. National media gave so little attention to the Pittsburgh or Harrisburg tax reforms that it is fair to say that a large majority of the well-read public, including those who worry about urban, environmental, and social problems, remained unaware that land tax measures were even a possible remedy for addressing such problems.

48. New York State in the 1990s permitted one city, Amsterdam, to use the two-rate tax. For the legislature to go that far was a victory in itself. But fierce legal and political attacks by opponents caused it to be repealed before it could be implemented. See Donald Reeb, *The Two-Rate Tax: The Amsterdam, NY Experience* (Cambridge, MA: Lincoln Institute of Land Policy, 1988).

49. Land tax reformers remain a distinct minority. America's spotlight in the 1990s focused on those who wanted a "flat" federal income tax (opposing progressive rates that rise with income), and on those who sought to replace it with a national sales or value added tax. Like land taxers, many other reformers called for returning federal power to localities. But they left out of the equation how cities, whose inequitable tax systems already are eroding their economies, are to pay for the higher expenditures this requires.

BEFORE: In the 1950s, the Rosslyn section of Arlington County, Virginia, directly across the Potomac from Washington, D.C., presented a low-rise jumble of pawnshops, industrial yards, paltry small businesses and vacant lots. Photo courtesy of Virginia Room, Arlington County Public Library.

AFTER: In the 1970s, Rosslyn boomed with high-rise commercial and apartment construction only a dozen years after higher land taxes unlocked the great growth potential of this prime real estate in the shadow of the nation's capital. Photo courtesy of Virgina Room, Arlington Historical Society.

PART THREE

EUROPE

Chapter 10

Denmark

BY OLE LEFMANN* AND KARSTEN K. LARSEN**

DENMARK WAS THE first country in Europe to put into practical operation the taxation of land values, and the first country in the world that had a political party of national influence whose chief aim was to make land value the principal and, if possible, the only source of tax revenue in the country.

I

Historical Background

THE PRACTICE OF land-value taxation is deeply rooted in Danish history, going back at least to the reign of Valdemar the Great (1157–1182), and possibly even antedating the Viking king, Sven Forkbeard (985–1014).[1] However, after the Valdemar kings, who

*Ole Lefmann is deputy president of the International Union for Land-Value Taxation and Free Trade. A diplomate of the Copenhagen Business School, he recently retired from the insurance business, having been previously engaged in both wholesale and retail commerce. For eight years he served as a member of the Assessment Committee of the Borough of Copenhagen. He has been honorary secretary of the board of the Danish Henry George Society, and for two periods edited its quarterly periodical, *Grundskyld*. Mr. Lefmann held various positions of responsibility in the Danish Justice Party, and stood for political office as its candidate on several occasions. He is author of *Three Synonyms: The Market Emancipated, the Economy Democratized, the State Based on Equal Rights* (1979), *Insurance of Private Liability* (1992), *Out With the Old Tax* (1993), and many articles in newspapers and magazines, especially the monthly, *Vejen frem*, and the quarterly, *Grundskyld*.

**Karsten K. Larsen earned a Master of Political Science degree from the University of Copenhagen. He serves as a section head for Statistics Denmark. He is a board member of the Danish Henry George Society, and editor of its quarterly magazine, *Grundskyld*, in which he has published articles. On several occasions, Mr. Larsen stood for Parliament as a candidate of the Danish Justice Party.

ruled until the middle of the 13th century, it seems to have fallen into disuse until the statesman, Hannibal Sehested, restored the national finances in the early 1660s after the disastrous war with Sweden. A key instrument in this restoration was the so-called "hartkorn tax," based on potential agricultural yield. In 1685, all land values were registered.

Yet, as in Europe generally, the vast bulk of the rural population was landless, and, moreover, subject to a form of serfdom. This situation obtained almost to the eve of the French Revolution, when the seizure of the regency in 1786 by Crown Prince Frederick (later Frederick VI) set in motion a series of sweeping and systematic reforms that, within just a few decades, not only did away with hereditary landed servitude, but created a class of independent smallholders numbering in the hundred thousands. At the same time, the modernization of agricultural techniques was encouraged, making for a shift toward dairying and the production of high-quality processed foodstuffs. In this, the celebrated "folk schools," or adult high schools, first established in the 1840s through the leadership of Bishop Severin Grundtvig, played a major role, for they helped the farmers gain intellectual and technical skills that enabled them to turn out superior products, and to compete successfully in overseas markets.

In 1802, the state minister, Count Christian Detlev Reventlow, submitted a memorandum to the king, calling, in language that anticipated Henry George, for a new hartkorn tax levied on top of the old one and broadened to include land under manor houses, which had hitherto been exempt.[2] Although the full implementation of the proposal took more than forty years, it was eventually accomplished. The tax at times accounted for more than fifty percent of the national revenues, and constituted more than half of the total land rent.[3] It was abolished in 1903 by the governing Liberal Party, which had once stood for enlightened policies, but had gradually come to represent the interests of the large landowners. The hartkorn tax was replaced by a combination of progressive income taxes and general property taxes, which greatly discriminated against the small farmers, with their highly productive holdings, typically intensively improved, not only with well-kept

buildings but with sophisticated agricultural and processing machinery.

Thus was the stage set for the enthusiastic reception of Georgism by the smallholders, just as they were organizing to oppose
the Liberals. The vehicle whereby this occurred was the agricultural folk high schools. Persons associated with the folk school
movement were, in fact, the first Scandinavians to learn about and
promote George's ideas. The young agriculture teacher, Jakob E.
Lange, had become acquainted with these ideas while studying in
England, and urged them vigorously among his colleagues in the
folk school organ, *Höjskolebladet.* The Norwegian folk school
principal and later president of Parliament, Viggo Ullman, produced the first Danish-Norwegian translation of *Progress and
Poverty.* With the formal adoption in 1902 of the concepts of land-
value taxation and free trade by the leading agricultural cooperatives, Danish Georgism acquired the needed critical mass for political action. After 1910, thanks to generous donations by the
American soap manufacturer, Joseph Fels, it also acquired the financial means to support an institute to propagate its doctrines.

The new movement split off from the now conservative Liberal
Party, to help form the Radical Liberals. By 1915, after earlier ex-
perimental legislation of a temporary nature, the Radical Liberals
were able to push through a law providing for a general reappraisal of all real property, with separate valuation of land and improvements. In 1922, the national general property tax was separated into two taxes, one on the value of the land alone, and the
other, at a lower rate, on the value of improvements. Shortly
thereafter, the local general property tax was similarly divided,
and at corresponding rates.

Meanwhile, an explicitly Georgist political party, the Justice
Party, had been formed in 1919, chiefly by disaffected Radicals
who advocated a bolder and more ideologically uncompromising
stand.

Seven years later, it was represented in Parliament. By 1948,
Georgist ideas had attained sufficient influence that the Government appointed a commission to consider the *full* taxation of land
values with corresponding reduction of taxes on industry, which
issued a favorable report in 1954. In 1957, the Justice Party joined

the Socialists and Radicals in a coalition known as the "Ground Duty Government." Although very much the junior partner in terms of the number of its parliamentary seats, it held three cabinet ministries, and was able to obtain a considerable increase in land-value taxation, with more or less concurrent decrease in other taxes.

Since 1916, the values of land and of improvements have been separately assessed with general assessment now made every four years, the latest one being in January 1999. Between the general assessments the valuations are regulated every year according to the compulsory registration of all sales of real property in Denmark. Both the land value and the total value are capital values (in fact, selling prices) and not annual or rental values. An annual tax on the assessed land values apart from improvements is levied.[4]

Table 1

TAXES AND LAND VALUES FOR SELECTED YEARS IN DENMARK, 1950–1995 (all figures at million Danish Kroner)						
Year	Real Estate Taxes	Of Which Land Taxes	All Taxes	Land Values	Land Improve-ments	Land Taxes as a % of All Taxes
1950	341	219	4,186	9,267	184	5.2
1956	562	363	7,216	12,504	571	5.0
1960	784	484	9,758	17,175	785	5.0
1965	997	684	20,154	41,078	1,878	3.4
1969	1,508	1,082	35,645	67,419	3,405	3.0
1973	2,617	2,130	73,429	103,484	6,040	2.9
1977	3,724	3,110	117,300	194,274	9,309	2.7
1981	5,540	4,671	185,379	229,650	8,182	2.5
1986	6,488	5,285	339,075	385,819	15,824	1.6
1992	8,973	6,895	419,883	429,154	17,601	1.6
1995	10,325	8,210	497,905	430,424	17,780	1.6
1997	11,720	8,229	557,820	463,677	17,313	1.5

Source: Statistics Denmark (The Danish Statistical Office).

Through the first part of the 20th century, three patterns may be traced in Danish fiscal policies in regard to land:

1. State[5] acquisition of land and its disposal on condition of payment of the economic rent.

2. Appropriation by taxation of some part of the increase in land values.

3. Shifting taxation from improvements and income to the value of land alone.

Each of these policies was actually implemented, and gave, up to the late 1950s, promise of further progress in their implementation.

II

State Acquisition

FOR SOME TIME after 1919, agricultural land belonging to or acquired by the state was used for the establishment of small holdings. Such land was not sold; instead the user paid to the government a rent calculated at four percent per annum of the assessed value on date of transfer, revised at each general assessment of land in the whole country.

Three land laws of October, 1919, accomplished this purpose. One of the laws provided that parochial or glebe land (agricultural) should be taken for the creation of small holdings; the particular church having the right to reserve seven hectares for its own use. Another of the laws provided that each entailed estate—that is, estate so restricted that it may be bequeathed only to a certain heir—might be freed from the burden of the entail if its owner agreed to pay the state one fifth of the value and surrendered one third of farmland against payment by the state of its assessed selling value. All owners of such estates took the opportunity offered. The third law and several laws passed later dealt with the disposal of the land acquired under the two acts, or of other agricultural land in the possession of the state, and with the financing of the erection of buildings, etc., on the new holdings.

However, later in the century, the system of State Rental Small Holders was abolished. The reason for this was that the State Rental Small Holders had to pay all the taxes levied on inhabitants of Denmark, on top of their paying the rent. As the value of their land increased, they were hampered in competition; and as they became annoyed with the double taxation, the legislators abolished the whole State Rental Small Holding system. The land was privatized and there was no enthusiasm later for returning to the previous approach, despite its many virtues.

The greatest influence on legislation for many years has come from the big farmers and their powerful trade organizations.

III

Appropriation of Part of Increases in Land Values

IN ADDITION TO the national and local taxes levied on land values, a national tax on increments in land values was collected under legislation effective in 1933 and revised in 1950. The rate of this tax was four percent annually. At first it applied to one half of the increase revealed at each general valuation made after the general valuation of 1932, but after the law was revised in 1950, the proportion of increase to which the land tax applied was enlarged to three quarters. Exemptions were allowed under complicated rules and the tax became of consequence only where there had been a considerable increase in land values caused by local or special circumstances, especially by urban development of agricultural land in the vicinity of the towns and near Copenhagen. Because of the exemptions, it did not generally effect ordinary agricultural land. However, where land did become liable to this increment tax, 45 percent of any further increase in value accruing before 1950, and 67.5 percent of the increase after 1950, in excess of the country-wide increase, was taken for state and local purposes.

The revenue from this increment tax was shared equally between the national treasury and the local rating authority in which it was collected.

An interesting feature to be noted here is that in the valuation of land, the incidence of this increment tax was disregarded. In other words, the land was valued as if the increment tax did not exist. In this respect, this taxation of increases in land value was treated quite as if a corresponding part of the land had been acquired from the state in the same manner as in the case of the small holdings.

In 1958, the tax on incremental land values was increased to comprise the full increment. In 1965, the tax on incremental land values was abolished.

IV

Shifting Taxation from Improvement and Income

A NATIONAL REAL estate tax on land plus improvements was imposed throughout Denmark as previously mentioned, since 1903, following the abolition of the hartkorn tax. It was in addition to a similar tax still levied by all local authorities. After 1922, the rate was lower for improvements than it was for land but the difference was not great. The tax on improvements in the counties was three fifths of the rate on land values, and elsewhere it was three quarters. This national real estate tax was, however, eventually abolished.

Local taxes on real estate are levied under the Act of 1933, which allows the councils in rural districts to fix their own rates and exemptions within the framework of the law.[6]

In 1954, the Parliament removed the upper limit for councils' levying tax on land values.

In 1957, the tax on improvements was frozen at its amount as of that date, and slated to be abolished gradually—which it indeed was.

In 1960, the limit for councils' levying tax on land values was restored. It was removed again in 1966, and several municipalities raised the ground duty (Danish: *Grundskyld*). For instance, Brondby Municipality in a couple of years levied for local use 4.7 percent of the assessed value of land (plus two percent for the county), which covered half the budgeted expenses of the municipality, and made it possible to reduce municipal income taxes.

Prices of land in Brondby Municipality did not decrease as predicted by the Georgists, probably because the citizens found that their total local tax on property and on income was unchanged.

But the Social Democrats in power in Brondby Municipality were able to document that the citizens benefited from the high ground duty and low income tax compared to a counter proposal offered by the non-socialistic opposition, according to which the citizens would pay lower ground duty and higher income tax. The Social Democrats published a folder showing in hard figures and drawings the advantages for representative groups of the citizens of the municipality.

Brondby's leading position in the public capture of land values was exceeded a few years later by the Municipality of Albertslund, which now levied ground duty of seven percent of the land values (plus two percent for the county). These rates were retained for several years but were later decreased.

It is difficult to decide whether the said percentages should be accepted as denominated, as the fact is that the taxpayers in those years could reduce the amount of their income tax by deducting in their tax declaration the ground duty paid the previous year. Further, there was a tax-equalizing arrangement between municipalities, transferring revenues from municipalities with a high income tax revenue per citizen to municipalities with a low income tax revenue per citizen.

In the 1970s, the upper limit of ground duty for local administration was reintroduced. In 1997, local administrations were required to collect at least 0.6 percent, but limited to collecting at most 2.4 percent (plus one percent for the county).

V
Tax on "Rental Value of Own Residence in Own House"

IN 1903, AT the same time as the income tax system was introduced, a peculiar tax was introduced as well.

It was levied as income tax on a small percentage (originally and for many years four percent) of the publicly assessed value (selling price) of the property (land plus buildings), when the taxpayer both owned and resided at the property.

As income tax was levied on capital yields by about 50 percent, the tax on the rental value of one's own residence in one's own house or apartment collected about two percent of this property value. In spite of the fact that it was levied on the value of land plus house or apartment, this tax was not registered by Statistics

Denmark (the Danish Statistical Office) as a property tax, but was rather classified as an income tax.

This tax was abolished in 1998 after being gradually reduced over a period of years. It had been in effect for almost a century. It was replaced by a regular property tax falling upon both land and buildings.

VI

Progress and Decline

THE PROGRESS OF the concept of collecting rent of land for public purposes went on in Denmark from 1880 to 1960. It culminated with the Ground Duty Government 1957–1960.

In 1960, at the new election of members of the Parliament, all the three parties of the Ground Duty Government (the Social Democratic Party, the Radical Liberal Party, and the Justice Party) lost seats, but the Justice Party lost *all* its seats.

The reason for this defeat was not the economic state of Danish society, as this was the best that could be wished for: a favorable balance of trade, almost no debt to foreign countries, virtually no unemployment, the highest real wages the country had ever known, and a dramatic increase in industrial production and personal savings and investment.

These claims are substantiated by Dr. Viggo Starke, late longtime leader of the Justice Party, member of parliament, and cabinet minister under the Ground Duty Government, in his book *Triumf eller Fiasko?* (Triumph or Fiasco?),[7] from which the following extract is taken:

The Foreign Exchange Deficit
Through a great many years, the balance of Denmark's annual account used to show a *foreign exchange deficit.*

In 1956, the deficit was DKK 250 million. In the Annual Statement of Activities of the Commercial Bank of Copenhagen [in the 1980s renamed the Danish Bank] the figures showed that from May 1957 (the month when the Ground Duty Government was established) the exchange reserves grew skyhigh, and rapidly deficit changed to a *foreign exchange* excess of more than DKK 1,000 mio.

Since 1960, there has been trouble with the foreign exchange balance, and every half year Denmark has "to be saved".

The Foreign Debt

In the period 1957–1960, [the period of the Ground Duty Government] the *foreign debt* of Denmark was reduced to the lowest amount in a generation. . . . Since 1960, the governments have borrowed money from abroad, partly for the purpose of showing off the stock of foreign exchange, and partly for the purpose of financing increasing public expenses. The result is that during these few years (1960–1970) the national debt doubled forty-fold.

Unemployment

When the Ground Duty Government was formed in 1957, there was considerable *unemployment* in Denmark. When the Ground Duty Government brought inflation to cessation, the increase of taxes ceased. Tax-free investments and tax-free depreciations were implemented, and land speculation was stopped. Wheels began to run again, and unemployment disappeared, practically speaking.

Real Wages

Under the Ground Duty Government, *real wages* went up four times as much as the prices went up. It was the greatest increase in real wages ever seen.

Taxes

The taxes implemented in June 1957 were levied to fill up the deficit left over from the four "old parties," and the imposed loan was soon paid back. Through the three following years, no further tax was levied.

The lowest earnings became tax-free and the highest earnings became taxed proportionally instead of progressively.

As the urban municipal ground duty was more than doubled, it was provided that the increased revenue should be used for reduction of the municipal income tax. As the wheel began to turn and the hands became employed, peoples' income raised, and because of the progressive tax system built up by the "old parties" the state revenue raised also.

But a family having in 1960 the same income and consumption as in 1957 would have had a tax reduction of more than 10 percent.

Industrial Production

Industrial production went up 32 percent. Industrial investments raised 135 percent. Private investments were three times as big as were public investments. Savings increased immensely, because it again became profitable to accumulate savings. Out of the savings were invested DKK two million.

In addition, at this time there was virtually no inflation, and no prospect of recession.

VII

Some Reasons for the Defeat

AS THE ECONOMIC state of Denmark 1960 was extremely good and its prospects even better, many people have been searching for the reason or reasons why the electorate in that year rejected the policies of the Ground Duty Government.

One of the present authors, Ole Lefmann, adds the following two reasons for the defeat in 1960 of the Ground Duty Government and especially the Justice Party:

1. *The Georgists were not prepared.*

When the Ground Duty Government took office in 1957, it increased land-value taxation considerably.[5] The immediate economic prosperity caught the Danish Georgists off their guard. They used to declare: "When we increase the land value tax, the prices on land will decrease." This correlation is theoretically correct when other factors are omitted, but now everybody could see that prices on land were rising, in spite of the fact that taxes on land values had been increased considerably and were expected to be increased further.

The Georgists also used to say: "When we increase the land value tax, we will reduce taxes on income." But initially, income taxes as well as land value taxes were increased under the Ground Duty Government, and most Danes failed to realize that by 1960 their total taxes were actually lower than before the increase.

Thus two key arguments previously used by the Georgists were now unusable: moreover, they could not agree mutually upon how to propose that the government dispose of the surplus, public revenues having surpassed public expenses.

Further, the Georgists could not agree mutually about such questions as: "Should compensation be given to the landowners when they could prove that the land-value tax caused them an economic loss?" and "Would the rent of land be sufficient to pay for all public expenses if other taxes were abolished?" And they were arguing bitterly as to whether they should call the collection of rent for public purposes a *tax*, or *duty*, or *charge*, or something else.

On top of that, there arose among people in the Justice Party internal quarrels that did not have anything to do with Georgist ideas, quarrels that took much energy and time that could have been better used for external propaganda. And (possibly in some cases due to frustration occasioned by these problems) during that period several of the best Georgist speakers died, became seriously ill, or withdrew from politics.

2. *The counteractions were strongly concentrated.*

The counteracting propaganda was sharp, severe, and harsh.

The opponents against the Justice Party and the Georgist ideas had no difficulty in raising money for their campaign, and they took full advantage of all the journalistic media.

The speakers in favor of land-value taxation were blamed for the technical provisions in the laws concerning ground duty and tax on incremental land values, that in some instances led to differences in the tax on obviously equal family houses, though most of these provisions were put into the laws to satisfy the opposition.

Members of the Justice Party were blamed by left-wing opponents for refusing to use the excess revenue for public (Welfare State) purposes, and by right-wing opponents for collecting more revenue than necessary.

The counteracting propaganda spoke energetically about the fear of the small householder who would be forced to leave his private home if he were unable to pay the increased land value tax.

The number of resident-owned houses in Denmark had increased immensely during the late 1950s (from 30 percent of all Danish homes to more than 50 percent), and the new homeowners found it easy to accept the harsh agitation against ground duty and the tax on incremental land values.

In October 1962, the Gallup Market Analysis Institute of Copenhagen[8] conducted a survey to determine what percentage of the Danish population would support a proposal to tax the full rental value of the land. The questions to which answers were elicited did not mention that the collection of the full rental value of land would imply proportionate reduction of the taxes on income and consumption. The Gallup Institute published in November 1962 its report, showing among other things that 12 percent of the voters favored the proposal, 17 percent opposed, and 71 percent did not know.

Professor Louis Wasserman in 1963 analyzed the survey in his unpublished, privately circulated essay, "Denmark: Land, Politics and Single Tax Sentiment."[9] In it he said that the land tax itself was not a relevant issue in the 1960 election, having been pushed out of focus by more contentious matters, but his analysis of the survey revealed that:

Only a few voters understood that they themselves benefited from land-value taxation.

Most voters looked upon land-value taxation as a tax like other taxes.

Of those voters who understood that a full land-value tax implied proportionate reduction in taxes on income and consumption, many doubted that such reduction would actually occur.

Several voters found it unfair to levy all taxes on land.

Very many voters were simply against the Justice Party.

Many voters wanted to punish the Justice Party because, in 1957, it established a government with the Social Democrats.

Wasserman emphasized that the Danish Georgists had not done a good enough job of educating the public in their principles: The underlying harmony between full land-value taxation and a strict free market stance was understood only by initiates; to most others, the two positions seemed incompatible. He also emphasized that the political chances of a single-issue party are remote, but that when such a party adds other issues to its program, it invites internal dissension and fragmentation.

VIII

The Land Bills of 1963

THE SOCIAL DEMOCRATS came into power in 1960 as the majority party of a new coalition. They had decided not to increase the taxation of land values, but they wanted to neutralize land speculation in another way. So, in 1963 they presented to the Parliament a series of bills which would accomplish this result, chiefly through greater ease of public acquisition, higher taxes on profits from the sale of land, new rules for valuation of agricultural land, and increased regulation of land use.

The bills were passed by Parliament, but a non-socialist opposition could demand that they be submitted to a public referendum. Knowing the result of the survey made by the Gallup Market Analysis Institute (mentioned above), the opposition raised an extraordinarily violent agitation against the bills, which were accordingly rejected by a vast majority in the referendum. But some years later, almost identical bills passed in Parliament one by one, without significant resistance.

IX

The Abolition of Tax on Incremental Land Values

ARHUS UNIVERSITY PROFESSOR Gunnar Thorlund Jepsen analyzed the reasons for the abolition in 1965 of the tax on incremental land values (TIL).[6] He criticized the fact that the TIL had been introduced without taking into account some essential technical problems, which he discussed. But he found that the reasons in 1965 for the abolition of the TIL were more political than economic. Our English summary of his book ends with the following:

The abolition of the TIL, however, was not due to these consequences [technical failures in the law, etc.] as much as to purely political reasons. In 1963, a referendum overthrew some land provisions suggested by the government. The revulsion of public feelings which followed in the wake of this referendum gave the opponents of the TIL an opportunity to abolish it completely. It is a paradox that this took place during the significant inflation of land values in the 1960s.

Nonetheless, the development during the 1960s created a political desire to tax particularly large capital gains on land. On the other hand, it was generally conceded that the Georgist way of taxing land was too unpopular to be tried again. It was felt that windfalls on land must be captured by a once-for-all levy, but that this levy should be designed in such a way that it would not impede trade or be passed on to the buyer. The result of these reflections was a combination of provisions:

1. A tax levied when land is released from agricultural use.

2. A tax levied at the first sale within urban areas.

3. An obligation on the part of the municipality to buy at the assessed price within four years after release from agricultural use.

4. An obligation on the part of the owner to offer his land to the municipality before selling it to private persons.

The first of these provisions will lower the price of land in agricultural areas. The second provision will force most of the land owners to sell their land just after it has been released for urban use, because the profit they might otherwise gain by postponing that sale is greatly diminished by the tax. In combination with the obligation of the municipality to buy, these provisions will undoubtedly cause the municipalities to take over most of the new land in urban areas. That the community is caused to take over the land and thus capture future rent is in harmony with the Georgist view. In some way, it is a paradox that a tax system which apparently is in much greater disharmony with the Georgist tax view than is the TIL, better fulfills in its effects the intentions behind this tax philosophy.

X

The Lessons and Consequences

WITH THE ABOLITION in 1965 of the tax on incremental land values, the Social Democrats proved that they had learned that the better part of valor was to accommodate the land owners and their supporters.

Had the tax on incremental land values been changed instead of being abolished, it would have levied sufficient revenue to avoid more taxes on income and consumption (Moms, a value added tax, was introduced a few years later, and today takes 25 percent of all spending on consumption). And it would have sharply discouraged the reckless assumption of indebtedness among farmers and others, who some years later came into troubles during economic crises. But of course, then the landowners would not have been able to collect the great boom in land values, that from 1960 to 1970 increased by 400 percent, and to 1995 by 2,500 percent.

Several Danish economists express now and then that they are well aware of the great advantages land-value taxation could provide for the nation's economy. But as long as the Danish population does not want increased land-value taxation, they say a proposal for it has no practical chances of success. This is notwithstanding the fact that because of land being immovable and impossible to hide away, from an administrative standpoint alone, land values are a much better source of taxation than income, consumption, and savings in the European Union with its loudly praised free mobility for money, goods, and labor.

The Justice Party today is not represented in the Danish Parliament, nor has it been for 15 years. In the mid-1990's, it decided to cease offering candidates for public office, and instead confine itself to endorsing sympathetic candidates from other parties. However, in the Autumn of 1999, the party decided to start collecting enough signatures to qualify it again for inclusion on the ballot in time for the next election of members to the Parliament.

In the Parliament, Danish Georgists can find supporters among Social Democrats, other socialist party members and the Radicals, who will maintain and protect the existing ground duty levied for local revenue, and therefore also maintain the existing Institute of Assessment and Valuation of Land.

However, on May 26, 1999, the Danish tax minister's website published the text of the report of his committee for modernizing the property tax system. It proposed the abolition of the separate assessment of land values, recommending that, in the future, land and buildings be lumped together for assessment purposes. The ostensible reason for this proposal was to meet the tax minister's desire for simplification, so as to forestall further complaints about the assessment of land values. According to the committee's report, people in general find it difficult to understand the concept of ground duty.

The Danish Georgists consider the report politically inspired, and dismiss the reason given for the proposal as shallow and implausible. They claim that combined assessment is no simpler than separate assessment to understand, and would elicit the same complaints. They make the point that if being difficult to understand were a valid reason for abolishing a tax, the income tax should be the first candidate for abolition, since very few people are able to calculate their own income tax.

Attempts launched by Danish Georgists to open a public dialogue on this issue have been ignored by politicians and news media alike. As of this writing, in the Spring of the year 2000, the proposal has not been debated either in Parliament or in the press. It should be mentioned that the tax minister, Ole Stavad, did dissociate himself from the proposal in answer to a question from a member of Parliament on September 6, 1999, but his statement was in no sense a categorical repudiation of it. Thoughtful observers fear that it will be passed as part of a packet of bills in the annual political tug-of-war over the budget, without ever having really been subjected to the attention and scrutiny of the electorate.

XI

Estimate of the Rent of Land in Denmark

THE ASSESSED LAND values (selling prices) should provide a base for estimating the rent of land. If we, for instance, assume that the land values express capitalization of that part of the annual rent that is not collected by public authorities, and the land is valued at 1,000, when the rate of interest is 10 percent, the uncollected rent would be 100. If the land value taxes are 50, the total rent would be 150. In this case, we have a situation where one third of the rent is captured by the system of land-value taxation.

Some might argue that all taxes work in the direction of decreasing the land values and so not only the land value taxes but all other taxes as well should be added to the rent. But our calculation does not take such aspects into account. The land value tax is taken, without question, from the rent. How other taxes might affect the rent is a much more complicated issue which goes beyond the purview of this chapter. The purpose here is merely to give an estimate of the rent, not to calculate what the rent could have been if circumstances had been different.

Table 2

								Land Taxes as % of Total Rent		Rent as % of GDP
Year	Land Values	Land Improvements	Value of Rude Land	Interest on Bonds	Untaxed Rent	Land Taxes	Total Rent		GDP	

<table>
<tr><td colspan="11" align="center">LAND VALUES AND RENT OF LAND IN DENMARK
FOR SELECTED YEARS 1950–1997
(Amounts in Mio. Dkr.)</td></tr>
<tr><td>Year</td><td>Land Values</td><td>Land Improvements</td><td>Value of Rude Land</td><td>Interest on Bonds</td><td>Untaxed Rent</td><td>Land Taxes</td><td>Total Rent</td><td>Land Taxes as % of Total Rent</td><td>GDP</td><td>Rent as % of GDP</td></tr>
<tr><td>1950</td><td>9,267</td><td>184</td><td>9,083</td><td>4.7</td><td>427</td><td>219</td><td>646</td><td>33.9</td><td>23,132</td><td>2.8</td></tr>
<tr><td>1956</td><td>12,504</td><td>571</td><td>11,933</td><td>6.2</td><td>740</td><td>363</td><td>1,103</td><td>32.9</td><td>33,380</td><td>3.3</td></tr>
<tr><td>1960</td><td>17,175</td><td>785</td><td>16,390</td><td>6.1</td><td>1,000</td><td>484</td><td>1,484</td><td>32.6</td><td>44,430</td><td>3.3</td></tr>
<tr><td>1965</td><td>41,078</td><td>1,875</td><td>39,200</td><td>8.2</td><td>3,214</td><td>684</td><td>3,898</td><td>17.5</td><td>76,065</td><td>5.1</td></tr>
<tr><td>1969</td><td>67,419</td><td>3,405</td><td>64,014</td><td>9.5</td><td>6,081</td><td>1,082</td><td>7,163</td><td>15.1</td><td>107,319</td><td>6.7</td></tr>
<tr><td>1973</td><td>103,484</td><td>6,040</td><td>97,444</td><td>12.5</td><td>12,181</td><td>2,130</td><td>14,311</td><td>14.9</td><td>172,860</td><td>8.3</td></tr>
<tr><td>1977</td><td>194,274</td><td>9,309</td><td>184,965</td><td>16.2</td><td>29,964</td><td>3,110</td><td>33,074</td><td>9.4</td><td>279,310</td><td>11.8</td></tr>
<tr><td>1981</td><td>229,650</td><td>8,182</td><td>221,468</td><td>19.0</td><td>42,079</td><td>4,671</td><td>46,750</td><td>10.0</td><td>407,790</td><td>11.5</td></tr>
<tr><td>1986</td><td>385,819</td><td>15,937</td><td>369,882</td><td>10.7</td><td>39,577</td><td>5,285</td><td>44,862</td><td>11.8</td><td>666,496</td><td>6.7</td></tr>
<tr><td>1992</td><td>429,154</td><td>17,728</td><td>411,426</td><td>10.3</td><td>42,377</td><td>8,338</td><td>50,715</td><td>16.4</td><td>887,868</td><td>5.7</td></tr>
<tr><td>1995</td><td>430,424</td><td>17,780</td><td>412,644</td><td>7.4</td><td>30,536</td><td>8,280</td><td>38,816</td><td>21.3</td><td>1,009,756</td><td>3.8</td></tr>
<tr><td>1997</td><td>463,677</td><td>17,313</td><td>446,364</td><td>6.2</td><td>27,675</td><td>8,229</td><td>35,904</td><td>22.9</td><td>1,114,332</td><td>3.2</td></tr>
<tr><td colspan="11">Source: Statistics Denmark (The Danish Statistical Office)</td></tr>
</table>

Table 2 shows a calculation of the rent by the means of the method described above. The value of improvements is deducted from the land values before estimating the rent.

The table should be taken as a very rough guess as to the size of the rent. One assumption is that if we double the rate of interest, the land value should be lowered by 50 percent. The rent is not affected. However, the table shows that when the rate of interest increases or decreases, the rent goes in the same direction. For instance, it is difficult to believe that the rent as a percentage of Gross Domestic Product was 11.5 in 1981, but only 6.7 in 1986. What is the reason for this bias? One explanation could of course be that the official land assessments are inaccurate. Another explanation could be that the selling prices of land change slowly as the rate of interest changes; if so, our calculation should be based, not on interest rate for the year, but rather on an average of interest rates for a number of years before the year in question.

However, such alternative calculations become very quickly pure guesses not better than the first guess. The general picture of the development seems clear. The rent as a share of GDP has increased since 1950 and reached a maximum in 1977–81. Since then the rent share has fallen again but it is probably not quite true when the figures show that the share has nearly returned to the 1950 level.

Some readers may wonder why the rent of land in Denmark in 1995 was only Mio. Dkr 38,816 and in 1997 only 35,904. The answer is that the rent of land will decrease when taxes are increased, and increase when taxes are decreased. Therefore, since the tax burden in Denmark is one of the highest in the world, the rent of land is correspondingly low.

Notes

1. Viggo Starke, *The History of Land Taxation in Denmark* (London: International Union for Land-Value Taxation and Free Trade, 1949), p. 3.

2. Kristian Kolding, *Danmarks Retsforbund* (Copenhagen, 1958), p. 24.

3. Michael Silagi, *Henry George and Europe* (Will and Dorothy Burnham Lissner, eds.; trans. from the German by Susan N. Faulkner; New York: Robert Schalkenbach Foundation, 2000), p. 141.

4. Detailed information about practical assessments of land values in Denmark was given by Anders Müller and Gregers Morch-Lassen in Ronald Banks, ed., *Costing the Earth* (London: Shepheard-Walwyn, 1989).

5. In this chapter, the term "state" is used as a synonym for national.

6. Up to this point, the text is largely based on that of K. J. Kristensen in the first (1955) edition of *Land-Value Taxation Around the World*.

7. Viggo Starke, *Triumf eller Fiasko?* (Triumph or Fiasco?) (Copenhagen: Vendelkar, 1970), pp. 205–209.

8. "The Gallup Institute of Copenhagen enjoyed a somewhat lesser confidence in its accuracy than did the leading American polling organization of that name. Its market analyses, however, were all well regarded; its monthly political samplings were carefully scanned by party leaders, and its election forecasts came considerably within the range of two to three percent of admissible error. The franchise for Copenhagen coverage was reserved for *Berlingske Tidende*, largest of the dailies." (Quotation from the below-mentioned essay of Louis Wasserman.)

9. Louis Wasserman was a professor of philosophy and government at San Francisco State College (now University). His essay, 20 pages in length, shows his profound knowledge of the historical, political, and economic background on which the land-value tax system of Denmark was developed.

10. At the establishment of the Ground Duty Government, the parties involved issued a statement in which (among other things) they promised to increase land-value taxation as much as possible.

11. Gunnar Thorlund Jepsen, *Fra grundstigningsskyld til frigorelsesafgift* (From tax on incremental land values to tax on release) (Arhus: Arhus Universitets Institut, 1970).

Count Christian Detlev Reventlow who, as state minister in 1802, called for a new hartkorn tax levied to cover the land under the manor houses, thereby anticipating Henry George.

Chapter 11

Estonia

BY AIVAR TOMSON*

ESTONIA IS A small Baltic republic with an area of 17,462 square miles and a population of 1,408,523. Except for a large Russian minority, its inhabitants are closely related to the Finns in race, language, and religion. Tallinn, the capital, is the largest city, with an estimated population of 423,990 in 1996. Between the 13th century and 1561, Estonia was ruled successively by the Danes, the Germans (Teutonic Knights), and the Poles. In 1561, it came under Swedish rule, but passed officially to the Russian Empire with the Treaty of Nystad, which ended the Great Northern War in 1710. It declared its independence during World War I, and remained free until 1940 when it was invaded by the Soviet Union, which annexed it as the "Estonian Soviet Socialist Republic." The following year it was occupied by Nazi Germany, which held it until it came under Soviet rule again in 1944. In 1991 it regained its independence.

*Aivar Tomson has been vice-director of Kinnisvarackspert Ltd., a valuation and market research firm, since 1993, except for a period during which he headed a country-wide mass valuation project for the Estonian National Land Board. Prior to 1993, he served as a specialist for the National Land Board, developing a cadastral register and mass valuation system. He is an engineering/land surveying diplomate of the University of Helsinki, where he also completed doctoral examinations. He is co-author, with Tambet Tiits, of the chapter, "Land Value Taxation in Estonia," in William McCluskey, ed., *Property Tax: An International Comparative Review* (1999), and author of numerous articles in his native language.

I

History and Exposition of the Land Tax

UP UNTIL ITS first modern period of independence, much of Estonia was made up of large estates owned by the nobility, which was of chiefly German ancestry. These were broken up after World War I, and the land distributed to workers on the former estates, as well as to men who had fought to gain the country's freedom. Under Communism, both agriculture and industry were nationalized. By 1950, four-fifths of the agricultural land had been turned into collective farms.

With the return of independence In 1991, private ownership began to be reestablished. The present land tax was introduced in 1993 as part of a monetary and fiscal reform carried out between 1991 and 1993. Its main characteristics are as follows:

- It is based on market value of the land only (i.e., exclusive of improvements).
- The tax is paid both by owners of private land and by users/occupiers of public land, since privatization has not yet been completed.
- Tax rates are determined annually by municipalities, and now vary between 0.5 and 2.0 percent. (Before 1997, the tax rates were between 0.8 and 1.2 percent.) Agricultural land is taxed from 0.3 to 1.0 percent until the end of 2000.
- Although the tax is national, 100 percent of the collected revenue is allocated to municipalities.
- Only limited groups of properties are entitled to exemption.
- Because of the absence of a complete national cadastre, municipalities keep land records (registers) at the local level, supplementing whatever information may be available from the national cadastre (which covered approximately half the total land area in mid-1999) with their own information. When the national cadastre is complete, this municipal responsibility will cease.
- The National Land Board is responsible for assessment, and the National Tax Board, for collection.

The land tax was introduced as a shared tax between local and central government. In 1996, it was decided to allocate the entire revenue derived from it to local government. Local authorities are under no special restrictions as to how it may be spent.

It is important to note the distinction between a land tax and a land-value tax, since historically there have been land taxes, such as the disastrous ryot tax in 19th century British India, which was a set amount levied without respect to the land's economic rent. In Estonia, although referred to simply as a land tax, the tax is defined by law as a land-value tax, since the statute bases it on market value. At the beginning, however, it did not really function as a genuine land-value tax. Although it was supposed to be based on market value, a true land market had not yet developed. Therefore, at least in urban areas, it fell on a fixed percentage attributed to the land component of real estate, using regional formulas that varied drastically from one region to another. In Tallinn, for example, it was assumed that the "relative price" of a site was twenty percent of the combined value of land and improvements; in Tartu, ten percent.[1] (At the time, there were no downtown land transfers, so the formulas made use of market information from surrounding areas, as well as from downtown transfers in foreign cities, etc.) By now, however, the real estate market has developed to the point where there is a sufficient record of genuine sales transactions on which to base land assessments. It is realized that in most cases downtown land values were underestimated, because the actual transactions that have now occurred there have been at a higher level.

Tax revenues from land are continuing to increase—from 118 million EEK in 1994 to 320 million EEK in 1999. (The EEK or Estonian kroon exchanged at 14.62 to the US dollar in September, 1999.) The increase is the result of higher tax rates, revaluation in 1996, and higher collection efficiency. The last revaluation took place in 2000, but figures for it were not available in time to be included here. The land tax represents 1.0 to 1.2 percent of all tax revenues and approximately 0.4 percent of GDP.[2] It accounts for only an average of 4 percent of local budget revenues, although it can run as much as 20 or even 30 percent in some rural and peripheral regions.

Apart from these minor exceptions (the population being nearly three-quarters urban), the percentages currently in place are scarcely high. Yet the collection even of such modest amounts reportedly has encouraged some property owners who stood to benefit by keeping their land idle under the restitution provisions of the Property Reform and Land Reform Acts of 1991, either to develop it or to sell it.

From the very outset, the Estonian system has availed itself of the support and technical expertise of various foreign and international organizations as well as of governmental agencies from certain Scandinavian countries. The deepest cooperation has been with OECD and PHARE with respect to tax administration, and with the Finnish government with respect to valuation.

II

Evaluation

THE ADVANTAGES OF Estonia's land tax may be summarized as follows:[3]

- It encourages more efficient and economical use of land.
- Its impact on the general economy is benign compared to the taxation of both land and improvements.
- It has the potential to serve as a useful instrument in land policy decisions.
- Its collection efficiency is very high (98 percent in 1998).

Despite these unexceptionable advantages, critics have objected to the land tax on the following grounds:

- It brings in less than two percent of the total tax revenue.
- Approximately one third of the revenue collected from it is in fact paid by the central government.
- The concept of ability to pay (which is how many public revenue theorists interpret the canon of tax equity) is better reflected by a property tax based on the combined value of land and improvements than by one based on the value of land alone.

The first objection is readily answered by pointing out that the problem is not with the tax as such, but with the fact that its rates are set too low. They could be raised to the full annual value of the land without distorting the economy. To the extent that they were raised and other tax rates proportionately lowered, productive activity would be stimulated and total tax revenue thereby increased.

The second objection has to do with unoccupied public land put up for auction. If it is posed merely to underscore what a small percentage of the total revenue is raised by the tax, the answer has been given in the paragraph immediately above. Otherwise, the objection must be, in fact, directed not to the tax but merely to the political decision to allocate 25 percent of the income from the auction of state land to local government—an issue that lies outside the purview of this discussion.

The third objection is more complicated. Generally speaking, a land-value tax tends to be more progressive than does a property tax based on the value of both land and improvements because it will be borne wholly by owners rather than being partly passed on to renters, who are, of course, less likely to be wealthy. The objection, however, has to do with special considerations such as the uneven development of a land market in Estonia, which puts taxpayers at a disadvantage in poorer, more rural, areas, where turnover is low yet agricultural and forest land are subject to taxation. At present, Tallinn and its neighboring municipalities, the nation's richest region, accounts for approximately 70 to 80 percent of the turnover, yet has about 40 percent of the total population and pays only about 30 percent of the land tax. With increasing privatization, a more uniform land market may be expected, and with it, the disappearance of such anomalies.

Notes

1. For a comprehensive discussion of the methods employed in estimating Estonian land values, see Kaisa Vuorio and Jussi Palmu, "Definition of the Market Value for Urban Land in the Absence of a Land Market," unpublished working paper, Helsinki, Huoneistomarkkinointi.

2. European Community Commission—PHARE Programme, Taxation of Land and Buildings in Estonia—Present and Future. An overall progress report submitted to Estonian authorities, June 1998. Contact person:

Anders Müller, Ministry of Taxation, Central Customs and Tax Administration, Copenhagen, Denmark.

3. Tambet Tiits and Aivar Tomson, "Land value taxation in Estonia," in W. McCluskey, ed., *Property Tax: an International Comparative Review* (Aldershot: Ashgate Publishing Ltd., 1999), pp. 383–384.

Chapter 12

Finland

BY PEKKA V. VIRTANEN*

THE PURPOSE OF this chapter is to describe the land-related taxes in Finland and recent changes in them, and to discuss some positive and negative effects of these taxes on land use policy.

Finland is a parliamentary democracy, one of Europe's Nordic countries, and since 1995 a member of the European Union. It was a part of Sweden until 1809, and from that time until 1917 a domestically autonomous Grand Duchy of Russia, with its own language, legislature, etc., but with a common foreign policy. It became independent in 1917.

Finland has a population of around five million and a land area of 305,000 sq. km. (as well as many lakes). This area is divided into 45² independent municipalities. In Finland, as in other Nordic countries, municipalities have a central and strong position in the

*Pekka V. Virtanen, who retired in 1995 as professor of urban and regional planning at the Helsinki University of Technology, received the Doctor of Technology degree from that institution in 1975. He began his career as a surveyor, and then spent 11 years as a regional planning director before entering the professoriate. He has written books on land and land use policy, valuation of urban land, regional and national physical planning, and rural planning. The number of his articles in professional journals exceeds 200.

The author is grateful to Ms. Eila Närhi and Mr. Kari Pilhjerta, National Board of Taxation, for checking to make sure that this chapter is up-to-date. In addition to those referenced in the endnotes, the following sources have been used: Johannes Hakala, ed., *Kaytännön metsätieto. Käsikirja metsänomistajille* (Handbook for Forest Owners) (Kajaani: Metsälehti, 1987); Komiteamietintö 1989-2, *Küntiestöverotoimikunnan meitintö* (Committee Report on Real Estate Taxation) (Helsinki: Painastuskeskus, 1989; Lasse Lovén, *Forest Taxation in Finland* (Stencilled copy, 1986); Ministry of Finance, *Taxation in Finland* (English original) (Helsinki: Painastuskeskus, 1995); and A. Rajamäki, O. Nykänen, and E. Laanterä, *Kiinteistöverotuksen käsikirja* (Handbook for Real Estate Taxation) (Jyväskylä, Suomen talokeskus, 1987).

administration system. This position is accentuated by the municipal income and property taxes.

Land ownership is predominantly private (60 percent); the state owns 29 percent, but the main part of this consists of the wilderness in the north (Lapland); big companies own eight percent, and the rest belongs to municipalities and church.[1] Even if the share of municipalities is very small compared to the whole of Finland, it is quite essential in the urban areas. For example, the city of Helsinki owns approximately 65 percent of all land inside its borders.

As to land use, Finland is mainly covered by forests (87 percent) and arable land (nine percent). Urban areas comprise one percent and the rest (three percent) goes for traffic, military purposes, etc..

I

Forest Taxation

TWO-THIRDS OF the total land area is so-called "actual forest land" which annually produces at least one cubic meter timber per hectare. Typical for Finland is the large number of small forest holdings. Traditionally, the most typical forest holding (or forestry unit) has been the forest of a farm, but the number of owners in other professions has increased continuously. Divisions of inheritance have resulted in the present situation where about one half of the privately-owned forests are owned by non-farmers.

Beginning in 1922, forest taxation in Finland was based on the estimated average value of the annual increment of the growing stock (=yield taxation). Forest income thus resembled capital income for taxation purposes. It could also be viewed as land value taxation in the spirit of Henry George since the "forest income tax" had to be paid every year regardless of whether timber was sold or not.[2] This old system had many advantages, but it was done away with a few years ago (Act 1535/1992, Income Tax Act). In the new system, the tax is based on the actual (stumpage) revenue and the tax rate is the same as generally in capital taxation (25 percent in 1995 and 28 percent in 1998). This new law began to be applied in the 1993 year's taxation, but forest owners could also choose the old system for a transition period which lasts until the year 2006, and approximately one third of them have done so.

Under the old system, the taxable income of the forest owner consists of the estimated average net yield of forest land and of the value of labor which he/she has performed by working on timber or transporting timber in connection with delivery sale from his/her own forest.

Net yield from forest land is determined as a result of five basic factors: (1) area and quality of forest land; (2) annual growth of the growing stock; (3) structure of timber yield; (4) value of "tax cubic meter"; (5) costs of timber production.

The quality of forest land is determined by a special forest assessment procedure called "tax classification." In it, forest land is divided on maps into five tax classes according to their productivity. The results of tax classification are collected into a special automatic data processing register. Reforesting of agricultural land and basic improvements of forestry land continuously increase the area of actual forest land and change its quality. Therefore, the tax classifications lag behind the real productivity, and thus forest lands have often been under-assessed.

Annual growth in different tax classes (measured in "tax cubic meters") is determined areawise by the central government on the basis of research done by the Finnish Forest Research Institute.

When the annual net yield is calculated, the forest owner is allowed to make certain deductions on the basis of average management and administrative costs. Also, some temporary tax exemptions are used in order to support certain positive measures concerning forests. When farmland is afforested or peatlands drained, the owner gets a certain tax relief. (New tax exemptions for drainage have not been admitted since 1988.) Also, the regeneration of forests is so important that certain kinds of tax relief are given to regeneration areas.

Since tax relief is given for regeneration as well as forest management, care, and administration, the tax falls chiefly upon the natural element (land in the economic sense), even though no formal or absolute distinction is made between virgin and planted timber. At the same time, inasmuch as improvements resulting from the application of labor and capital continuously increase the quality and hence the tax classification of forest parcels, assessments (while generally lagging behind actual gain in productivity) tend to counteract this state of affairs by more and more reflecting improvement value rather than land value strictly understood.

In the new system, which is based upon the actual revenue from the sale of timber, the income is seen as income from capital. For tax purposes, it is calculated so that from the gross income the owner can deduct all expenses connected with that income. They may relate to forest management, care, and administration, and they are deductible according to the documents in bookkeeping.

Because all capital income of the taxpayer is handled as a totality, it is not possible to say in blanket terms how severe this taxation of forest really is. If, for example, a forest owner also has some rentable apartments he/she can deduct repair costs of these apartments even from the forest income. The capital tax rate was 25 percent in 1995 and increased to 29 percent by 2000.

A comparison of the two systems would seem to indicate that the old system was more favorable to the reasonable and effective use of forest land. Also, some evidence exists that the changeover to the new system has encouraged efforts to abuse it.

II

Taxation of Agricultural Land

BEFORE THE YEAR 1968, agricultural land was taxed in the same way as forestry land in the "old system," i.e., according to the estimated average yield. For that purpose, agricultural lands were classified according to their productivity, and the taxable income and capital were then calculated according to a certain system. Since 1968, the income taxation of agriculture is based upon real income which is shown by bookkeeping.

III

Taxation of Capital

ACCORDING TO THE Capital Tax Act (1537/1992), land is included in the term "capital." One basic rule in the taxation of capital is that real estate (i.e., land plus improvements) is assessed at its market value. There are some exceptions, and the most important ones are those concerning forestral and agricultural lands. This tax—as well as above mentioned taxes on forests and agricultural land—is a national tax, and thus differs from the municipal real property tax.

The determination of the value of forest for capital taxation is a purely political decision, with little weight given to the real capital value (market value). On the average, the taxation value of the forest is about 1/3 of the market value, but the variations are great depending upon the growth phase.

In the taxation of capital, the assessed value of agricultural land is determined by a certain calculation which has no real connection with the actual capital value (market value), but is much lower. In practice, the taxable value of agricultural land in Finland is about five percent of market value. This has, together with some other factors, resulted in rather high prices of agricultural land. (Another reason for that has been the ample state subsidy to agriculture, but now this situation may change as a result of the European Union).

The tax scale for the taxation of wealth (=net wealth) was for the year 1998 as follows: Taxable wealth of less than 1.1 million FMK (about 0.25 million US dollars) is free from taxation. For wealth of 1.1 million FMK, the tax is 500 FMK (or about 0.05 percent) and for a wealth exceeding this limit, the tax rate is 0.9 percent. This rate applies to individuals and the estates of deceased persons; for corporate bodies, the rate is one percent.

IV

Tax on Sales Profits

IN THE RATHER new Income Tax Act (Tuloverolaki, Act 1535/1992), there are rules about the taxation of sales profits. It is a national tax applied to the profits coming from the sale of capital goods including land. In principle, the sales profit is defined as selling price minus acquisition cost. If that cost can not be found, or in certain other cases, this profit is determined by fixed rates of calculation.

For example, with property acquired from 1999 on, the calculated "acquisition cost" is always at least 20 percent of the selling price, and if the seller has owned the property ten years or longer, this deduction is at least 50 percent.

Some sales profits are tax-free. The most important case is when one's own dwelling is sold; these sales are wholly tax-free if one has lived in that dwelling at least two years. Then there are partially tax-free sales when property is expropriated or could have been expropriated. In these cases, the exemption from taxes is implemented so that at least 80 percent is deducted from the selling price. This latter rule is good for municipal land policy because land owners then prefer selling to municipalities. In order to discourage landowners from waiting to do so, since some municipalities are in urgent need of suitable sites for housing and urban development, the Income Tax Act was amended in 1990 to provide that this partial exemption of sales profits cease on 30 June, 2000.

V

Real Property Tax

In 1992, Finland got a new Act on Municipal Tax on Real Property (Kiinteistöverolaki, Act 654/1992). This is an annual municipal tax which is put on most building sites. (All other taxes dealt with in this chapter are national ones.) Forests and agricultural areas are exempt as well as military areas, churches, cemeteries, and foreign embassies. The limits for tax rates are given in the law, and municipal councils can make their decisions inside these limits.

The "general tax rate" is valid for the specified land and many buildings. It was originally limited to 0.2–0.8 percent of the assessed value, but after two amendments (in 1998 and 1999, respectively), until 2000 to 0.2–1.0 percent, and from 2000 onward to 0.5–1.0 percent. However, there are some exceptions: The rate for buildings for permanent housing was 0.1–0.4 percent until 2000, and 0.22–0.50 percent from 2000 onward. But buildings for other than permanent housing may be given a higher tax rate within certain limits. In practice, this applies mostly to summer cottages.

Still higher rates (up to 2.2 percent) apply to power plant buildings.

The most recent amendment also contains a new section providing for a special "penalty tax" on vacant lots in urban areas, raising their tax rate to 1.0–3.0 percent-representing, at the highest end, a trebling of the normal tax. The purpose, of course, is to bring such lots into the market or spur their owners to develop them.

VI

Assessment of Building Land

THE ASSESSMENT OF building land is discussed here in its own section because the results of this assessment are applied to all taxes where building land values are needed, e.g., tax on capital, tax on sales profits, real estate tax, inheritance and gift tax, and transfer tax. These objects are assessed only once (periodically) even if taxes go partially to the national government and partially to the municipality.

According to the old Income and Wealth Tax Act of 1974, building land should be assessed at its market value. In practice, this goal was not achieved. The assessed values lagged behind for two main reasons. First, central taxation authorities abandoned the goal written in the law, and, instead of market value, they tried to set a level of 70 percent of the market price (in order to protect taxpayers against possible over-assessment). Second, there was for a long time a certain nonchalance about legislation among those local taxation boards which, in earlier years, determined the assessed values.

To help the local taxation boards in their work and to make this taxation more uniform, in 1981 the National Board of Taxes prepared, with the help of the Technical Research Center of Finland, directives for assessment of building land. These directives are based on normal real estate valuation principles and are appended with land maps for each urban area.

The basic idea of the National Board of Taxes was that the under-assessed values should be gradually raised so that they could rather quickly reach the goal level. Another idea was that those land value maps should be checked every five years, and that no annual adjustments are needed during interim periods. This resulted in continuous lagging behind the market value.[3] In practice, these reassessments after 1981 took place in 1986 and 1994.

To correct the existing defects, some new rules have been adopted. In 1988, a new Income and Wealth Tax Act was stipulated (1240/1988) and it changed the assessment rules so that since 1989 the directives given by the National Board of Taxes are binding on the local taxation boards; they must follow the values given in (renewed) value maps. The last renewed value map was given for the 1994 taxation year, and that is based upon the market value. Since 1994, these value maps have been revised annually, and the amendments have been small.

Building sites in rural areas are assessed normally as building land, not as agricultural or forestry land. The "target value" is here, as in urban areas, 70 percent of market value. So-called "raw land" or future development land (which has not yet a town plan, but which already is sold at rather high prices) is normally under-assessed, i.e., assessed as agricultural or forestry land.

VII

Other Land-Related Taxes and Payments

A. Inheritance and Gift Tax

There is a special Inheritance and Gift Tax Act (Act 378/1940, last amendment 1561/ 1995). According to this act, real property must be assessed according to the market value. The inheritance tax is graduated into three classes according to the "nearness" of family connection. The nearest relatives pay about 10–16 percent and the most distant heirs, threefold. The gift tax is determined according to the same rules as inheritance tax.

B. Stamp Duty (or Transfer Tax)

The buyer of real estate must pay this "tax" when he/she applies for the obligatory official registration of ownership. The amount to be paid as of 1998, is four percent of the selling price (or market value).

There is also a transfer tax for the conveyance of shares, and it is only 1.6 percent of the purchase price (or of the assessed value). This has offered a way to avoid the normal- and higher-transfer tax for real estate deals: the owner sets up a company to own the given real estate, and then he/she can sell the shares of his company instead of selling the actual real estate. The saving—2.4 percent of the price—is normally divided between buyer and seller.

To sell shares is also easier than selling real estate *per se* because real estate must be sold according to special legal rules; e.g., the deal must be confirmed by a notary public, and the deal is registered in the official market price register for real estate. The selling of shares is free of such regulations.

VIII

Some Conclusions

THE ROLE OF land value taxation in the Finnish tax system has been quite essential because of the "old forest tax." Disregarding the warning of many experts, this tax was removed in 1992. The same year, Finland got a new Municipal Act on Real Property which gives municipalities a right to put a higher tax rate on land as compared to improvements. Even if the tax rates are quite modest, the impacts of this tax can be seen to be positive.

The yield of the real property tax was 2.7 billion FMK in 1998, which makes about five percent of the total municipal tax revenue; about 25 percent of that tax comes from land, and 75 percent from improvements.[4] The state collects many taxes which, for some part, are based upon land values (e.g., income, capital, inheritance, and gift taxes) but there are no statistics to show the land's share in these. The total state tax revenue in 1997 was roughly the following:[5]

Income and wealth taxes	53 billion FMK
VAT	54 "
Import duties	4 "
Sumptuary taxes	5 "
Others (transfer taxes, etc.)	9 "
Total	145 billion FMK

The above mentioned sums do not include any pension or health insurance payments.

The assessment of land values has not been problematic in theory, but in practice it has lagged some years behind the real price development.

Pollution taxes or other payments based upon environmental degradation do not exist yet in Finland, but they are under discussion now.

Notes

1. Pekka V. Virtanen, *Maankäytön perustiesta* (Basic Facts of Land Use). (Hämeenlinna: Otatieto, 1995), p. 163.

2. Lasse Rauskala, *Forest taxation and roundwood supply in Finland.* (Helsinki: Metsäntutkimuslaitos tiedonanto 176, 1985) pp. 1–2.

3. Pekka V. Virtanen, "Rakennusmaahan kohdistuva verotus ei ole tasapuolista" (Taxation of Building Land is Not Equitable), *Verotus*, No. 5, (1985).

4. Suomen Kuntaliitto (Finnish Association of Local and Regional Authorities), Kunnallinen verotilasto 1998 (Municipal Tax Statistics, 1998) (Internet, 1999).

5. Valtiovarainministeriö, vero osasto (Tax Department, Ministry of Finance), Tilastotietoja veroista vuodelta 1997 (Tax Statistics, 1997), (Stencil, 1999).

Urban landscape.

Forest landscape.

Chapter 13

Germany

BY JÜRGEN G. BACKHAUS*

LAND-VALUE TAXATION in Germany has a very long and multifaceted history. This history began several centuries before Henry George's writings appeared. His work was, however, well received in Germany, and he became part of a larger intellectual movement, which also gathered political momentum. This political momentum translated into imperial and municipal legislation. The land reform movement, of which Henry George's ideas became an integral part, had a dual focus: to offer a solution to the problem of urban squalor, and to present a developmental strategy for optimal resource use. The latter aspect, in Germany, became particularly pressing after two economic catastrophes following military defeats suffered by the nation in 1918 and 1945. The task of reconstruction required specific tools of taxation. Similarly, re-unification of Germany in 1990 presented the country with the massive challenge of reconstructing the East after the collapse of the German Democratic Republic which had, in particular during its last years, practiced massive disinvestment.

This historical and intellectual situation in Germany just broadly outlined, suggests the following structure of this chapter: In the

*Jürgen G. Backhaus, professor of public economics, Maastricht University, holds both Ph.D. and J.S.D. degrees from the University of Constance. In 1994, he founded (with Frank Stephen) *The European Journal of Law and Economics*, of which he is managing editor. He is sole author of eight, co-author of four, and editor or co-editor of 11 books; not to mention 102 book chapters and articles in refereed journals. Among his books are *Public Enterprise: Forms and Functions* (rev. ed., 1980), *Co-determination: A Legal and Economic Analysis* (1987), and *Werner Sombart: Social Scientist* (3 vols., 1996).

The author wishes to thank Reginald Hansen for extensive suggestions and other help.

first section, the intellectual roots of Georgist ideas in German literature are traced. Secondly, the specific issue of land-value taxation, and in particular land-value increment taxation is explored in some detail.

Thirdly, however, the core of Georgist or quasi-Georgist tax legislation in Germany lies not in the taxation of land per se, but rather in the income tax code as it interconnects with business investment decisions, in particular investment in real estate. The issue has, to the present writer's knowledge, been overlooked in the literature so far. Therefore, section three is devoted to explaining the system theoretically, and illustrating how it operates in practice.

I

Intellectual Roots of German Land Taxation

MAKING LAND RENT a basis for taxation is by no means a modern concept; it has played a significant role in European economic history, at least from the times of the Middle Ages. For example, farm sizes and levies depended on the fertility of land, not the actual product, during feudal times in the Holy Roman Empire (established in the year 800). This indicates that the imputed or economic land rent, and not the income from land use, was the determining factor. The reason for this arrangement, it should be kept in mind, was not equity in taxation. Equity in taxation, as understood by most professional economists but not by Georgists, would have called for basing levies on ability to pay, such as real yields, number of people to be maintained, or other such considerations. Yet household size became an endogenous variable, as marriage licenses were only given upon proof of sufficient means of subsistence and a need for the labor of the likely offspring. Taking the land rent into consideration was a matter of efficiency rather than of equity, since those farmers who did not produce sufficient yields to pay the tax were driven off their farms. In this sense, Schumpeter is perfectly justified in calling the gist of Henry George's proposal "obvious wisdom."[1]

When George's *Progress and Poverty* appeared in German in 1880,[2] it met with widespread approval and appeal.[3] The way in Germany had been paved before George by Friedrich List in 1845. This source is well worth mentioning, because it emphasizes again the efficiency aspect of George's proposal over the equity aspect. Equity had been dominant in John Stuart Mill's writings on taxation, and was also later in those of Adolf Wagner. Curiously, the German literature seems to assume that George accepted the Smithian view of equity as ability to pay, when actually he explicitly rejected it in favor of the principle of payment for benefits received.[4] Friedrich List was writing about the economic development of the Kingdom of Hungary in 1845.[5] Specifically, he said: "If the Hungarian state increases the land rent many fold by undertaking improvements in water and transport infrastructure, the increase often being twenty fold, then the state should at least take half of the added value by means of a tax advance upon the occasion of the transfer of such real estate."[6] This highly specific and sophisticated tax instrument, which shows List as a shrewd expert in public finance, we shall meet again, two generations later and implemented not in Hungary but in China.

In modern legislative history, Napoleon Bonaparte seems to have prefigured List's idea through the so-called "swamp decree" of September 16, 1807, which provided for taxing half of the increase in value of land due to public measures such as draining of wet lands, irrigation of dry lands, building of roads, and establishing public places, etc.[7] None of the early German advocates of land and tax reform went so far as to subscribe to George's notion of limiting the state to only one form of public revenue, i.e., a tax falling wholly on land rent. When this aspect was discussed at all, it was typically dismissed as impractical or otherwise insignificant, or in outright contradiction to received tax theory.[8]

Finally, another factor needs to be addressed which characterizes not only the German literature here surveyed, but with a very few exceptions also the American literature on Henry George's contribution.[9] The land rent which serves as the tax base for George's single tax is defined in terms of a very specific concept of land which is not identical to either soil or the surface of the earth. Yet, the entire literature in Germany to which George is seen to have made an intellectual contribution uses a narrow concept of land (*Boden*) and argues for land reform (*Bodenreform*). Let us first consider how George himself defines his crucial concept of land.

In order to document this important definition, we must look at the precise way in which George sets it forth:

> Land, labor, and capital are the three factors of production. If we remember that capital is thus a term used in contradistinction to land and labor, we at once see that nothing properly included under either one of these terms can be properly classed as capital. The term land necessarily includes, not merely the surface of the earth as distinguished from the water and the air, but the whole material universe outside of man himself, for it is only by having access to land, from which his very body is drawn, that man can come in contact with or use nature. The term land embraces, in short, all natural materials, forces, and opportunities, and therefore, nothing that is freely supplied by nature can be properly classed as capital. A fertile field, a rich vein of ore, a falling stream which supplies power, may give to the possessor advantages equivalent to the possession of capital, but to class such things as capital would be to put an end to the distinction between land and capital, and, as far as they relate to each other, to render the two terms meaningless. The term labor, in like manner, includes all human exertion, and hence human powers whether natural or acquired can never properly be classed as capital.[10]

The reduction of Henry George's residual category of land which includes all natural resources, to land in the colloquial sense of the word, as far as the German literature is concerned is not due to any defect in the translations. Both Gütschow and Dobbert translated the crucial part of the second chapter of Book I of *Progress and Poverty* (quoted above) correctly; hence other reasons must be responsible for this incomplete reception of George's theory. Reducing the category's applications to just land in the sense of the surface of the earth, as the land reform movement did in Germany, substantially curtailed the impact of George's message.

Whereas in the Anglo-Saxon world, George's message was taken up on the one hand by the land reform movement, (John Stuart Mill after all in 1870 had himself founded the Land Tenure

Reform Association) and on the other hand by the single tax movement in America, in Germany it was translated into the demand for a set of specific taxes on incremental land value. Already in the seventies Adolf Wagner had defended taxing the added value of land during the meetings of the *Verein für Socialpolitik*, a demand he later would integrate into his public finance textbook, which appeared in many updated editions. Later, Michael Flürscheim advanced the same ideas,[11] and after the publication of Henry George's *Progress and Poverty*, Adolf Damaschke, a former school teacher,[12] propagated the idea of land value increment taxation specifically and land reform more generally, with great popular success.

After the introduction of a successful scheme of land-value taxation in the German protectorate of Kiao-chau in China, the idea took hold in the German mother country. At the end of 1910, not less than 652 municipalities and counties in the German Reich had adopted a land-value increment tax. The first German city to introduce such a specific tax was Frankfurt-am-Main in 1894, prior to the Kiao-chau experiment. It was abortive, but a repeated effort in 1904 met with success. The Reich similarly instituted a national land-value increment tax, passed on the 15th of February, 1911, and replacing specific state taxes of, for instance, Hamburg, Lübeck, Lippe, and Hesse. This act was complicated, as the municipalities and counties had to participate in the revenue according to different rules, and it turned out that the tax revenue for the Reich was so insignificant that only two years later, in 1913, on the third of July, the constituting states of the Reich and the municipalities and counties received their taxing authority back. The Reich then proceeded to tax wealth, and the act, which remained on the books, became meaningless after the hyper-inflation of 1923.

An interesting feature of tax avoidance appeared along with the rise in municipal land-value increment taxes. Corporations (both joint stock and limited liability) began to form, having as their assets land holdings assessed in their balance sheets at the expected values after development. On the basis of these balance sheets, stock was issued and thereby the capital raised for the planned development. In 1907, 174 such corporations existed in Berlin alone. This form allows for an almost complete sheltering of the added land value from taxation.

Although the successful tax legislation in the German protectorate of Kiao-chau precipitated the spate of municipal and county land-value increment taxes introduced in the first decade of this century in Germany, the political background of the Kiao-chau case is altogether different from and not even comparable to the standard municipal tax. As the consequence of a treaty between the German Empire and the Chinese Empire in 1898, Germany took possession of the harbor of Tsingtao and the area called Kiao-chau[13] in the north of China in order to develop this natural harbor for industry, commerce, and coal mining. Coal having been found a little further inward, a railroad line was soon to be established, allowing its transport to the harbor and then on to world markets. The treaty called for the protectorate to be returned to China after a period of 99 years of successful economic development.[14] Since the land to be developed had been leased and not bought, it made sense from the start to distinguish between the improvements to be made and the land itself. Hence, the Georgist distinction between land rent and improvement value had a natural counterpart in this particular legal arrangement. The implementation rule was simple, and echoes the one suggested by Friedrich List in 1845. Thirty-three and a third percent of the resale value of any piece of property had to be paid to the government upon sale of the property, from which some documented value of improvements could be deducted plus six percent of the total sales price. In addition, every twenty five years, one third of the land-value increase had to be paid as well. These levies were not handled as taxes, but rather held by the government as mortgages, secured by the land title. Now we can realize how this system operated as a developmental strategy. From the very start, the developmental authority, in this case the governor at Tsingtao, held mortgages the value of which depended on the success of the developmental strategy. The mortgages in turn, could be used as collateral for incurring credit, for instance in order to secure bonds. Hence, the funds for the developmental strategy are immediately available upon the start of the developmental activity, that is, when the plan has been finalized and buyers have become interested in the land to be covered by the plan.[15]

II

General Characteristics of German Land Taxation

IN GERMANY, THE system of land taxation in general remained extremely variegated until 1936. Even after the Reich had effectively abandoned its own land taxation in 1913 and assigned the revenue to the municipalities and counties, different constituent states of the Reich still practiced largely different systems, and municipal autonomy including autonomy of taxation had not been carried through in the strong form in which it had existed since the Stein-Hardenberg reforms in early 19th century Prussia.

A common characteristic of land taxation, however, obtained in Germany, and that was its independence from actual realized income or profit from the land. Ever since the medieval form of the land tax, the Bede, efforts were made to establish set charges for each piece of land in view of its ability to produce income, a clear approximation of the land rent. In this very general and somewhat tenuous sense, German land taxation has always been a taxation of the land rent and not the improvements. In 1936, the Prussian minister of finance, Johannes Popitz, also professor of public finance at the University of Berlin (who was later to perish due to his involvement with the coup attempt of July 20, 1944), succeeded in carrying out a real estate tax reform for the entire (now centralized) Reich, assigning the tax revenue to the municipalities and counties. Framework legislation was a function of the central authority, but determination of tax rates a function of the local authority. This is still the system that we have today in the Federal Republic of Germany. More specifically, real estate taxation in Germany is subject to competitive legislation, which means that either the federal government or one of the sixteen constituent states can legislate, but the legislation of the federal government will prevail if both have legislated. The federal government has legislated the real estate tax law (*Grundsteuergesetz*), the assessment act (*Bewer-tungssgesetz*), the personal income tax code

(*Einkommenssteuergesetz*), and the wealth tax act (*Vemögens-steuergesetz*). All these are in different ways relevant for real estate taxation, as are several other acts, such as those relating to succession duties, etc.. The purpose of this legislation is to establish a general framework under which, according to the same basic principles and rules, real estate taxation can take place as set forth by the different municipalities where the real estate is located and to which the tax accrues.

The value of the real estate is, principally, the unitary value established through the procedure set forth in the assessment act. This unitary value, a set number in euro terms, is relevant for all manner of taxation, not only real estate taxation. The unitary value of real estate, for instance, is also relevant for corporate accounting. The unitary value is not a market value. The market value has to be used as a fair market value (*gemeiner Wert*) in case a unitary value has not been established. And third, there is the partial value, (*Teilwert*) in case a particular piece of property is used by different economic entities, conceivably for different purposes.

Real estate is generally classed into three different categories, which then result in two different tax categories. Real estate can conceivably be used for either agriculture or forestry (Tax Category A); or as private property (in household use) either with or without improvements, where the improvements are simply thought to be constructions; or else as property for business use. This can be for commerce, production, or some other legitimate business. These latter two categories of either household or business-related real estate fall under the Tax Category B. The state legislatures can, but need not, legislate the relationship of tax revenues from Tax Categories A and B for the particular municipalities or counties. Here ends the legislative function. At this point, the municipalities and counties enter, and they, using the set of instruments so far described, set the tax rates (*Hebesätze*) for their particular tracts of real estate within their jurisdictions. Hence, since the local communities have to create the circumstances under which successful farming, forestry, commerce, and business can take place, and they therefore largely determine the size of the land rent; they are also able to tax this land rent that they create to the extent that they actually create it.

In conjunction with the local corporate tax (*Gewerbesteuer*), these two tax instruments (Categories A and B) in the hands of the municipalities and counties, provide for a system of fiscal federalism that invites the municipalities and counties to compete for the business of their choice, for which they then through their active governing can create the conditions under which that business may prosper.[16]

Currently, the yield of the property tax is about 2 percent of the total tax revenues, or, in 1999, 16.9 billion marks. While this may not seem a very significant percentage, among the multifarious taxes in the Federal Republic it ranks ninth, which is relatively high. What is more important is the fact, mentioned earlier, that in Germany it is the distinctively structured income tax which, to a greater degree than any other, satisfies the efficiency criterion of Georgist theory. Economic efficiency is, to be sure, a key aspect of the Georgist paradigm. But equity—conceived as the right to keep the product of one's legitimate efforts, coupled with the obligation to pay the community for socially-produced advantages and benefits—is more than a key aspect; it is its very soul. An intriguing topic for conjecture is whether a better understanding of George's view of equity might have led to greater reliance on land-value taxation and less on income tax in Germany.

III

The German Income Tax as a Quasi Land-Value Tax

DURING THIS CENTURY, Germany has suffered two crushing military defeats. The first one led to the Treaty of Versailles, the economic consequences of which had been presaged by John Maynard Keynes.[17] This peace set enormous indemnities for several generations to come, i.e., a staggering penalty that the Reich had to pay to the victorious powers. The policy of the Reich was that which any tax payer would adopt: seeking a compromise between compliance and avoidance. This led to several highly idiosyncratic features that still characterize German economic policy. More specifically, the Reich on the one hand had to secure raw materials not only to feed the population, but also to allow production to generate enough exportables to pay the indemnities. Germany had not only lost its military but also its commercial navy; it was in urgent need to attract capital for building shipping capacity. On the other hand, the same policies had to somehow be successful in proving Germany's inability to pay. A system was therefore designed which creates commercial credit through the income tax code. The same system was later to be perfected after World War II. Let us describe this system of credit through the income tax code with the example of creating shipping capacity.

When personal incomes need to be declared for tax purposes, obviously business losses can be taken off the income to be declared. Herein lies the purpose of creating losses that can be used for tax purposes, but do not by themselves constitute a sacrifice in the sense of wasting resources. Take an individual with an income in the relevant tax bracket of one million marks. This disregards, for our purposes, the income that falls under the lower tax brackets. From an economic point of view, only the marginal income is relevant, that is the income in the highest tax bracket. If the tax rate is 50 percent, of this one million marks, five hundred thousand marks can be put at the disposal of a business enterprise, if an offsetting loss of one million marks can be shown. In fact, an individual with respect to this personal income tax situation is indifferent, under these assumptions, between investing five hundred thousand marks in an enterprise that produces a loss statement of one million marks or paying the 50 percent income tax. Let us now generalize this statement and collect investments from high income clients for the purpose of building the shipping capacity in question. Building ships is obviously an enterprise that under no circumstances during its first year can yield a sizable profit. It almost certainly yields a substantial loss. However, the nominal loss can be increased if the shipping capacity we are in the process of creating can be depreciated rapidly. This is where accelerated depreciation comes in. The principle means that the shipping capacity that we are in the process of building is being depreciated in value to its nominal value, let us say one mark, upon completion of the ship, when the ship actually has its highest market value. This system of accelerated depreciation therefore is able to produce substantial book losses, when in fact substantial investments are being made. Let us now assume the prudent tax avoiding investor puts one hundred thousand marks into the ship building enterprise. He thereby reduces his disposable income by one hundred thousand marks, but his taxable income remains at the original one million under the 50 percent tax rate. But if he receives a loss statement in relation to this one hundred thousand mark investment share of two hundred thousand marks in the first year, that loss statement reduces his tax debt by the same amount of one hundred thousand marks he actually invested in buying the share of the ship. This means that with this loss assignment, he is indifferent between investing one hundred thousand marks in the ship or paying the tax. Actually, he is not quite indifferent, because in paying the tax he receives nothing in return, whereas in investing in the share of the ship, he might conceivably earn something once the ship is set afloat.

What has been dubbed a "scheme," of course, needs to be approved by the tax authorities. By approving these constructions, the tax authorities essentially assign away taxes owed to very specific projects which the government cannot itself conceivably undertake. And, indeed, German shipping capacity in the early 'twenties rose miraculously through this procedure.

In 1945, Germany had lost not only its navy, both military and commercial, but essentially everything, and the country lay in ruins. What industrial capacity there was still remained subject to *demountation*, that is, the disassembling of industrial plants and removal of productive capacity. These demountations actually continued well into the early 'fifties, after the establishment of the Federal Republic in West Germany in 1949, and the currency reform of 1948. The allied occupying powers had also insisted on a stiff progressive income tax rate of up to 90 percent. Such an income tax rate, of course, stifles efforts at earning income, and therefore stifles efforts at leading the country through reconstruction into economic prosperity. By insisting, however, on such a stiff income tax rate, the allied powers had created ample opportunities for the scheme just described. Not only commercial ship building capacity had to be created, millions of homeless people who had either lost their homes through the bombing raids or had arrived in West Germany as refugees, needed living space. Hence,

provisions were entered into the tax code allowing for special deductions for ship building, the creation of residential rental housing, etc., these being the amendments to Article Seven of the income tax code, creating special opportunities for deducting losses
from commercial activities.

These losses in an accounting sense could, of course, be shown
to have occurred, because long term investments had been made,
where the investment comes first and the yield will appear over a
long period of time. By allowing these deductions, and in addition
accelerated depreciations, the fruits from these investments were
made tax free, and the wealth created through the investments
would also remain tax free if only the scheme of the income tax
code were to continue indefinitely. Thus, German economic recovery received a strong impulse in two ways: High income earners faced a zero income tax (in the relevant tax brackets) if only
they were willing to re-invest their income in those preferred investment areas, such as housing, real estate development, shipping, and various others. And these indicated commercial areas
received an almost unlimited supply of credit, a supply of credit
restricted only by the income earning capacity of the high income
earners.

If we look at this phenomenon from the point of view of Henry
George's distinction between land value and improvement value,
we notice that the improvements, even in the area of real estate
development, remained tax free. George's theory is, however, not
only about improvements remaining tax free. It is about a tax constitution that balances government's revenues with a government's ability to stimulate rents of natural resources, and it is about
economic development. These two elements are remarkably present in the provisions of the German income tax code (amendments to Article Seven) as described here. Indeed, the income tax
code was designed to become an engine of economic development, the credit for which development was created by taxes not
collected. These tax deductions should, indeed, not be seen as tax
expenditures, rather they were investments in the tax base. The
creation of residential housing, for instance, involves multiple
transactions which are all subject to the value added (or formerly
sales) tax, and this tax has proven to be a most fertile revenue

source. Yet, many of these transactions would never have taken place if the specific incentive structure embodied in the amendments to the tax code had not been conceived.

After the collapse of the German Democratic Republic, the reconstitution of the five new states and their accession to the Federal Republic, Germany faced the daunting task of reconstructing a landscape that had over the last decades been subject to massive disinvestment. Again, recourse was taken to the same scheme just outlined. This is also the reason why income tax legislation is exempt from European Union harmonization. The German income tax system, due to its "Georgist" elements, is so unique and dissimilar to other systems, that it is not possible to enter it into a process of harmonization while the reconstruction of East Germany has yet to be completed. In order to show how this is done in practice, a document is here reproduced which consists of a prospectus or invitation to invest in a particular real estate development program in Jena in Thuringia.[18]

The document, of course is in German, but it need not be translated here. Instead, we shall simply point out its most salient features. The purpose of the investment is described as creating a service center with office and shop space in Jena. The manager of the enterprise is described as being Dr. Lothar Späth, a former prime minister of the State of Baden-Württemberg known for his inventive use of tax and other incentives to lure major investments into that booming state. The total loss assignments are given by year, the first year yielding 144.55 percent and the last year still some 9.73 percent, the total being 234.15 percent. Given a tax rate of 53 percent, this investment still yields an after tax return of 18.87 percent. But after five years, the share in this real estate project, by then no doubt developed and leased, can already be sold. As pointed out before, the profit from the sale can be tax exempt if it is re-invested into a similar scheme.

Figure 1

Anlagen ＞4.

Anlage 23

Vereinsbank

BAYERISCHE
VEREINSBANK AG

Immobilien – Leasing – Fonds
Beteiligung an der HETTA Verwaltungsgesellschaft mbH + Co. Vermietungs KG

Mindestzeichnungsbetrag DM 1 Mio

Mindesteinlage   DM 1 Mio (Bareinlage) = 43,51 %
Fremdfinanzierung   DM 1,3 Mio – 56,49 %

(In Ausnahmefällen jeweils die Hälfte; ist mit Herrn Gersthewohl MUC/–3809 abzustimmen)

Objekt ist ein Dienstleistungszentrum mit Büro– und Ladenflächen in Jena.

Generalübernehmer ist die Jenoptik Bauentwicklung GmbH.

Leasingnehmer ist die Jenoptik GmbH, Jena, die zu 100 % dem Land Thüringen gehört. Geschäftsführer ist Dr. Lothar Späth.

Steuerliche Verlustzuweisungen

     1994 = 144,55 %
     1995 = 10,43 %
     1996 = 9,30 %
     1997 = 8,79 %

Weitere Verlustzuweisungen für die Folgejahre.

     Gesamt 234,15 %

Die Verluste aus der Beteiligung können vom Gesamtbetrag der übrigen Einkünfte in 1994 abgezogen werden. Die den Gesamtbetrag übersteigenden Verluste können gemäß § 10 d EStG wahlweise auf die beiden Vorjahre verteilt werden; evtl. dann noch verbleibende Verluste lassen sich auf die Folgejahre vortragen.

Aufgrund der hohen Verlustzuweisungen läßt diese steuerorientierte Konzeption nur geringe Ausschüttungen zu.

Zins und Tilgung werden vom Leasingnehmer bezahlt. Das Zinsänderungsrisiko trägt auch der Leasingnehmer.

Bei einem Steuersatz von 53 % ergibt sich eine Rendite von 18,87 % nach Steuern.

Die Bindung des Eigenkapitals beträgt nur 5 Jahre.

..l2

IV

Conclusion

THIS PARTICULAR EXAMPLE shows that the concept of land-value taxation in Germany needs to be considered with respect to the most peculiar circumstances under which Germany has developed and the sometimes creative reactions to adverse constraints. The Georgist program involving the distinction between the rent of natural resources on the one hand and the value of improvements on the other, with the stipulation that the land rent should be taxed totally whereas the improvements should remain totally untaxed, thus creating a tax constitution designed for economic development, can be shown to exist in modified form in real estate taxation in Germany. But it still figures much more compellingly in the interplay between the income tax code and corporate investment in specifically designated areas, including real estate development, to be sure, but also other areas such as shipping or any specific focus that might gain priority in economic policy.

Notes

1. Joseph Alois Schumpeter, *History of Economic Analysis* (New York: Oxford University Press, 1954), p. 865.
2. Henry George, *Fortschritt und Armut* (translated by C.D.F. Gütschow; Berlin: Staude, 1882 [with a preface by Henry George himself in German, dated San Francisco, August 10, 1881]). There is another even more beautifully produced edition based on a different translation: Henry George, *Fortschritt und Armut* (translated by F. Dobbert; Halle: Hendel, no year [1891]), in a series called Complete Domestic and International Library, with each volume selling (at the time) for 25 pfennig.
3. See for instance the long review article by Gustav von Schmoller himself, "Henry George," in Gustav Schmoller, *Zu Literaturgeschichte der Staats und Sozialwissenschaften*, (Leipzig: Duncker & Humblot, 1888). The original is dated 1882 and is a review of the Gütschow translation of 1881.
4. See *Progress and Poverty*, Book VIII, chap. iii, sec. 4.
5. Friedrich List, *Gutachten über die wirtschaftliche Reform des Königsreichs Ungarn*, 1845.
6. The original German text reads: "Erhöht der ungarische Staat durch Wasser—und Verkehrsanlagen vielfach die Bodenrente auf das zwanzigfache, so soll—natürlich bei Gelegenheit künftige Verkäufe—der Staat mindestens die Hälfte der Wertsteigerung an Steuer vorwegnehmen."

7. Wilhelm Gerloff, "Die Wert zu Wachssteuer in Literatur and Gesetzgebung," Schmollers Jahrbuch für Gesetzgebung, Verwaltung und Volkswirtschaft im deutschen Reiche (37, 1913), pp. 1485–1497.

8. This fairly extensive literature has been ably surveyed. See Fritz Stier-Somlo," Grundsätzliches und Tatsächilches zu Wertzuwachssteuer," Jahrbücher für Nationalökonomie und Stastik (1909), p. 1. And the article by Gerloff, cited in the previous note.

9. Jürgen Backhaus and J. J. Krabbe, "Henry George's Contribution to Modern Environmental Policy: Part One, Theoretical Postulates, *The American Journal of Economics and Sociology*, Vol. 50 No. 4, (October 1991), pp., 485–501. Jürgen Backhaus, J. J. Krabbe, "Henry George's Contribution to Modern Environmental Policy: Part Two, An Application to Industrial Siting," *The American Journal of Economics and Sociology*, Vol. 51, No. 1, (January 1992), pp. 115–127.

10. *Progress and Poverty* (2ⁿᵈ ed., 1880; rpt. New York: Schalkenbach, 1979), pp. 38–39. Oddly, in both the Gütschow and the Dobbert translations, the quote can be found on page 31.

11. Michael Flürscheim (born 1844) was the manager of iron works in Gaggenau and produced several pamphlets (*Auf Friedlichem Wege, Der Einzige Rettungsweg, Deutschland in Hundert Jahren*), and a monthly paper called *Deutsches Land*, all arguing for land reform. This led to the constitution in 1888 of the Deutsche Bund für Bodenbesitzreform. Flürscheim also tried an experiment in the Mexican state of Sinola, which failed. See for details, Adolf Damaschke, *Geschichte der Nationalökonomie* (Jena: Fischer, 1909 [3]), pp. 392–393.

12. See Adolf Damaschke, *Die Bodenreform* (Jena: Fischer, 1916).

13. The best account can be found in Ludwig W. Schrameier, *Aus Kiau Tchau's Verwaltung, Die Land-, Steuer-, und Zollpolitik des Kiau Tchau Gebietes* (Jena: Fischer, 1914), The author is there described as privy councilor in the Imperial Navy, formerly imperial commissioner of the Kiau-chau protectorate and holding a doctorate in philology.

14. The terms of this treaty suggested by the Germans to the Chinese government, were soon thereafter reflected in the renegotiated treaty between the British Crown and the Chinese Empire.

15. See for further details, Karl Bräuer, "Wertzuwachssteuer (Grundsstücksgewinnsteuer)," *Handwörterbuch der Staatswissenschaften* (Jena: Gustav Fischer, 1928 [4]) Vol. 8, pp. 117–142.

16. For further details, see Karl-Heinrich Hansmeyer, "Grundsteuer, *Handwörterbuch der Finanzwissenschaft*, (Stuttgart: Fischer, Tübingen: Mohr, Göttingen: Vandenhoeck and Roeprecht [3], 1981 [2]), pp. 726–743; and V.G. Peterson, "Germany," in Harry Gunnison Brown, Harold S. Buttenheim, Philip H. Cornick, and Glenn E. Hoover, eds. *Land Value Taxation Around the World* (1ˢᵗ ed.; New York: Schalkenbach, 1955).

17. John Maynard Keynes, *The Economic Consequences of the Peace* (New York: Harcourt Brace and Howe, 1920).

18. See Reginald Hansen, *Die praktischen Konsequenzen des Methodenstreits: eine Aufarbeitung der Einkommensbesteuerung* (Berlin: Duncker & Humblot, 1996), p. 547. Many other examples can be found in the appendix to this book which describe in great detail the intellectual foundations and practical realizations of the German income tax code.

Chapter 14

Great Britain

BY OWEN CONNELLAN* AND NATHANIEL LICHFIELD**

THREE STRANDS MAY be discerned in the history of land-value taxation in Great Britain: land tax gathering for public revenue purposes, development value capture for the benefit of the community, and recoupment of infrastructure costs. This chapter describes the three in sequence.

Of these three strands, only the last is currently in place in Britain under circumstances of private ownership. However, although to do much more than mention it would carry us too far afield, there has also grown up a method of development value capture with which Britain has had great experience since World War II— namely, capture as a consequence of prior public acquisition of

*Owen Connellan is a chartered surveyor and valuer who has specialized in real property taxation and is a member of the International Association of Assessing officers (USA). He was engaged extensively in professional practice privately and with commercial property organizations before pursuing an academic career. Currently, he is a research fellow of Kingston University near London, where he was formerly head of the School of Surveying. Among his publications are five monographs on land-value taxation and related topics, co-authored with Nathaniel Lichfield for the Lincoln Institute of Land Policy, Cambridge, MA. He holds the B.Sc. From the University of London.

**Nathaniel Lichfield, Ph.D., University of London, has been chair of the program there in the economics of environmental planning since 1966. He has had practical experience as a town planner and urban economist at both local and central government levels, and is currently a principal in the consulting firm of Dalia and Nathaniel Lichfield and Associates. In 1968, he was appointed president of the Royal Town Planning Institute of Britain. Prof. Lichfield is co-author of numerous books and reports, including, with Haim Darin-Drabkin, *Land Policy and Planning* (1980), *Economics in Urban Conservation* (1988), and *Community Impact Evaluation* (1996). Since 1996, he has collaborated with Owen Connellan on five reports related to land-value taxation, commissioned by the Lincoln Institute of Land Policy, Cambridge, MA.

land for development and subsequent renting or leasing, by which increasing land values flow to the public purse. Under this approach there has been a huge program that includes, for example, the redevelopment of bomb-damaged and obsolete areas after the war;[1] the building of some thirty new towns, starting in 1946;[2] the redevelopment/regeneration of obsolete areas by Government-appointed Development Corporations;[3] and also value capture from the nationalization of natural resources, as in coal[4] and oil/gas.[5]

In the first three of these examples, significant land value rises were captured by the legislation fixing levels of compensation for the purchase which did not reflect the expected potential rise from the development envisaged. In the latter two, the principles were different; however, both, of course, involve remuneration to the public for both the right to extract the resource, and for the quantity extracted. In relation to coal, nationalization of the underground deposits, with compensation paid to the owners, was initiated in the 1930s, so enabling the National Coal Board to grant licenses for the use of the nationalized rights subject to obtaining a planning permission. As to open cast mining, which was begun during the war, the same system applies but no compensation was paid to the landowners. For oil/gas, the government assumed ownership of both on-shore and off-shore deposits. It was thus able to grant licenses to explore, and then, when appropriate, to operate, and to garner income from them in the form of royalties. The principles of the latter two are currently being applied in relation to licenses for the spectrum of radio waves. These are the subject of open auction bidding by intending licensees to run the next generation of mobile 'phones.

I

History of Land-Value Taxation in Britain

AN UNDERLYING PRECEPT of the administration of the Roman Empire, which included what is now Britain, was a codified system of property jurisprudence, at the heart of which the control, transfer and ownership of rights over land were clearly evident. The Romans also recognized land as a target for measurement and assessment by surveyors for taxation on a quinquennial basis,[6] which would have been a normal part of their imperial taxation during the four centuries of their occupation in the first millennium. Subsequently land continued to have a fiscal role.

After the collapse of the Roman Empire, the outstanding feature of Europe was the feudal system. Thenceforward until the late Middle Ages, land paid virtually all the costs of government in England and indeed throughout most of Europe.[7]

It was with the disintegration of the feudal system that land increasingly became treated as "absolute private property free from obligation, [leading to] increasing dependence of government upon other sources of revenue."[8]

From Britain's past, Wilks[9] summarized what little fleetingly remains of land taxation by confirming that there were very minor residual taxes still existing based on the value of bare land. These were known as Danegeld, land tax, and Queen Anne's Bounty. His view was that for all practical purposes these may be forgotten, being the residue of a system that was in force seven hundred or more years ago. And indeed, vacant land in Britain became entirely tax free in 1923.[10]

Despite this, the basic arguments for a return to land taxation were extensively promoted by classical political economists in the nineteenth century (for example, David Ricardo and John Stuart Mill). In Britain, in the latter part of that century, Henry George fueled the debate when he visited Britain five times, three on extended speaking tours.[11] His impact was considerable amongst progressive thinkers. Testimonials by such eminent Fabians as Bernard Shaw, Sidney and Beatrice Webb, and H. G. Wells explicitly credit George with being the most potent single instrument in the conversion of both individuals and the working class itself to trade unionism and socialism,[12] even though he viewed trade unions as having but limited value, and advocated socializing only natural monopolies.

The influence of George's ideas in Britain has endured. While no economist accepted his total framework, and most rejected much of it, his stress upon the idea of a tax on land values persisted in the minds of some 20th century economists, and even his all-out notion that it should be the *single* tax still has adherents. Consequently over the past century there have been many attempts at legislative action in Britain to promote land-value taxation as a source of government revenues; these are tabulated in the appendix to this chapter. This shows that there was considerable activity, right up to the beginning of the Second World War, by expert bodies, members of Parliament and municipal authorities to persuade Parliament to allow local governments to levy rates on land values. None succeeded. And there were also attempts by Central Government to introduce land value duties as taxation for national and local purposes but only two succeeded in becoming Acts of Parliament: The (Lloyd-George) Finance Act of 1909–10 from the Liberals, and the (Snowden) Finance Act of 1931 from the Labour Party. Although enacted, these measures were abandoned before they could be fully implemented.[13]

However the pressure for some introduction of land-value taxation did not abate. In 1942 and 1952 two Government-appointed committees reported relevant findings regarding the possible introduction of land-value taxation: Uthwatt by the war-time Coalition and Erskine Simes by the Conservatives.

The Uthwatt Committee (Expert Committee on Compensation and Betterment, 1942), which really focused on the compensation and betterment problem, positively recommended a form of site-value taxation in its proposal for a levy on enhanced annual site values as a practical method of recouping betterment. The levy was to run alongside the existing rating system as based on assessments for combined values of land and buildings. The recommendation was that in the valuation lists made for rating purposes there should be provided an additional column in which should be entered quinquennially the annual site value of every hereditament separately assessable for rates.[14] As a proposed solution it was never taken up.

Very little comment on this proposal can be gleaned from later examinations of the prospects of introducing site-value taxation, although a brief reference appeared in the Report of the Simes Committee of Enquiry but without any evaluation of its possibilities. This committee had the following charge: "... to consider and report on the practicability and desirability of meeting part of local expenditure by an additional rate on site values, having regard to the provisions of the Town and Country Planning Acts and other factors."[15]

The Simes Committee took four and a half years to produce its report, and was divided in its conclusions. A majority of six members found that meeting any part of local expenditure by site-value rating, having regard to the Town and Country Planning Act 1947 (which had already legislated for a development charge for the recoupment of betterment), was neither practicable nor desirable. Three members dissented and submitted a minority report in favor.

A. Summary of Existing Situation on Land-Value Taxation

What emerges from this history is there has been a distinct lack of success during the century with successive Governments in bringing site-value rating/taxation within their armory of tax-gathering methods to supplement local and national revenues. Why has this been so?

The evidence points to a lack of political will-power in the face of opposition from various professional groups and land-owners, each having its own taxation agenda. Some notable exceptions apart,[16] modern British economists have tended to rally against Georgist doctrines, even though proposals under consideration by Parliament were far from embracing George's root and branch single-tax panacea. The relevant professions (the rating valuers and surveyors) have stressed the difficulties of site valuation, despite the findings of the successful pilot surveys carried out by Wilks[17] and supported their traditional preference for the long established rating procedures for a tax on the occupation of combined hereditaments of both land and buildings.

Yet, on the other hand, it is interesting and significant to note that, even after a hundred years, the supporters of the Henry George tradition in Britain, as well as in various groupings of societies and foundations around the world, are still actively pursuing George's precepts on land taxation and arguing his case. The United Committee for the Taxation of Land Values was founded in 1907. It is now known as the Henry George Foundation and publishes the quarterly journal, *Land and Liberty*, which celebrated its 100th anniversary in 1994. Other active groups in Britain include the Land Value Taxation Campaign, the Land Policy Council and the Scottish Ogilvie Council.

II
Community Betterment (Value Capture) from Development Value in Britain

HAVING EXAMINED THE attempts at public revenue raising by means of direct land-value taxation, we now turn to the second strand of Government measures, namely, development value capture, or the effort to recover "betterment"—i.e., increased value from development activity.

A. Early Provisions for Betterment

Two threads in the fabric of the history of this country indicate the application of the principle of betterment for the community:

(i) payment *according to* benefits received or dangers avoided—being benefits which were the *deliberate* objective of the projected improvements—most frequently represented by sewers and drainage rates; and

(ii) payment (whether by direct charge or set-off against compensation) *in respect of* benefits received by public improvements—being benefits which were *incidental* to the direct objective of the projected improvements—e.g. through the widening of roads.

The first thread remains unbroken from the Middle Ages to the present day, when it is represented by differential rates under the Land Drainage Act, 1930. The second thread first appeared in 1662, but after a few years is broken and does not reappear until about 1830.

The earliest statute giving effect to the principle of assessment of contributions according to benefits was an Act of 1427 (6 Henry VI, c.5) appointing Commissioners of Sewers for ten years to supervise works for sea defence wherever they might be required. The principle on which the sewage rates were levied under a later Statute (of 1531) was that "everyone whose property derives benefit from the works of the Commissioners may be assessed to the rates they impose." Some authorities have doubted whether this is an example of the principle of *betterment*, for the sewer rate was in fact in the nature of an improvement rate levied over the area (or, in some cases, on the individual properties) adjudged to be benefited by the sewage works, and not necessarily only upon areas or properties for whose benefit the works were deliberately executed. But it certainly appears to contain the germ of the principle of betterment, and it is clear that the principle is by no means a recent innovation. It was adopted by Parliament as long ago as 1662 in the Act 13 & 14 Charles II, c.2, though the word used is not betterment but melioration. The Act provided (inter alia) for the widening of certain streets in London and provided powers to assess upon owners and occupiers of such houses, "such competent sum or sums or annual rent in consideration of such improvement and melioration as in recent and good conscience they shall judge and think fit." A similar provision was included in the Act for the Rebuilding of London after the Great Fire, 1667 (18 & 19 Charles II, c.3).

III

Betterment and Compensation in the Planning Acts

A. Town and Country Planning Act 1947

Although within the last hundred years the principle of betterment was reflected in the Town Planning Acts of 1909–1932, it did not really come into its own until after World War II. Based on the principles of the Uthwatt Report but not on its precise precepts, the post-war Labour Government's Act of 1947 nationalized development rights and introduced compensation betterment provisions which were quite different from that in the pre-war Town Planning Acts of 1909–1932. Beyond minor exceptions, no development was allowed without the permission of the local planning authority. If permission were refused, no compensation would be paid, except in a limited range of special cases. If permission were granted, any resulting increase in land value was to be subject to a development charge.[18] The land owner had the right to continue the existing use of land so that any interference by the State would attract compensation.[19]

Betterment could be claimed as a development charge so far as the value of land was enhanced by the grant of permission.[20] In other words, it was conceived as "any increase in the value of land (including the buildings thereon) arising from central or local government action, whether positive, for example by the execution of public works or improvements, or negative, for example by the imposition of restrictions on other land."[21] The development charge was assessed on the development value, *and* on one hundred percent of the increase in value due to the permission to develop. Thus there was no incentive to develop, since all profit on development was theoretically taken away.[22]

Under the 1947 Act, loss of development value due to the nationalization of development rights (which was calculated to be the difference between the unrestricted value and the *existing* use value) attracted compensation. This was based on admitted claims to an ex gratia fund of £300 millions, plus one-seventh for the accrued interest on the amount of the claim. When all claims had been received and examined, the previously set £300 millions would be divided between them according to the respective proportion of their value of July 1st 1948, and paid together with interest. In the event the total of all claims amounted up to £380 millions, very close to the preliminary estimate.[23]

The Town and Country Planning Act of 1947 thus brought about a major change. Whereas in the 1909–1932 Acts the landowner had his development rights granted to him in the local planning scheme, after 1947 the landowner had no rights, minutiae apart, until they were granted to him by the planning permit, except in the case of reinstatement of established buildings.[24]

The 1947 Act did not work as expected. Land was being widely offered, and still worse, bought, at prices including the full development value, even though developers were to pay a development charge amounting to one hundred per cent of the increase in the value of land resulting from development.[25] This was largely due to the severe restrictions imposed on building, because of resource limitations. Building licenses were scarce, and developers able to obtain them were willing to pay a high price for land upon which to build.[26] Purchasers other than developers often found themselves forced to pay more for land than its existing use value, which in logic was all they should have been ready to pay.[27]

The greater the amount of planning control, the greater did the gap between existing use and market values become. As a result of the 1947 Act, owners who were forced to sell their land to public authorities at existing use values considered themselves to be very badly treated in comparison with those who were able to sell their land to others at increased prices, resulting partially from the planning restrictions on other sites.[28]

B. Unscrambling the 1947 Act: The Acts of 1953, 1954 and 1959

The new Conservative Government (1951) unscrambled the scheme by a series of measures taken by the Town and Country Planning Acts of 1953, 1954 and 1959. One of these was the abolition of the development charge. The abolition caused land speculation. As long as owners could expect to receive only existing use value there was little point in buying land to hold in anticipation of a price rise. But when development values were given back to private sellers the prospect of speculative profits emerged again.[29]

With the new scheme, the £300 million compensation fund was extinguished as well. Instead of the compensation for development rights lost in 1947 being paid on a pro rata basis out of the fund, it was to be paid only when the loss was actually realized on refusal of permission. The local authority was made responsible for the payment of this compensation in cases where the claim attached to a site which was being compulsorily acquired. In other cases it was the central government's responsibility.[30]

The owners who sold their land privately in the market were now placed in a privileged position compared with owners whose land was subject to compulsory purchase.[31] The former received the full market price for their property and retained the development value. On the other hand, until the 1959 Act the latter only received existing use value because, in principle, the development rights belonged to the State. The Act of 1959 re-established market price as the basis of compensation for compulsory acquisition.[32] An owner could thus obtain the same price for his land irrespective of whether he sold it to a private individual or to a public authority, at least in theory. For the public authorities, land purchase suddenly became extremely costly.[33]

But the law as to the *ownership of the development rights* survived the Acts of 1953, 1954 and 1959, and has endured ever since. They are still separated from the balance of the ownership title and are owned by the Government, so that the denial of compensation for refusal of permission, or imposition of unsatisfactory conditions, still largely prevails as in the 1947 Act.

C. Land Commission Act of 1967

The Labour Government of 1964 made another, quite different, attempt to secure the return of a substantial part of the development value created by the community to the community, and the reduction of the cost of land to authority for essential purposes. To pursue these policies, a Land Commission was created to buy or compulsorily purchase land suitable for development with the objective of supplementing the local authority's powers to facilitate an orderly program of development. The Land Commission was designed to be a site assembler; a planning agency to determine land use; and to manage, dispose of or develop land, whether by itself or by engaging either private or public developers. Thus a central government agency was established to compete with the local authorities in determining where and how land should be used.[34]

A betterment levy was introduced which was equal to a proportion of the development value on all land sold, either in the open market and paid as a tax, or in a sale to the Commission and used as a deduction against purchase at market value. Initially the rate of the betterment levy was to be forty percent but in order to encourage early sales the percentage would increase over time.[35]

This "betterment levy" was in fact the "development charge" reinstated, but this time at only forty percent. However, the Land Commission Act of 1967 was repealed in 1971 by the Conservative Government.[36]

Together with the betterment levy, the Labour Government established a Capital Gains Tax (CGT) as well, by the Finance Act of 1967. The CGT was charged on the increases in the existing use value of land only, and not on the increases in the development value as in the betterment levy.[37]

D. Development Gains Tax

On 17 December 1973, a Conservative Chancellor announced the only Conservative Party proposal relating to land-value taxation. This was to introduce legislation for a form of Development Gains Tax related to substantial capital gains arising on the disposal of land and buildings with development value or potential, or on the occasion on which a building (other than one used for residential purposes) was first let following material development.

However, there was soon a change of Government following the general election in February 1974, and it fell to a new Labour Chancellor to put these proposals into legislative clothing (Part III and Schedules 3 to 10 of the Finance Act 1974). This was regarded by the Labour Government as an interim measure only, to bridge the gap until a more far-reaching one could be found in the Development Land Tax Act.[38]

E. Community Land Scheme

The Labour Government that took office in 1974 returned to the charge. It introduced its Community Land Scheme in two parts. The first was the Community Land Act of 1975, which provided wide powers for compulsory land acquisition, and the second was the Development Land Tax Act of 1976 which provided for the taxation of development values for "returning development values to the community."[39]

The Community Land Scheme differed from the previous attempts in two ways. The first is that the provisions dealing with the taxation or recoupment of betterment were separated from provisions dealing with the public acquisition and development of land. The second is that the local authorities became the vehicles for exercising power in respect to this function rather than the Central Government.[40] The increased power given to the local authorities was also conceived as a contribution aimed at strengthening the more "positive planning" introduced in the 1947 Act by comparison with the "negative planning" of the 1932 Act.[41]

The objectives of the Community Land Scheme may be grouped into two: enabling the community to control the development of land in accordance with its needs and priorities; and recouping to the community the increase in the value of land arising from its efforts. The first objective arose from the difficulties in achieving "positive planning." The rise of the second objective stemmed, following the repeal of the Land Commission Act, from the absence of any specific means of channelling some part of this increase to public hands, other than through general taxation.[42] Following these objectives, the intentions of the Scheme were identified as the passing through local authority hands of all land for development and renewal in the country, and the passing into public hands of all rises in land values which resulted from such development.[43] Exempt development, which was outside the coverage of the Community Land Scheme, included development for which permission was given by a General Development Order, and development for purposes of agriculture and forestry.[44]

In terms of land acquisition, under the Community Land Act a local authority could purchase land for the purpose of private-sector development either compulsorily or by agreement. If the authority gave permission for relevant development, it had the option to acquire the land for subsequent disposal. The local authority could then dispose of land to the private sector by leases, in general up to ninety-nine years. The choice of developer to whom the local authority leased the land was affected by "prior negotiating rights."

Land acquisition under the Community Land Act would be financed by borrowing, and all costs of this borrowing, as well as the costs of management and of land improvements, would be met from the proceeds of land disposal.[45] Only when it was fully profitable would it be possible to transfer surplus funds from the "community land accounts" to other local authority sectors. However, this held true only for thirty per cent of the surplus. Forty percent had to be paid to the central government and the rest into a fund from which allocations would be made to local authorities whose community land accounts were in deficit.[46] Under the Development Land Tax Act of 1976, development gains were calculated as the difference between the market value (the net proceeds of disposal) and either the current use value or the cost of land acquisition plus special additions (whichever was the highest). The tax would be paid when there was development on the land, or when the land was sold or leased.[47]

The Community Land Scheme was expected to rectify certain features of the private sector development process. The first of these features would be the reluctance of landowners to make their land available for development, both because of the possibility of the exercise of compulsory purchase powers and the liability for development land tax. The second feature would be the unwillingness and inability of the developers to undertake the obligations and risks of major schemes in the new climate. Finally there was the unwillingness of financial institutions to make funds available in the circumstances now prevailing following their experience with developers over recent years.[48]

The scheme, like its two predecessors, had little chance of proving itself. The economic climate of the first two years of its operation could hardly have been worse, and the consequent public expenditure crisis resulted in a central control which limited it severely.[49] The Community Land Act was abolished by the Thatcher Government in 1979. But it left in existence the Land Authority for Wales which had been created in the 1975 Act "to perform the functions as those allocated to the local authorities in England." Subsequently it was merged with the Welsh Development Agency.

F. Summary of Existing Situation on Betterment

The three post-war measures for betterment tax on development value in Britain, introduced by successive Labour Administrations, have all been withdrawn by the succeeding Conservative Administrations. Blundell[50] opines that the Acts failed for a variety of reasons. They were complex pieces of legislation and created confusion, and their effect was to deter development and the better use of land, to encourage land hoarding by owners and to produce an artificial scarcity of sites. But another major reason was that they were all repealed before they had sufficient time to settle down.

However, one critically important feature of the 1947 Act remains unaffected, namely that the ownership of all landed property development rights continues to vest in the Crown. Despite the amending planning legislation of subsequent Governments these rights were not given up and returned to the property owners. Consequently there is now no compensation problem to form the other side of the betterment coin. If a planning application is refused or granted with conditions, no claim for loss of development rights can be admitted. Prest puts it succinctly: "*But at least one thing does seem clear in the fog: the issue of planning compensation for planning refusal can be considered truly dead and buried.*"[51]

This has now an additional importance beyond the solution to the compensation problem when land value is mooted as a new taxation base. Any objections from land owners, for example, to a betterment tax on the development rights which they do not own but nevertheless can enjoy (as discussed in the Uthwatt Report),[52] hardly makes for a credible case at the Court of Equity.

IV

Recoupment of Infrastructure Costs

WE NOW TURN to the third strand. On the repeal of the third Labour Government attempt to recoup community benefit from rising land values, and the absence of any development land tax, a serious anomaly became apparent. On the one hand the economy was prospering so that land values (untaxed except for capital gains tax) were rising significantly to the benefit of the landowners/developers; while on the other hand local authorities were finding themselves even more squeezed in terms of the amount of financial support from Central Government. Out of this anomaly arose the common sense response of authorities to go outside the prevailing arrangements for payment for physical and social infrastructure, and look for extra sources of contribution from the landowners/ developers.

They sought to do so by use of their powers to enter into contracts with landowners/ developers outside the planning system, but related to it. The development rights, being still owned nationally, were dispensed locally, without financial charges through planning permissions, which were of great value to the landowners and developers who were anxious to obtain them in order to reap the uplift in land values consequent upon the grant. From this arose a bargaining situation. Where they chose to do so, the local authorities could pressurize the landowner/developer to make his contribution towards the cost of infrastructure (sometimes interpreted very broadly), which would be occasioned by the development for which permission was sought, and which would otherwise fall on the hard-pressed local government financial resources.

The machinery for doing so was initiated by local authorities and regularized by Government policy, under rubric initially of "planning gain" and then "planning obligations."[53] In economic terms, the exaction which was being delivered could be thought of as a tax on land value or recoupment of community benefit. But strictly it is neither; it is a shift in the burden of infrastructure financing from the public to the private landowner/developer sector. And furthermore it is capricious in its incidence. Just how it became divided between the two depended very much on the relative strengths of the landowner as vendor and the developer as purchaser, in the local land market. Just where it would be levied depended on the strength of the market and the anxiety or otherwise of the local authority to obtain the development.

A. Summary of Existing Situation on Recoupment of Infrastructure Costs

In practice, the planning gain/obligation system has offered a useful and flexible tool for redressing the public/private balance in land development.[54] But it has made for considerable confusion, and has attracted many suggestions for improvement, such as toward the direction of the US impact fees. The debate continues.

V

Conclusions

DESPITE THE NUMEROUS difficulties and disappointments recorded in the foregoing history, there is now a growing swell of opinion and debate from diverse political sources in Britain on the possibility of re-introducing land-value tax principles as part of the country's fiscal system. Whether this discussion will blossom into political action it is too early to prognosticate, but the signs are there and perhaps the next edition of this book will have a more positive story to tell of solid achievements rather than heroic attempts. Toward this end, the present authors have developed proposals that spacial constraints preclude from being included in this chapter, but to which the attention of interested readers is directed.[55]

Notes

1. Town and Country Planning Act, 1944; Town and Country Planning Act, 1947.
2. New Towns Act, 1946.
3. Development Corporation Act, 1980.
4. Coal Industry Act, 1949; Opencast Coal Act, 1958.
5. Gas Petroleum (Production) Act, 1944; Continental Shelf Act, 1964 (for off-shore); Oil Gas (Enterprise) Act, 1982 (for on-shore).
6. Edward Gibbon, *The Decline and Fall of the Roman Empire* (1776–1788; London: J. M. Dent & Sons, Ltd., 1951), II, 124.
7. Kenneth Jupp, "European Feudalism from its Emergence through its Decline," in R. V. Andelson, ed., *Land-Value Taxation Around the World* (2nd. ed.; New York: Robert Schalkenbach Foundation, 1997), p. 37.
8. Ibid.
9. H. M. Wilks, *Some Reflections on the Second Valuation of Whitestable* (London: Land & Liberty Press, Ltd., 1975), p. 1.
10. Haskell P. Wald, *Taxation of Land in Underdeveloped Countries* (Cambridge, MA: Harvard University Press, 1959), p. 23.

11. Nathaniel Lichfield and Owen P. Connellan, "Land Value Taxation in Britain for the Benefit of the Community: History, Achievements and Prospects." Working paper issued by the Lincoln Institute of Land Policy, Cambridge, MA, 1997, p. 10. For a detailed account, see Elwood P. Lawrence, *Henry George in the British Isles* (East Lansing, MI: Michigan State University Press, 1957).

12. Elwood P. Lawrence in Will and Dorothy Burnham Lissner, eds., *George and Democracy in the British Isles* (New York: Robert Schalkenbach Foundation, 1992), p. 83.

13. Roy Douglas, Land, *People & Politics: A History of the Land Question in the United Kingdom, 1878–1952* (London: Allison & Busby, 1976), chaps. 8–12.

14. Uthwatt Committee (Expert Committee on Compensation and Betterment), Final Report (Ministry of Works and Planning; London: H. M. Stationery Office, Sept., 1942).

15. Simes Committee (Committee of Enquiry), The Rating of Site Values (London: H. M. Stationery Office, 1952), p. 4.

16. E.g., A. R. Prest, *The Taxation of Urban Land* (Manchester: Manchester University Press, 1981).

17. H. M. Wilks, *The Rating of Site Values: Report of a Pilot Survey at Whitstable* (London: Rating and Valuation Association, 1964), and *The Rating of Site Values* (London: Land Institute, 1974).

18. B. Cullingworth and V. Nadin, *Town and Country Planning in Britain* (London: Routledge, 1994), p. 107.

19. J. P. W. B. McAuslan, "Compensation and Betterment," in Charles M. Haar, ed., *Cities, Law & Social Policy: Learning from the British* (Lexington, KY: D. C. Heath and Company, 1984), p. 84.

20. Ibid., p. 78.

21. Cullingworth and Nadin, p. 107.

22. McAuslan, p. 78.

23. Cullingworth and Nadin, p. 107.

24. Nathaniel Lichfield and H. Darin-Drabkin, *Land Policy in Planning* (London: George Allen & Unwin Ltd., 1980), p. 137.

25. Cullingworth and Nadin, p. 10.

26. Ibid., p. 108.

27. McAuslan, p. 78.

28. Cullingworth and Nadin, p. 109.

29. H. Ronald Parker, "The History of Compensation and Betterment Since 1900," in P. Hall, ed., *Land Values* (London: Sweet & Maxwell Limited), p. 67.

30. Ibid. p. 66.

31. Ibid.

32. Ibid. p. 67.

33. Cullingworth and Nadin, p. 110.

34. McAuslan, p. 78.

35. Ibid.

36. Ibid.

37. Cullingworth and Nadin, p. 111.

38. Prest, p. 96.

39. Cullingworth and Nadin, p. 114.

40. McAuslan, p. 79.

41. Lichfield and Darin-Drabkin, p. 4.

42. Ibid. p. 169.

43. Ibid. p. 4.

44. Ibid. p. 171.

45. Ibid. p. 173.

46. Ibid. p. 174.

47. Ibid.

48. Ibid. p. 181.

49. Cullingworth and Nadin, p. 114.

50. V. H. Blundell, *Essays in Land Economics* (London: Economic and Social Science Research Association, 1993), pp. 5–12.

51. Prest, p. 189.

52. Uthwatt Committee, pp. 135–54.

53. Department of the Environment, Circular 22/83: Planning Gain (London: H.M. Stationery Office, 1983) and Circular 16/91: Planning Obligations (London: H.M. Stationery Office, 1991); Cullingworth and Nadin.

54. Nathaniel Lichfield, "From Planning Gain to Community Benefit," *Journal of Planning and Environmental Law*, 1989, pp. 1101–1204; "From Planning Obligation to Community Benefit," *Journal of Planning and Environmental Law*, 1992, pp. 65–144.

55. Nathaniel Lichfield and Owen Connellan, "Land Value and Community Betterment Taxation in Britain: Proposals for Legislation and Practice." Working paper issued by the Lincoln Institute of Land Policy, Cambridge, MA, 1999.

Appendix

HISTORY OF ATTEMPTS AT LVT IN BRITAIN Schedule of Legislative Proposals			
Proposal	**To Meet Local Expenditure**	**Levied on Annual or Capital Value**	**Limitation on Amount of Rate**
Royal Commission on Housing of Working Classes, 1885	Part of it	-	-
L.C.C. Evidence to Royal Commission on Local Taxation, 1899	Part of it	Capital	6d. in £,. (2.5%)
"Separate Report" of Royal Commission on Local Taxation, 1901	Part of it	Annual	To be fixed by Parliament
Judge O'Connor's Minority Report (Royal Commission on Local Taxation), 1901	Whole	-	-
L.C.C. Bill, 1901	Part of it	Annual	2s. in £,. (10%)
Mr. C. P. Trevelyan's Bill, 1902	Part of it	Annual	2s. in £,. (10%)
Dr. T. J. MacNamara's Bill, 1903	Part of it	Capital	1d. in £,. (0.42%)
Mr. C. P. Trevelyan's Bill, 1904 and Sir John Brunner's Bill, 1905	Part of it	Annual, defined as 3% of capital value	Same rate on improved value of occupied, and unimproved value of occupied land
Land Values Taxation (Scotland) Bill, 1905	Part of it	Annual, defined as 4% of capital value	2s. in £,. (10%)
Select Committee on Land Values Taxation (Scotland) Bill, 1906	Whole	Annual	-
Finance (1909-10) Act, 1910	Part proposed but undetermined	Capital Annual	Incremental and Reversionary duties (10%) Levy on undeveloped land (0.21%)
Departmental Committee on Local Taxation, 1914 (Minority Report)	Part of it	Capital	10% of amount raised in rates plus half of any future increases
Manchester Bill, 1921	Part of it	Annual, defined as 5% of capital value	-
Finance Act, 1931	-	Capital	1d. in £, (0.42%) originally proposed
Mr. J. C. (later Lord) Wedgewood's Bill, 1932	Whole or Part of it	Capital	-
Mr. A. MacLaren's Bill, 1937	-	Annual	-
L.C.C. Bill, 1938-39	Part of it	Annual	2s. in £,. (10%)
Source: Simes Committee Report (1952: 23-24			

Chapter 15

Hungary

BY BALÁZS KÓNYA*

BEFORE WORLD WAR I, Hungary was the food provider of the Austro-Hungarian Empire. The distribution of landed estates was inequitable because a few hundred landlords—forming the aristocracy—held in check with their privileges millions of "dwarfholders" as well as the landless laborers. The number of medium-sized farms was relatively small.[1]

Urgency to solve the land question had increased at the turn of the century due to the fact that, through the impact of the Industrial Revolution, the standard of living of the agrarian population was further lowered. So the annual rate of emigrants, mainly to the United States, was considerable at this time.

Among those who tried to find a solution to this problem were a group of young Hungarian free-thinkers who formed the Galilei Circle and who were glad to hear about the very popular speeches and writings of Henry George in which he supplemented the Physiocrats' views with new social and economic arguments.[2] Between 1909 and 1914, the sociologist Robert Braun, who maintained a close relationship with some American Georgists, had brought out Magyar versions of *Protection or Free Trade* and

*Balázs Kónya, a Doctor of Laws from the University of Pécs, served as a department head at the Hungarian Chamber of Commerce, and then as a special researcher at the Scientific Institute of the Hungarian Planning Office. He is editor of the *Hungarian Economic Thesaurus* (1985), and author of articles in Hungarian economics journals and daily newspapers. His Study on Henry George's Philosophy (in Hungarian) is available on the Internet at the website of the Budapest University of Economic Sciences.

This chapter owes much to the invaluable counsel of Dr. Károly Ravasz, which the author takes pleasure in acknowledging.

Progress and Poverty. These Hungarians also established contacts with the *Bodenreform* movement in Germany.[3]

I

Dr. Julius J. Pikler and the Land Taxes
of 1917–1921

BUT THE ASTONISHING, albeit short-lived, success of Georgism in Hungary was almost wholly due to the drive and persuasive logic of a truly remarkable individual– the physician and statistician, Dr. Julius J. Pikler, who had learned about the doctrine through Braun shortly before World War I. As deputy director of the Budapest Public Statistics Office, he commanded a respectful audience, and conducted a virtual one-man campaign for the idea of the land-value tax, writing articles for leading periodicals, and speaking wherever opportunity afforded. He made no effort to found a movement or organization, but relied solely on his ability to convert persons of influence and authority through rational argument. However, he had considerable support within the Social Science Society and among the Hungarian Freemasons.

Pikler's first victory was in the Transylvanian city of Arad (now in Romania) in May of 1917. This was followed, in November of the same year, by a breakthrough in Budapest. There, an ordinance for the taxation of land-values was passed by a large majority of the City Council, and a special Land Valuation Office was created, with Pikler as director. After this triumph, he traveled throughout Hungary promoting the concept.

According to the Budapest decree, an annual tax of one half of one percent was levied on land values, whether the land was used or not, and there were no exceptions allowed except for publicly owned sites. At the same time, the "rent-penny"—a three percent tax on rents collected for the use of buildings—was reduced to 1.5 percent.[4] Valuations were to be made every three years with the greatest possible publicity, each citizen having the right to petition and each owner to appeal.

To be sure, the rate on land values set by this decree was low. But considering that this was the first time that an ad valorem tax ever had been placed upon land in Hungary,[5] and taking into account the resistance of the real estate interests to such a tax, the step was significant. Also it was hoped that it would be the beginning of a program for the fuller collection of land values, and it served notice on speculators that henceforth, they would be required to contribute to the upkeep of the community from which they benefited.

Unhappily, such good effects as might have stemmed from the change were to a large extent nullified by the fact that in 1919, when the collection of the tax began, inflation had already depreciated the Hungarian currency considerably. Nevertheless, the principle upon which the tax was based had been established, and the example set by Arad and Budapest was soon followed by the cities of Debrecen, Szeged, Kaposvar, Györ, Sopron, Ujpest, and Marosvásárhely (Târgu-Mures). During 1918, an appraisal was made in all applicable cities of the value of all real estate property—without consideration for their use, possible construction, or improvements.[6]

It is worthy of note that the municipalities of Debrecen and Szeged at that time were essentially farm communities, consisting of enormous agrarian acreage centered by relatively tiny urban cores. Instead of being frightened by the bogey of taxing land, the small farmers proved especially receptive to Pikler's arguments. But the influence of this brilliant advocate was not confined to Hungary. Invited to speak in Vienna, he (although Jewish) won over the Christian Socialist mayor and the latter's deputy, and a law largely modeled after that of Budapest was passed by the City of Vienna in 1919. It was revoked by the Marxist Socialists in 1923.

In Hungary, the notion of a national land-value tax was included in the program of the short-lived republican regime of Count Michael Károlyi, but that regime was overthrown in March of 1919 by a Communist uprising under Béla Kun. In August, the White army, headed by Admiral Nicholas Horthy, seized power in a rightist counter-revolution. Horthy restored the monarchy but left the throne vacant, with himself as regent. The relatively liberal self-governing bodies in the cities were supplanted by ones that reflected his conservative outlook. The tenement house owners' lobby now instigated a campaign against the land tax, using the effective if irrelevant argument that it had been supported by Freemasons and Jews.[7]

In the chaos and upheaval of the post-war years, it is scarcely surprising that Pikler's successes were reversed. Two of the cities that had adopted a measure of land-value taxation were annexed to Romania. In 1921, the conservative majority on the Budapest City Council, without rescinding the ordinance, suspended the collection of the tax indefinitely. In other cities, land-value taxation was either suspended or abolished outright.

II

Land Reform, 1921–1947

THE CONSERVATIVE GOVERNMENT did try to solve the land question in the twenties, but its endeavor failed because it only meant the dividing up of some large estates. The new laws aimed only to increase the ability of certain special groups (e.g., war orphans and war widows) to acquire land, without making the fulfillment of their claims obligatory. Nevertheless, under the law of 1920— which was further amended in 1922 and 1924—about one million acres were distributed to landless peasants and 400,000 acres more were given in tenure and lease.

In the years that followed, nowhere was any determined move made for a revival of the land-value taxation system. The idea might indeed have died but for a group encouraged and taught by Dr. Pikler through whose efforts the re-establishment of land-value taxation in the cities and its general introduction were several times proposed in Parliament.

> Up to the end of World War II, Hungary was a land of large estates; dominant among the owners were the descendants of aristocratic families whose properties had come down to them in entail from the Hapsburg monarchs. The need for a sweeping land reform became again the most urgent question to solve in the country.[8]

The provisional National Assembly in 1945 passed Law Number 6 which was promulgated on the 15th of March, the most important Hungarian national holiday since 1848. In two years, four million acres changed ownership with the result that approximately

650,000 landless peasants with their families became owners of plots of seven acres on average. The land reform affected all the communities of the country. Simultaneously, some three million acres of forests, fisheries, and large estates were nationalized.

III
Land Policies Under Communism

WHEN, IN MID-1947, the Communists (who had won only about 22 percent of the popular vote) menaced many influential parliamentary members of his Smallholders Party (FKgP), Prime Minister Ferenc Nagy, who was abroad, decided not to return home. A new coalition government was formed with Communist participation, and came gradually to operate under Soviet directives. This process was facilitated by the presence of Soviet troops. The following year, with the forced resignation of President Zoltan Tildy, Communist power was fully consolidated.

The goal of the Communist Government's land policy was to "dispose of" the new dwarfholders by the forced collection of their agricultural products so that they might be unable to survive outside the agrarian cooperatives (*kolkhoz*). While the majority of Hungarian peasants stood firm against the kolkhoz despite the heavy pressure which was exerted on them, by the end of 1952, 25 percent of the arable land had been forced into the cooperatives and the state became owner of another 12.7 percent.

The 1956 Revolution put in front the agricultural conception of Prime Minister Imre Nagy, whose principal aim was the voluntary formation of cooperatives to replace the former movement based on coercion.[9]

After the reoccupation of Hungary by Soviet troops, the newly installed Communist government led by János Kádár, to placate the village population, abolished the laws ordering the forced collection of agricultural products and canceled all the arrears of the peasants due to previous delivery obligations. The enforced collectivization was abandoned, but instead the cooperatives received important subsidies and the collectivization was strengthened later using both the stick and the carrot.

Under the Kádár regime, the main characteristics of the collective farming model were the following: (1) collective (both state and cooperative) ownership of the farm land and of the means of agricultural production; private ownership being limited to household plots; (2) management according to the socialist farming model of the whole agrarian sector including both productive and non-productive functions; and (3) centralized planning of the whole economic environment through the bureaucratic allocation of resources at artificially fixed prices.[10]

From the point of view of mere production, a successful period was to be registered from 1965 to 1985, the foundations of which were the combination of the large farming estates and private enterprises (household plots), and also the background which was provided by the COMECON market. In fact, Hungary became the agrarian mainstay of the East European countries as it used to be a century ago in the Austro-Hungarian Empire.[11]

However, family farming traditions were replaced by the management model followed in large estates where the laborers work under the centralized leadership of experts, losing on the way the former multidimensional competence needed in farming on a family scale. Besides the introduced subsidies and taxation system,[12] the members of the cooperatives as well as the employees of the state estates had their rights to employment and to minimal wages legally guaranteed.

In the cities, the state building projects provided fewer homes for the workers, and the building of family-owned homes became dominant. The acquired (allocated by local municipalities) homes or flats could be exchanged or sold by the tenants. So, under the Kádár regime, a speculative land market began to develop in the cities as well as in the case of household plots or holiday cottages, and especially around cities where rezoning could be anticipated.

Meanwhile, the market for agrarian produce narrowed step by step because the importing socialist countries lost their ability to pay, and the European Community blocked Hungarian agricultural exports. Nevertheless, agriculture remained an important occupational factor of the economically active population, providing the subsistence of 4,000,000 out of the total 10,000,000 inhabitants of the country.

In 1989, the two above-mentioned agrarian models still worked in symbiosis, namely the smallholders' farming model based on private ownership, which was maintained though legally restricted, and the dominant one, namely the big-farming model based on collective ownership.[13]

IV

Post-Communist Land Programs

AT THE TIME of the 1990 parliamentary elections, the Smallholders Party (FKgP) proposed to reestablish the situation prevailing in 1947. In the first program of the FKgP, adopted in 1988, a land tax based on periodically reassessed market value was included, but this stressed the legal restitution to all those who were cheated out of their possessions by the Communist regime, and it was later silently disregarded.

It was hoped by the FKgP that all those who were forced into the cooperatives might take advantage of the entrepreneurial farming model based on private ownership. However, the majority of the laborers and employees working previously in the socialist agrarian sector were unprepared to try this model and unwilling to face the risks and responsibilities inherent in such a venture, to say nothing of the lack of financial support for investments in machinery, building projects and the purchase of fertilizers, pesticides, etc..

The opposite view was proposed by the Socialist Party (MSzP), which broke away from the Communist Party (MSzMP) led by Kádár. Its proposal excluded any legal restoration and precluded the break-up of the undivided collective ownership of the cooperatives.

The Liberal Party (SzDSz), which in 1990 became the most important opposition party, refused the two extreme proposals and envisaged a step-by-step privatization with the elimination of the agrarian monopolies within the framework of the newly created agrarian free market. Several members of Parliament of this party became members of the Hungarian Henry George Society, and advocate to this day the rating of land values by municipalities.

The standpoint of the Conservative Party (MDF) led by Prime Minister József Antall, the biggest force in the governmental coalition, was pragmatic and was changed several times. It rejected the outright reprivatization of land and introduced instead "compensation bonds" as a more or less symbolic indemnity for the illegally confiscated properties. The law concerning "compensation bonds" was first issued in June 1991 and subsequently modified according to the interests of the prevailing pressure groups. Since the land bases to satisfy the needs of the holders of these bonds were inadequate, the bonds began to depreciate as the land auctions had to be postponed.

After the 1994 elections, the Socialist Party (MSzP) obtained a majority (54 percent) in Parliament and formed a coalition government with the Liberals. The most urgent task in the agrarian sector was to clarify the intricate situation created by the contradictory trends produced by the execution of the laws concerning compensation bonds and the privatization of land. Really, the bureaucratic regulations stemming from the in-themselves inconsistent laws were in contradiction with the just-beginning market processes.

By the mid-nineties, the land owned by the former cooperatives had been distributed among some 1,500,000 owners—some 300,000 active agrarian workers obtaining one third of the total. The remaining two thirds are now in the possession of 600,000 retired persons and another 600,000 former cooperative members or their heirs who have no ties anymore with the agrarian sector and as stockholders are only concerned to obtain land rent or life-annuity.

The consequence of this fact—namely that 70–80 percent of the new landowners are only passively engaged in the cooperative movement—is that leasehold farming is now prevailing in the agrarian sector at a rate exceeding the European average.[14]

In the election of 1998, the left-wing government was defeated and replaced by a new coalition of the center-right, under the leadership of Viktor Orban of the Young Democrats (Fidesz). The new coalition promised fundamental changes, including a re-shaping of the complicated system of taxation. One of its constituent parties, the Smallholders Party or FkgP, again sought to reform the agrarian system, which had been neglected by the previous governments since 1990. However, the flood and other calamities prevailing in 1999, as well as the Kosovo War involving neighboring Serbia, prevented the immediate execution of such reforms. For example, the government's intention was to amend the 1993 Law on Land, but although the amendment (which might have been a step in the direction of land-value taxation) was introduced in Parliament in May, 1999, discussion of it was postponed. In the words of Prime Minister Orban, it "stirred up a hornet's nest." However, the municipalities continue to have the ability to determine local taxes, and this includes the taxation of land, either including or excluding its improvements, and either according to market value or at a fixed rate.

V

The Hungarian Henry George Society

IN 1989, DURING the last months of the Kádár regime, the Hungarian Henry George Society (MHGT) was formed as an independent association and tried to introduce a law concerning land-value taxation in cooperation with the political parties. The Liberal Party (SzDSz) was willing to submit a bill, which was however rejected in Parliament by the conservative parties forming then the majority. As a distortion of this proposal, the law concerning the financial resources of the self-governing municipalities contains the legal possibility either to tax vacant building plots or buildings.[15] Nevertheless, this seemed to provide an opportunity to widen further the legal basis for land-value taxation by the new coalition government formed by the Socialists and the Liberals in 1994.

Prime Minister Gyula Horn announced his intention to introduce a property tax. The economic experts of both parties studied the problem; in the meantime the government has decreed the computerization of the land registry system, which is now under way and which would form a basis for assessment.

The MHGT extended its activities to the experts of the most important ministries (Finance, Interior, Environmental Protection) with which it cooperates in matters relating to regional development. The self-governing municipalities are becoming gradually aware of how to make optimal use of the resources at their disposal. The MHGT participated in a countrywide conference organized by the Regional Research Center of the Hungarian Academy of Sciences for the municipalities. The main lectures of this conference were published in a study including an assessment of the land situation and also what may be done to promote the introduction of land-value taxation at the local level.[16]

The main political issue is now the reshaping of Hungary's Constitution. In this question, good collaboration has been achieved with some important non-governmental organizations recognized by the United Nations on the basis of a resolution concerning the missing clause in the UN Declaration of Human Rights.[17]

Hungary's historic Constitution, dating back to the sainted King Stephen I early in the 11th century, affirmed the ownership of all land by the Holy Crown, i.e., the nation as a whole. Over the ensuing centuries this principle remained theoretically authoritative even if ignored in practice. The MHGT's standpoint is that the equal right to land should be secured by requiring of all land holders the payment of a percentage of the full rent of the land held, whether it be used or not, and excluding the value of the improvements thereon.

The denial of validity of common rights is practiced by monopolistic capitalism, and the denial of individual rights is characteristic of modern communism. The MHGT asserts that the exercise of both common and individual rights is essential to a society based on justice. The introduction of this clause in the Constitution would be, of course, of great importance.[18]

Notes

1. More than a century earlier the enlightened Hapsburg monarch Joseph II was acquainted with the Physiocrats' views, and, after abolishing serfdom in 1785, he tried to introduce land-value taxation by decree, but was forced to repeal all his edicts before his death in 1790.

2. The following works of Henry George were translated into Hungarian at the beginning of the 20th century: *Progress and Poverty*, *Social Problems*, *Protection or Free Trade* and *The Condition of Labor*.

3. Adolf Damaschke, *Die Bodenreform*, 1902, trans. Imre Déri (Budapest; Stephaneaum, 1916), p. 182.

4. The "rent penny" produced only part of the total taxes levied on rents, and lowering it by half does not mean that the total tax on rents was cut by that proportion. Actually, the reduction represented roughly what would have been raised by the new site or land-value tax; that is, about a tenth of the total revenue of the city.

5. Under the old cadastre system which had operated and is still in force elsewhere in the country, agricultural land was taxed according to its fertility—estimated in the 1880s—and there was no tax on non-agricultural land in the cities.

6. Michael Silagi, *Henry George and Europe* (Will and Dorothy Burnham Lissner, eds.; trans. from the German by Susan N. Faulkner; New York: Robert Schalkenbach Foundation, 2000), p. 128.

7. Ibid., p. 129.

8. Robert Major, "Hungary," in H. G. Brown et al, eds., *Land-Value Taxation Around the World* (1st edition; New York: Robert Schalkenbach Foundation, 1955), p. 175. Paragraphs 5–8 have also been reproduced or paraphrased from this source.

9. Imre Nagy (1896–1958), who as minister of agriculture distributed land in 1945, was aware that the peasants would adhere to their newly received plots. So he opposed the compulsory collectivization of the whole agrarian sector. In his opinion, both tilling models, individual as well as collective, were necessary simultaneously. He was acquainted with Henry George's ideas but did not speak up in their favor, while some of his followers—sentenced after 1956—did.

10. No law ever abolished the property right of the members entering in the cooperatives in which they continued to till their own household plots. Otherwise, the property right concerning the land ceased not only as "usus" but also as "fructus"—which means the possession of the products of the land—and which was replaced by the payment of land rent (by the cooperative) having however only symbolic value. The "abusus"—which means the free disposal of wealth—was also canceled. Only its limited inheritance was permitted, but it did not automatically give membership in the cooperatives to the heirs.

11. István Berényi, "Expected Situation of the Structure of Land Use of the Great Hungarian Plain", TET (*Space and Society*), 7, No. 3–4, (1993), p. 75.

12. The above-mentioned old cadastre (see Note 5) served as a basis for the appraisal of both subsidies and land taxation. "Hungarian agrarian policy, although a single case, might be called a 'third' type and indeed is pictured as such in some Soviet and East European publications." Karl-Eugen Wädekin, "Determinants and Trends of Reform in Communist Agriculture: A Concluding Essay", in *Communist Agriculture*, edited by Karl-Eugen Wädekin (London and New York: Routledge, 1990), p. 323.

13. Marie-Claude Maurel, "Privatization of the Agriculture: Specialties of the Hungarian Approach", TET (*Space and Society*), 7, No. 3–4, 1993, pp. 126 and 129. See also: A földtulajdon és a mezögazdasági struktura talakitása (Property in land and the transformation of agricultural structure), edited by Böla Csendes (Budapest: Agrárkutató Intézet, 1990), pp. 306–308. Vol. 3.

14. Gyula Vargo, "A fekete leves még hátre van!" (The Worst is still to Come!), Figyel" (*Economic Observer*) (October 27, 1994), pp. 28–29.

15. Josef Sivok, "Economic Transition: Challenges in Financing Local Government—The Hungarian Response," Lecture held at the IRRV Second International Conference, Budapest, May 24–27, 1993.

16. Mária Máthé, ed., *A Területféjlesztés Es Területhasznositás Arának, Adójának Meghatározása* (Determination of the price of tax on the development and use of territory). (Györ: Regional Research Center of the Hungarian Academy of Sciences, 1944).

17. Bent Straarup, "The Missing Clause in the UN Declaration of Human Rights, and Profit Sharing of the Resources of Nature Instead of Social Subsidies and Taxes." Paper delivered at the Conference of the International Union for Land-Value Taxation and Free Trade, Roskilde, Denmark, 1995.

18. The MHGT (Hungarian Henry George Society) proposal has been submitted to the Preparatory Commission for the Elaboration of the Constitution. Work in the Commission is now in abeyance, as a two-thirds majority in Parliament is required to amend or replace the Constitution, and the possibility of such a majority has not existed since 1998.

PART FOUR

AFRICA

Chapter 16

Nations of Eastern Africa

BY REXFORD A. AHENE*

THE HISTORY OF land taxation in east Africa reveals a chronology of incremental adjustments to European settlements in the region since the beginning of the century. The process can be divided into two broad phases. The first phase was a period of increasing European homesteading induced by colonial economic aspirations, and its accompanying need to define policies for land resource management. The second phase began with the attainment of independence in the 1960s. For most African states, this was an era of budget deficits, as governments consistently spent much more that they were able to raise from domestic sources despite their high levels of taxation.[1]

In addition to the common British colonial heritage shared by the countries included in this survey, a wide variety of obstacles has stymied the attempt to tax real property. First, pre-colonial East Africa was characterized by the complete absence of urban settlements; few areas in Africa had such complete dispersal of population. Cities such as Nairobi, Entebbe, Kampala, Lusaka, Blantyre, Harrare, and Dar es Salaam were started by European and Arab settlers. Second, African traditional ideas of property ownership are often obscured, and there are, in most rural areas, no clear distinctions between private and community land

*Rexford A. Ahene, associate professor of economics and director of the African Studies Program at Lafayette College, Easton, PA, earned his Ph.D. at the University of Wisconsin. He is co-author of *Privatization and Investment in Sub-Saharan Africa* (1992), and *Valuation Procedures and Practice in Tanzania* (1996), and author of many articles and reports mostly dealing with economic issues in Africa. He is also a staff consultant for the World Bank and the governments of Malawi and Uganda, and has worked for the United Nations Development Program and for the African Development Bank.

ownership. Normally, land boundaries are not surveyed and land tenure terms are not specified. Thus, within the indigenous land tenure framework, title registration was of little significance to the management of land resources. Land registration was also introduced, in large measure, by Europeans as the tenure system in urbanizing areas, but was sporadically enforced or largely ignored in the rural areas. Consequently, the rudimentary cadastral requirements for levying a tax on real property have evolved slowly in Africa, and the land tax experience is limited, for all practical purposes, to urban land and improvements.

The relative importance of land value taxes as a source of public revenue is difficult to establish in Africa because only rough estimates exist for a few countries on an aggregate, nationwide basis. Furthermore, financial accounts of local governments are rarely available and, as illustrated in Appendix A, land-based taxes provide a very small percentage of central government revenue. John F. Due's 1963 observation is still valid: "African property taxation, except for the European areas in Kenya, is almost solely urban taxation; nowhere is African-owned farm land subject to significant tax."[2] Thus, although real property is one of the components of the tax base in most African countries, the taxation of land values is feasible only when a well-defined registration system can be made possible. In spite of these limitations, we will endeavor to review the significance of land taxation in Kenya, Tanzania, Uganda, Malawi, Zimbabwe, and Zambia.[3]

I

Background to Land Taxation in
Colonial East Africa

SOME FORM OF land taxation was already present in the Kingdom of Buganda before Britain took over effective administration beginning in 1900. The Buganda Kingdom started as a small nation comprising a few counties—namely Kyadondo, Busiro, and Mawokota in the 15th century. The ruling elite, headed by the *kabaka* (king) collected rent from all land-holding subjects of the Buganda Kingdom. This levy was an obligatory tax collected from each man who owned a homestead and was married. Thus, when the

Uganda hut tax was introduced, it was clear that the concept of taxation was discernible to most Ugandans.

As early as 1901, the hut tax was proposed as the only practical way to raise revenue from the African rural sector. Though some scholars believe this tax was introduced to induce Africans to work on European farms, in reality the hut and poll taxes were crude wealth taxes that also served as a proxy for property rating to rural areas. The 1901 Hut Tax Regulation imposed a tax of one rupee, payable in kind or labor, upon every native hut in British East Africa. A subsequent amendment to the law allowed the tax to be levied specifically upon the owner of the hut. By 1910, other special provisions were added to the Native Hut and Poll Tax Ordinance to provide for the distress of property, or three-months imprisonment for nonpayment of tax due. However, the direct taxation of land values in Africa has a close nexus with the large scale alienation of land in the settler economy.[4] The protectorate government in East Africa argued in early 1908[5] for preserving the means of obtaining some share of any future appreciation in the value of the land, particularly because much of the land acquired by settlers was not being developed.[6] Thus, when the Crown Land Bill was presented in 1908, it became the first legislation to propose the levying of a graduated land tax on individual holdings as a sound basis for land policy in East Africa.[7]

The 1908 Bill defined important aspects of the new system of land taxation. In the first place, any Crown land lease rated at more than Ks 180 rent would be charged a land tax in addition to such rent at the rate of six cents for every 75 cents of rent.[8] (The colonial currency then in use has been translated into its present-day equivalents. Refer to the East African currency units and exchange rates in Table 1.) The Bill also provided that whenever any individual or corporation held more than 50,000 acres; the land tax would be increased by four times the amount that would otherwise be payable. Section 137(c) further provided that an individual or corporation holding more than 100,000 acres should be compelled under penalty of Ks 325 per day to divest himself of such surplus land.

Table 1

CURRENCY UNITS AND EXCHANGE RATE PER US DOLLAR			
Country	Currency	Currency Units Average 1995	1987
Kenya	Kenya Shillings (Ks)	51.43	17.75
Malawi	Malawian Kwacha (MK)	15.28	2.21
Tanzania	Tanzanian Shilling (Tsh)	574.76	64.26
Uganda	Ugandan Shilling (Ush)	968.90	106.10
Zambia	Zambian Kwacha (ZK)	1200.00	8.89
Zimbabwe	Zimbabwean Dollar (Z$)	11.55	1.80

Source: Africa South of the Sahara, 1997.
Historical Statistics: National Accounts Statistics of the United Nations.

The Crown Land Bill was rejected in 1908 because of strong opposition from the settlers. A subsequent proposal that eventually became the Crown Lands Ordinance in 1915 conceded to the settlers' demands by deleting the provisions for land taxation. However, the 1915 Ordinance helped in shaping current land policy throughout the region: It helped the emergence of a land market by legalizing the free transfer and mortgaging of land. It also allowed land leases to be granted for 99 years, and rent reassessments at one percent and two percent of the unimproved value of the land during the 33rd and 66th year respectively. The Ordinance allowed the colonial government to promote the systematic registration of urban lands and the privatization of land rights throughout East Africa. Furthermore, it promoted commercial agriculture and urbanization that served as the catalyst for defining individual and private family rights to land in more exclusive terms. In spite of its strong legacy, the 1915 Ordinance failed in one important respect: Although occupiers were required to make improvements to the land within a specified period and to maintain such improvements after that, it did not include any provisions against speculative accumulation of land.[9]

The above historical profile shows that the colonial administration in East Africa recognized both urban and rural land as a tax base. Between 1910 and 1938, land-based taxes went through many changes. With few exceptions, the practice of differential property rates, sometimes favoring land over buildings, was used throughout East Africa. From 1939 to 1960, significant changes were made to the hut and poll taxes to include the taxation of employee incomes. The most notable change occurred in 1958, when the law was changed to replace the hitherto flat rates with a graduated tax schedule.

Rating is the assessment of property tax payable by applying a monetary charge in the form of a rate to the value or values appearing in a Valuation Roll. Variants of the property tax or rating systems used in East Africa included applying the *rate* or *tariff* to land only; also called land or site-value rating. Alternatively, the rate may be applied to land and improvements, improvements only, services, and annual rental value. As in the British practice, taxes on urban property in East Africa are generally referred to as *property rates* and are a source of public finance. Furthermore, rates are imposed predominantly on land, although in most East African urban areas, a differential rate, significantly higher on land than on improvements, is the preferred practice. The patterns of land taxation specific to the countries reviewed are now considered in turn.

II

Kenya

A REVIEW OF the current practice of applying property rates to land in Kenya reveals that very little has changed since the original rationale for imposing a tax on rent was proposed shortly after the turn of the century.[10] All local governments in Kenya have taxing authority, including the right to levy a tax on property. The municipality of Nairobi, for example, is one of the six municipal governments and seven other county councils, which have relied on land taxes to stimulate local development since the 1940s. In these parts of Kenya, policies to encourage land registration and settlement have historically influenced land ownership patterns and the emergence of a land market. Nairobi was sufficiently urbanized to begin rates on land values in 1921 and Mombasa followed suit in 1949. Currently, there are 19 urban councils, 13 town councils, 20 municipal councils, and 39 county councils that comprise the local government system in Kenya. All have the same taxing powers, including the power to levy differential rates favoring buildings over land. Thus, after more than fifty years of practice, property values have been compiled from sale transactions in all the taxing jurisdiction in Kenya.

Unlike the rental income or imputed owner-occupied property income tax practice bequeathed by the British to most of her former colonies, the system of property taxation adopted in Kenya is a land (or site) value tax system. The law required the application of property rates, using site value basis, to all land held by individuals and private corporations. Property belonging to the government or used by public and charitable organizations are exempted, although housing estates developed on city-owned land are required and presumed to include a tax element in the rent charged to tenants. The tax is imposed on land or site value only, irrespective of structures on the land. The basis is what the vacant land would sell for if offered for sale in the open market.

Kenya law requires that all land parcels should be surveyed and registered. This requirement is more strictly enforced once an area is declared a planning area. The law also requires a copy of all land transactions, including evidence of land sales and leasehold terms, to be sent to the valuation office in the taxing jurisdiction. Revaluations are required every five years, although in Nairobi, mass valuations are performed every three years. Valuation estimates derived are used in Nairobi and other cities to establish a citywide map of localized values per square foot. The information obtained is then used to establish standardized land tax rates for freehold and leasehold interests in the appropriate tax jurisdiction. Care is taken to recognize the lesser value of the leaseholder's interest in property having similar characteristics. Assessed values become effective only after the estimates have been checked by an expert valuation officer and approved by the Valuation Court. Typical rates are also established by government valuers for townships and for special classes of property. In rural areas, however, a paucity of land market activity forced the county governments to resort to a flat rate schedule, sometimes made more regressive by declining the rate as the size of holding increased.

The Nairobi site-value tax rate was set at two percent by the municipal council in the 1960s and remained unchanged for several years. Even before 1963, Nairobi generated about Ks 87.5 million a year (using nominal 1996 exchange rate of US$1 = Ks 15.23), or approximately 45 percent of its total revenue from site rating alone. According to more recent data provided by the World Bank, property tax revenue of local governments in Kenya was Ks 152 million in 1977, Ks 323 million in 1981 and Ks 573 million or 42 percent of total local government revenues in 1985. Local authorities are convinced the system of applying property rates to land and site value only has been a major factor in the rapid development and modern appearance of Nairobi and other major cities in Kenya. In a survey conducted in the mid-1970s to examine the potential development effects of a switch from a pure land value base to an annual value base, the Nairobi City Council concluded that the inclusion of improvements in the tax base would reduce the potential return accruing to property owners under a site value system by more than 5.2 percent.[11] The system also makes a small contribution to central government revenue.[12] The aggregate land-based tax revenues for 1977–1987 are reported for the countries in this review in Appendix A.

On the whole, land-value taxation appears to function satisfactorily to finance a significant portion of local government expenditure in Kenya. The existing legislation allows the taxation of improvements as well, although most councils have chosen the valuation simplicity of rating land rather than improvements. However, certain limitations continue to constrain its general effectiveness as an efficient tax system. A major limitation of the system is the absence of a comprehensive cadastral information system for identifying each ratable unit and for classifying land uses. The values that are the intended base of the tax are supposed to be determined free of all encumbrances. However, this cannot be ascertained without a legal cadastre in most African rural areas. Other questions arise about the value of unsold rural and peri-urban land parcels, and about the appropriate capitalization rate to use in most areas outside the highly urbanized and actively traded urban council rating areas.

Additional complications may be attributed to the fact that most industrial sites are owned by the government or held by some parastatal organization without any specified terms and cannot be sold outright. The special valuation conditions created by the large number of public/private joint venture investments in development cannot be ignored. In response to these limitations, the County Councils in Kenya employed a flat sum per acre, classified by broad land use categories and adjusted to account for differences in size of holding.[13]

III

Tanzania

ALTHOUGH TANZANIA HAD experiences that paralleled the introduction of the hut and poll taxes in other East African colonies from the beginning of the 20th century, the first comprehensive tax regulation appeared at the outbreak of the Second World War. In 1939, Tanzania and Uganda governments introduced tax legislation that defined real property income as income from dividends or interest, royalty or rent.[14] Before 1958, the Act imposed a tax on rent less any expenses incurred in the production of the income. However, the law has undergone profound changes in the area of taxation of rents. Between 1959 and 1964, average land rent contribution to GDP was 4.1 percent. However, when Tanzania adopted socialism in 1967 and proceeded to nationalize all private property in the state, Section 8 of the Act under which rents were brought into the concept of income was effectively abandoned.

Statutory taxation of property rates was possible because of the high standards of surveying and registration established in Tanzania and the entire East African region in the 1920s. Site-value rates similar to those used in Kenya were also introduced in Dar es Salaam and eleven autonomous urban councils in 1955. Rating in the remaining parts of the country was conducted by government appointed councils.[15] Each autonomous council, including Dar es Salaam City Council, was required to set its own rate applicable to the unimproved land values only. However, the rate proposed was subject to approval by the minister of the local government.

Throughout the 1950s, the average rate for Dar es Salaam was 2.6 percent, although most of the remaining local councils set property rates ranging from 2.5 percent to 3.5 percent. Revaluations were undertaken every five years by certified government valuers from the Valuation unit of the Ministry of Land and Surveys.

Tanzania passed the Rent Restriction Act of 1962, which, among other things, set a ceiling on chargeable rent and prohibited the eviction of tenants except in extreme cases. The law also had the unfortunate effect of curbing any expectation of rental growth and thus effectively undermined the operation of an active rental market in Tanzania.

Conditions in Tanzania were further complicated by a system of laws that redefined land tenure and property relations based on socialism. During this period, all land in Tanzania was nationalized and presumed leased at full economic rent. Consequently, taxation based on land value ceased to apply from 1974. Lacking an active rental market and evidence of transactions at market rates of interest, chronic market distortions occurred, as government valuers resorted to using proxy measures that required considerable adjustment to arrive at market rents.[16]

An attempt to replace the shortfall created by the loss of revenue from site-value rating resulted in the passage of the Land (Rent and Service Charge) Act of 1974. However, lacking reliable market values, statutory rents were used. Currently, the Urban Authorities (Rating) Act of 1983 governs valuations for rating in Tanzania. As illustrated in Appendix B, the law reintroduced property taxes based on annual rental value[17] and permitted rating authorities to set property tax rates according to the authorities' financial needs.

There is renewed optimism in Tanzania due to the passage, in May of 1995, of a new land policy reversing the socialist policies of the past decades.[18] The new policy is the result of a careful research and public inquiry into land matters initiated in 1989. Because of this exercise, the new land policy has reintroduced private property rights and legalized market alienation of land. The 1995 policy also strongly recommended the introduction of land-value rating not only as an efficient source of revenue for local governments, but also as the preferred policy instrument for managing the development of urban sites and speculative land holding throughout Tanzania. These policies are currently being carried out.

IV
Uganda

UGANDA IS UNIQUE among African countries because of its long history of title registration leading to the conversion and individualization of African customary tenure in rural areas. The government of the Uganda protectorate took precautionary measures to protect native lands from alienation in 1906. This was followed by the registration of *Mailo*[19] land titles in Buganda and the establishment of freehold estates as a first step in the administration of direct taxes on land. Because of these early policies, Uganda has excellent land maps, adequate records of land ownership and field boundaries to administer urban property rates and rural land tax in some areas. Considering that all the existing urban places in Uganda were started by the British, rating in Uganda is as old as the municipalities in which they are used.

Currently, the local government system consists of Kampala City Council, nine municipalities, 33 districts, 32 town councils, and 23 town boards. Except Entebbe which taxes on an annual value basis, the municipalities of Kampala, Jinja, Masaka, and Mbale employ differential rates equal to 1.5 percent on the capital value of land, and 0.25 percent on improvements. The basis was shifted from annual rental value to market value under normal conditions of sale between 1947 and 1948.[20] Fifteen other towns became autonomous taxing jurisdictions in 1962, however, these towns tax on annual value basis only.

Uganda has also had substantial land under individual and registered tenure. Under the Uganda agreement of 1900, the mailo tenure system created freehold tenure by allocating land in square mile blocks to the kabaka, political nobles, missionaries, and white settlers. The system was used as the backbone for introducing hut and poll taxes in the region. More recently, however, rural land registration and the preparation of property registers allowed the identification of taxable fields and taxpayers in the

Kigezi District in 1958. The area has since been subdivided into three local authorities, namely, Kabale, Rukungiri, and Kisoro. Landowners are classified for purposes of rural tax on the basis of soil quality and acreage. According to Due,[21] the three rate classifications used are Ush 1.50 for the lowest grade of arable land, Ush 5.0 for average quality land, and Ush 25.0 for the highest quality land. However, because rural land registration exists only in mailo land tenure areas, the land tax is not a major revenue source. Although a sound foundation was established before 1960, after independence Uganda was unable to replace the technical expertise provided by the British colonial government for maintaining the cadastral system. The task was made more daunting by the destruction of the National Land Registry by fire in the late 1970s. Thus, in the absence of local experts and resources for maintaining an accurate fiscal cadastre, Uganda's approach to rural taxation now relies solely on imputed land-based income as a proxy for annual rental value.

Ironically, Uganda's economy began to unravel in the early 1970s due to several factors. According to evaluations by the World Bank, economic and socio-political cohesiveness in Uganda was completely shattered by the economic mismanagement and extensive destruction that occurred during this period, which more or less coincided with the dictatorship of Idi Amin. This era was also characterized by an unprecedented abuse of property rights that culminated in the nationalization of all land in Uganda under the 1975 Land Reform Act. Today, the tax base remains narrow and excessively dependent on income taxes and the graduated personal tax.[22] According to the World Bank, fiscal deficits remain high because of Uganda's low tax burden as a percentage of GDP. Furthermore, as indicated in Appendix A, data on property tax revenues in Uganda were sporadic throughout the 1970s and 1980s.

Table 2

TOTAL RECURRENT REVENUES, UGANDA 1985/93 (Billions of Ush)				
Revenue Source	1985/86	1990/91	1991/92	1992/93
Income Tax	156.3	13869.6	23638.6	37756.5
Export Duty	1914.8	12729.7	2005.0	0.0
Customs Duty	176.4	49581.9	76588.2	122839.5
Sales Tax	422.3	36558.4	43318.1	76927.0
C.T.L.*	22.7	3055.2	5417.7	8160.0
Other Taxes	151.3	21013.0	36933.0	41428.2
Total	2843.8	136807.8	187900.8	287111.2

Source: Ministry of Finance and Economic Planning. 1992/93 Projections as of June 1993.
*Commercial Transactions Tax

There is no disputing the fact that Uganda's current tax effort at six percent of GDP since 1989 is far lower than the average of approximately 18 percent for other Sub-Saharan African countries. As Table 2 shows, the principal sources of revenue for the government of Uganda are income tax and customs and excise tax, sales and commercial transactions tax, and graduated personal taxes. However, the Uganda Revenue Authority is currently considering the use of land-value taxation as a more fundamental solution to its chronic revenue shortfall. The principal advantages of property rating most attractive to the URA are related to its appropriateness for: (a) determining ability to pay taxes, (b) identifying property owners as beneficiaries of public expenditure on social and economic infrastructure, and (c) superior (relative to income taxes) neutrality with respect to resource allocation. However, in Uganda, as in other countries where property rates are used, land tax revenues are expected to be employed in combination with other taxes to provide the necessary variety of public services.

V

Malawi

MALAWI HAS AN impressive array of natural resource and land use laws dating back to its early federation with Zimbabwe and

Zambia. Formerly known as Nyasaland, Malawi was a member of the Federation of Rhodesia and Nyasaland under British colonial tutelage. Consequently, the Rhodesia Municipal Ordinance of 1914 introduced land-value taxation in both Malawi and Rhodesia. At the time, the basic policy followed on property rates permitted municipalities to differentiate between the taxation of land and improvements. Arthur W. Madsen's account of land taxation in Eastern Africa revealed that urban centers in the Federation maintained a four-to-one ratio between the tax rate on land and improvements from 1915 until 1953.[23] The city of Blantyre, for example, had a population of 50,000 residents and was fiscally dependent on the site rate system for a significant proportion of the cost of municipal services by 1945. Three municipal councils centered in Zomba, Mzuzu, and Lilongwe are also governed by the Local Government (Urban Areas) Act which contains provisions for rating land values. However, in the predominantly rural hinterlands, town councils applied property rates to the capital value of land and buildings because of the unsettled conditions in these areas.

Although the municipality of Blantyre has continued to use the site rating system, the total yield from property rating as a share of the cost of public and municipal services has declined (see Appendix A). Since 1971, the administration of land-based taxes has been coordinated by the central government through the Ministry of Land and Valuation from Lilongwe. However, government finance statistics show that taxes on property accounted for only 2.7 percent and 3.3 percent of government revenues in 1977 and 1981 respectively.

The decline in site-value rating is, however, not due to a decline in the privatization of land titles in Malawi. On the contrary, the government in the early 1970s directed all agencies responsible for land to accelerate the privatization of customary communal land titles for three main reasons. It enabled the government to: (a) add some customary land to the tax roll by creating statutory leaseholds; (b) levy and periodically review ground rents on leasehold titles as a significant source of revenue; (c) exercise control through covenants contained in leases, including the right to revoke a lease for non-payment of rent. Thus, the ministry responsible for land and valuation was authorized to create private *presumptive* titles in communal tenure areas by granting leases, reserve a rack rent, impose a financial penalty of 10 percent on all monies due for late payment of rent, and to revoke leases created on formerly customary communal lands. The Act also empowers the minister to re-enter any private land for non-payment of taxes.

There is abundant evidence that Malawi has defined more land and property interests in law in urban and rural areas than have most African countries of equivalent size. Furthermore, Malawi has the legislation and registration machinery necessary for administering land taxation. The history of rent taxation in the country also shows that either a rental value or a capital value system can work, and there is certainly no presumption that a site or land-value rating cannot be applied to both freehold and statutory leaseholds throughout Malawi. However, Malawi lacks the work force and political will to recast the existing system nationally along the lines of land-value rating, despite the clearly demonstrated advantages of that approach.

Table 3

NOMINAL AND REAL VALUES OF GROUND RENT LEVY PER HECTARE IN MALAWI (1985–95)		
Year	Nominal Value (MK)	Real Value (MK)
1985	10.00	10.00
1990	20.00	12.60
1993	30.00	11.37
1995	36.80	4.04

Less than 50 percent of the urban property rates are collected in Blantyre and less than 10 percent of the leasehold rent due is ever paid. As far as revaluations reflect rising land values, none has occurred in recent years. Since 1991, the World Bank has emphasized, without success, the expedience of a fourfold increase in leasehold rent and a more effective collection system as a necessary precondition for stimulating effective land utilization in Malawi. One might argue that the real value of the ground rent levy in Malawi has declined due to the combined effect of currency revaluation and the government's failure to revise leasehold rents. In the absence of conclusive data explaining the trend for ground rent over the years, the currency exchange rate from 1985 to 1995 (Malawi Kwacha to the US Dollar) may be used as a fairly reasonable way to determine this trend. Using 1985 as the base year, the currency index for 1995 was 910.35. Thus, according to the values indicated in the table above, nominal rent has increased from MK 10.00 per hectare in 1985 to MK 36.80 in 1995, but the real value of leasehold rents has declined in real terms from MK 10.00 to MK 4.04. per hectare at 1985 prices.

In the meantime, a very vocal opposition from commercial farmers owning extensive freehold and leasehold estates has stymied efforts by the Ministry. Because freehold land in rural areas in Malawi is not subject to property rates, it is especially conspicuous in the densely populated districts of Thyolo and Mulanje in the Southern Region. The credibility of former colonial allotments of tribal land to European commercial farmers is being undermined by land invasion, encroachment on private land, and demands for restitution. A feasible policy solution is to impose a rural land tax that would force all estate owners to release under-utilized land for use by the landless. Finally, the continuing tax-free treatment of commercial freehold estates and lax collection of leasehold rents in Malawi may also be due to conflict of interest—most senior officials of the government are also major land owners. Thus, the Land Ministry's claimed inability to generate an accurate list of registered title holders on demand should be viewed with suspicion. Perhaps the most important point that can be made for Malawi is that the framework for a national land taxation system exists there. However, no amount of striving for technical competence in tax administration will be worth much unless it has the backing of the government.

VI

Zambia and Zimbabwe

THE RE-INTRODUCTION OF land taxation in Zimbabwe remains an integral part of the long term strategy for economic management presented by the government in 1982. A basic policy on property rates was in existence as a crucial feature of land alienation in Zimbabwe (formerly Southern Rhodesia) from 1910 until 1965. The process by which African communal land areas were alienated and converted into white freehold estates or some variant of state property is well documented.[24] By 1931, white settlers held 50 percent of the land under freehold, small scale commercial (black) farms held five percent, while the South African Company managed 23 percent of the land under a variety of leasehold arrangements for the colonial state.[25] In fact, Zambia (formerly Northern Rhodesia) and Zimbabwe had the largest European settlements outside South Africa during this period.

Both Zimbabwe and Zambia also had several urban places where differential property rates were the principal source of revenue for town councils. Under the Rhodesia Municipal Ordinance of 1914, differential rates were allowed. By 1915 and 1917 respectively, Harare (formerly Salisbury) and Bulawayo local authorities began to apply property rates to the capital value of land and buildings, by setting the tax on improvements at 25 percent of the site-value rate. The municipalities of Gwelo, Kwekwe, Gatooma, and Hwange soon followed, and property rates were of substantial importance in 23 other urban communities in Zimbabwe.

Throughout the period leading to independence for Zambia in 1964 and Zimbabwe in 1980, the existing law supported the application of property rates to actual freehold sale value. However, no adjustment is made when title is a leasehold since the tax is a levy on the registered owner. Local councils in both countries were permitted to set the rates according to local fiscal need; however, each council's rate proposal needed the approval of the minister for local government to become law. Table 4 reveals differences in the rate on land and improvement employed in some Zambian towns in the 1960s. According to Due,[26] the higher rate on land was designed to discourage land speculation and to help building development.

Table 4

Differential Property Rate in Zambia—1960		
	Rate on Land	Rate on Improvement
Lusaka	Zsh 2.0	Zsh 0.10
Ndola	Zsh 1.75	Zsh 0.65
Kitwe	Zsh 2.0	Zsh 2.50
Highest Rate		**Zsh 2.50**
Lowest Rate		**Zsh 0.25**
Source: John F. Due, 1963., op. cit.		

Harare and Bulawayo operate fully staffed and independent valuation units. However, valuation in the remaining municipalities is made by the valuation unit in the Ministry of Local Government. In addition, rural road councils in the former European areas were permitted to levy a flat betterment tax against each piece of property, regardless of size. Revaluation is conducted every three years although required by law only every ten years. New buildings are added to the Valuation Roll every six months or whenever the Valuation Office believes substantial changes in property values have occurred.

The full sale price, based on open market transactions, is the preferred standard for tax valuation. However, the value of the improvement is ascertained by subtracting the land value from the total. In practice, the valuation office establishes standard values per acre from land sales for use as the basis for mass valuation. Commercial property rates are computed by the capitalization of net rents when the required information is readily available. The more common practice is to use the cost approach to value new buildings. The data required is compiled from information submitted to the deed registry and retained by each municipality. In both Zambia and Zimbabwe, unpaid tax is recorded as a lien and the municipality can repossess the property following a decision by the court. Very few problems of delinquency were reported since much of the tax is paid together with mortgage payments in both countries.

In 1986, the report of the Chelliah Commission of Inquiry into Taxation suggested that the existing local authorities' rates were inadequate for attaining fiscal autonomy in Zimbabwe. Thus, in 1990, following the implementation of a new land policy, the government established a Land Tax Committee to draft a land tax bill. The government believes that "the force of taxation can be applied to increase the momentum of the effort to bring back into full production land that is underutilized and to maximize the productive use of this scarce national resource."[27]

VII

Concluding Observations

VARIOUS STUDIES ON land policy reform and taxation in Africa have pointed to the efficacy of a general land or site-value tax system for stimulating land use.[28] There is no disputing the fact that Africa's current tax effort is far lower than the average for other developing regions. The principal factors contributing to this poor tax performance, according to the World Bank and evidence provided by revenue authorities in 1994, include: (a) poor compliance in the informal sector economy, (b) narrow coverage of the existing tax instruments, and (c) poor administration and tax collection efforts. However, fundamental solutions to these and other problems are currently being contemplated. Recommendations have emerged suggesting the desire by local authorities to adopt land value taxes designed to: (1) encourage the development of both rural and urban land, (2) broaden the revenue base of local government, (3) provide opportunities for streamlining the country's land tenure and cadastral records system, and (4) streamline fiscal structure and provision of public services.

The application of the land or site-value tax system is regarded as a highly satisfactory method that penalizes development less. From the fiscal point of view, differential property tax initiatives in East Africa have been credited with the intensity of development and the attractive appearance of cities in the region. In addition, land policy reform measures taken to strengthen cadastral records and tax administration in Tanzania, Uganda, and Zimbabwe since 1991/92 have resulted in visible improvements in collection efficiency. However, measures to increase local government decentralization, or to control expenditure in response to revenue shortfall have not been adequate in improving public sector provision of services and/or tax equity. Further action is required to broaden the tax base, and to ensure that public investments are compatible with the expected delivery of public services. To this end, research and data management systems for comprehensive and accurate valuation are critically needed. The institution of a land tax to be based on the rated value of output in the rural land sector and a flat rate for common areas are under consideration in Zimbabwe.

Classifying soil according to its productive capacity has some precedence in most parts of East Africa where property rates are employed. Although production and consumption taxes impede economic growth, most African governments find them relatively easier to administer than a tax on land. Consequently, the potential for increasing the tax yield without impeding incentives, by encouraging further development of urban and rural land taxation, has been overlooked. Furthermore, most governments lack the political commitment and financial resources to undertake systematic adjudication of titles and registration in rural areas. Fortunately, current technology for aerial mapping and Geographic Positioning Survey methods can be used to overcome cadastral limitations quickly and at a considerable cost and time savings over other geodetic survey methods. Using land attribute classifications similar to those proposed in Zimbabwe will involve a change in the mode of expressing the tax base and will also require a more comprehensive land information system. This can be accomplished quite easily and cheaply by making land taxation a top priority wherever land policy reforms are contemplated.

Notes

1. African governments have come to rely more on direct and indirect taxes on production and expenditure and have, in the process, failed to invest in cadastral systems necessary to improve the taxation of land and

improvements. See V. Tanzi, "Structural Factors and Tax Revenue in Developing countries: A Decade of Evidence," in I. Goldin, et. al. (eds.) *Open Economies: Structural Adjustment and Agriculture* (Cambridge, England: Cambridge University Press, 1992).

2. John F. Due, *Taxation and Economic Development in Tropical Africa* (Cambridge, MA: MIT Press, 1963), p. 102.

3. According to Bekele Muleta, identified only as "a high government official in Ethiopia," that nation has been implementing a form of land-value taxation since January, 1966: "We let out vacant land for the highest bidders, and raise the annual rent on existing landowners four fold." (*Incentive Taxation*, May, 1997, p. 5.) Efforts to obtain details have proved, unfortunately, unavailing.

4. H.W.D. Okoth-Ogendo, *Tenants of the Crown: Evolution of Agrarian Law and Institutions in Kenya* (Nairobi: ACTS Press, 1991), p. 27.

5. See Lord Elgin's despatch dated 19th March, 1908. *Official Gazette of the East African Protectorate*, 19th March 1908.

6. Based on early communication between settlers in the East African region and the British Foreign Office, that dealt with the problem of unproductive accumulation of land.

7. That this Bill may have been influenced by the ideas of Henry George is shown by the following statement in Lord Harcourt's despatch to Sir Percy Giroward, the governor: "As to the proposal for a graduated land tax, it has been brought to my notice that of the land in the protectorate for white settlement some 4,000 square miles has already been sold or leased and that it is estimated that only about 4,000 square miles still remain for disposal. The present white population is stated by you to be 1,200. It will be seen therefore that the idea of a large white population in the Highlands may be seriously prejudiced unless the government retains some means of restraining undue accumulation of land. The graduated land tax proposed in Lord Elgin's despatch, is, in my opinion, well designed to secure this object." See Lord Harcourt's despatch dated 3rd February, 1911 to Col. Sir Percy Giroward, the Governor, on account of the Rental Bill, *Official Gazette of the East African Protectorate*, 7th March, 1911.

8. Based on calculations by W. McGregor-Ross, Sections 137(a) and 137(b) of the Fifth Schedule to the Bill provided the basis for taxation. See *Kenya from Within: A Short Political History*. (London: Frank Cass, 1968), pp. 72–73.

9. Ibid., p. 75ff.

10. The acceptance of site-value taxation in East Africa arose from the spread of the single tax idea of Henry George which was proposed in the Crown Land Bill of 1908.

11. See Roy W. Bahl and Johannes F. Linn, *Urban Public Finance in Developing Countries* (A World Bank Book; New York: Oxford University Press, 1992), pp. 175–177.

12. Due, op. cit., p.110.

13. According to John F. Due, the typical county rate schedule for a small holding of up to 20 acres is Ks 2.0 per acre; 20–50 acres, Ks 1.5; 50–100 acres, Ks 1.0; 100–500 acres, Ks 0.60; beyond 500 acres, Ks 0.10. Ibid., p.112.

14. Income Tax Act (25) Section 3 (2) defines the income coming from property as dividends or interest, Section 6 goes further to include in this definition royalty, rent, premium among others. The rates, premiums, and interest are the gains from corporeal property and usually accrue to a tax payer for allowing use or occupation of his property by another.

15. Due, op. cit. 113.

16. The current basis of valuation of rent assessment in Tanzania is made under Section 17 of the 1984 Rent Restriction Act. The act defines standard rent as: "The annual rent assessed by the Rent Tribunal, and not to exceed the total amount equal to 14 percent of the replacement value of the premises in the case of residential premises, or 18 percent in the case of commercial premises."

17. The 1983 Act replaced the Land (Rents and Service Charge) Act of 1974, which was, until then, the authority under which land rent and service charges were levied. Similar authority for rating was established under the Local Government (District Authorities) Act of 1982. The act empowers urban and township authorities to levy a tax on any improvement which is capable of use or occupation and which is of a sufficiently permanent nature as normally to pass with land on disposition.

18. Refer to the following documents produced by R. Ahene, senior land policy advisor and team leader, Ministry of Lands, Housing and Urban Development (MLHUD), and published by Tropical Research and Development, Inc., Gainesville, Florida, 1994–1996: (1) *Privatization and Investment in Sub-Saharan Africa*, by Rexford A. Ahene & B. Katz, Praeger Inc., New York, (1992), (2) "Property Tax Modifications for Improved Land Stewardship in Uganda" National Environment Management, Action Program for the Environment, *Tropical Research and Development Report*, Gainesville, Florida, March, 1995, (3) "Valuation and Observable Land Market in Tanzania" Tropical Research and Development Report, Gainesville, Florida, October 1994, and (4) "Local Government Responsibility for Implementing Economic Reforms in South Africa" in *Regional and Local Taxation in a Future South Africa*, ed., R.C.D. Franzsen, Center for Human Rights, Pretoria, South Africa, October 1994. See also, Report of the Presidential Commission of Inquiry into Land Matters, 1992. MLHUD and the Scandinavian Institute of African Studies, Uppsala, Sweden.

19. Mailo tenure is a form of absolute ownership created by the Uganda agreement of 1900 as the highest and most ample estate in indigenous clan land in Uganda. It is based on square miles of land; thus the tenure form under which it is held.

20. Due, op. cit., p. 110.

21. Ibid.

22. The graduated personal tax or GPT is a crude wealth tax with origins in the Native poll and hut tax.

23. Arthur W. Madsen, in Brown et. al. (eds.), *Land-Value Taxation Around the World* (1st edition, 1955), p. 46.

24. S. Moyo, *"The Land Question" The Political Economy of Transition in Zimbabwe.* (Harare. Government Printers, 1987).

25. S. Moyo, "Land Tax Proposal for Zimbabwe." in R.C.D. Franzsen and C. H. Heyns (eds.), *A Land Tax for the New South Africa?* (Pretoria: Center for Human Rights, University of Pretoria Press, 1992), pp. 92–110.

26. Op. cit., p.115.

27. Financial Bill, Hansard, July 1982.

28. Refer to "Land Tenure and Agricultural Development in Uganda," MISR/LTC, June 1988; *Uganda: Possibilities for Tax Reform*, Walter Mahler, et. al., 1993; *Access to Land and Other Natural Resources: A Research and Policy Development Project*, Jerome French and Cornelius Kazoora, eds., MISR/LITC, May 1992.

Appendix A

LAND BASED TAXES AND REVENUE SOURCES: EAST AFRICA

Country: Kenya (Millions of Kenya Shillings)

	1977	1978	1979	1980	1981	1982	1983	1984	1985	1986
(A) Central Government										
Current Tax Revenue (Total)	6.147	9.181	9.833	11.823	13.567	14.874	16.154	17.772	19.926	23.357
Taxes on Property	11	14	13	36	12	29	11	12	4	3
Estate, Inheritance	11	14	13	36	12	29	11	12	4	3
(B) Local Government										
Taxes on Property	152	159	172	182	323	436	441	399	572	–
Entrepreneurial Property Income	334	368	443	485	460	598	678	561	578	–
(total Local Govt. revenue)	620	643	714	787	903	1203	1280	1083	1362	

Local Government in Kenya Comprises: 39 county councils, 20 minicipal councils, 13 town councils, and 19 urban councils.

Country: Tanzania (Millions of Tanzania Shillings)

	1976	1977	1978	1979	1980	1981	1982	1983	1984	1985
(A) Central Government										
Current Tax Revenue (Total)	3411	4470	5474	6855	7408	8393	–	–	–	–
Tax Revenue				5835	6931	6054	9182	10880	13480	17197
Taxes on Property	7	49	47	68	41	47	57	49	66	190
Estate, Inheritance	2	8	2	–	4	6	2	8	2	6
Commercial Property Income	173	460	140	379	266	196				
rent (Buildings)	14	28	28	26	20	2				
Other Property	85				53	32				279
Royalties and Rent	85				53	11				

Local Government comprises of 20 regions.

Appendix A

LAND BASED TAXES AND REVENUE SOURCES: EAST AFRICA

Country: Uganda (Milians of Uganda Shillings)

	1977	1978	1979	1980	1981	1982	1983	1984	1985	1986
(A) Central Government										
Current Tax Revenue (Total)	34.39	57.93	26.31	40.48	30.91	276.64	536.78	937.6	668.9	228.1
Taxes on Property	-	-	-	-	-	-	-	-	-	-
Commercial Property Income	0.72	0.19	0.07	0.25	0.61	1.59	2.52	5.62	-	-
(B) Local Government										
Taxes on Property				0.6	0.84	1.93	19.6			
(total Local Govt. revenue)					14.28	27.82	40.06			

Local Government in Uganda Comprises: 33 Districts, 1 city council, 9 municipalities, 32 town councils and 23 town boards.

Country: Malawi (Millions of Kwacha)

	1977	1978	1979	1980	1981	1982	1983	1986
(A) Central Government								
Current Tax Revenue (Total)	109.07	142.4	176.21	192.24	214.08	231.97	276.54	479.22
Taxes on Property	0.08	0.06	0.09	0.07	0.02	0.14	0.27	0.41
Tax Revenue Rents	1.26	1.46	1.94	1.61	1.81	2.29	2.29	6.49
(B) Local Government								
Taxes on Property	3.13	3.94	5.23	6.83	4.7			
Entrepreneurial Property Income	0.45	0.41	0.34	1.46	1.14			

Local Government in Malawi comprises: 3 cities, 7 town councils, 24 district councils, and 1 municipality.

Appendix A

LAND BASED TAXES AND REVENUE SOURCES: EAST AFRICA

Country: Zambia (Millions of Zambian Dollars)

	1979	1980	1981	1982	1983	1984	1985	1986	1987	1988
(A) Central Government										
Current Tax Revenue (Total)	539.6	709	751.1	776.2	958.6	1017.4	1427.1	2800	4027	4501.1
Taxes on Property	0.1	0.4	0.3	0.4	0.4	2.2	3.2	14.1	6.3	6.4
Estate, Inheritance	0.1	0.4	0.3	0.4	0.4	2.2	3.2	0.6	1	0.8
Commercial Property Income		32.1	28.4	22.7	30.7	16.5	28.4	65.8	53.7	45.2
Other Property	6.4	2.3	1.5	10.9	1.3	1.7	7.9	2.8	1.9	1.9
Land Rent	–	–	–	–	–	–	0.7			
(B) Local Government										
Current Revenue (Total)	29.2	28								
Taxes on Property	21.8	20.7								
Entrepreneurial Property Income	3.4	3.5								

Local Government in Zambia comprises: 55 district councils.

Country: Zimbabwe (Millions of Zimbabwe Dollars)

	1978									
(A) Central Government										
Current Tax Revenue (Total)	572.7	1.6	2.8	1.9	4	5.7	8.4	2114.8	–	–
Taxes on Property	1.7	1.6	2.8	1.9	4	5.7	8.4	7.8	–	–
Estate, Inheritance	1.7							7.8	–	–
(B) Local Government										
Taxes on Property	22.6	23.1	24.8	32.3	38	48.2	52.2	57.4		
Entrepreneurial Property Income	22.8	26.3	28.3	30.5	44.4	51.5	58.5	75		
(total Local Govt. Revenue)	217.9	253.5	310.5	324.7	474.4	567.6	692.3	804		

Local Government in Zimbabwe comprises: 12 town councils, 55 district councils, and 48 rural councils.

Source: IMF, Government Finance Statistics Yearbook, 1988

Appendix B

PROPERTY TAX RATE DETERMINATION:
An Example from Tanzania

Suppose in the Mwanza municipality there are **30,000** squatter type of properties, each unit averaging a value of Tsh **2,500,000** and **10,000** medium quality houses averaging a value of Tsh **6,000,000** and **4,000** commercial or high quality buildings with an average value of Tsh **40,000,000**.

Suppose that the municipality anticipates to raise Tsh **5,000,000,000** from property taxes to finance its expenditure for the 1996/97 year and it anticipates that only **40 percent** of this can be raised from local sources and government grants, what tax should the various property owners (i,e., of low-cost, medium-cost and high-cost houses) select to pay in property rates in the next financial year?

Assessment of Rate Payable

Budget Expenditure (E):	Shs 5,000,000,000
Less	
Other Anticipated Revenues (S):	
5,000,000,000/=@40%	Shs 2,000,000,000
Amount to be raised from property tax (T):	Shs 3,000,000,000
Divide by total assessed property values:	
Squatter Houses	
30,000 @ Shs 2,500,000	Shs 7,500,000,000
Med quality Houses	
10,000 @ Shs 6,000,000	Shs 6,000,000,000
High Quality Houses	
4,000 @ Shs 40,000,000	Shs 160,000,000,000
Total Value of ratable properties (B)	Shs 173,500,000,000

$$
\begin{array}{r}
0.0173 \\
\times\,100 \\
\hline
\text{Rate} \quad 1.73
\end{array}
$$

Multiply by 100 to get Rate Payable

Since the Rate $R = [(E - S) \times 100] \div B$
Thus $R = (T \div B) \times 100$

Chapter 17

Republic of South Africa

BY GODFREY R. A. DUNKLEY*

THE REPUBLIC OF South Africa (RSA) is among the world leaders in collecting municipal or local government revenue from the capital value of land. Looking at the country as a whole, some 70 percent of city revenue has been collected by site-value rating where there is no revenue collected from improvements. For the remainder, a larger portion has come from land values than from improvements, with only two major cities collecting an equal percentage from both land and improvements, i.e. flat rating.

For the most part, there is a distinction between rates and services. Services are normally charged as close as possible to cost and capital replacement/amortization, and contribute little towards general municipal revenue or expenditure. However, there has been a major upset to this principle in recent years because of political agitation and the growth of a new culture of non-payment. This has reached serious proportions to the extent that the central power supply authority, Eskom, has at times been forced to cut off power supplies to large areas. Local authorities have also cut off water supplies, and are threatening to do so again. Many local authorities are effectively bankrupt and this could affect current thinking on municipal revenue systems.

---

*Godfrey R. A. Dunkley qualified as a mechanical and electrical engineer after study at Whittoms Engineering College. For 25 years, he was employed by Mobil Oil in various parts of South Africa. In 1980, he became national president of the Institution of Certified Mechanical and Electrical Engineers. From 1993 to 1997, he served two terms as president of the International Union for Land-Value Taxation and Free Trade. Mr. Dunkley is author of the book, *That All May Live–Guidelines Towards a Better Society* (1990), and a booklet, *Land Tenure: A Time Bomb Ticking in South Africa* (1991).

There has been a strong move towards redistribution of land and restitution of land rights that were taken away from large numbers of people during the days of the apartheid policy of moving blacks from white areas to black homelands. Much of the confiscation is being reversed by court decisions, and the Ministry of Land Affairs is working towards introducing a land tax in rural areas. This tax is being opposed by all farming organizations.

With the above overview of present conditions in the RSA, it may be useful to go back to some of the earlier history of land taxation in the country.

I

History of Land Taxation

SOUTH AFRICA HAS a long history of collecting a portion of land rent as revenue. In 1652, the Dutch East India Company asserted its right to the land in the western Cape. Under Jan van Riebeeck, the settlers had only tentative rights to the land at the discretion of the governor, for which they paid a land tax or quitrent, according to the agricultural quality. In 1714, a fee of twelve riksdollars per annum was charged for grazing land, and a tithe of one tenth of the crop for sowing land. In 1731, farmers were allowed to register land in erfpacht for fifteen years with an annual payment of twenty-four riksdollars for a sixty morgen farm. Some were later converted to freehold with a minimum payment of twenty-four riksdollars per annum plus an additional amount on the more valuable farms, to be assessed by officials.[1]

Sir John Cradock introduced perpetual quitrent in 1813, allowing holders of land on loan to establish security. The maximum size of a farm was to be three thousand morgen and the annual fee not to exceed two hundred and fifty riksdollars, but this could be increased at a later date.[2]

As the Boer farmers gradually migrated to the east in later years, the British government followed with a demand for land tribute which resulted in the Great Trek into the hinterland, namely the Orange Free State and the Transvaal, where for a while they were free. With the establishment of both these territories as republics, farms were laid out on the principle of putting in four pegs during a one hour gallop on horseback. "First come" got the best land. Their payment was rent in the form of service, that is, the provision of one man, one horse, and one rifle when needed to preserve the peace or defend the land. As in Europe, this service gradually gave way to other forms of taxation.

After the establishment of the Union of South Africa in 1910, most municipal ratings were based on the total value of both land and improvements. At that stage, the Labour Party of South Africa included the taxation of land in its manifesto. In 1912, a Provincial Commission was set up by the Transvaal to investigate the franchising and rating of leasehold plots or stands in Johannesburg, where rates were being paid by the stand holders. After a stalemate situation, the late Justice Frank A. W. Lucas proposed that rates should be levied on the site value of land with the recommendation that, despite anything to the contrary in the titles, the freehold owner should not be allowed to recover the rates levied on him from the leaseholder. The Commission recommended this proposal.

About this time, several Labour candidates, including Lucas, were elected to the Johannesburg Town Council. They were pledged to press for the rating of site values and the exemption of all improvements. A resolution to this effect was adopted and submitted to the province. However, the Provincial Council consisted mainly of large landowners and disregarded the recommendation.[3]

In 1914, following strike action, the Labour Party took control of the province with a majority of one. This allowed it to pass the necessary Transvaal Provincial Ordinance No.1 of 1916, which allowed for site-value rating and prevented flat rating. This ordinance (in 1933 consolidated into Ordinance No. 20) had the effect of ensuring a higher rate on land than on improvements, by one penny in the pound. This provision was removed in the new Ordinance No. 11 of 1977, where the emphasis is still on rating of land but allows equal rating of improvements under certain conditions. However, rating on improvements can never be higher than on land. The 1916 Transvaal Ordinance acted as a model for much of the country.

Some details of this ordinance were given in the first edition of *Land-Value Taxation Around the World* (1955), but warrant repeating in part. Site (land) value is defined as follows:

> "Site value of land" shall mean the capital sum which the land or interest in land might be expected to realize if offered for sale on such reasonable terms and conditions as a bona fide seller would require, assuming that the improvements, if any, thereon, or appertaining thereto, had not been made. The site value of land shall include any value due to any franchise, license, privilege or concession attaching to the site for the time being.[4]

The earlier Transvaal Ordinance effectively prevented flat rating or total value rating. Johannesburg was the first to adopt site-value rating in 1918, followed by other municipalities. By 1955, there were 20 of the 60 urban municipalities on site-value rating and by 1979, all the major municipalities in the Transvaal had followed suit.

The other provinces gradually followed the lead of the Transvaal. By 1979, 60 of the 125 largest municipalities in South Africa were on site-value rating, and by 1984, of the 112 cities with a total value of over R30 million, 62 were on site-value rating. These accounted for 70 percent of the total value of rating in the RSA. By then, only two of these largest cities were still on flat rating, namely Cape Town and Port Elizabeth. The others, on composite rating, all collect a larger percentage from land values than from improvements. It would be safe to say that less than 15 percent of the total rates in the RSA come from improvements. Towns and villages with a total value of less than R30 million only account for 2.4 percent of the municipal revenue in the RSA so can have little impact on conclusions given. A large percentage of these low value, low growth towns are on flat rating.[5]

Two surveys on rating in South Africa by the present author show that the cities which collect rates on site value only have drawn twice the percentage of increased capital investment compared to those which rate total value. The first survey covered a twenty year period from 1959 to 1979, and the second a ten year period from 1974 to 1984. The second survey was staggered by five years from the first to allow for differences in updating of valuation rolls. The Transvaal Ordinance calls for a three year update while the Cape Province allows for ten year updating. This staggering had little effect on the results.

II

Rating Surveys

THE FINDINGS OF the two surveys on rating in South Africa are given in Chapter Fourteen ("Effects of Municipal Rating on Progress") of *That All May Live*,[6] and may be summarized as follows:

a. In the period 1951 to 1984, the number of cities and towns on flat rating reduced from 187 to 61, while those on site-value rating increased from 36 to 98 in the same period. Some changed to and some from composite rating and a few were absorbed into larger towns in that period.

b. In the first survey—1959 to 1979, the cities on flat rating showed a total value increase of 536.5 percent over the twenty year period, while those which were on site-value rating for the full period showed an increase of 940.3 percent. Those which changed to site-value rating showed an even larger increase, namely 1,013.2 percent.

c. The corresponding increases for the ten years of the second survey, 1974 to 1984, were 171 percent for flat rating, 328 percent for site-value rating, and 357 percent for those changing to site-value rating.

d. The growth is even more remarkable when excluding the land values and considering the increase in capital investment as a percentage over the ten year period. This study was confined to the 48 largest cities, each with a total value over R200 million in 1984. Of these, 33 were on site-value rating and showed an aggregate growth of 413 percent compared to 282 percent for the 13 on composite rating and 189 percent for the two remaining cities on flat rating. This is valid evidence showing that the rating of improvements provides a strong incentive for capital investment to go elsewhere, namely to those cities which collect their rates from site value only.

e. A large number of small towns on flat rating in the Cape showed very little growth. This could be partly due to their geographic position and partly due to their system of rating all improvements.

It is interesting to note that the remaining two large cities on flat rating are Cape Town and Port Elizabeth, both major ports and tourist cities and one the legislative capital of the Republic. They should logically have kept pace with the average growth of major cities. However, their percentage growth in all instances has been low compared to the average for the RSA and particularly for those cities on site-value rating.

The other cities, which rate land at a higher percentage than improvements, showed growth in both total value and capital investment approximately in proportion to the incidence of rates on land vs. improvements. As a group, their growth was between those on site-value rating and flat rating under all the different conditions considered.

III

Changes in the New South Africa

FUTURE STUDIES COULD be complicated by a variety of changes which have taken and are taking place in the RSA. To start with, all the independent homelands have been reincorporated into the Republic. This has made a big difference to government statistics and in particular to the total population. It has also allowed for major changes in the population distribution, and increased city population beyond normal growth because of squatters.

A population census has just been carried out, the results of which will give a better picture of the population distribution.

At the national level, the four former provinces together with the former independent homelands ("Bantustans") have now been consolidated and split into nine provinces with mainly new boundaries except for the Free State. In addition, many predominantly lower priced and black squatter areas have been incorporated into formerly all-white cities, and in many cases completely new city boundaries have been established.

The struggle for land ownership and the right to land tenure is reaching serious proportions. In the past, this was partly hidden by the controls of apartheid. With the removal of Influx Control, squatter camps started growing around many towns and villages as well as major cities throughout the Republic. The independent homelands had been heavily subsidized by the RSA and were thus able to operate on a different and lighter tax structure than that in the RSA. This was a deliberate attempt to encourage the growth of industry and other employment opportunities in areas which would have been close to marginal because of their adverse location relative to markets, and their lack of infrastructure.

When the above areas were reincorporated into the Republic in 1993, these subsidies were reduced or removed and the former independent homelands came under the Republic's tax structure which immediately had the effect of shifting the economic margin of production.

Viable industries and business undertakings were rendered unprofitable. The increase in taxation had the effect of placing them beyond the new economic margin.

A typical case is Fort Jackson, a border industrial area near East London which previously came under the Ciskei homeland tax structure. Until 1994, it had approximately thirty thriving industries employing thousands of local blacks. Within three years only about eight of these industries were still operating, the others having been destroyed by the new taxes. Thousands of laborers became unemployed with no alternative employment in the area. Many other areas have suffered a similar tragedy. The Department of Finance and its tax consultants refuse to address this problem. In desperation, the unemployed continue to migrate and settle in squatters camps around the cities, and have added an unprecedented economic burden to those cities. In spite of the current housing policy and the fact that tens of thousands of small houses have been constructed, there are still millions of squatters in the RSA.

The minister of land affairs is aware that a proposed land tax should apply to all land including urban land, and that it should be offset by a reduction in value added tax or other taxes which impose a burden at the margin of production. However, the land affairs portfolio only covers rural land, and the minister has no say over urban or mining land.

The Tax Commission was appointed by the national government on June 22, 1994, under the chairmanship of Professor M. M. Katz, to investigate and report on the overall tax structure of the RSA, together with recommendations. In its Third Interim Report, dated November 28, 1995, under the heading "Land Tax," page 29, the following appears:

> 4.2.3 The Commission does not recommend a national land tax in the short to medium term.
>
> 4.2.4 However, the commission believes that there is sufficient evidence to justify the possible implementation of a rural land tax at a local government level.

The Tax Commission has subsequently recommended an additional tax of two percent on all rural land and improvements without any talk of off-setting it against other existing taxes. Its tentative views as of October 1996, include the following:

- The market value of land and improvements should form the tax base.
- Valuations should take place at least every five years.
- The owner of the land should be liable for the tax.
- The tax rate should not exceed two percent a year.
- Relief through the use of rebates and referrals should be kept to a minimum.
- The tax should be levied annually but could be collected at shorter intervals.

Here are the main respects in which these tentative views differ sharply from the recommendations submitted to the Commission on behalf of the International Union for Land-Value Taxation and Free Trade:

- The tax is on both land and improvements rather than solely on land.
- The tax is on rural land only rather than on all land.

- The tax does not replace existing taxes that contribute to unemployment by their effect upon the margin of production.
- The tax is limited to two percent.

At local government level, vast changes are taking place rapidly. At this stage, only a couple of items can be included in this report.

Throughout the country, many of the smaller municipal areas were incorporated into larger cities, and some then subdivided along different boundaries. This has made it virtually impossible to compare city statistics in order to ascertain growth trends. An extra complication is that the Cape Town Valuation Roll is now sixteen years out of date and reflects wildly inaccurate values which vary between some five percent and 50 percent of the actual market value.

A Greater Cape Metropolitan Area was established which brought together thirty-nine former municipal areas with a population of approximately two and a half million people, covering an area approximately 120 kilometers from north to south and 60 kilometers across. It was then subdivided into six municipal areas. Each included a number of totally different valuation rolls that varied vastly, some nearly twenty years out of date, as well as a mixture of different rating structures with different percentages of composite rating and flat rating. Both the complexity and the severity of the situation created an opportunity for introducing the site-value rating system. First the South Peninsula Municipality appointed a Rating Committee under the chairmanship of Councilor W. Stibbe. Information about site-value rating was provided to him by the present writer, and presentations were made by a number of Cape Town planning and rating officials who favored going directly to SVR in order to simplify and update the valuation rolls. After a few meetings, the Committee recommended that (single) site value rating be introduced in July, 1998. This was then approved by the South Peninsula Council.

This Rating Committee subsequently influenced the Cape Metropolitan Council to resolve in favor of a similar system in October 1996, but three municipalities declined to adopt it at that stage, as they already had mainly updated valuation rolls and did not wish so soon to assume the considerable expense of new ones.

Before site-value rating could be implemented, large numbers of properties had to be revalued and many of the existing valuation rolls updated. Cape Town and two adjoining municipalities, South Peninsula and Blaauwberg, undertook the preparation of new valuation rolls based on site values only. On nearing completion, these new rolls were challenged by landlords on technicalities, some possibly valid. Costly litigation could have resulted. For this reason, coupled with various factors mentioned below, the new rolls were discontinued.

In the meantime, the central government had announced steps to create five mega-cities—Johannesburg, Pretoria, Durban, Cape Town, and Port Elizabeth. New municipal boundaries have been drawn, and rural areas including farming land have been incorporated into these new municipal areas. All will become liable for paying rates. This process is in diverse stages of implementation. Great confusion exists, and strong objections have been voiced. The farming communities are very upset, as most of them have never paid rates, and believe that they will receive little of value in return.

For some years there has been talk of a tax on the value of rural land. The argument has been advanced (by this writer among others) that the tax should be on the value of all privately-held land throughout the nation, and that it should be offset by a reduction in other taxes, particularly the 14 percent value added tax.

The Eighth Interim Report of the Katz Commission, under the heading, "The Implications of Introducing a Land Tax in South Africa," has, on the other hand, recommended that a land tax on rural land be implemented at the local government level only, and incorporated into municipal valuation rolls and rating.

This report discussed at length the use of market value compared to use value as the basis of valuation for farming land, holding that market value can be badly distorted by potential use value near thriving urban areas. It then recommended (current) use value, with the proviso that municipalities may apply to change to market value where more applicable.

Four different applications of a land tax were considered: 1.) It may be regarded as an additional tax that could have adverse effects upon farming and employment. 2.) It may be treated as an additional input cost when assessing income tax. 3.) It may be off-set against income tax in the form of a minimum tax. 4.) It may be regarded as a provisional payment against tax payable. The Commission recommended that it be treated similarly to urban property rates, and constitute a deduction from income for income tax purposes.

Revaluation was recommended at intervals of no longer than five years, and preferably fewer where the cost is not disproportionate. The rating percentage was left flexible, but a guideline of two percent was suggested. The method of rating was discussed, but preference given to total value rating—i.e., rating based on the total value of a site, including both land and improvements.

A new valuation bill is scheduled to go before Parliament in the near future, but as of this writing (mid-March, 2000) the final draft had not yet been circulated for public comment. In October, 1999, a draft of this bill was aired, along with the Eighth Interim Report, at a public hearing held in a Parliament committee room in Cape Town, and chaired by a top official from the Department of Finance. Discussion papers were presented by various interested government departments and by private organizations such as the South African Agricultural Union, the Chamber of Mines, and sundry Chambers of Commerce. Presentations were made by Michael Jacques and Peter Meakin in favor of a land tax, and this writer took part in the discussions. The occasion was the first time that so many interest groups had been assembled to discuss aspects of a land tax.

There is much uncertainty as to the eventual system of rating to be adopted. Despite the fact that site-value rating has proved to be so successful and accounts for at least 85 percent of the country's total rates, it is unlikely to be legislated as the preferred system. The idea of a tax so broadly based as to include everybody in its net seems to weigh more heavily than do traditional concepts of equity as proportionate to either benefits received or ability to pay.

Over the last decade in South Africa, most cities and towns have been invaded by squatters and hawkers, not only from the former homelands but from other African nations. With them has come crowding, crime, and filth. People of even modest affluence no longer venture into many of the former central business districts, and most offices and better shops have moved to the suburbs. Downtown Johannesburg, once the pride of the entire continent, has become a slum; even high-class international hotels there have closed down, and vast office towers now stand virtually empty except for their basements and rooftops where squatters have set up housekeeping. This situation is, of course, in no sense attributable to site-value rating, which accounted in large measure for the city's erstwhile affluence, but rather to a well-meaning but foolish decision by a former municipal administration regarding parking spaces, and the fact that the cruel rigidity of apartheid has now given way to an official culture of permissiveness that protects criminals at the expense of law-abiding citizens, both black and white. It is evident that the national government has major problems to solve, and that this will not be accomplished unless good intentions are accompanied by both insight and firmness.

IV

Conclusion

THE WHOLE SITUATION is in the melting pot, with relatively few knowledgeable and dedicated advocates of site-value rating and fewer all-out Georgists resident in the country. The system has amply demonstrated its worth in practice, but (as in so many instances) few of its beneficiaries understand or are even aware of it. However, contact has been established with a number of key officials. The near future could give rise to very interesting developments.

In can be shown that, in the absence of a land tax, the present taxes continue to contribute to unemployment and mass migration to squatter camps. Value added tax can be shown to be a tax on labor which has to be met by additional wages, a cost to the employer. At each level of production, from primary industry to finished product and marketing, approximately half the value added is due to labor. So all materials and services purchased have many layers of labor included in their cost and each layer of labor has its cost increased by 14 percent value added tax (RSA 2000). In effect, the value added tax imposes a tax of approximately 87.5 percent of 14 percent after three levels of production or 12.25 percent on all material and services input. This is in addition to the 14 percent on labor at that stage of production. This is enough to put most semi-marginal industries and a large number of farms out of business.

Further estimates show that the rental value of land in the Republic in 1986 was of the order of 64 percent of the 1986–87 national budget.[7] As all taxes eventually come out of rent, the economic rental value is what is left after the existent taxes have been extracted from the economy. If the sum of all existing taxes at a particular point in time is added to the total annual rent of a nation at that same point in time, the final quantity or sum would give a fair indication of the total rent that would be available within that nation without those taxes. For South Africa, the 1986–87 figure would have been 164 percent of the budget. If 70 percent of this total economic rent were collected by the government in lieu of other taxes, the figure would exceed the budget of that period. (164 × 70% = 114.8% of budget.)

The subjects of a land tax and of site-value rating are more in the public dialogue now than in many a decade, and many people in government realize that something has to be done about distribution of land ownership and land tenure. It is only a pity that there is not a strong organization to lobby the cause of a land tax to replace all existing taxes.

Notes

1. T. R. H. Davenport and K. S. Hunt, *The Right to the Land* (Cape Town: David Philip, 1974), p. 3.

2. Ibid., p. 6.

3. Frank A. W. Lucas, *"Justice and Social Reform," Land and Liberty* (London) April, 1957.

4. Arthur W. Madsen, "The Union of South Africa", in H. G. Brown et al, eds. *Land-Value Taxation Around the World* (1st edition; New York: Robert Schalkenbach Foundation, 1955), p. 41.

5. Godfrey Dunkley, *That All May Live* (Roosevelt Park, RSA: A. Whyte, 1990), pp. 120–121.

6. Ibid., pp. 119–127.

7. Godfrey Dunkley, *Land Tenure: A Time Bomb Ticking in South Africa* (Cape Town: Dunkley, 1991), p.15.

PART FIVE

ASIA

Chapter 18

Abu Dhabi

BY ROBERT V. ANDELSON*

PRIOR TO THE commencement of oil production in 1962, Abu Dhabi was one of seven impecunious desert sheikhdoms known collectively as Trucial Oman or the Trucial States, the others being

*Robert V. Andelson, professor emeritus of philosophy, Auburn University, and distinguished research fellow, American Institute for Economic Research, holds a Ph.D. from the University of Southern California. He is sole author of *Imputed Rights: An Essay in Christian Social Theory* (University of Georgia Press, 1971), joint-author (with J. M. Dawsey) of *From Wasteland to Promised Land: Liberation Theology for a Post-Marxist World* (Orbis/Shepheard-Walwyn, 1992), and editor and co-author of *Critics of Henry George* (Fairleigh Dickinson University Press/Associated University Presses, 1979), *Commons Without Tragedy* (Barnes & Noble/Shepheard-Walwyn, 1991) and of the 2nd edition of *Land-Value Taxation Around the World* (New York: Robert Schalkenbach Foundation, 1997). He is a director of the corporation and a member of the editorial board of *The American Journal of Economics and Sociology*, to which he has contributed numerous articles. His articles have also appeared in other scholarly periodicals including *The Personalist* (on the editorial board of which he served for its last five years of publication), *Modern Age, The Southern Journal of Philosophy*, and *The International Journal of Contemporary Sociology*. He is also author of several booklets, among them the widely-circulated *Henry George and the Reconstruction of Capitalism*.

Dr. Andelson is current president of the International Union for Land-Value Taxation and Free Trade, vice president of the Robert Schalkenbach Foundation, an adjunct faculty member of the Ludwig von Mises Institute, and was twice president of the Alabama Philosophical Society. Early in his career, he spent three years as executive director of the Henry George School of Social Science in San Diego. In 1964, he founded the Tax Reform Association of Louisiana (TRAL), which, during its brief existence, produced a study of the potential impact of land-value taxation on the city of Natchitoches, LA.

The author gratefully acknowledges a grant from the Lincoln Institute of Land Policy which enabled him to do field research in the UAE in 1993. For a fuller treatment of the topic, see his article, "The Single-Tax Limited in Abu Dhabi: Problems and Perils of a Petrolocracy," *International Journal of Contemporary Sociology*, Vol. 34, No. 1 (April 1997).

Dubai, Sharjah, Ajman, Umm al-Qaiwain, Ras al-Khaimah, and Fujairah. Aside from Dubai City, a trading center which was then by far the largest town, they subsisted primarily on date production, fishing, pearling, and, for some centuries, piracy. (At one time, they were frequently referred to as "the Pirate Coast.") Their population was sparse, consisting, as late as 1965, of no more than about 86,000 altogether.[1] (Since then, they have experienced a collective increase greater than 27 fold.) In the 19th century, the sheikhdoms came under the influence of Britain, which assumed responsibility for their defense and foreign affairs, including the regulation of their relations with one another. By the time Britain withdrew in 1971, the sheikhdoms (now styled "emirates") had formed a federation, the United Arab Emirates (UAE). (Bahrain and Qatar participated in the preliminary negotiations and agreements but ultimately decided to "go it alone"; Ras al-Khaimah remained outside the Federation until several months after it was officially proclaimed.) Each emirate is more or less autonomous, with the highest federal authority consisting of the emirs in council, and the highest federal positions divided, by agreement among the emirs, between the princely houses of Abu Dhabi and Dubai. Sheikh Zayed ibn Sultan an-Nahayan, emir of Abu Dhabi, who was the leading force in the formation of the UAE, has been its president since its inception.

The emirates cover an area of some 32,000 square miles along the lower Arabian (Persian) Gulf, with a shorter coastline on the Gulf of Oman, adjoining Qatar to the northwest and Oman to the southeast, and bordering Saudi Arabia inland on the west. Abu Dhabi, the most westerly emirate, occupies something in excess of two-thirds of the total. Despite its relatively larger area, Abu Dhabi, with the least rainfall and few oases, was poorer than some of the other sheikhdoms, although they were all extremely poor—especially after the market for natural pearls dried up in the 1930s. This situation was dramatically reversed with the development of its oil deposits, which account for approximately 85 percent of total oil production in the emirates.[2]

In 1961, the year before oil was first exported, Abu Dhabi City (the provisional capital of the UAE since its formation, and likely to remain the capital) had a population of 1,500—almost entirely

Abu Dhabi citizens. Today, the population is close to 800,000—but it is made up overwhelmingly of foreigners. In fact, UAE nationals currently comprise fewer than 20 percent of the inhabitants of Abu Dhabi Emirate, and many of them are citizens of other emirates belonging to the Federation. (Throughout this study, the term "citizen" is used to denote status within the discrete emirates, "national" to denote status in the UAE at large, and "expatriate" to denote foreigners in the UAE.)

I

The Single-Tax Limited in Abu Dhabi

IN 1977, OTHER than a trivial percentage derived mainly from investment dividends and UAE stamps and customs duty, public revenue in Abu Dhabi came entirely from the government's 60 percent share of the profits from crude oil and gas production, and from corporate income taxes and royalties that went to foreign interests.[3] More recent discrete figures for the emirate are difficult where not impossible to come by, but one may safely assume that any changes are to the government's advantage. Doubtless, investment dividends have increased as a percentage; however, inasmuch as the invested funds consist of oil and gas revenue, this does not change the picture in any way germane to the present analysis. Since foreign companies invest virtually all the oil production capital, the share of profits received by Abu Dhabi must be virtually all rent. What relatively little capital (mainly infrastructure) is provided by Abu Dhabi is paid for out of oil rent.

In what is by some standards an absolute monarchy, where such a high percentage of wealth is channeled through the government, it is not easy to draw a clear-cut line between public and private expenditure. For purposes of this discussion, let us classify as "public expenditure" spending for goods and services provided by the state to the general population of the emirate, to all qualified UAE nationals in the emirate, to all citizens of the emirate, to holders of public office by virtue of functional relatedness to their duties, and to foreign aid. Under the category of "private," let us place spending not subsumed under these headings, even when allocated by the state. Although some public functions are still carried on at the emirate and municipal levels, more and more are being administered by the Federation government, which is largely subsidized by Abu Dhabi. For all practical purposes, public revenue in Abu Dhabi may be said to consist of oil money collected by the emirate government, regardless of what jurisdiction may administer its spending.

In addition to providing for defense and for the maintenance of law and order, for an elaborate infrastructure including first-class roads and airports, seaport facilities, a massive desalinization system, etc., and for such amenities as parks, zoos, cultural and sports centers, and street beautification—benefits shared by all inhabitants, this revenue furnishes excellent education and health care free to UAE nationals and at minimal cost to expatriates serving in the military or as civilian government workers. It subsidizes housing without charge to citizens, who are also eligible for no-interest loans with which to erect approved commercial structures such as office and apartment buildings. It supports social security benefits to certain groups of needy citizens, "need" being interpreted so liberally as to render even nominal work by citizens a matter of volition rather than of necessity.[4] ("The relatively small number of federal employment seekers from Abu Dhabi is attributed in part to the extremely generous welfare and social security benefits in this particular emirate, which leave little incentive for the pursuit of public employment."[5]) Needless to say, it pays for the palaces, jets, luxury automobiles, residences abroad, swarms of skilled retainers, and all the countless indulgences enjoyed by members of the princely and other influential families. It underwrites the salaries of cushy public jobs, for which citizens are customarily given first preference, followed by other Emirians, and only then by expatriates. It funds mosques and other Islamic institutions. It covers at least 75 percent of the cost of the Federation budget, more than half of which goes to the poorer northern emirates on top of the substantial disbursements they receive directly from Abu Dhabi. Finally, it accounts for billions of dollars of foreign aid outside the UAE—e.g., to less developed countries, to the Arab League, and to the Palestine Liberation Organization.

In view of the above, it is evident that Abu Dhabi is a single-tax state, since the cost of all legitimate public services (and of some the legitimacy of which may be open to question) is met essentially by a species of land rent. Its single-tax is, however, a *single-tax limited*, since even though public expenditure goes well beyond what Thomas G. Shearman (who coined the latter term) would have considered necessary or probably even legitimate, a considerable rent surplus is either left in or channeled into private hands. This surplus represents not merely direct, but also and perhaps more importantly, *indirect* oil income.

The stratospheric rise in land prices, while it may initially have been precipitated by the discovery of the mere presence of oil in the ground, was, of course, heightened many fold by the staggering population influx brought about by oil production. Since foreigners (who constitute well over 80 percent of the population) are not permitted to own land in Abu Dhabi, but cannot avoid using it, if only for a place to spread their sleeping mats, the fortunate local who holds title to a quarter acre or so in even one of the less desirable districts of Abu Dhabi City or the interior oasis city of Al Ain might nearly as well be in possession of a gusher. And on the receipts from it he is not taxed a single dirham. The results of this are poignantly described by Suzanne St. Albans:

> The driver thoughtfully allotted to me by the Ministry is a Palestinian who speaks English well. As he crouches over the wheel, slumped with gloom and cares, I try to cheer him up and ask about his family. This releases a floodgate of woes. Life is very expensive for foreigners, who, unlike [citizens], have to pay for their lodgings. The prefab in which he and his family live, and which he took over as a bare shell, and entirely fixed up, fitted and painted himself, laying on water, power and plumbing, is going up in rent. The owner, who had been calmly watching and waiting for his property to go up in the world, came to him when all was finally finished and said, "You've done a good job here, and made this into a very valuable property, worth twice the former rent. You must pay double from now on." And in spite of vigorous protest at the flagrant injustice, he has to comply or get out.[6]

Ironically, the prefab in question was, in all likelihood, one of the myriad low-cost dwellings built by the government and presented free to Abu Dhabi citizens in the late 1960s, together with the land beneath them. As Heard-Bey remarks, many recipient families, "soon became affluent enough to be able to build their own houses and to let the low-cost house to expatriate tenants; this activity was never officially condoned, but it was a recognized way of enabling the local [native] population to participate in the emirate's wealth."[7]

With respect to the new and immensely superior houses now given by the government to local citizens, the practice of letting to expatriates is today forbidden and this prohibition strictly enforced. Also, "whole quarters near the center of town built in the late 1960s are now being demolished; the owners are given very generous compensation and land on which to build new homes."[8] None of this, of course, is any help to the expatriates; it merely increases their rent and makes for still worse crowding in whatever lodgings remain available to them.

Still, the lot of the expatriates is pitiable only in contrast with the self-indulgent, ostentatious lifestyle of the locals.[9] The expatriates earn considerably higher wages than they could in their own countries, on which they pay no taxes. The crowded conditions in which they live are, in many cases, at least partly due to their propensity to send a large portion of their earnings home, or to save them for investment upon their return. And even in the slums, they may enjoy unaccustomed luxuries; the present writer saw an air conditioning unit on nearly every hovel in the slums he visited. No doubt the denizens of these hovels are better off than they would be in Karachi or Calcutta, where they might well be sleeping in the streets. Yet this is cold comfort to those who watch the locals flaunting wealth that they did nothing to produce.[10]

II

Conclusions

THE UNADULTERATED SINGLE-TAX theory is predicated on the moral principle that the earth and its resources are the rightful heritage of humankind as such, and that their market value (economic rent), being a social product, ought to be appropriated by society in lieu of imposts upon labor and its fruits. From this standpoint, in a perfectly just world, oil in the ground would be viewed as a global resource. Abu Dhabi citizens, who, after all, had nothing to do with the existence or presence of the oil, would not regard the direct profit from it as their exclusive perquisite; rather, it would be classified as "world territorial rent," to be divided equally among the world's inhabitants. By the same token, Abu Dhabi would share proportionately in the profits attributable to natural resources, fertility, and such locational factors as access to navigable waters, elsewhere on the globe.[11] However, "the component of rental value arising from current and historical urbanization would be the product of the labor and capital of current and past generations in a given region," and would therefore remain in that region.[12]

Since past generations made a negligible contribution of labor and capital to the rental value arising from urbanization in Abu Dhabi, that value, expressed in surface rents (which do not there reflect natural locational factors to anything like the same degree as they do urbanization), would, under an order of perfect justice, be equally divided and/or shared in common among all members of the current regional population that produced it, regardless of their place of origin. The members of the expatriate community "play crucial roles in each and every facet of economic life in the UAE. Indeed, one may venture to assert that without their expertise and physical power, socioeconomic development in the emirates would probably come to a halt."[13] This being so, the bulk of the surface rents would go to them. Abu Dhabi City is located on an island, which has been and is being considerably expanded artificially with public funds. The rent of this "made land" would of course, accrue to the community that made it.

Since we don't live in a perfectly just world, the unadulterated single-tax has not been implemented anywhere (nor could it be in its entirety with respect to world territorial rent unless it were implemented everywhere). It would scarcely be fair to fault the government of Abu Dhabi for failure to do something no other government has done, and which it has probably come closer to doing than has any other government.

The unification of the emirates (as a perceived necessity for defense against aggressive designs by such regional powers as Iran) is understandably Sheikh Zayed's number one priority. To this end, he has frequently declared that "Abu Dhabi's oil and all its resources and potentialities are at the service of all the Emirates,"[14] and followed these words with deeds. He has also stated that "money is of no value unless it is used for the benefit of the people."[15] The obvious question is: What people? For Sheikh Zayed, the term embraces, as we have seen, all Emirians, not just Abu Dhabi citizens. But its scope, for him, does not stop there. He has, in fact, shared oil profits with the broader world, especially the Moslem world, to an extent that may be, proportionately, unparalleled. In the peak year of 1974, when the price of oil was at its zenith, Abu Dhabi contributed approximately 28 percent of its income to foreign aid, on top of meeting most of the federal budget—a combined contribution representing nearly half of its total disbursements for the year.[16] Such a massive distribution of "world territorial rent" is, one dares say, without precedent: percentage-wise, it makes the Marshall Plan look like peanuts!

It is in the distribution of rent attributable to urbanization that Abu Dhabi would appear furthest from the ideal standard. Although the unification of the emirates and their citizens is a sound and understandable priority, real-politik as well as justice would seem to call for certain adjustments to modify the severe population imbalance and sharp disparity between the living standards of nationals, especially citizens, and of most expatriates. For example, instead of allowing surface rents to be appropriated by privileged natives, they could be used for the benefit of all inhabitants—perhaps by the extension of free education and health care. Such a policy would help to relieve the shortage of affordable housing for expatriates by squeezing the speculative water out of surface rents.

The issue of population imbalance presents a knottier dilemma. Even if they had not been spoiled by privilege, Abu Dhabi natives are too few in number to do the work of the emirate; all the native Emirians combined would not begin to suffice. So the policy has been to employ large numbers of expatriates, permitting naturalization only in rare and exceptional cases. On the one hand, fear of social instability has led increasingly to the employment of non-Arab Asiatics, who are seen as less potentially threatening to the existing order than are non-Emirian Arabs, since their main interest is to accumulate a nest-egg and then return home. This has reached a point where the population of the UAE is now 68 percent non-Arab, and (although official figures are not maintained for the disparate emirates) one may safely surmise that the percentage in Abu Dhabi is even higher. On the other hand, the existence of a situation in which more than two-thirds of the population is composed of persons of alien language and culture is scarcely conducive to the building of national unity.

In a letter written to William Lloyd Garrison II in 1893,[17] Henry George asserted the right of peoples to maintain their cultural and territorial integrity by excluding foreigners, so long as they do not arrogate to themselves disproportionate access to the opportunities afforded by Nature, i.e., so long as they share their world territorial rent with those excluded. This Abu Dhabi has done as fully as could be asked of it in today's world. But, as we have seen, exclusion ceased to be a viable option when Abu Dhabi (yielding to the inevitable) decided to exploit its petroleum resources and become part of the developed world. The answer to the question of how it might best distribute that portion of its rent that reflects urbanization is thus complex, for it must take into account not only the rights of the expatriates, by whom that rent was very largely produced, but also the right of Abu Dhabi (and, by extension, the UAE) to preserve its historic ethnic character and identity. It would be folly to expect that it could long preserve that character and identity with such a preponderance of inhabitants who are not merely alien in cultural attributes and loyalties, but who quite properly regard themselves as merely temporary residents.

The long-term solution to this dilemma would seem to be twofold: First, more liberal opportunities for naturalization might be afforded to Arab expatriates who had worked in Abu Dhabi for a given number of years, and who were not perceived as potential threats to the regime; and further immigration might be limited, except in special cases, to approved Arabs with the same opportunities for eventual naturalization. This would permit the gradual emergence of a homogeneous population with essentially the same basic cultural attributes that historically belonged to the natives of the emirate. Second, the free housing, no-interest loans, and preferential pensions that allow native citizens to live in easy idleness might be phased out, and (as has already been suggested above) all surface rents appropriated by the government for general public use. The last of these policies, by eliminating the speculative element in surface rent, would (at least initially) reduce the surplus, affording fewer temptations for conspicuous consumption.

It is easy to propose; to implement is quite another matter. Earlier in this chapter, Abu Dhabi was described as "by some standards an absolute monarchy." This locution was used advisedly. It is an absolute monarchy in the sense that there are few constitutional restrictions upon Sheikh Zayed's authority. Yet this does not mean that he is subject to no practical constraints, for he depends upon the support of his extended family, other powerful families, tribal leaders, and rulers of other emirates—all of whom must be kept appeased. (This explains why the highest appointments seldom go to persons best qualified in terms of education and ability.) Otherwise, he could be replaced by a palace coup, just as he replaced an older brother, Sheikh Shakhbut, who was deemed insufficiently friendly to development. He may well sympathize with the policy proposals made above, but feel that, if their implementation were to be attempted now or in the very near future, it would arouse dangerous opposition among those who could depose him and undermine his present primary objective of welding the emirates into a united modern nation that commands international recognition and respect.

Implicit in Henry George's strictures against land monopoly is a recognition that each generation has an obligation to safeguard the right of coming generations to natural opportunity. A portion of the wealth derived from the earth's resources must be invested against the day when they are exhausted or their value seriously eroded. At present levels of consumption, crude oil reserves in the UAE (of which Abu Dhabi accounts for some 85 percent) are estimated to last for more than 100 years.[18] But at some point before their exhaustion, it is not improbable that the demand for Abu Dhabi oil might plummet drastically due to the discovery of major deposits elsewhere or the development of some cheaper substitute for oil. (The fate of the pearl fisheries is analogous: The Gulf is still a rich potential source of natural pearls, but with the development of the cultured pearl industry in Japan, demand for them has all but disappeared.)

Sheikh Zayed has, in most respects, been an enlightened and farsighted ruler, as well as exhibiting remarkable generosity and talent for conciliation. His statesmanship is perhaps open to question primarily with respect to provision for a future no longer lavished with oil wealth. To spend money (that might have been invested profitably abroad) unstintingly on decorative verdure which must be irrigated with costly desalinated seawater, or upon showy building projects (such as the half-billion dollar officers' complex or the unbelievably opulent international airport in Abu Dhabi City) in a region where extreme heat and humidity, salt air, and brackish ground-water close to the surface render the lifespan of even the most solidly-constructed edifice no more than forty years at most, suggests a penchant for present luxury at the possible expense of future sufficiency. Yet, even this criticism should be advanced only tentatively and with caution. For here again, the emir/Federation president may see these expenditures as ways of forfending local opposition to Abu Dhabi's munificence toward the other emirates, and its open-handedness in foreign aid.

Notes

1. *World Almanac*, 1965.
2. Ahmad Mustafa Elhussein, "Manpower Nationalization in the United Arab Emirates: The Case of the Banking Sector," *Journal of Developing Societies*, Vol. 7, fasc. 2 (July–October), 1991.
3. Mana Saeed Al-Otaiba, *Petroleum and the Economy of the United Arab Emirates* (London: Croom Helm, 1977), pp. 43, 250.
4. Abdullah Omran Taryam, *The Establishment of the United Arab Emirates 1950–85* (London: Croom Helm, 1987), pp. 267–68.
5. Ali Mohammed Khalifa, *The United Arab Emirates, Unity in Fragmentation* (Boulder, CO: Westview Press, 1979), p. 61.
6. Suzanne St. Albans, *Green Grows the Oil* (London: Quartet Books, 1978), p. 27.
7. Frauke Heard-Bey, *From Trucial States to United Arab Emirates* (London: Longman, 1982), p. 386.

8. Ibid., p. 483, note 145.

9. See Taryam, op. cit., p. 260.

10. Something of an analogous situation obtains in Fiji, where British colonial rulers, alarmed at the encroachments made by European planters on Fijian land, sought to ensure the protection of native rights by registering 83 percent of the island as inalienable *mataquali* (communal kinship group) lands. These lands are leased out by a government agency for up to six percent of their unimproved value, which is then remitted, minus administrative costs, to the mataquali. This system has obviated the need for indigenous Fijians to engage in business or productive work, "as they can exist on the rents of those who do." (David Lea, *Melanesian Land Tenure in a Contemporary and Philosophical Context* [Lanham, MD: University Press of America, 1997], p. 54.)

"Those who do" consist primarily of the descendants of indentured East Indian laborers, imported in the late 19th century to cultivate the sugar cane plantations. These industrious and enterprising folk now comprise a slight majority of the population, and are mainly responsible for the socially-generated value of the land, yet own only 1.7 percent of it, and are legally unable to acquire more. Per capita income in Fiji (US$1930) is highest of all the independent islands of the South Pacific (excluding Australia and New Zealand), and the Indians are, by and large, far better off economically than they would be in their ancestral homeland. However, their desire for a greater share of the wealth that they produce is surely understandable. Moreover, their status has become precarious since the elected government was overthrown in 1987 by a military coup, followed in 1990 by a new constitution favoring the indigenous minority.

11. See Nicolaus Tideman, "Commons and Commonwealths," in R. V. Andelson, ed., *Commons Without Tragedy* (Savage, MD/London: Barnes & Noble/Shepheard-Walwyn, 1991), pp. 118ff.

12. Ibid., p. 19.

13. Khalifa, op. cit., p. 112.

14. Quoted in Heard-Bey, op. cit., p. 349.

15. Quoted in John Daniels, *Abu Dhabi: A Portrait* (London: Longman Group, Ltd., 1974), p. 1.

16. Heard-Bey, op. cit., p. 381.

17. Quoted in Charles Albro Barker, *Henry George* (New York: Oxford University Press, 1955), p. 135.

18. Central Intelligence Agency, *The World Factbook 1993–94* (Washington, DC: Brassey's, 1993).

Chapter 19

Republic of China (Taiwan)

BY ALVEN H.S. LAM*

THE HISTORY OF real property taxes in China can be traced back to four thousand years ago when farmers contributed one-eighth of their crop to the government. The practice at that time was to subdivide a square piece of land into nine plots of equal size, with two plots on each side of the square, and one in the middle. Then eight families were assigned the rights to cultivate the eight outside plots. Each of these eight families had an obligation to cultivate the centrally located ninth plot. Since all the plots were equal in size, the products from the ninth plot were the eight farmers' annual contribution, or taxes, to the government. Each family's contribution, or tax rate in modern terms, was about ten percent of its production income.

The modern Chinese property tax system was designed by Dr. Sun Yat-sen, the Republic's founding father. Dr. Sun's ideology was called the Three Principles of the People. His land and taxation philosophy was heavily influenced by the turn-of-the-century American economist, Henry George. In 1912, Dr. Sun responded to a question from a group of American reporters by saying: "The

*Alven H. S. Lam, a specialist in urban and regional design, holds a doctorate from Harvard University. He is advisor to the US-China Housing Initiative, Office of Policy Development and Research, US Department of Housing and Urban Development, and a fellow and faculty member of the Lincoln Institute of Land Policy, Cambridge, MA. He has served as dean of the Land-Reform Training Institute, Taiwan, as a policy advisor and project coordinator for various government agencies in Taiwan, as a land policy specialist for the US Agency for International Development, and as a consultant to the US Environmental Protection Agency. He is author of some 15 monographs, book chapters, articles, and working papers, including "The Impact of Urban Landscape on Urban Land Value" (1988), "Geographic Information Systems in the Context of Land Use Policy" (1990), and "Policies and Mechanisms on Land Value Capture in Asia" (1997).

teaching of your single taxer, Henry George, will be the basis or our program of reform. The land tax as the only means of supporting the government is an infinitely just, reasonable, and equitably distributed tax . . ."[1] The emphasis of Dr. Sun's philosophy on property taxation was later stipulated in China's Constitution.

For thirty years after the Republic of China was proclaimed in 1912, the country was under constant hostilities among warlords and from Japanese invasion. As warlords ruled the country in the name of the Republic but in defiance of its Constitution, Chinese people and government systems were exploited without mercy. After Dr. Sun's death in 1925, his political successor, Chiang Kai-shek, was so preoccupied with trying to control the warlords, resist Japanese conquest, and stave off Communist revolution under Mao Tse-tung that he had little opportunity to implement large-scale land reform on the mainland.

The enforcement of Dr. Sun's land policies, had it been possible, could well have thwarted the eventual Maoist takeover by correcting the popular grievances that fueled it. Chiang's force withdrew from Mainland China to Taiwan in 1949, and the Statute for the Equalization of Urban Land Rights was enacted in 1954 to reaffirm Dr. Sun's land taxation ideology. The Statute was intended to achieve four objectives: (1) fair assessment of land value; (2) taxation according to declared value; (3) government optional purchase at declared value; and (4) public enjoyment of future land value increment. These objectives became the guidelines of all property taxation laws in later years.

In 1977, the Land Tax Law was passed to provide stronger regulatory and enforcement power for land-related taxes. Two major land-related taxes were defined in the laws: land-value tax and land-value increment tax. The land-value tax was developed to expand the local government revenue base. The land-value increment tax was designed to ensure the public enjoyment of future land value increment. In other words, land-value increment tax's objectives are to assure the equal distribution of future benefits from land and to control land speculation. For the effectiveness of implementing the laws, both land-value tax and land-value increment tax are carried out within local jurisdictions.

The land- and building-related taxes in Taiwan include land-value tax, agricultural land tax, land-value increment tax, deed tax, house tax, and estate and gift tax. Agricultural land tax was suspended in 1986. Estate and gift tax is a central government tax. Deed tax accounted for 8.5 percent of prefectural and municipal revenues in 1995 and was relatively less significant in the revenue system in Taiwan. The primary focus of this chapter will be on land-value tax, land-value increment tax, and house tax. These three kinds of taxes in Taiwan are commonly called property taxes in other countries around the world.

I

The Current Revenue Structure in Taiwan

IN FISCAL YEAR 1995, national taxes accounted for 53.8 percent of total national revenues, while provincial and city taxes accounted for 20.4 percent; and prefectural and municipal taxes accounted for 20.9 percent.[2] In the same fiscal year, 75.3 percent of total prefectural and municipal tax revenues came from land taxes in which the land-value tax accounted for 14.9 percent and the land-value increment tax accounted for 60.4 percent (see Table 1). The statistics show the importance of land taxes, especially the land-value increment tax, in a local government's revenue base. Between 1985 and 1990, annual total revenue growth was 18 percent; whereas the land-value increment tax increased 28.6 percent annually. Although the annual growth rates for all taxes became stable between 1990 and 1995, the total amount of land-value increment tax continued to climb from NT$82.9 billion in 1990 to NT$155.3 billion in 1995. The peak of land-value increment tax collection was in 1992 when the land-value increment tax accounted for 71 percent of total local revenues.

Table 1

PROPERTY TAX AND PREFECTURAL AND MUNICIPAL REVENUES (Unit: NT$ Billions)											
Total Revenue			LVT			LVIT			House Tax		
Fiscal Year	Amount (NTSB)	% Inc. Yr.	Amount (NTSB)	% of Total	% Inc. Yr.	Amount (NTSB)	% of Total	% Inc. Yr.	Amount (NTSB)	% of Total	% Inc. Yr.
1985	77.5		10.9	14.4		34.1	45.2		18.8	25.5	
1990	143.6	18.0	22.6	15.7	21.5	82.9	57.8	28.6	27.4	19.1	9.1
1995	257.2	15.8	38.2	14.9	13.8	155.3	60.4	17.5	40.2	15.6	9.3

NT$: New Taiwan Dollars: US$1 was approximately equal to NT$27.5 in 1995
LVT: Land Value Tax
LVIT: Land Value Increment Tax

Source: Yearbook of Tax Statistics, Republic of China, Ministry of Finance, 1996

II

Property Taxation and Assessment

LAND-VALUE TAX, land-value increment tax, and house tax are the major property taxes in this country. Each has its own rates and assessment practices.

A. Land-Value Tax

The land-value tax is levied according to the Official Declared Value (ODV) of land. The ODV is assessed once every three years by municipalities. Market information is used in the assessment. The Ministry of Interior provides technical assistance to local assessment. A Land Value Assessment Commission is established by each local municipality with the responsibility of evaluating official assessed value. After the approval from the Commission, the assessed value is announced as ODV.

Land-value taxation is based on progressive tax rates of one percent, 1.5 percent, 2.5 percent, 3.5 percent, 4.5 percent, and 5.5 percent. A Starting Accumulative Value or SAV, is assigned as the starting base for taxation. For an ODV less than the SAV, the tax rate is one percent. For the portion exceeding the SAV, but less than 500 percent, the tax rate is 1.5 percent. For the portion exceeding the SAV, but less than 1,000 percent, the tax rate is 2.5

percent. For the portion exceeding the SAV, but less than 1,500 percent, the tax rate is 3.5 percent. For the portion exceeding the SAV, but less than 2,000 percent, the tax rate is 4.5 percent. Value at higher levels is taxed at 5.5 percent.

B. Land-Value Increment Tax

The land-value increment tax is levied on realized gains from land transactions. It is sometimes imprecisely characterized as a "capital gains" tax. The gains from land sales in Taiwan, however, have special land policy implications. In Dr. Sun's ideology, it is important that "the increment of land price should belong to the society rather than the landlord." He believed that the increase of land-value is attributable to social development rather than work from the landlord or investors. The profits from land should be returned to the society through the land-value increment tax. The land-value increment tax became a powerful policy tool to regulate the equity of income distribution and to control land speculation. The seller must pay the land-value increment tax before the land transaction is completed.

For taxation purposes, the land-value increment is measured by the difference between the Official Declared Present Values (ODPVs) at the current and last transfer. The assessment of the ODPV is announced on July 1 of every year. Since land-value increment tax is a tax on gains in asset income or value, all the occurring costs and fees are deductible from the gross income. The formula to calculate the net increment is:

> Land-value increment
> = declared present value at the transfer
> - original decreed value or the assessed value at the last transfer
> × consumer price index adjustment
> - land improvement costs + construction benefits fee paid
> + fee paid for land consolidation.

The tax rates are 40 percent, 50 percent, and 60 percent. When the increment is not in excess of 100 percent, the tax rate is 40 percent. If the increment is between 100 to 200 percent, the tax rate is 50 percent. If the increment reaches more than 200 percent, the tax rate becomes 60 percent.

C. House Tax

The house tax can be traced back to China's T'ang Dynasty (A.D. 618–907). Current house tax is levied according to the value of the house (House Tax Act, 1967), assessed by a local real estate assessment committee. The values must be publicly announced by the committee.

House tax rates vary depending upon the purposes of use. For residential use, the tax rate should be higher than 1.38 percent and lower than 2.0 percent of the current value. The rate for owner-occupied houses should not exceed 1.38 percent. For commercial use, the rate is from 3.0 to 5.0 percent. For non-profit use such as hospital or civic organizations, the rate is 1.5 to 2.5 percent. Local government is responsible for setting the house tax rates. Once the local Peoples' Assembly has approved the rates, they are submitted to the provincial government. After approval from the Provincial Assembly, the tax rates are sent to the Ministry of Finance for the record.

III

Evaluation of the Current Property Tax System

THE MOST UNIQUE characteristic of the Republic of China's property tax system is its constitutionality. The implementation of the equalization of land rights is stipulated in the Constitution. The main objective of the equalization of land rights is to redistribute profits from land through the measures of land-value assessment, declared land-value, land-value taxation, and land-value increment taxation. Hence property taxation becomes a local government function with its objectives stipulated by the national Constitution. The administrative structure to implement such a unique taxation program has evolved into a very complicated and inefficient bureaucracy in Taiwan.

Although property taxes generate revenues for local governments, local tax officials have never implemented a taxation policy as a revenue-generation tool. The bureaucracy through which central government controls local revenues and expenditures gives little incentive for local officials to seriously monitor the effectiveness of the property taxation system. Land-related taxation was designed and implemented with regulatory, political, and social objectives. Although property tax revenues continue to grow and are often seen as a healthy revenue source, the reality is that a significant portion of gains from land sales escape through regulatory loopholes. For example, land transactions within the annual assessment period are not subject to land-value increment tax even if sales value has increased significantly within the year.

The land-value increment tax has unique objectives as mentioned earlier: to capture the gains from land sales, to distribute the benefits to the public, and to control speculation. The objectives have been difficult to fulfill due to the complexity of regulatory, political, and social conflicts.

A. Capturing Gains from Land Transactions

Taiwanese assessment practice was never able to reflect the real market values of land, and consequently never able to measure the real gains from transactions. The publicly declared land values are approximately 50 percent of market values. If the local government does not reassess land value, then the ODPV will not be changed. In this case, no land-value increment taxation is collected. Even though the government reassesses land values every year, a seller can still escape paying land-value increment tax by buying and selling land before the new ODPV is announced. For example, if the ODPV is announced on July 1 every year, someone can buy a piece of land on July 2 and then sell the land on June 30 of the next year. The person makes a huge profit, but does not need to pay land-value increment taxation because the ODPV has not changed. As a result of such practices, when the real estate market skyrocketed in the early 1990s, significant land-value increment taxation revenues were never captured.

B. Distributing Benefits to the Public

The intergovernmental revenue and expenditure-sharing mechanisms allow limited power to distribute benefits from land sales to the public. Local governments are allowed a portion of land-value increment taxation revenues to be allocated for public housing and other urban and community development projects. The intention was to distribute benefits to needy people such as low income families or disadvantaged groups so as to give them a competitive edge in the society.

In the early 1950s, the benefit distribution mechanism in the land reform program was to offer land to the tillers. When land becomes scarce, distributing land becomes an impossible mission. Distributing tax revenues through providing urban services evolved as a natural solution. However, projects to provide urban services often require strong political commitments as well as effective technical and administrative expertise. As some projects fail, the idea of distributing benefits evaporates. The land-value increment taxation revenues, in these circumstances, had to be reallocated to other municipalities or to be returned to the provincial or central government. As revenues shift to other jurisdictions, the original objective of sharing the benefits tends to be forgotten.

C. Controlling Land Speculation

Controlling land speculation has never received strong endorsement within the current political structure. Neither government nor the private sector has significant interest in implementing this policy. For the private sector, the political power of the land owner tends to overwhelm most of the other powers in society. For the public sector, government agencies that own land are interested in using profits from land development to reduce agency deficits or raise revenues. In either case, regardless of lip service to the principle, the political will to prevent land speculation is disappointingly feeble. Nevertheless, while far from perfect, the land taxes are at least somewhat effective in this regard, especially in contrast with arrangements in most other countries.

IV

Conclusions

THE IMPLEMENTATION OF a program of land and tax reform inspired by Dr. Sun's ideals played a major and indispensable role in building a strong foundation for both economic development and social justice in Taiwan. The population gained equitable access to land and other production utilities. In the 1950s and 1960s, Taiwan was transformed from an impoverished agricultural backwater to a thriving industrial state with one of the world's strongest economies. Income levels increased dramatically, with far less disparity in distribution than in most other countries.

By the mid-1980s (about ten years after the death of Chiang Kai-shek), the system had begun to show its imperfection. Rapid urbanization had created a shortage of suitable land supply. Fast-accumulating international trade surpluses stimulated private investment in land, especially by the ruling party and its leading members. Ironically, the Kuomintang, the party founded by Sun and carried on by Chiang, which had enshrined the Three Principles of the People in its platform, became in time the greatest obstacle to their effective operation. Having gained possession of the most valuable locations, the party and its leaders became immensely wealthy. Their profits from land speculation undermined the government's original policy goals by sapping any initiative to rectify weaknesses in the administrative mechanism, and the gap between the very rich, on the one hand, and middle and lower-income citizens, on the other, began to widen.

In the early 1990s, a social movement arose demanding a "Second Land Reform" to close the loopholes in the existing regulations. Although it was active for several years, it was unable to overcome the landed interests' stranglehold on the government—as evidenced by the sacking of a cabinet minister who proposed an increase in the land-value tax.

However, the political landscape changed radically in March 2000, when the ruling Kuomintang was defeated in a national election, marking its first time out of power in the half-century since Chiang and his forces had withdrawn to Taiwan from the

Mainland. It is too soon to tell whether the new administration, led by President Chen Shui-bian, will revive and effectuate the Second Land Reform, but the situation is not without grounds for optimism.

Notes

1. *The Republic* (Chicago), April 12, 1912, p. 349.

2. The city taxes and municipal taxes discussed here are levied from two different levels of governments. The two major cities, Taipei and Kaoshiung, are cities at the provincial level which is under the central government's jurisdiction. Their taxes are in the category of provincial and city taxes. Other local level governments are called prefectures or municipalities which are under provincial government's jurisdiction. Their taxes are in the category of prefectural and municipal taxes.

Chapter 20

Hong Kong and Singapore

BY SOCK-YONG PHANG*

THERE ARE MANY similarities between Hong Kong and Singapore. They have both enjoyed high rates of economic growth over the past three decades, averaging six percent a year in real terms. The two have become known as "East Asian Tigers," having made the transition from poverty to newly industrialized economies in a relatively short time. Both started off as British colonies, with British legal and administrative systems, and made their living as trading ports serving their respective regions. Singapore has been an independent republic since 1965; Hong Kong was returned to China on July 1, 1997. While Hong Kong and Singapore are now the busiest ports in the world in terms of throughput, they have divested from their reliance on trade since the 1960s, climbed the industrial ladder, and are now important international financial centers as well.

Hong Kong and Singapore are both densely populated cities. Land is a scarce resource and land and property prices are high even when compared to prices in the Organization for Economic Cooperation and Development countries (with the exception of Japan). "Speculating" or "investing" in the property market in both cities is indeed a favorite pastime of risk-loving locals and

*Sock-Yong Phang, Ph.D., Harvard University, recently accepted appointment as associate professor of economics in the School of Business, Singapore Management University, having occupied a similar position at the National University of Singapore. She has served on the boards of Singapore's Urban Development Authority and Land Transport Authority, and has also been involved with a number of World Bank projects. She is the author of *Housing Markets and Urban Transportation: Economic Theory, Econometrics and Policy Analysis for Singapore* (McGraw Hill, 1992). She is the coauthor of *The Singapore Experience in Public Housing* (Times Academic Press, 1991).

foreigners alike. The two cities are well known for being free traders as well as international financial centers with few restrictions on trade and capital flows, which are many times their GDP. However, what is less well known is the fact that the state owns all land in the case of Hong Kong, and four-fifths of the land in the case of Singapore. There is no hint of Henry George's distinctive methodology if one examines the technical procedures for deriving revenue from real estate in Hong Kong and Singapore. This is especially true in that no attempt is made to separate site-value from the improvements on land. The assessment systems in both cities are derived from the British rating system and are basically annual value systems. Even though Singapore and Hong Kong depart from the method of land-value taxation that George advocated, they have accomplished to a significant degree the capture of land values for the public, along with the reduction of tax burdens upon industry—which together constitute George's key policy proposal.

Hong Kong and Singapore capture economic rent primarily by nationalizing land and leasing it out. In *Progress and Poverty* (Book VIII, chapter ii), Henry George contends that this approach is "perfectly feasible," and that it satisfies the "laws of justice" and "meets all economic requirements." However, he goes on to say that there is a "simpler, easier and quieter way," namely, to leave land in private hands while using the tax mechanism to appropriate its economic rent for public purposes.

Yet, (except maybe for minor considerations of administrative efficiency) it should not be taken for granted that he necessarily considered the second way superior to the first for every situation. His statement assumes a context such as that which obtained in the US and most of the Western world both then and now, in which private property in land is the norm. Whether he would have viewed land-value taxation as superior to nationalization in contexts such as Hong Kong and Singapore, where such a high proportion of the land (not merely in area, but also in value) was public from the outset, is by no means clear.

While the state is the largest landowner in Singapore and the only landowner in Hong Kong, the inefficiencies that could have resulted from state ownership have been minimized through the creation of markets for state land and property leases. Unlike the socialist city where the absence of land markets had very negative impacts on efficiency, productivity, and environmental quality,[1] property markets are active in Hong Kong and Singapore and transmit important information to both users and urban planners. Also, the public leasehold system, where the government plays a major role in land use planning and resource allocation, works in Hong Kong and Singapore because the public sector institutions in both cities are efficient and non-corrupt. These institutions in both cities benefit from adequate checks and balances, merit-based recruiting, and pay scales high enough to reduce the temptation to corruption.

I

Hong Kong

HONG KONG'S STATUS as a British colony ceased on June 30, 1997. However, the 1984 Sino-British Joint Declaration guarantees that the legal system that was in place before the resumption of sovereignty by China will continue for a period of fifty years beyond the date of the resumption.

In 1998, Hong Kong's land area of 1,095 square kilometers and her population of 6.6 million were both approximately twice those of Singapore. Owing to historical reasons, Hong Kong's land-tenure arrangements produce an effect comparable to that of straightforward land-value taxation.

The former colony of Hong Kong comprises three main regions: Hong Kong Island, Kowloon Peninsula, and the New Territories. Hong Kong Island was ceded by China to Great Britain in 1841 during the First Anglo-China Opium War, while the Kowloon Peninsula and Stonecutter's Island were ceded to Britain after the Second Anglo-Chinese War in 1860. In the late nineteenth century, after China's defeat by Japan in the war of 1894–95, the British government took advantage of the situation by demanding the lease of the New Territories together with 235 islands from China for 99 years from July 1, 1898. Under the terms of the Sino-British

Joint Declaration of 1984, all three regions reverted to China on June 30, 1997.

The British government, on taking over Hong Kong Island in 1841, recognized immediately the importance of controlling land. In 1843, it proclaimed that all land belonged to the Crown and that the government would not allow any private ownership of land.[2] No freehold estates were to be granted. Leases for building land were to be for 75 years (the length of time considered necessary to induce tenants to erect substantial buildings) and other land for 21 years. Leases were sold at public auctions or granted directly for the payment of an annual rent. Unhappiness with the relatively short 75-year leases resulted in the British government relenting and allowing the extension of existing leases to 999 years in 1848. At that time, the practice of annual rents being fixed at auction was replaced with a system of nominal ground rent subject to the payment of a premium. For the next five decades, most land leases were granted for 999 years.

After the ceding of Kowloon Peninsula to the British in 1860, new leases for 999 years were granted to Chinese owners of land who remained in possession. Compensation was paid to owners of land who were dispossessed. In 1898, the Hong Kong governor was instructed by the British government to require new leases to be of 75 years duration and to stop the practice of granting 999 year leases. The resulting major protests resulted in a compromise where leases were to be of 75 years with a right of renewal for a further 75 years. Since 1898, 75 years became the standard duration of leases.

Land tenure arrangements in the New Territories differ from the rest of the colony. Hong Kong and Kowloon were relatively uninhabited when they were ceded to the Crown. When the New Territories were leased to the British, a large area of land was already held by Chinese owners and had been farmed for centuries. A land court was subsequently set up which granted rights to leases involving 354,277 lots after the completion of a survey. All unclaimed land in the New Territories was held by the Crown for disposal. The longest Crown leases in the New Territories expired three days before June 30, 1997.

A. Technical Provisions for Land Value Capture

There is no site-value taxation as such in Hong Kong. Owners of income-yielding land leases or buildings are charged a standard rate of 15 percent on the annual rental income of their properties. Rates are levied on landed property (whether income-yielding or not) and are 5 percent of the estimated annual rental value. Lease-owners of income-yielding landed property therefore have to pay both property taxes on the actual yield and rates on the annual value; however, rates may be deducted to arrive at "net assessable value" (actual rental yield minus rates paid and a 20 percent allowance for repairs and other outgoings on the balance). Government rent is payable from July 1, 1997, for all land leases granted on or after May 27, 1985, and on the extension of non-renewable leases. The rent is equivalent to 3 percent of the rateable value. In 1996–97, receipts from property tax totaled HK $1.6 billion, while that from rates totaled HK $15.6 billion.[3] The government also collected $9.3 billion, amounting to about 5 percent of its total revenue, from investments and rents from government properties.

According to Cruden,[4] Hong Kong's political and economic climate is not favorable to the growth of compulsory government planning powers. Formal town planning in Hong Kong dates from 1939 when the Town Planning Ordinance was enacted. However, it has not been central to the implementation of land policy, as it provides only guidelines and there are no enforcement provisions. Instead, enforcement powers for land use decisions are found in the Building Ordinance and contractual powers in Crown leases.

The Hong Kong government leases land based on its land contracting system. It collects land premia from the initial land auctions, modifications of lease conditions, and contract renewals. Land leasing is an important tool in managing urban growth as well as in raising public funds in Hong Kong. The government stipulates the restrictions on uses, height, plot ratio, and building design in the Conditions of Sale when contracting to lease a parcel of land. The contract is sent to all interested land developers who will then bid for development rights of land in the public auction. A land lease sales program is issued at the beginning of each financial year and shows the details of public auctions and tenders for each month.

A leaseholder who subsequently wants to modify any of the conditions has to apply to the Lands Department for official permission. The approval of the application requires the leaseholder to pay an additional premium which is based on the enhancement in the land value deriving from modification. A new set of covenants would also be imposed on the modified contract. Lease renewals represent another opportunity for land-value capture by the Hong Kong government.

In 1984, under Annex III of the Joint Declaration, the British and People's Republic of China governments had agreed that all land leases which expired on or before June 27, 1997, would be renewed for another 50 years. Leaseholders are only required to pay a new levy of rent set at three percent of the rental value of their properties. The Declaration also limited the colonial government to total grants of new land not exceeding 50 hectares a year, and with leases for terms expiring not later than June 30, 2047.[5] This limit excluded land grants to the Hong Kong Housing Authority for public rental housing. Moreover, half of the premium income from land transactions had to be set aside for the then-future Chinese Special Administrative Region government to fund land investment and infrastructure expenditures after 1997. A Land Commission comprising officials from the two governments was set up in 1985 to implement the provisions of Annex III. The Land Commission could increase the 50 hectares annual limit, and did so regularly. The land disposal limit for 1994–95 was in fact 1,411 hectares—in large part for developments relating to the new airport. Between 1985 and its dissolution on June 30, 1997, the Land Commission agreed to the disposal of almost 3,000 hectares of land.

When land is needed for public purposes, the Hong Kong government obtains the land through compulsory resumption. Unlike Singapore, compensation is paid to the leaseholder based on the open market value of the land resumed.

B. Land Value Capture and Economic Development

Income from land transactions is an important source of government revenue in Hong Kong. A study by Hong[6] shows that the Hong Kong government was able to capture 39 percent of land-value increments occurring between 1970 and 1991 from land leased in the 1970s. Land revenue from the initial auctions, rather than from lease modifications and renewals, was the most important source of land revenue. This captured value financed an average of 55 percent of the annual infrastructure investment during the same period. Hong also estimated that combined land-related revenues could recover, on average, 79 percent of the annual costs of public infrastructure investment.

The current profits tax rate for corporations is 16.5 percent. Profits from unincorporated businesses are taxed at 15 percent. Salaries tax rates range from two percent on the first HK $30,0000 of net income, to eight percent and 14 percent on the second and third segments of $30,000 each, respectively, and then to 20 percent on remaining net income, subject to the limitation that the total tax paid shall not exceed l5 percent of gross income. Due to generous personal allowances, about 53 percent of the labor force does not pay any salaries tax.[7] The low level of tax rates and their lack of progressivity have contributed to the economic dynamism of Hong Kong, encouraging work effort, investment, and enterprise.

Moreover, generous depreciation allowances encourage new capital investment in the industrial sector. In order to promote Hong Kong's status as a financial center, there is no interest withholding tax on foreign currency deposits.

Since 1973, the Hong Kong government has also assisted selected industrial ventures by its provision of land for their needs via private treaty instead of public auction. In 1977, the Industrial Estates Corporation was set up to provide land at a price which reflects only the cost of formation and servicing for industrial processes which could not be carried out in multistory industrial buildings. These industries include land-intensive ones such as gas, telecommunications, oil refineries, and electricity. The land premia are decided by negotiation rather than auction with the objective being to foster industrial growth and develop public utilities. Land grants of this category include leases for the development of industrial estates and the new airport, the expansion of container terminal facilities, and for the development of hospitals and other nonprofit community ventures.

Similar to Singapore, Hong Kong has a large subsidized public housing sector which has been made possible partly by state ownership of land. In 1994, over three million people (or half the population of Hong Kong) resided in some 879,000 public housing flats. Some 2.5 million live in 685,000 rental units while 593,000 live in purchased flats.[8] In 1998, public rental housing accommodated about 2.5 million people (39 percent of the population) compared with 1.7 million in 1975. Since 1978, the government has built more than 240,000 subsidized flats for sale under various ownership schemes. In early 1998, the new government announced a new housing strategy that included an annual supply of 85,000 flats from 1999, and a target of increasing the overall homeownership rate from 52 percent to 70 percent by 2007. Inasmuch as all the land is state owned, the government does not have to purchase land from private landowners to build public housing for the lower income group. In addition, the government further subsidizes the provision of public housing by providing grants and loans at concessionary interest rates to the housing authority.

According to Ho and Castells, Goh, and Kwok,[9] subsidized housing had a significant impact on economic development through its initial dampening effect on the cost of living and wages. By holding wage costs down, the government enhanced the price competitiveness of Hong Kong's exports and facilitated economic growth.

II

Singapore

SINGAPORE IS A small island city state with a total land area of 648 square kilometers and a population of 3.9 million. It was founded as a British trading post in 1819 by Sir Stamford Raffles. Under

Raffles and for some time afterward, ground rent was virtually the sole source of public revenue except for sumptuary taxes on opium and liquor. This has long ceased to be true, but a combination of unusual circumstances and technical provisions produced an effect comparable to that of straightforward land-value taxation.[10]

Soon after his arrival, Raffles established a formal plan for the town in 1823. In 1824, a treaty between the British and Malay rulers ceded perpetual title to Singapore and all islands within 10 miles of her shores to the East India Company and its heirs. In 1826, English statutes in force on November 26, 1826, and the principles of common law and equity were received as part of the law in Singapore. This meant that English doctrines of tenure and estates operated in Singapore and all land was, in theory, vested in, first the East India Company, subsequently the British Crown, and currently the Republic.[11] Grants of land were subsequently made which transferred much land in Singapore into private ownership and leaseholds. These grants ranged from those of unlimited duration, to leases of 999 years, to temporary licenses.[12]

Singapore remained a British colony until 1959 when it achieved internal self-government. The People's Action Party which was elected in 1959, has been returned at every election since. Singapore joined the then newly formed Federation of Malaysia in 1963, but withdrew in 1965, becoming an independent republic. Upon receiving its independence, the Singapore government was confronted with a host of political and economic problems which were soon compounded by the closure of British military bases there. Rapid population growth, a severe housing shortage evidenced by chronic overcrowding in dilapidated buildings and squatter slums, and the need for employment creation topped the list of problems. There was a sense of urgency resulting from the crises of separation from Malaysia and the withdrawal of British troops. The majority of the population then was comprised of low income and fairly recent immigrants; there were few large landowners. These factors aided in enabling the government to push through legislation for urban land reform.

In 1960, the state owned 44 percent of the land in Singapore. By 1985, the proportion of land under state ownership had increased to 76 percent. This dramatic increase in the state's landholding was effected via land reclamation (reclaimed land automatically becomes state land), and, most importantly, eminent domain provisions that made it easy and cheap for the republic to reacquire land for development purposes. Legislation under the State Land Rules provides for state land to be leased for a term not exceeding 99 years.[13] The next section describes the process through which land-value capture has been effected in Singapore.

A. Technical Provisions for Land Value Capture

There is no site-value taxation as such in Singapore. A flat rate of 12 percent on the annual rental income of commercial property has applied since July 1, 1996. There is a concessionary tax rate of four percent of the estimated annual rental value for owner-occupied residential properties. Unlike other East Asian countries such as South Korea, Taiwan, and Japan, there is no capital gains tax on private sector real estate transactions.[14] The Singapore government has instead relied on the process of nationalization of land on a selective basis to effect the process of land-value capture.

The central piece of legislation for land nationalization and rent capture is contained in Singapore's Land Acquisition Act of 1966. Between 1963 and 1965, when Singapore was part of the Federation of Malaysia, Article 13 of the Constitution of Malaysia provided that no person should be deprived of property except as specified by the law, and that no law shall provide for compulsory acquisition without adequate compensation. The new independent government of Singapore was, however, strongly committed to the idea that urban land should, with few exceptions, be owned by the state; this was due in no small part to the extreme scarcity of land in the island republic. The Land Acquisition Act of 1966, which became operative from June 17, 1967, conferred powers on the state and its agencies to acquire land for any public purpose, or for any work or undertaking which is of public benefit, public utility or public interest, or for any residential, commercial or industrial purpose. An amendment in 1973 set compensation for acquired land at the market value as of November 30, 1973, (the statutory date) or at the date of gazette notification, whichever was lower. Thus, the rate of compensation made no allowance either for appreciation or for the landowner's purchase price. Subsequent amendments fixed the statutory dates as of January 1, 1986, for property acquired on or after November 30, 1987, but before January 18, 1993; as of January 1, 1992, for property acquired on or after January 18, 1993, but before September 27, 1995; and January 1, 1995, for property acquired on or after September 27, 1995.

A related piece of legislation which further depressed land prices for acquired land was the Control of Rent Act. Rent control was introduced in Singapore in 1947 by the British colonial government in the aftermath of World War II to protect tenants at a time when there was a severe housing shortage. The statutory rent was set at the rates which existed on August 1, 1939, and affected privately owned premises built on or before September 7, 1947. It remained generally in effect for the next 40 years. Block decontrol for 32 hectares of prime land located in the central business district was introduced in 1969. Vacant decontrol was introduced in 1980 and rent control began being phased out in stages in 1988. Rent control, however, enabled the government to acquire controlled premises for public sector projects at 1973 prices (before 1987), prices which had been further and substantially depressed by rent control.

Some 18,000 hectares of land were acquired by various government agencies between 1959 (internal self-government) and 1984. This exercise wiped out land rent increases for affected landowners, some of whom suffered actual losses, having purchased their land at prices above the 1973 price. Some such landowners had to carry on with loan repayments for land which had already been acquired by the government. This apparent disregard for losses incurred by unfortunate landowners is completely in line with Henry George's uncompromising stand that rents paid to individual landowners were unfair even if capitalized in the purchase price.

Another land-related class of policies involved those pertaining to the taxation of motor vehicle ownership and usage. To the extent that road usage rights represent rights to the use of a land-related resource, the taxation of that right is completely in line with George's prescription for land-related taxation. Motor vehicle taxation in Singapore represents a form of regulatory capture which is related to land use. Road space is a valuable resource in this land-scarce city state and is priced accordingly for private motor vehicle owners and users. As a result, congestion is not an occurrence which motorists generally expect. Road usage pricing has been implemented since 1975. There are other onerous charges relating to vehicles which may or may not be consistent with George's ideas.[15]

B. Land-Value Capture and Economic Development

As a result of successful land-value capture, revenue from land leasing and motor vehicle-related charges are important sources of revenue. Singapore has a high ratio of non-tax revenue to GDP. The ratio is partly dependent on the volume of government land leases for the year. In 1994, revenue from government land leasing was S$8.7 billion, exceeding the income (corporate and personal) tax revenue of S$8.3 billion. Revenue collected by the Registry of Vehicles amounted to S$4.2 billion. (GDP in 1994 was S$105 billion).

The Singapore government has enjoyed healthy budget surpluses since 1968. Tax rates on income and profits have been steadily reduced over time. In 1966, the marginal personal income tax rate varied from six to 55 percent, with the highest marginal rate being applied to chargeable income of S$750,000 and above. In contrast, at present, the marginal tax rate varies from two to 28 percent; and the highest marginal rate is applicable to chargeable incomes above S$400,000. Generous tax relief and rebates provide incentives for higher income women to have more children.

The corporate income tax rate was 40 percent between 1966 and 1986. It has since been reduced to 26 percent, with 25 percent as the eventual target set by the Ministry of Finance. However, numerous schemes for tax exemption, tax deduction, and tax concessions exist which have been introduced as part of Singapore's industrial policy to attract direct foreign investment.[16] Tax incentives were introduced in 1959 and liberally extended to promote industrial investments. Pioneer tax incentives as well as expansion incentives provide tax holidays of varying duration. Selective tax incentives have also been liberally used to encourage the development of various activities or sub-sectors of the economy. Industries which qualify under these schemes enjoy zero or concessionary income tax rates. More recently, fiscal incentives were introduced to encourage firms to invest outside of Singapore.[17]

To facilitate foreign direct investment in the manufacturing sector, the Economic Development Board, which was established in 1961, developed industrial sites on state-owned land at various locations throughout Singapore. In 1968, the Jurong Town Corporation (JTC) was established as a separate statutory board to manage and develop industrial estates. The JTC leases land or facilities to individual industrial tenants. JTC land leases are normally for either 30 or 60-year terms. Large tracts of land for industrial purposes were thus made available at low cost through the Land Acquisition Act.

Despite its small domestic market, Singapore has developed into a major international financial center. Offshore financial activities relating to foreign exchange, futures, loans, and deposits are handled by both domestic and a host of multinational financial institutions. Asian Currency Units handle designated international assets and liabilities and enjoy preferential regulatory and tax conditions. Futures traders and fund managers in Singapore also enjoy preferential tax rates. The government's efforts to develop Singapore as an international financial center date back to 1968 when tax incentives were introduced for the establishment of an Asian Currency Market in Singapore.

The Urban Redevelopment Authority (URA) was given the task of planning and redeveloping the city in a comprehensive manner. To facilitate private sector redevelopment, legislation for block decontrol of 770 privately owned properties on thirty-two hectares of commercial land in the heart of the central business district was introduced in 1969. The tract of land subsequently became known as the Golden Shoe due to its high value and shape. Land acquired by the government in and around the central area was leased to private developers (usually for 99 years) through a public tender process. The URA specifies the desired type of development as well as the design guidelines. Through the URA sale of sites programs, offices, hotels, shopping centers, warehouses, and recreational facilities as well as residential projects were built by private developers who were successful in the tender process. The difference between the price paid by private developers for state land leases and the compensation (at 1973 prices until 1987) given to dispossessed landowners represented the land-value captured by the government.

The public housing program in Singapore is well known and is a source of great pride for the government. Eighty-six percent of the population resides in public housing. Public housing in the Singapore context refers to housing built by the state which is either rented or leased on a 99-year basis at subsidized prices to eligible households. Home ownership in this context refers in most cases to ownership of a residential lease. The overall home ownership rate is above 90 percent. The large public housing sector has served to cushion the impact of inevitably rising prices of land and housing on the cost of living in a rapidly growing economy where land is a scarce commodity. This in turn has helped to dampen wage increases, improved international competitiveness, and promoted economic growth.

Notes

1. Alain Bertaud and Bertrand Renaud, "Cities Without Land Markets: Location and Land Use in the Socialist City" (World Bank Policy Research Working Paper 1477, 1995). See also Yu-Hung Hong, "Myths and Realities of Public Land Leasing: Canberra and Hong Kong," *LandLines*, newsletter of the Lincoln Institute of Land Policy (March 1999); and Sock-Yong Phang, "Urban Transportation and Land Regulations in Singapore," a paper prepared for the World Bank's World Development Report 1999/2000 workshop, February, 1999.

2. Gordon N. Cruden, *Land Compensation and Valuation Law in Hong Kong* (Singapore: Butterworths, 1986), chapter 1 for details.

3. Hong Kong Government, *Hong Kong—A New Era* (Hong Kong: Government Printer, 1998), pp. 62.

4. Cruden, chapter 18 on Town Planning.

5. Cruden, chapter 21 for details of the provisions for land leases under the Joint Declaration.

6. See Yu-Hung Hong, op. cit., and "Can Leasing Public Land be an Alternative Source of Local Public Finance?" Working paper issued by the Lincoln Institute of Land Policy, Cambridge, MA, 1996.

7. Tax rates are for 1997 and further details may be found in Hong Kong Government, op. cit., pp. 61–63.

8. Ibid, p. 181–190.

9. P. Sai-wing Ho, "A Ricardian interpretation of the provision of public housing services in Hong Kong", *Cambridge Journal of Economics* (June 1996), pp. 207–225; and M. Castells, L. Goh, and R. Y. W. Kwok, *The Shek Kip Mei Syndrome: Economic Development and Public Housing in Hong Kong and Singapore* (London, UK: Pion Limited, 1990).

10. F. T. Hodgkiss, "Raffles of Singapore," *The Freeman*, March, 1942; A. R. Hutchinson, "Sir Stamford Raffles in Indonesia," *Progress* (Melbourne), February, 1968; Robert V. Andelson and James M. Dawsey, *From Wasteland to Promised Land* (Maryknoll, NY.: Orbis Books/London: Shepheard-Walwyn, 1992), p. 95.

11. W J. M. Ricquier, *Land Law*, (2nd ed.; Singapore: Butterworths, 1995), p. 6 and 11.

12. R S. J. Braddell, *The Law of the Straits Settlements* (Kuala Lumpur: Oxford University Press, 1982), p. 53.

13. Ibid., p. 18.

14. There is a capital gains tax for certain transactions involving the sale of subsidized housing built by the public sector. From May 15, 1996, capital gains from all properties sold within three years after they were purchased are subject to income tax. Additional stamp duty is also levied on the seller of such properties.

15. Taxes and charges associated with car ownership include an import tax, registration fees, annual road taxes, and a Certificate Of Entitlement (COE) which is required for the registration of any new vehicle. A COE may be obtained in a public tender for a predetermined quota which is held each month. The COE is valid for a period of ten years. In 1998, an electronic road pricing system comprising electronic gantries, vehicle transponders and pre-paid cash cards replaced the previous manually enforced paper license (on windscreen) system.

16. Chong-Yah Lim et. al., *Policy Options for the Singapore Economy* (Singapore: McGraw Hill, 1988), p. 258.

17. Since 1988, Singapore's gross national saving has exceeded gross capital formation. This is partly a result of persistent and large budget surpluses as well as a high rate of compulsory savings. In 1995, gross national saving was 50.8 percent of GNP and gross fixed capital formation was 33.4 percent of GNP. Since Singapore has become a net lender to the rest of the world, the government has adopted an industrial strategy of providing tax incentives for firms to invest overseas. For details on the various tax incentives, see Ministry of Trade and Industry, Singapore, *Economic Survey of Singapore, 1993* (Singapore: SNP Publishers, 1994), pp. 44–45.

Singapore: The Philips factory at the Toa Payoh Industrial Park provides employment opportunities for residents of Toa Payoh town. Toa Payoh town was built by the government on state owned land. It is one of more than 20 Housing and Development Board towns that together house 86 percent of Singaporeans.

Singapore: Tampines new town was built by the government on state owned land and is home to some 250,000 people. It is one of more than 20 Housing and Development Board towns that together house 86 percent of Singaporeans. The Tampines regional center provides employment and shopping opportunities for residents, who also have access to excellent public transport services.

Chapter 21

Japan

BY YOSHISABURO YAMASAKI* AND ROBERT V. ANDELSON**

WHEN COMMODORE MATTHEW Perry's warship anchored in Edo (Tokyo) Bay in 1853, Japan was a hermit country, ruled by a hereditary generalissimo, the Tokugawa Shogun, in the name of a powerless emperor. Its economy was predominantly agrarian, farmers being outranked only by warriors among the four traditional classes of society, with artisans below them and merchants at the very bottom. Land was held in customary tenure, the largest

*Yoshisaburo Yamasaki holds the degree of Doctor of Economics from Kōbe University, where he served as professor of social policy in the faculty of economics from 1953–1971. Upon being made professor emeritus at Kōbe, he taught 11 more years at Kinki University. His chief publications are *Henry George's Theory of Land Reform* (1961), *Land Problems and Land Policies* (1972, revised and enlarged in 1987)—both in Japanese, and a Japanese translation of Henry George's Progress and Poverty (1991). He also supervised the translation of George's *Protection or Free Trade* (1990).

**Robert V. Andelson, professor emeritus of philosophy, Auburn University, and distinguished research fellow, American Institute for Economic Research, holds a Ph.D. from the University of Southern California. He is sole author of *Imputed Rights: An Essay in Christian Social Theory* (University of Georgia Press, 1971), joint-author (with J. M. Dawsey) of *From Wasteland to Promised Land: Liberation Theology for a Post-Marxist World* (Orbis/Shepheard-Walwyn, 1992), and editor and co-author of *Critics of Henry George* (Fairleigh Dickinson University Press/Associated University Presses, 1979), *Commons Without Tragedy* (Barnes & Noble/Shepheard-Walwyn, 1991) and of the 2nd edition of *Land-Value Taxation Around the World* (New York: Robert Schalkenbach Foundation, 1997). He is a director of the corporation and a member of the editorial board of *The American Journal of Economics and Sociology*, to which he has contributed numerous articles. His articles have also appeared in other scholarly periodicals including *The Personalist* (on the editorial board of which he served for its last five years of publication), *Modern Age, The Southern Journal of Philosophy*, and *The International Journal of Contemporary Sociology*. He is also author of several booklets, among them the widely-circulated *Henry George and the Reconstruction of Capitalism*.

holdings by 250 *daimyos* (feudal lords), each with his retinue of dependent *samurai*. Rents and taxes were paid in kind by peasant cultivators.

This backward and static system was ill-equipped to cope with the challenge presented by the opening of Japan to Western trade that followed Perry's visit; moreover, the national humiliation attendant on the imposition of commercial and extraterritorial treaties through the implied threat of force spelled the end of the Tokugawa Shogunate. In 1867, a group of progressive nobles from western Japan persuaded the young emperor, Mutsuhito, also known as Meiji (Enlightened Rule), to reassert an authority that had been dormant for centuries. Under this pressure, the last shogun resigned, and imperial troops easily subdued such Tokugawa forces as resisted.

These pivotal events, which have been designated the Meiji Restoration, set the stage for a program of modernization that enabled Japan quickly to negotiate for itself an end to such Western political incursions as extraterritoriality that had eroded the sovereignty of China and other Asian nations, and to emerge within the next quarter century as a world power, both militarily and economically.

I

The Meiji Land and Tax Reform

THE MECHANISM THAT made this program possible was a reconstruction of the land tenure system, embodied in the Land Tax Revision Act (Chiso Kaisei Jōrei) of 1873 (the sixth year of Meiji),

---

Dr. Andelson is current president of the International Union for Land-Value Taxation and Free Trade, vice president of the Robert Schalkenbach Foundation, an adjunct faculty member of the Ludwig von Mises Institute, and was twice president of the Alabama Philosophical Society. Early in his career, he spent three years as executive director of the Henry George School of Social Science in San Diego. In 1964, he founded the Tax Reform Association of Louisiana (TRAL), which, during its brief existence, produced a study of the potential impact of land-value taxation on the city of Natchitoches, LA.

which provided secure legal title in place of merely customary title to land, permitting sale, division, annexation, mortgage, and lease. Above all, it abolished the tax in kind (rice) paid to feudal lords, and replaced it with a tax in money, paid to the central government. "Rent which had formerly been levied upon the rural peasants to support the warrior class and its conspicuous consumption was switched into the coffers of the nation's exchequer and used to finance an industrial revolution."[1]

Thus the 19th century "Japanese miracle" was achieved, at the outset, on a foundation of land-value taxation.[2] An efficient centralized bureaucracy was set up. A modern army and navy were established. Compulsory education was introduced. Manufacturing, mining, transportation, and banking were promoted, frequently with advice from European and American experts. And a bicameral Diet or Legislature was formed, with an elected House of Representatives.

However, from the standpoint of social justice, the assessment formula embodied in the Land Tax Revision Act was severely flawed, in that it gave landlords a tax advantage over owner-cultivators. This was not the intention of the technocrats who devised it, for they had no personal bias toward landlordism. The tax was meant to fall on net produce (i.e., economic rent) in contrast to the Tokugawa land tax, which was a proportional levy on gross farm produce. But the assessment formula used to value holdings was faulty.

Assuming that the income of a tenant was one-third and rent two-thirds of a parcel's yield, they decided that, in arriving at the assessed value of a tenant-cultivated holding, rental income should be capitalized at two-thirds (four percent) of the figure used to capitalize owner-cultivated land (six percent).[3] The effect of this was to deduct from the landlord's property value and hence his taxes the wages (and other inputs) retained by his tenants, but to include the owner-cultivator's wages in his property value and hence his taxes. The Meiji land tax was thus a true land-value tax only with respect to land cultivated by tenants; for owner-cultivators, it was also a tax on wages. One can only hazard the guess that the reformers simply failed to grasp the concept that the yield attributable to the labor input of an independent worker on his own land is a form of wages.

The disadvantage of the owner-cultivators did not cause them serious harm so long as the price of rice remained high, but when it began to decrease (due to a policy of currency deflation) in 1881, reaching its low point in 1887, they found themselves hard-put to pay the tax, which (unlike the Tokugawa land tax) was inflexible, making no allowance for lean years. This put the landlords, whose tax obligation was a third lower, in a position to buy out the distressed independent cultivators, and led to concentration and speculation. A great many of the independent cultivators were thus reduced to tenancy, and some, together with tenants who had been deprived of the right of cultivation, drifted into the cities to join the ranks of the emerging proletariate.[4]

In 1878, the national land tax was reduced from three to 2.5 percent of capital value, but rents were not reduced for tenant farmers. The proclamation of the Constitution in 1889 institutionalized the political power of a landowning class that now held private legal title free of feudal obligations. Franchise in national elections was granted to males over the age of 25 who paid taxes at or above a specified minimum. Inasmuch as 97 percent of the electorate qualified on the basis of land tax rather than income tax payments, this gave landowners effective control of the Diet, where "their main interest was directed toward reducing their tax burden."[5] Independent smallholders, understandably, were no less zealous in this respect than were great landlords.[6] Accordingly, whereas in 1872, land taxes accounted for 72 percent of total government revenue, this share declined to about 46 percent in 1890, and again to 15 percent just prior to the First World War. It might, of course, be possible to interpret this decline in share to the parallel development of industry and consequent increase in the proportion of voters paying income tax. Yet this fails to explain why the fiscal surplus attributable to the reduced military spending occasioned by the London Naval Conference of 1930[7] was used to lower the land tax even more drastically than before. In 1931 (the sixth year of Shōwa), the Land Tax Revision Act was replaced by the Land Tax Law (Chiso Hō), which mandated, instead of the previous tax on the capital value of land, a 3.8 percent levy on *annual lease rent*—an extremely smaller base.

The Meiji land tax made possible Japan's transformation into a modern capitalist power, but, as we have seen, only at great cost in human welfare. Fred Harrison's apt verdict provides a fitting coda to our consideration of the subject:

> The Meiji land tax . . . has been criticized on a number of counts. These criticisms . . . have been misdirected; they imply, or explicitly state, that the land tax per se is a deficient instrument for accomplishing the desired goals. But on the contrary, problems arose in Japan because the tax was technically inadequate and incomplete.[8]

II

Agricultural Land Reform under the Allied Occupation

BY THE ADVENT of World War II, concentration of agrarian land-ownership had become a major problem in Japan. Fifty percent of the farms were owned by absentee landlords, 70 percent of the farmers were tenants, and 68 percent of the total farm yield was paid to landlords in rent. Such circumstances, needless to say, had a disincentive effect upon agricultural production. And it takes no stretch of the imagination to surmise that this artificial contraction of lebensraum in a country where it was naturally in short supply exacerbated already existing widespread land-hunger and thus helped to fuel support for the militarist program of territorial expansion.

The Agricultural Land Adjustment Law (*Nōchi Chōsei Hō*) promulgated in 1938 (the 13th year of Shōwa, during the premiership of Prince Konoye), was a largely ineffectual effort to address the problem by encouraging independent cultivators, strengthening arrangements for the mediation of tenancy disputes, and establishing provisions to safeguard tenants' rights.[9]

After the war, the need for stronger measures had become clearly evident. Accordingly, the Agricultural Land Reform Bill was drawn up on its own initiative by the Ministry of Agriculture and Forestry, and enacted by the Diet in December, 1945, as an amendment to the Agricultural Land Adjustment Law. It provided for a number of regulations designed to improve the status of independent farmers, to democratize local agricultural administration, etc.[10]

However, between the preparation and the passage of this bill, the Headquarters of General Douglas MacArthur, Supreme Allied Commander of the Occupation Forces, had addressed to the government a "Memorandum for Rural Land Reform," calling for more sweeping legislation. Inasmuch as the Occupation Headquarters did not consider the act an adequate response to this memorandum, the government postponed enforcement of most of it, and promulgated the "Second Agricultural Land Reform" on October 21, 1946 (the 21st year of Shōwa). This actually consisted of two statutes—the Independent Farmer Establishment Special Measures Law (*Jisakunō Sōsetsu Tokubetsu Sochi Hō*), and the second amendment to the Agricultural Land Adjustment Law.[11]

The Second Agricultural Land Reform broke up the huge agricultural estates, virtually obliterated absentee landholding, created a large and politically potent class of independent smallholders, and greatly improved the position of farm tenants. All cultivated land leased out by absentee owners, as well as any cultivated land exceeding one *chobu* (about one hectare), or, in the northern island of Hokkaido, four chobu, was subject to compulsory sale to the government. Almost all the land thus purchased by the government was then sold on easy terms to the tenants. Thus, by mid-1950, a total of 1,742,000 hectares of cultivated land had been transferred to 4,478,000 tenant or tenant-and-independent farm households. Eighty percent of the former tenant farms became the property of their cultivators, and in the remaining ones the well-being of the tenants was powerfully improved by the strengthening of cultivation rights and the lowering of rents.[12]

Afterward, in 1952 (the 27th year of Showa), the Agricultural Land Law (*Nōchi Hō*) was enacted to maintain the results of the Agricultural Land Reform.[13]

Although the postwar land reform brought tremendous changes to the national structure of landownership, and gave new vitality to agricultural growth, it had two very significant shortcomings: First, it applied only to cultivated acreage, and had no bearing upon either urban or forest property. Second, even in the agrarian sphere, it failed to provide for the social capture of the unearned increment of land, the truly fundamental basis for a just and efficient economic order. Again, Harrison's comments are worth quoting:

> The postwar reform sought to eliminate the despised landlords by increasing the number of owner-occupiers (a policy orientation that can be traced back to the Hirota Cabinet of 1936). But in merely transforming tenants into owners, the 'reform' succeeded in consolidating the system of land monopoly, with the privileges enjoyed by an enlarged class. There is no such thing as a society free of landlordism when the benefits of publicly-created land values are privately appropriated. When the fiscal system permits monopolists [regardless of how numerous] to exploit the land market to their advantage, society becomes the tenant of the owner-occupiers.[14]

For one thing, peasant proprietors near urban areas tended to hold their acreage for speculation, keeping it ostensibly in agricultural use so as to enjoy the minuscule tax rate on agricultural land, while it appreciated in value. Meanwhile, much-needed residential development was stymied for lack of suitable space, and industries found it difficult to expand facilities. For another, the cost of food was kept unnaturally high by agricultural import barriers imposed at the behest of farm constituencies. Thus, while nominal wages came to rival those in the US, their value is considerably lower because of the percentage the average Japanese is forced to spend on food and housing.

Leaving aside the flawed and ultimately abandoned Meiji land tax, the concept of land-value taxation was not unknown in Japan, for the system of Henry George had been vigorously advocated there in detail by Sentaro Jo as early as 1891, and slightly later by the missionary, Charles E. Garst. Moreover, at least one Georgist sympathizer, Wolf Ladejinsky, played a key role in setting up the land program under the Occupation. Then, if ever, was a signal opportunity to lay the groundwork for a genuinely thoroughgoing reform in keeping with the complementary ideas of free enterprise and equal access to natural opportunity. Why it was not taken, we shall probably never know.

III

Later Developments

BECAUSE JAPAN IS a densely populated, mountainous archipelago, very little of which is suitable either for human habitation or for agriculture, the value of usable land would be naturally high even without monopoly or speculation. But, as might have been anticipated, the post-war industrial boom gave rise to a speculative binge that drove land prices through the roof in 1972–73. Seeking to dampen speculation, the government introduced a progressive sales tax on land transactions in 1974, but by then the surge in land prices had already peaked, and the only effect of the tax was to encourage large speculators to withhold land from the market.[15]

Land prices started escalating upward again in 1977, thanks in part to large-scale public sector spending (especially on housing). They were further spurred by liberal credit policies introduced in 1979 and expanded in 1985. Also contributing to this spiral was the inherent resilience of the economy, based on traditional Japanese habits of hard work, cooperation, and a propensity toward systematic saving and investment despite high living costs, together with a literate and well-trained labor force and strong corporate emphasis on research and development. The surging Japanese economy became the envy of the world. Land prices, however, outpaced production, causing alarm on the part of the government.

Accordingly, between 1988 and 1992, a series of measures was instituted to discourage speculation and moderate the inflated land market. These measures included: (1) Local "surveillance" (control) of prices on parcels above a certain size at time of sale. (2) Planning and regulation of land use. (3) Sharp restrictions on the size of real estate loans banks were permitted to make, coupled with general increase in interest rates by the Bank of Japan. (4) Increase in assessment ratio for local property taxation. (5) An increase in the capital gains tax. (6) A national tax on land value, exclusive of public and residential lands.

In 1990, the economy turned downward, and the nation has been in recession ever since. Land prices began declining in

Tokyo and other cities around the end of the same year, and continued to do so during the course of the next.

It was the contraction of credit more than anything else that burst the Japanese land bubble. The land-value tax (*Chika Zei*) did not come into operation until 1992 (the fourth year of Heisei). Moreover, it did not apply to residential holdings, and its rate was insignificant—0.2 percent the first year, 0.3 percent the second and third years, and a minute 0.15 percent thereafter.[16]

In 1996, Koichi Mera (then a visiting professor at the University of Southern California) produced a working paper, "The Failed Land Policy: A Story from Japan," the main thesis of which is that Japan's prolonged recession was primarily caused by the government's deflationary land price policy. Mera concedes that his is decidedly a minority position among scholars who have studied the recession.[17] His paper would scarcely deserve notice were it not for the fact that it was issued by the Lincoln Institute of Land Policy, a respected think-tank supported by a foundation that was established to advance the economic philosophy of Henry George. (Of course, to issue a working paper is not necessarily to endorse its contents.) Patently, the minuscule land-value tax, which was not instituted until two years after the recession had commenced, could not have caused it. Other absurdities in Mera's paper have been noted in a memorandum by the distinguished land economist, Mason Gaffney.[18]

In 1997, the government announced plans to suspend the land-value tax for three years. This was done, and, as of this writing (April, 2000), the tax has not been reinstated. If the government imagined that the suspension of this tax, even in combination with lowered interest rates, would reverse the recession, it was mistaken. Consumption continues to decline, as does the real estate market. The stock market is rising, but only because US and other foreign investors are taking advantage of new legislation that enables them to buy cash-strapped Japanese firms at distress prices.

IV

Conclusions

FROM THE ABOVE account emerges the conclusion that, despite periodic land reforms, Japan's only real experience with land-value taxation was in the early decades of the Meiji Restoration. Because it relied on a technically flawed assessment formula and failed to allow for lean years, the tax unintentionally favored absentee landlordism and caused great hardship and loss to small working farmers. Nonetheless, for all its manifest faults (none of them intrinsic to the theory or practice of land-value taxation per se), it played an indispensable role in laying the groundwork for Japan's emergence as an economic power-house.

Political realities make it unlikely that the government will soon cease its futile tinkering with short-term palliatives, and instead institute a perfected version of the program that could have given the nation economic justice and stability as well as dynamism had it been correctly implemented. Yet the Japanese people have demonstrated historically an unrivaled capacity to subordinate private interests for the sake of collective goals. If they only can be made to see its potential benefit to the whole society, it is not too much to hope that they may force a change in political realities so as to revive, after all, the principle of the Meiji land tax, suitably corrected in the mechanics of its application.

Notes

1. Fred Harrison, *The Power in the Land* (London: Shepheard-Walwyn, 1983), p. 153.

2. E. H. Norman, *Japan's Emergence as a Modern State* (New York: Institute of Pacific Relations, 1940), p. 141; R. P. Dore, *Land Reform in Japan* (London: Oxford University Press, 1959), p. 15; and T. Fukutake, *Japanese Rural Society* (Ithaca, NY: Cornell University Press, 1967), p. 10.

3. J. I. Nakamura, *Agricultural Production and the Economic Development of Japan 1873–1922* (Princeton, NJ: Princeton University Press, 1966), p. 190.

4. Goro Hani and Kimio Izu, *Meiji-Ishin Ni Okeru Seido Jō No Henkaku* (The Institutional Changes in the Meiji Restoration), contained in *Nippon Shihonshugi Hattatsu Shi Kōza* (The Series on the History of the Development of Capitalism in Japan) (Tokyo: Iwanami Shoten, 1932), p. 26.

5. R. P. Dore, "Land Reform and Japan's Economic Development," *Developing Economies*, Special Issue, Vol. 3, 1965, p. 385. Page reference is to reprint in T. Shanin, ed., *Peasants and Peasant Societies* (Harmondsworth, UK: Penguin Press, 1971).

6. Yoshitarō Hirano, *Nippon Shihonshugi Shakai No Kikō* (The Structure of Capitalistic Society in Japan) (Tokyo: Iwanami Shoten, 1950), p. 189.

7. Kenji Yamaguchi, *Tochi Wa Kōkyōzai* (Land is a Public Good) (Tokyo: Kindai Bungei Sha, 1996), pp. 203f.

8. Harrison, op. cit., p. 155.

9. Takekazu Ogura, *Agrarian Problems and Agricultural Policy in Japan: A Historical Sketch* (Tokyo: Institute of Asian Economic Affairs, 1967), p. 10.

10. Ibid., pp. 20, 21.

11. Ibid.

12. Ibid.

13. Hiroshi Mizumoto, Shūzō Toda, and Eiji Shimoyama, eds., *Fudōsan Hōsei Gaisetsu* (An Outline of Real Estate Laws) (Tokyo: Seirin Shoin, 1995), p. 254.

14. Harrison, op. cit., p. 168.

15. H. Tsuboi, "Japan's Land Development Policy and the Real Estate Industry: Problems and Prospects." Paper presented to the 20th Annual Congress of FIABCI, the International Real Estate Federation, Tokyo, June 1, 1979, p. 6.

16. Mizumoto et al, eds., op. cit., pp. 276–77.

17. Koichi Mera, "The Failed Land Policy: A Story of Japan." Working paper issued by the Lincoln Institute of Land Policy, Cambridge, MA, 1996, p. 2.

18. Memorandum from Mason Gaffney to R. V. Andelson, dated 11 March, 1997. For example, on p. 6 of his paper, Mera asserts that "the mere fact that the price of land went down suggests that the asset value of the people in Japan was reduced, as land is an important component of the total asset." Gaffney comments: "Overpricing land does not make it more productive. High land prices are simply redistributive, widening the gap between the haves and the have-nots. They make it even harder for the have-nots to buy land, without making it easier for the haves, who, if they sell one piece to buy another, are no better off."

Chapter 22

Kiao-chau

BY V. G. PETERSON* AND TSENG HSIAO**

KIAO-CHAU WAS A German protectorate from 1898 to 1915, located on the Yellow Sea coast of China. It occupied some 200 square miles on the Shantung Peninsula around and including the city of Tsingtao, leased to Germany for one hundred years by the imperial Chinese government. When Germany acquired the region, Tsingtao was an obscure fishing village, and the total population in the area was only 83,000. When Germany withdrew in the second year of World War I, Tsingtao had become the fourth most

---

*V. G. Peterson (Violetta G. Graham) was for many decades executive secretary of the Robert Schalkenbach Foundation. Upon retiring, she was elected a director of the foundation, in which capacity she served until her death.

**Tseng Hsiao, a founder of the department of land administration at Chengchi University, Taipei, also founded the Chinese Research Institute of Land Economics and the China Land Reform Association. His numerous publications include *The Fundamentals of Equalization of Land Rights, Theoretical Framework for the Equalization of Land Rights*, and *The Theory and Practice of Land Reform*, all in Chinese. He studied at Beijing University and (under the noted Bodenreformer, Adolf Damaschke) at the University of Berlin. His students marked his 70th birthday by publishing a collection of his writings consisting of 70 papers. Also in recognition of the occasion, Kon-Kul University in Korea awarded him an honorary Ph.D. in economics.

This chapter combines material from Miss Peterson's chapter on Germany in the original (1955) edition of *Land-Value Taxation Around the World*, with material by Tseng Hsiao not available to her when she wrote that chapter. Tseng Hsiao's contribution is from "Land Tenure in Tsingtao and Henry George's Ideals," in Richard W. Lindholm and Sein Lin, eds., *Henry George and Sun Yat-sen: Application and Evolution of Their Land Use Doctrine* (Lincoln Institute Monograph #77-12; Cambridge, MA: Lincoln Institute of Land Policy, 1977), pp. 122-127. In this edition, the chapter has been amplified with information from Michael Silagi, *Henry George and Europe* (Will and Dorothy Burnham Lissner, eds., trans. from the German by Susan N. Faulkner; New York: Robert Schalkenbach Foundation, 2000), chapter 8.

important trading port on the China coast, and the area's population had increased to 275,000.

The pleasant climate and scenic setting of Tsingtao made it a natural site for a resort, and with its location at the mouth of Chiao-chou-wan, one of the best naval harbors in northern China. The Germans developed the harbor, constructed a railroad to Tsinan, and built many resort facilities.

I

Land-Value Taxation in Kiao-chau

KIAO-CHAU WAS HELD under the jurisdiction of the German Navy Department, not the Colonial Office, due to the efforts of the navy secretary, Alfred von Tirpitz (later to become grand admiral), who held the policies of the latter in low esteem. Tirpitz was sympathetic to progressive socio-political thought, and with his encouragement "the Navy Department became a sort of stronghold of land reform ideas."[1] Adolf W. F. Damasche, whose persuasive and organizational talents later built the *Bund deutscher Bodenreformer* (German Land Reform League) into a powerful body with something like 100,000 members, was able to win over a number of high naval officers to the cause, who became members of the Bund. One of these was Admiral Otto von Diederichs, whose forces had conquered and occupied Kiao-chau, and who served as its military governor. Diederichs and Tirpitz were determined that land speculation, which severely afflicted the German colonies in East Africa, not be permitted to take hold in the new protectorate.

Speculation had begun as soon as it became known that extensive improvements would be undertaken by the German authorities. To curb it and at the same time help finance the development, the Reichstag (doubtless on the Admiralty's recommendation) enacted a law in 1898 which provided for the compulsory sale to the government at pre-occupation prices of all land the government deemed necessary for possible public works. The land was then replotted, and parcels not needed were resold at a profit. Land in rural areas was not compulsorily purchased, and remained in private hands.

All private land was taxed according to its assessed value at an initial rate of six percent, and subjected to an increment tax of one third of the net profit when sold. After 25 years had elapsed, reassessment was to take place and the increment tax levied on any increase in value regardless of sale. (This provision, of course, was never implemented, as the colony came under Japanese occupation after only 17 years, and its distinctive land tax system was abolished.) In transfer of ownership, the government had the prior right of purchase at the price reported, thus discouraging anyone from reporting a lower sales price in order to reduce his increment tax. The land-value increment tax in Kiao-chau was the first to be adopted anywhere in the world,[3] although there had been tentative anticipations of it earlier in Germany.[4]

In 1903, a method of increasing the annual tax on vacant or underdeveloped land was adopted. Land not utilized for the purpose for which it had been purchased from the government was taxed after 1906 at nine percent instead of the usual six percent, with a three percent increase every three years thereafter until an annual tax of 24 percent had been reached. When properly improved, its tax would revert to six percent.

These policies proved most effective in Kiao-chau. Once they were implemented, there was no more land speculation, and economic growth was very rapid. Most important, the increment resulting from growth and development was applied to the welfare of the whole population of the colony. The success of the increment tax in Kiao-chau led to its being widely adopted in Germany itself—by several hundred cities and towns, including Frankfurt-am-Main (which had introduced it for a brief time even earlier), and in 1911 on the federal level. (See the chapter on Germany for further details.)

II

Ludwig Wilhelm Schrameier

THE DETAILS OF the Kiao-chau Land and Tax Statute were based upon a memorandum by Dr. Ludwig Wilhelm Schramaier, a foreign service official versed in Oriental languages, who was serving as Admiral Diederich's interpreter when Kiao-chau was occupied. (He had previously held consular positions in Shanghai and Canton.) Subsequently, Schramaier was named civil commissioner, and entrusted with the administration of land affairs in the protectorate. He was undoubtedly the driving force behind the system described above, although, of course, he would not have gotten very far without the strong backing of Diederichs and Tirpitz.

For all practical purposes, the system may be, and, indeed was, regarded as the essential realization of the single-tax doctrine of Henry George. This was conceded by Schramaier himself, although he claimed not to have been influenced by Georgism directly, but by the practical necessities of administering the territory.[4] Be that as it may, he was familiar at the time with its basic principles, and became active in the Bund deutscher Bodenreformer on his return to Germany.

In the early 1920s, Schrameier was retained as a consultant by Dr. Sun Yat-sen, who had known him in Shanghai and was familiar with his work in Kiao-chau. He went to Canton to oversee the drafting of the land law and the land registration regulations. These documents were nearly completed when, on January 5, 1926, Schrameier was fatally injured upon being hit by a street-car.

Notes

1. Michael Silagi, *Henry George and Europe* (Will and Dorothy Burnham Lissner, eds.; translated from the German by Susan N. Faulkner; New York: Robert Schalkenbach Foundation, 2000), p. 89.

2. Tseng Hsiao, "Land Tenure in Tsingtao and Henry George's Ideals," in Richard W. Lindholm and Sein Lin, eds., *Henry George and Sun Yat-sen: Application and Evolution of Their Land Use Doctrine* (Lincoln Institute Monograph #77-12; Cambridge, MA: Lincoln Institute of Land Policy, 1977), p. 124.

3. V. G. Peterson," Germany," in H. G. Brown et al, eds., *Land Value Taxation Around the World* (1st ed.; New York: Robert Schalkenbach Foundation, 1955), p. 194.

4. Silagi, pp. 93ff.

Chapter 23

Republic of Korea (South Korea)

BY TAE-IL LEE*

FROM AS EARLY as 50 B.C. (the Three Kingdom period), payment of land tax has been one of the basic duties Korean citizens have had to perform, along with military service and service for public works. The ownership of land was traditionally considered to be in the hands of the royal dynasty and the king, and the land tax was an in-kind charge for the right to cultivate assigned farmlands. Although the structures and the implementation schemes differed substantially from dynasty to dynasty, and even during different periods of the same dynasty, a similar principle more or less persisted until the end of the 19th century.

With the opening of the 20th century, modern techniques of land resource management were eventually introduced to Korea by the Japanese colonial government (from its own motives of pillage); these include a cadastral survey of the entire country, land-value taxation, and a land use planning system. In the course of the first national cadastral survey (1910–1918), the primitive, loosely organized land ownership pattern that had prevailed previously virtually disintegrated, and a clearer land title concept was enforced, with corresponding tax liability. In this modern concept of real-estate as introduced to Korea, the land and its improvements

*Tae-Il Lee, Ph.D., Texas A&M University, is the director of the Chungbok Development Institute. He served for 15 years as senior research fellow and director of the Land Policy Research Division, Korea Research Institute for Human Settlements; and has been an advisor to the Minister of Construction, a visiting scholar at the Harvard Graduate School of Design, and a visiting fellow at the Lincoln Institute of Land Policy. His publications include a book, *The Land Policy Problems in East Asia: A Search for New Choices* (1994), and various book chapters, articles, and working papers dealing with Korean land policy.

were treated as separate entities, and property taxes thus levied separately upon them.

I

Land-Related Tax System in Modern Korea[1]

A. An Overview of Land Taxes

As is the case for most other countries, land taxes by the central government in Korea are basically imposed on the income stream from the property and the capital gains realized at the time of transaction, while the local property taxes are levied on acquisition and registration, and on ownership. Table 1 shows the array of different land taxes currently being imposed on Korea in each sequential stage of land ownership cycle.

Table 1

LAND TAXES IN KOREA (As of April 1996)		
Imposed On	National Tax*	Local Tax
Acquisition	Inheritance Tax Gift Tax	Acquisition Tax Registration Tax
Holding	Income Tax** Corporate Income Tax** Land-Value Increment Tax	Comprehensive Landholding Tax City Planning Tax
Transfer	Transfer Income Tax Special Surtax on Corporate Income Tax Corporate Income Tax	
Notes: *Stamp Tax is surcharged. **Imposed on rental income.		

It should be noted that, before the beginning of the local autonomous political system in 1995, the central government made virtually all the rules in Korea. Instead of having governors, mayors, and county heads appointed by the Ministry of Home Affairs (MOHA), local citizens now elect their administrators through direct vote. Besides these elections, however, not many changes have been made yet in overall local administration.

B. Administration of Property Tax

MOHA is the central government agency responsible for overseeing the activities of the local governments, and even for taxes labeled as local taxes. Tax codes used to be and are still largely established by MOHA, which defines the details of tax bases, rate structures, exemptions and reductions, and collections as well as appeal procedures. Formerly, local property taxation in Korea was simply an extension of the central government's activities, part of it (e.g., collection) being delegated to municipalities and counties. The levying and management of property taxation, which usually constitutes a major portion of any local government's revenues,[2] did not at all reflect each locality's distinctive financial situation.

As has already been pointed out, all the property-related local taxes in Korea make a clear distinction between land and buildings. The distinction apparently is not derived from the influence of Henry George, since buildings are also taxed, possibly at even higher rates, by the same property taxes as those on land. Currently, the land portions of the property tax are levied in the spring of each year and the building portions in the autumn.

II

Public Concept in Land (To-Ji-Gong-Gae-Nyom)

A. Background

The bad memories of nation-wide land speculation in the late 1970s had scarcely faded when land prices soared again in the late 1980s. Although the rate of increase was not the highest Korea had ever seen, the absolute level of prices was such that the social and political problems generated posed a serious potential threat to the national integrity. For example, the total sum of the value of the nation's landed resources was estimated to be more than nine times the size of the GNP in 1990,[3] much higher than the figure for most other countries and even higher than in Japan.

The magnitude of the "capital" gains from the price appreciation in the year of 1989 alone was estimated to be 35 percent more than the local aggregate income earned by all urban workers in the same year. For a number of reasons, however, most of these unearned gains were virtually free from the recapturing efforts of tax authorities.

The government recognized that, if not properly taken care of, these issues could not only shatter the nation socio-politically, but also create a bottleneck for future economic growth. Thus from 1987 to early 1989, when the land price increase began to show signs of letting-up again, the government introduced a set of new policies, popularly known by the comprehensive term, "To-ji-gong-gae-nyom" (Public Concept in Land).

Interpreted as measures to enhance pubic interests in land-related matters, they include: the comprehensive landholding tax, a new system of land assessment, a reinforced land title registration system, and three completely new measures which some regard as rather radical—the ceiling on urban residential land per household, the development charge, and the land-value increment tax. However, since the ceiling on urban residential land, and the development charge are not exactly tax measures, they will not be discussed in this chapter.[4]

B. Comprehensive Landholding Tax

Korea's landholding tax used to be levied at fixed rates on the value of each land parcel. In the late 1980s, a broad consensus emerged that this tax should be increased to deter speculative withholding. Also, as the true dimension of ownership concentration became evident, a heavy tax burden was called for also to discourage large land holdings.[5] For these reasons, the comprehensive landholding tax was introduced in 1988.

Thus, the levying scheme of the conventional property tax (land portion) has been revised so that progressive rates could be applied for large holdings. Basically, it is a tax on the sum of the value of landed parcels all over the country registered under the same owner. A progressive rate structure is certainly not desirable in terms of neutrality, horizontal equity, administrative costs, or the fiscal autonomy of local jurisdictions, but the decision was made to selectively increase the tax burden of large land owners so as to render them more likely to dispose of their excess holdings. It was anticipated that this would lessen the concentration of ownership and at the same time lower the market price of land.

Table 2

RATE STRUCTURE OF THE COMPREHENSIVE LANDHOLDING TAX			
Classification	Land Type	Number of Tax Brackets	Rate (%)
Fixed Rates	Factory site		0.3
	Farmland tilled by owner		0.1
	Luxury property		5.0
Progressive Rates	I. Speculative land and residential land	9	0.2-5.0
	II. Commercial land	9	0.3-2.0

It was clear from the beginning of this measure that the tax burden on ordinary homes, agricultural lands owned by working farmers, and factory sites in operation would not increase and, indeed, would sometimes even decrease. In its final form, the measure constituted an amalgam of three principles: first, the indiscriminate aggregation of all land holdings registered under the same owner; second, the penalization of "obviously speculative" holdings; and third, opposition to any tax increase for "innocent" holdings.[6] The tax rate structure includes three fixed rates and two progressive rates as shown in Table 2. Low fixed rates for factory sites and farm land, and a high rate for luxury land are the same as in the old property tax, but now residential land, commercial land, and land held presumably for speculation are subject to one of two progressive rates.

The first progressive rate, which applies to speculative land as well as residential land is a penalty only to the truly large land holders, since it reaches a one percent marginal rate only when the assessed value is as high as 500 million Won (roughly US$650,000). The second progressive rate with more mild progressivity is applied to commercial building sites which usually occupy expensive land in downtown areas.

Applying progressive rates is most feasible when the ownership of all land is computerized nationwide. After five years of preparation, the Ministry of Home Affairs currently runs a computerized land ownership record system and determines the amount of tax for each individual. The amount of land owned is then divided in proportion to land values among localities in which the owner holds land, and each local government is responsible for collecting its share.

C. The Tax Base and Assessment Ratio

At the core of the problems of land taxes, both national and local, is the issue of assessment. For the purpose of local taxation, Korea's local government officials are supposed to assess the unit value of each land parcel every year and set the Standard Value for Taxation (SVT), which is then written on the official record of the parcel. However, until recently, local governments had not bothered to accurately assess land values. Even when land prices increased rapidly, the SVT was raised only slightly, partly because of political reasons but also because of the knowledge that much revenue shortfall would be supplied by the central government anyway.

Nationwide, the SVT ranges somewhere between 15 and 20 percent of the market price. As we have seen, holding tax rates are quite low for most properties, but it is the low assessment ratio that makes the tax almost insignificant to landowners and renders land taxation ineffective in achieving any policy goal. Table 3 shows the effective average tax rates for eight land values which correspond to the bracket boundaries of Progressive Rate I. In 1990, 93.56 percent of taxpayers belonged to the lowest rate bracket, and over 99.9 percent of them paid less than 0.09 percent of their land values. Whatever the policy objective of the tax may be, it cannot be achieved with such a low effective rate.

Another problematic aspect is that the present assessment ratio shows a great deal of variation among regions, land uses, and individual parcels. Usually, when there is a time lag between the actual market price change and the assessment, land with higher prices and higher rates of price increase tends to be assessed at a lower ratio; thus, the wealthy pay relatively less tax. In addition to the inequity problem, lack of assessment uniformity poses an obstacle in using the tax as a land policy tool.

Table 3

AVERAGE EFFECTIVE RATES OF COMPREHENSIVE LANDHOLDING TAX[7] (Progressive Rate I) (Unit: Million Won)				
A. Tax Base (Assessed Value)	B. Amount of Tax	C. Market Value of Land	D. Average Effective Tax Rate (B/C, %)	E. Cumulative Rate of Taxpayer (1990, %)
20	0.04	133.3	0.03	93.56
50	0.13	333.3	0.04	98.42
100	1.38	666.7	0.0	99.46
300	1.78	2,000.0	0.09	99.91
500	11.28	6,666.7	0.17	99.98
3,000	51.28	20,000.0	0.26	100.00
5,000	111.28	33,333.0	30.33	100.00

Notes: 1. Assessment Ratio is assumed to be 15 percent. Number of total taxpayers subject to the Progressive Rate I was 7,549,350.
2. 1 million Won is equivalent to approx. 1,280 Dollars (US$1 is approx. 780 Korean Won).

D. Land-Value Increment Tax

One of the most controversial of the new measures adopted was a new tax called land-value increment tax. The land-value increment tax was to institute and, in fact, to strengthen the windfall recapture system by taxing away a significant portion of the unearned income from land value appreciation even before it is actually realized, thus deterring landowners from holding onto lands because of speculative anticipations.

The lands which are subject to this tax are basically unbuilt, idle lands and non-business lands owned by firms, and excess residential lands beyond the permitted ceiling. This tax is normally levied at three year intervals, and a flat 50 percent rate is applied to the "excessive profits from lands" (land value increase over the national average during the three year period). However, when the land value increase of a certain district is so rapid that it exceeds 1.5 times the national average (speculation prone districts), the land in question is taxed annually instead of every three years.

The new tax was levied for the first time in June 1991 with 27,441 individuals and firms being affected. It exhibited a tremendous impact on the real estate market, sharply reducing speculation-oriented land ownership. As might be expected, it did not meet with universal approval. It was criticized for being levied on unrealized gains and for violating the principle of "ability to pay." Actually, according to the initial version, an owner might have to reduce the number or size of his housing plots or farming paddies just to pay the tax.

Also, there have been numerous successful instances of evasion by landowners who managed to avoid the "idle lands" classification by building unnecessary and often unsightly "improvements." Besides being an aesthetic blight, during a period in 1990–1992 much of this building exacerbated a shortage of materials and skilled labor that might otherwise have been used for genuinely needed construction.[8]

Strong and organized complaints from the landowners culminated in their bringing the issue of land-value increment tax to the constitutional court in 1995. The court eventually ruled that the tax was not conforming to the spirit of the Constitution and ordered a substantial modification. Besides, the stabilized land market since 1991 made the number of taxable cases decrease rapidly and, at the moment of this writing, the practical viability of the land-value increment tax in the future is rather slim.

E. Unified Official Land Price Assessment System

There were in the past a number of different official land price quoting systems by different agencies or ministries corresponding to the needs of their respective functions. Problems with these existing official land prices were two-fold. One was that, although each agency had its own rationale, ordinary citizens were confused as to how the government was assessing the value of their properties and were reluctant to accept the official prices, especially since they varied widely from one agency to another. Also, land was so grossly under-assessed (roughly 15–20 percent of the market value), any policy tools—taxes being most critical—could not exert their intended effects. Even the most stiff nominal tax rate would turn out to be a very meager tax burden for landowners.

These problems of assessment were well recognized, and the Ministry of Construction managed to get a law passed in 1989 to improve land assessment. Under its provision, all these official land prices were unified to one single system, and more importantly, full market value was made the criterion for land assessment.

The first nationwide assessment of all private lands, under the new criterion, was completed during the summer of 1990, and from 1991 national taxes on land have been imposed on that base. To-ji-gong-gae-nyom measures have also adopted the new assessment base. The government, however, failed to link the new assessment system with the comprehensive landholding tax because of objection from the National Assembly which feared that the new assessment standard would abruptly raise the tax burden. The government nevertheless planned to adopt the new assessment system as the base for the comprehensive landholding tax by 1998. But, it also planned to simultaneously adjust the nominal tax rates lest the change in the assessment standard should result in a sudden tax increase for most land owners.

F. Land Title Registration System

Formulation and implementation of any policy requires accurate information, but the current land-related record system needs a great deal of improvement. Currently, two official records exist for each parcel of land. One is used for taxation and other administrative purposes, and the other, kept by the judicial courts, shows various legal property rights related to the parcel and concerned individuals. The problem is that one or both of the records may frequently contain defective information, and they often conflict with each other.

The proposals made for improvement include: first, unification of the two records into a single system, correctly representing all related information; second, computerization of the information with a broader scope (links to resident identification card and household database, and to building records); and third, the initiation of a Land Census which will update necessary information once and for all.

As the first step toward improvement, the National Assembly passed the Compulsory Property Registration Act in July, 1990, which makes non-registration of property a criminal offense. Despite some doubts of its conformity to the principle of free transaction, this law will deter major causes of tax evasion and enhance the effectiveness of land taxes.

III

Financial Crisis and Recent Changes in Land Policy

THE BAILOUT BY the International Monetary Fund in November 1997 marked a critical turnover in the nation's overall economic policy environment. Originating from the mismanagement of excessive short-term borrowing from abroad by local financial institutions, the crisis swept through the entire spectrum of the economic system, quickly drying up the financial market. Faced with severe lack of liquidity, business firms hurriedly let go of their real properties, and the banks also poured real properties and other assets held as collateral into the market. The real estate market in general and the land market in particular thus suddenly became flooded, and prices dropped to fire-sale levels. Since a large proportion of their portfolios consisted of real properties, this asset deflation further aggravated the threat to financial institutions. It also posed a threat to average families that held their savings in the form of housing.

This vicious cycle of problems caused serious concern on the part of government policy makers, who swiftly relaxed much real estate related regulation in order to buoy up the market. This approach mainly took the form of permitting foreigners (who had previously been excluded) to buy real estate, and of various exemptions and reductions in transfer income tax. In addition, the urban residential land ceiling regulation and the land value increment tax, both part of the Public Concept in Land package introduced in the late 1980s, have been lifted. The development charge, also part of the package, was temporarily halved until the end of 1999.

Another line of policy change consisted of the introduction of mortgage-backed securities (MBSs) and asset-backed securities (ABAs), to make real estate a more easily assessable option to the general investor. With this move, the real estate and financial markets have slowly begun to be integrated.

IV

Summary and Conclusions

KOREA'S PAST LAND policy was so obsessed with the speculation problem that the land-related taxes were primarily regarded as measures for recapturing the unearned "capital" gains between the transactions; e.g., transfer income tax and special surtax on corporate income tax. However, due to the numerous cases of exemption and defective market information, these taxes were not able to hold down speculative transaction and ownership.

The To-ji-gong-gae-nyom policy package was thus introduced in the late 1980s as an effort to rectify the situation by structurally affecting the land ownership pattern itself. The comprehensive landholding tax, which is a much reinforced version of the already existing local property tax (land portion), was adopted to increase the tax burden of those with large holdings. The land-value increment tax was also introduced for recapturing unearned land price appreciation regardless of transaction. The focus has, therefore, shifted from the transaction point to the holding stage of the land ownership cycle.

While the rationale behind the comprehensive landholding tax is relatively well received by the public, some problems still persist including the argument about the nature of this particular tax, namely that local taxes such as the comprehensive landholding tax should not carry too heavy a national policy objective. Uneven level of assessment is another problem that has to be solved for the effective administration of the comprehensive landholding tax. The land-value increment tax, on the other hand, is facing a serious setback by a rule of the constitutional court which could dwindle its viability.

In general, the importance and effectiveness of the landholding tax depend largely upon the share of the tax among local revenue sources. If it is a major revenue source with high effective rate, every minute detail of the tax code will draw attention from tax-payers and the tax will have significant effects on the economy. However, in many developing countries, the landholding tax is only a minor revenue source and the effective tax rate is low for various reasons: the ownership of the land may be unclear, record keeping defective, identification of land parcels difficult, and assessment techniques primitive. Under such conditions, the government's efforts should be focused on building up an essential information base to make the tax workable. A number of measures taken by the Korean government during the late 1980s and early 1990s such as mandatory title registration and an improved assessment system, reflect such endeavors.

The government should also refrain from using the landholding tax as a tool for too many policy goals, especially when the effective tax rate is low. If a tax measure carries diverse motives, it becomes unmanageably complicated, and altogether ineffective. Also, when the central government has the power to institute tax exemptions and reductions for national purposes, it can further distort the proper tax administration and may cause revenue loss for the local governments.

Notes

1. From this point on, the name "Korea" refers only to the non-communist part of the divided nation, or South Korea.

2. Property tax (land and building portions together) makes up roughly 30–80 percent of each local government's annual revenue.

3. Since then, the ratio between land value and GNP has shown a declining trend; in 1995, it was estimated to be around five to one.

4. For detailed discussions on the background and mechanisms of each measure, see Tae-Il Lee, "Selected Papers on Korean Land Policy." Working paper issued by the Lincoln Institute of Land Policy, Cambridge, MA., 1993.

5. A government statistic on land ownership, first revealed in 1988, indicated that 65.2 percent of the nation's total landed resources was owned by the top 5 percent of landowners in the country.

6. Jae-young Sohn, "Land Development, Taxation, and the Role of Local Government: Lessons from Korean Experiences," in *Land Policy Problems in East Asia: Toward New Choices*, ed. Bruce Koppel and D. Young Kim (Seoul: East West Center and Korea Research Institute for Human Settlements, 1993), p. 273.

7. Ibid., p. 276.

8. Such difficulties exemplify the pitfalls of introducing roundabout methods such as classification to try to achieve the benefits of straightforward land-value taxation. If all parcels were assessed at full market value and taxed at the same percentage thereof, with improvements exempted correspondingly, no owner would have any incentive to erect unnecessary and shoddy structures, but neither would he be penalized for erecting high-grade ones that serve a useful purpose.

Chapter 24

Papua New Guinea

BY H.J. MANNING* AND CIARAN O'FAIRCHEALLAIGH**

PAPUA NEW GUINEA (PNG) comprises the eastern half of the island of New Guinea, the second largest island in the world. Size it undoubtedly has, for from the country's western border with the Indonesian province of Irian Jaya to Rossel Island and the Pacific Ocean in the east, the distance is 1,500 kilometers.

*H.J. Manning is a fellow and medalist of the Australian Institute of Valuers, and served in important capacities both in Australia and in other countries, including chief valuer and chief assessor of Singapore, and three advisory appointments with the Royal Thai Government. Among his publications are "The Case for Centralization of the Assessment Function" (1970), "Urban Renewal and Property Taxation: Some Impressions of Practices" (1976), and "Small Town Financing: Where Does the Money Come From?" (1984). In 1970, Mr. Manning's paper, "Property Taxation Singapore Style," won first prize in the Donahoo Essay Contest of the International Association of Assessing Officers.

**Ciaran O'Faircheallaigh is professor in the School of Politics and Public Policy, Griffith University, Brisbane. He holds a Ph.D. from the Australian National University, and previously occupied research and teaching positions there, as well as at the University of Papua New Guinea, and Queen's University in Ontario. He has published numerous articles and several books in such fields as public policy, resource economics, social impact assessment, and indigenous studies, including *Mining and Development* (1984), and, with J. Wanna and P. Weller, *Public Sector Management in Australia* (1999). Prof. O'Faircheallaigh has worked as a consultant for many organizations in both public and private sectors, such as the United Nations, Greenpeace International, the governments of Australia and Papua New Guinea, and resource development companies in Australia and Canada. For the past ten years, he has advised various indigenous bodies in Queensland and the Northern Territory regarding matters related to native title, regional agreements, and exploration and mining.

Ciaran O'Faircheallaigh contributed the section on Mineral Taxation. He wishes to express appreciation to the Internal Revenue Commission of the Government of Papua New Guinea for assistance in providing recent information.

Within these limits lies a country of 462,840 square kilometers. This includes the large islands to the north in the Bismarck archipelago, viz. New Britain and New Ireland, and the many lesser islands of the Admiralty and Saint Mathias groups as well as those to the east including the large island of Bougainville, the most northerly of the Solomon Islands chain. Indeed, a total of 1,400 islands is within its borders.

But to think in terms of size only is not to grasp a true understanding of PNG. It is a harsh and rugged country. About two-thirds of its land area comprises an immense chain of overlapping mountain ranges in which 28 mountains exceed 3,700 meters in height and Mount Wilhelm, the tallest, rises to 4,509 meters.

Moreover, this rugged and mountainous country, including most of the larger islands, is scarred and intersected by steep-sided valleys, riven by turbulent rivers and streams all constantly fed by heavy persistent tropical rain, which also nurtures thick, sometimes impenetrable rain-forests. To this unprepossessing mélange, add some 100 active volcanoes. As could be expected in such a rugged country, air transport is essential. So there are 452 airfields, varying from steeply sloping mountain airstrips to seven international airfields.

Within this harsh environment live only some four million people, mostly in widely scattered village communities, each, at least in the past, seeking by means of hilltop locations fenced with high palisades, protection from inter-tribal raiding.

When to this fragmentation and among such a relatively small population is added a multitude of separate and often mutually unintelligible languages, it can be seen that PNG, socially, is a very divided society. But, with the slow spread of education, the old inter-tribal language of pidgin English is being replaced by widely spoken and understood standard English. Indeed, it seemed possible to discern the emergence of a "togetherness" so that, for example, the Motuan of Port Moresby were beginning to think that the Kukukus of the highlands or the Tolai of New Britain were not, after all, far distant in kinship.

Unfortunately, these fragile and tentative approaches to unity were not sufficient to preclude a secessionist rebellion on Bougainville that started in 1987 and lasted for a decade. Charges of corruption in connection with the hiring of mercenaries to suppress it, led to an investigation of the then prime minister, Sir Julius Chan, and leading members of his cabinet. Those charged stepped down from office pending a decision by the Commission of Inquiry, but were duly cleared. However, after a period in which the acting prime minister refused to stand aside to permit Sir Julius to resume his post, the latter lost his seat in Parliament. Bill Skate, himself still fighting a bribery charge, was elected prime minister by the new Parliament in July of 1997. He remains in office as of this writing.

The earliest known connection of PNG with world history followed soon after Vasco da Gama's epochal 1498 voyage to India, for, as early as 1520, the name Papua began to appear on Portuguese maps. Papua (a Malay word meaning "frizzled") because its dark, fuzzy-haired people so reminded the early Portuguese navigators of the people they had encountered when sailing down the west coast of Africa. Not long after, in 1569, the name New Guinea appeared on Mercator's world map.

From then until the south-eastern portion of the island became a British protectorate in 1884, and the north-eastern portion the German Territory of New Guinea, the people of the eastern half of New Guinea, disturbed only by some scattered religious missions and gold seekers, continued their centuries-old stone age life. Then in 1902, British New Guinea was transferred to the then newly-established Commonwealth of Australia and became the Territory of Papua.

Next, in 1914, on the outbreak of World War I, an Australian naval and military force, in order to preempt its use by German naval forces then operating in the Pacific, invaded and occupied German New Guinea. This occupation of German-claimed territory was changed in 1921 when Australia was given a mandate to administer the area under a League of Nations Covenant.

Slowly then, under Australian auspices, a system of national control and development began. Only in the Trobriand Islands could administration be pursued through traditional tribal chiefs. For the rest of New Guinea, territorial government was exercised through district and sub-district offices mostly by young Australian officers bringing by long, arduous, lonely patrol, pacification, medical aid, and administration to some 11,920 villages. The *kiap* system, as it was called, appointed to each village a *luluai*, through whom control was administered, and in Papua a village constable.

The Japanese invasion of New Guinea in December 1941 and of Papua in April 1942, put an end to separate civil administration of the two territories. Military control took over both territories in a single military government, the New Guinea Australia Administration Unit (ANGUA) which continued until war's end in 1945.

At the conclusion of hostilities, the two territories combined were placed under a United Nations trusteeship, with Australia accepting the obligation to prepare the people of the Trust Territory for self-government or independence. The task was to bring a country of disunity, of a multitude of languages, and without any heritage of common historical experience to nationhood.

The patrol system of bringing government to the people, of suppressing inter-village and inter-tribal raiding, and of penetrating the remaining remote restricted areas was continued. Education was encouraged, a national code of laws drafted, and gradually the PNG people were prepared for self-government, which was accorded to them in 1973.

Finally, a national coalition government accepted the responsibilities of full independence which was passed over by Australia on September 16, 1975. At no time did Australia exercise the mandate or the trusteeship with the wish or expectancy that it would continue as a colonial power.

PNG is a parliamentary democracy. It is under the nominal rule of a governor general elected by Parliament to represent Queen Elizabeth II of England, the head of state. The members of Parliament are elected by universal suffrage from 20 provinces and 89 districts, plus 19 representatives from the National Capital District of Port Moresby. The government is headed by a prime minister.

Within the national boundaries are 34 urban centers, although of these the only sizable cities or towns are Port Moresby (190,000), Lae (72,800), Madang (23,000), Goroka (25,000), and Rabaul (20,000)—the latter figure as recorded prior to the nearby volcanic eruptions of September 1994.

I

Land Tenure

IN A COUNTRY so dominated by village and tribal life, it could not be expected that there would have developed a widespread pattern of clearly-defined and survey-identified land ownerships. Moreover, the exceedingly rugged terrain would have greatly complicated ownership or boundary identification, while the existing social circumstances would probably have made any such action unwise and probably unworkable. Not surprisingly, therefore, clan and kinship community groups occupy, without precisely defined title, some 97 percent of the land area of PNG.

Nevertheless, rights to use certain roughly defined areas for village gardens or houses are held by individuals, and can be transferred to descendants, but rarely to persons living outside the village area. Knowledge of these rights is passed on by word of mouth from one generation to another. Inevitably, many disputes over ownerships and ownership boundaries arise, especially in areas where populations are growing rapidly. Some of these disputes are settled by village elders, unless there are Land Councils when attempts are made to work out peaceful solutions.[1]

Some 160,000 hectares of PNG land, however, are owned in freehold title by private individuals or by religious missions, who obtained their legal title ownerships early in the colonial era.

II

Property Rating

PNG'S ADOPTION OF site-value property taxation (or rating as it is called there) had its origin in Australia's pre-independence administration, and the proximity of Australia to PNG. The influence of Australian law and practices was especially pronounced on visiting PNG scholars and researchers (one of whom, for example, is now senior lecturer in law at the University of Canberra).

Property taxation is levied on land owned in freehold title, and is based on the unimproved value of each parcel of taxable land.

Values are determined by a government-appointed valuer general. His values can be appealed against.

The "unimproved value" is defined as "the capital sum that the fee simple of the land might be expected to realize if offered for sale on such reasonable terms and conditions as a bona fide seller would require assuming that the improvements on the land (if any), other than ground improvements, did not exist at the date to which the valuation relates, less the Ground Improvements Allowance (if any) applicable to that land."

Ground improvements relate to those improvements made to land for its better use and/or development such as the felling and clearing away of trees or native shrubs; the removal or leveling of stone which exists naturally on land; and the leveling or filling of land. The definition of the Ground Improvement Allowance puts a 15 year time limit within which the allowance can be enjoyed after the works have been completed, or earlier if the land is sold or passes out of the ownership of the owner or owners who originally carried out the improvement works. It can be inferred that this time limit has been applied by the PNG legislators in the belief that this is a sufficiently long period during which those who carried out the works might obtain adequate recompense for their expenditure.

However, the definition further adds that "the sum so to be deducted shall not exceed the estimated increase which the expenditure has made to the value of the land as at the date of valuation." For example, if the expenditure is considered to have been either totally or partially of an unwise or improvident nature and therefore not responsible for a like increase in the value of the land then the allowance is to be adjusted accordingly.

The unimproved value as defined follows closely those applicable in most of the Australian states and in New Zealand. In consequence, there is a considerable volume of Australian and New Zealand case law further refining the definition of unimproved value.

One of the basic aims of the property taxation system as applicable in PNG is to raise revenue as based solely on the value of land, and not intermingled with the value of any improvements on the land. Nevertheless, where many small houses tend to spring up within or adjacent to serviced urban land ("squatter" colonies as they are often called, usually built on customary tribal or government land in respect of which there is little prospect of gaining permanent ownership) then legislation provides that property taxation may be levied on the value of such buildings. However, four conditions restrict this power.

The first of these requires that the building has been registered, and has thus some official standing. The second is that it must be occupied by a person other than of the state, or an authority or instrumentality thereof.

A third, quite important, provision is that the tax as based on the value of the building cannot be more than if based on the unimproved value of the land on which the building stands. A final provision is that the tax can only be applied if the building is within an urban area, and thus has some access to urban-type services such as water and electricity. Hence, this excludes from any application of the tax the thousands of village houses, (many erected at or near mountain tops) all over PNG, because they are not within an urban area.

The revenue derived from property taxation is regarded as an important contribution to local government revenues.

The present writer attempted to ascertain the amount of local revenue in PNG raised by rates on land values, and the approximate percentage this represents of local revenue from all sources. Repeated efforts on his part and on that of the editor to obtain this and other information from the secretary of the Department of Provincial and Governmental Affairs yielded no response. This failure to respond to inquiries is no doubt related to the political turmoil and governmental breakdown to which allusion was made earlier in this chapter.

III

Mineral Taxation

PRIOR TO SELF-GOVERNMENT, the mining industry in PNG was largely in the hands of a single company, Bougainville Copper Limited (BCL), which extracted substantial quantities of copper and gold, and played an important part in the economy. Its operations were located on the island of Bougainville, recently the scene of armed secessionist activity. It functioned under an agreement negotiated by the Australian colonial administration, which the new government considered unduly generous to the company.

The agreement was accordingly renegotiated, with input from two economists, Ross Garnaut and Anthony Clunies Ross, who recommended use of a resource rent tax (RRT) to be collected at progressively higher rates after a certain threshold rate of return on funds invested had been realized. Public appropriation of mineral rents will not deter mine investment, since by definition rents refer to income in excess of that required to attract such investment. The government would thus receive a large portion of the profits from highly successful mining projects, yet investment in apparently marginal projects would not be deterred since little or no tax would be levied until adequate compensation for outlay had been attained.

However, to design and administer a tax system that will capture a large proportion of resource rents alone is difficult and complex as compared to other options which have, moreover, the advantage of being able to generate public revenue from projects that are only marginally successful.

The PNG government accepted the underlying principle of the recommendation by Garnaut and Clunies Ross, but negotiated an agreement with BCL that, instead of providing for a "pure" RRT system, combined several taxes: the existing 1.25 percent ad valorem royalty; a flat profits tax at the standard company tax rate (then 33.3 percent); a dividend withholding tax of 15 percent on dividends paid to foreign shareholders; and an additional profits tax (APT). All told, this combination would yield a total tax rate of 70 percent on profits above a return to BCL of 15 percent on funds invested. (BCL suspended operations in 1987 when the rebel forces on Bougainville became too threatening. Although the agreement described above is technically still valid, resolution of the Bougainville situation will doubtless require a change in the agreement to satisfy rebel demands for a bigger share of revenue from the mines if and when BCL resumes extraction on the island.)

A generally applicable model based on this arrangement but with certain technical refinements was subsequently developed by the government for the taxation of large mining projects. It has been applied to various mines on the mainland island, including the large Ok Tedi mine run by Australia's company, BHP Ltd. The refinements (chief of which are accelerated depreciation allowances for marginal mines, and wider application of the APT) facilitate rapid recovery of initial investment and reduce the risk of tax-driven loss to the company, yet guarantee that profitable operations quickly yield a high tax return.

A tax regime similar in concept to that for mining, but using different rates of tax and threshold rates of return, has been developed for petroleum. In addition, operational experience, as well as political conflicts involving landowners affected by Bougainville and Ok Tedi and the large Porgera gold mine, have resulted in further adjustments to the tax regime for mining and to substantial changes in the distribution of tax revenues between the national government, provincial governments and local landowners. While the remaining paragraphs describe major features of the regimes for mining and petroleum taxation at the end of 1999, the present author has no reason to believe that they have ceased to be current as of this writing (March, 2000).

For both mining and petroleum, a royalty of 2 percent of the value of net smelter value or well head value applies. Royalties are distributed to provincial governments, local level governments, and project landowners. The apportionment of royalties is determined by a development agreement between these parties, or, in the absence of an agreement, on a basis decided by the national minister for mines or the minister for petroleum.

In addition, the national government provides "special support grants" to provincial governments to assist with provision of infrastructure in areas where major mining projects occur. These grants are based, not on a fixed percentage of mineral revenue, but on annual budget allocations, which are negotiated between the national government and relevant provincial governments. There are no special support grants for petroleum or gas projects. Instead, project developers pay a development levy of 2 percent of the well head value of all petroleum produced from a license area directly to the affected provincial government or governments.

Companies operating major mining projects pay a corporate tax rate of 35 percent, while petroleum companies pay 50 percent. Additional profits tax is applied to mining companies at a rate of 35 percent when "net cash receipts" are positive, in other words when the sum of assessable income less allowable deductions (which exclude interest and depreciation charges) exceeds capital expenditure and income tax paid. When "net cash receipts" are negative they are carried forward at an annual accumulation rate of 20 percent or US prime rate plus 12 percent. The cumulative amount is also adjusted for changes in the exchange rate between the US dollar and the PNG currency.

Petroleum companies pay APT at a rate of 50 percent, but they enjoy a higher accumulation rate (27 percent) than do mining companies. The higher corporate tax rates and APT rates for petroleum companies reflect a belief that investment in petroleum offers the prospect of higher rates of return than does investment in mining, but petroleum investment is also seen as involving a greater degree of risk, reflected in the higher accumulation rate.

An unusual aspect of PNG's tax system is the concept of Prescribed Infrastructure Development. Mining and petroleum companies can devote a portion of the money they would have paid in company tax (currently 2 percent of their assessable income for tax purposes) to infrastructure projects (such as schools, hospitals or roads) designed to benefit residents of the areas in which the companies benefit. The selection of infrastructure projects involves representatives from village groups, local level governments, provincial governments, the national government, and the mining or petroleum companies. From the companies' point of view, the advantage of this provision is that it allows local people to derive additional benefits from their operations. From the PNG government's point of view, a significant benefit is that mining or petroleum companies can use the expertise they have available to assist in carrying out the infrastructure projects. This reduces the overall cost of projects to the government, and increases the likelihood that tax revenues devoted to infrastructure provision will be utilized efficiently.

Note

1. For a detailed account of customary land tenure in PNG, see David Lea, *Melanesian Land Tenure in Contemporary and Philosophical Context* (Lanham, MD: University Press of America, 1977), especially chapters 1–4, and pp. 112–118. The land-related background of the Bougainville revolution is treated on pp. 25–45 (chapter 2). An interesting discussion on pp. 49–71 and 176, suggests certain parallels between the problems arising from Fijian land tenure and those exhibited in Abu Dhabi as recounted in chapter 18 of the present work. Lea is a lecturer in politics and administration at the University of Papua New Guinea. His book (probably based on a doctoral dissertation) contains elaborate discussions of property rights doctrine as set forth by such thinkers as Locke, Kant, Hegel, etc., as well as by contemporary theorists.

PART SIX

THE ANTIPODES

Chapter 25

Australia

BY GEOFFREY A. FORSTER*

THE COMMONWEALTH OF Australia is a federation which was established on January 1, 1901. It consists of six states, all previously separate British colonies—New South Wales, Queensland, Victoria, South Australia, Western Australia, Tasmania—and the sparsely populated Northern Territory which now has a territorial government elected by its own citizens. The total area of the Commonwealth is 2,974,581 square miles. At the time of federation, the designation of "colonies" was changed to "states" for all but the Northern Territory, which retained its original designation.

The Commonwealth also includes the 940 square miles of the Capital Territory in which the national capital, Canberra, is located, and which also has a locally-elected government.

There are three levels of government in Australia, and three levels of financing: federal, state, and local (municipal, shire, borough, etc.). In Australia, federal land tax was abolished early in 1952; reasons alleged for this vary. All states have a state land tax, but with variations in implementation. They all have varying exemptions and gradations. Finally, at the local government level, municipal property rates may be based on site-value only, or else or equally on the value of the site and its improvements (capital improved value or net annual value), or occasionally on a "shandy" system—a mixture of two. In recent years, in most states,

*Geoffrey A. Forster holds bachelor's degrees in both arts and sciences from the University of Melbourne, and an L.Th. from the Melbourne College of Divinity. Much of his professional career was spent as managing editor of *The Australian Journal of Agricultural Research* and *The Australian Journal of Soil Research*. He was co-editor of *Progress* (Melbourne) from 1968 to 1994, has been a member of the management committee of the Land Values Research Group (Melbourne), and is secretary of Tax Reform Australia.

there has been a tendency to weaken site-value rating, e.g., by supplementing or replacing it with fixed charges for specific purposes.

The main functions of local government in Australia are to provide and maintain roads, street lighting, rubbish collection and disposal, maternal and child health care centers, libraries, and recreational facilities. It may also subsidize certain educational and counseling services, although education is not regarded as primarily a local responsibility. Nor is public security. Some local functions are supported, not through property taxation, but through user charges.

I

Historical Development of Land-Value Taxation

SOME AUSTRALIAN MUNICIPALITIES were rating on unimproved land values as early as the 1850s. But as a result of the impact of Henry George's writings, single-tax leagues, as they were often called, began proliferating about 1890. The concept was spread by such able and energetic advocates as Max Hirsch, who abandoned a successful career in commerce in order to do so. George's three-month speaking tour in Australia in 1895 accelerated this trend. Its growth was halted by the outbreak of World War I, and from then on, exacerbated no doubt by the welfare state, a decline in the number and membership of the leagues set in.

Almost from the beginning, some land value capture for public benefit in Australia has been obtained through the leasing out of Crown lands (i.e., public lands once owned by the British Government and now by the Commonwealth).

A graduated federal land tax was introduced in 1910, with the stated intention of breaking up the large estates. The first £5,000 of unimproved value was exempt, and the rates were low except for very large estates, the owners of which frequently escaped the tax by nominally subdividing them among family members.. As mentioned above, it was abolished in 1952.

State land taxes were introduced into the six states in the following order: South Australia, 1884; New South Wales, 1895;

Tasmania, 1907; Western Australia, 1907; Victoria, 1910; and Queensland, 1915. They vary considerably, apply only to certain properties, and suffer from serious administrative defects.

By far the most important are the local land taxes or "site value rates." All six states permit their adoption by local option; Tasmania is the only one in which no jurisdiction has availed itself of this choice, although strong efforts have been made there to promote it. Its use began in New South Wales and Queensland in 1890, and is universal in both states; in Western Australia it began in 1902, and is predominant there. In South Australia and Victoria net annual value rating is predominant, but site value rating has existed in the former since 1893, and in the latter since 1919.

Canberra, the national capital city, which now covers most of the Australian Capital Territory (transferred to the Commonwealth by New South Wales), was established in the late 1920s on a leasehold system, involving a rental payment to the federal government. After the site was chosen for the capital territory in 1909, an international competition to plan the city was won by a Georgist, Walter Burley Griffin of Chicago, for whom Canberra's central lake is named. The leasehold system applied to the entire ACT, not merely to the city. Although 99-year leasehold remains nominally in effect, it became for all practical purposes a "dead letter" when payment of residential leasehold rents was abolished by then-Prime Minister John Gorton on January 1, 1971, a move intended, according to his opponents, to rally public support for his reelection. "It was estimated that the government transferred 100 million Australian dollars in equity to lessees at that time, resulting in the loss of an important source of revenue."[1] However, site-value rating, which was introduced in 1927, continues throughout the territory. The history of Canberra's land tenure system is presented in an excellent book by Frank Brennan, *Canberra in Crisis*.[2]

II

Earlier Studies

SEVERAL ATTEMPTS HAVE been made to estimate the yield of site-value revenue in Australia since the first edition of this book in

1955. In addition, the main study referred to in that survey has to some extent been updated. The following is extracted from the 1960 publication, *Public Charges Upon Land-Values*,[3] by the Land-Values Research Group (LVRG), Melbourne, under the direction of A. R. Hutchinson. A comparative study of the six Australian states, this little work, restrained and sober almost to the point of dryness, constitutes perhaps the most compelling empirical brief ever presented for the practical social benefits to be derived from the public appropriation of land rent.

The states were grouped and will be referred to as Group One and Group Two. In the first, are Queensland and New South Wales, where unimproved value rating is universal on the local level, and Western Australia, where it is predominant. The second group takes in South Australia and Victoria, where both systems are operating, and Tasmania, where annual value rating only is used. From the following comparisons of key indicators of prosperity, it will be seen that the development shown by the land-value rating group was greater than that of the other states.

Table 1 demonstrates this with respect to agricultural development. While other factors (e.g., climate, crop seed varieties, fertilizer application, population changes, etc.) undoubtedly had an influence in various ways, the consideration that the same trend occurred in two separate periods seven years apart creates a presumption that the rating systems constituted an extremely significant if not decisive determinant, and is, moreover, consistent with numerous indicators, several of which are mentioned subsequently in this chapter, while others are omitted for reasons of space.

The most significant single indicator of progress is to be found in the increase in the number of dwellings that are built in any country. This is at once an indicator of the extent of real settlement and of the general level of prosperity, for the building industry is a basic one, and activity in it is reflected in many dependent industries.

Table 1

COMPARATIVE AGRICULTURAL DEVELOPMENT				
STATE		Acreage Under All Crops		
A. Depression Period Land-Value Rating States (U.C.V.)	Season 1929–30 acres	Season 1938–39 acres	Change acres	acres
Queensland	1,046	1,734	+688	(+68%)
New South Wales	5,501	7,049	+1,548	(+22%)
West Australia	4,566	4,719	+153	(+3%)
Group Figures	11,113	13,502	+2,389	(+21%)
Improved Value Rating States (N.A.V.)				
South Australia	4,967	4,724	-243	(-5%)
Victoria	5,579	5,019	-560	(-10%)
Tasmania	265	243	-22	(-8%)
Group Figures	10,811	9,986	-826	(-8%)
B. Post-War Years Land-Value Rating States (U.C.V.)	Season 1946–47 acres	Season 1958–59 acres	Change acres	acres
Queensland	1,617	2,841	+1,224	(+76%)
New South Wales	6,512	6,825	+313	(+5%)
West Australia	3,590	6,135	+2,545	(+71%)
Group Figures	11,719	15,801	+4,082	(+35%)
Improved Value Rating States (N.A.V.)				
Queensland	3,885	4,147	+262	(+7%)
New South Wales	5,103	4,792	-311	(-6%)
West Australia	361	339	-22	(-6%)
Group Figures	9,349	9,278	-61	(-1%)

In making interstate comparisons, some modifying factors must be considered. It is not sufficient merely to compare dwelling increase with population increase to establish a stimulating effect owing to taxes on land values. Account must be taken of the age composition of the population, for clearly, where the increase is mainly of infants by procreation, fewer new houses are required than where the increase is of adults. These difficulties of comparison are overcome if we compare dwellings built with the marriages taking place in any period. In the following table, this comparison was made for all states for the period 1921 to 1958:

Table 2

COMPARISON OF DWELLINGS BUILT WITH NUMBER OF MARRIAGES				
STATE	Dwelling Increase 1921–58	No. of Marriages 1921–58	Increase in Dwellings per Marriages*	
Land-Value Rating States (U.C.V.)				
Queensland	224,500	340,800	66.0	[59.0]
New South Wales	607,200	946,600	64.5	[59.8]
West Australia	121,500	175,400	69.0	[61.0]
Group Figures	953,200	1,462,800	65.4	[60.0]
Improved Value Rating States (N.A.V.)				
Queensland	141,400	227,000	62.0	[50.1]
New South Wales	431,900	706,900	61.1	[55.5]
West Australia	45,800	84,300	56.1	[52.0]
Group Figures	619,100	1,017,200	61.0	[54.5]
*Bracketed figures exclude Government-built homes.				

These figures show that the land-value rating group had a dwelling-construction activity greater than that for the annual value rating group for the same period. Not only that, but the activity in each of the states in Group One is above that of any state in Group Two.

Further still, some of the districts in South Australia and Victoria rate upon the land-value basis, while in Tasmania, none at all do this. It is significant, therefore, that Tasmania is at the bottom of the list.

The direct connection between the rating systems and dwelling construction may be pursued still further within the two states that have some districts rating land values. It is then seen that these are the districts which contributed most to their states' better showing than Tasmania.

In Victoria, although at the 1921 census only 16 percent of the state's population was in the 14 districts rating land values, these districts accounted for 46 percent of the total increase in dwellings for the state between the two census years. Moreover, in Melbourne (Victoria), over the 20-year period from 1921 to 1940, the municipalities rating land values built 2.12 times as many houses per acre available for building as did their counterparts rating on the annual value system. Similarly, evidence submitted to the Commonwealth Housing Commission in South Australia showed that dwelling construction in the districts rating only land values was markedly superior to that in the districts rating both land and improvements under the annual-value system.

The Melbourne Metropolitan Statistical District is of particular significance because it is made up of a large number of local government authorities, almost equally divided between those using site-value rating and those using annual-value rating. A study of this district by Kenneth M. Lusht, chairman of the department of insurance and real estate at Pennsylvania State University, using data reflective of the 56 local government authorities through 1989, concluded: "There is evidence of a long-run association between the use of the site value tax and the intensity of development, and indicates that the use of the site value tax stimulates faster development."[4]

The ratio of the value of improvements to unimproved land value in 1939–40 was 151 percent in the land-value rating states to only 79 percent in the others, and it was highest, 198 percent, in Queensland, where the land-value tax is highest. Further, the average total value of improvements per land taxpayer was fully twice as great in the Group One states as in the others. This would seem to indicate that the exemption of improvements has tended to encourage the construction of not only more, but better, improvements, and that these benefits are directly related to the weight of taxation placed upon land values.

The average annual wage paid to adult male workers in factories, according to the *Commonwealth Year Book* for 1938, was £237 for Group One, and the real wage index, having regard to changes in the cost of living, drawn from the same source, was 1,274. For Group Two, the group average wage was £219 and index figure 1,160 (the year 1911 as base 1,000).

Similar conclusions were derived from comparing the two groups of states in terms of such other factors as development of manufacturing industries, volume of retail sales, home ownership as opposed to tenancy, assets of financial institutions and cooperative societies, and population gain or loss resulting from migration. Indeed, what makes this study so impressive is the wide range of data upon which its findings rest.

III

Mid-Seventies Study

IN THE MID-SEVENTIES, another important study was made by Hutchinson; this time, his figures were for 1976–77.[5] Due to a change in government methods of gathering and compiling statistics, data that might have enabled him to reproduce his earlier findings were no longer available for many of the factors in his index. Hence the scope of this later study was restricted to determining: (1) how much site rental was being collected for public purposes in the Australian states and territories; (2) the total potential for site rental as public revenue in Australia; and (3) how far the latter would go in lieu of taxes on labor and capital in meeting the legitimate costs of government at all levels.

Table 3

	SUMMARIZED 1976-77 TOTALS OF PUBLIC REVENUE COLLECTIONS OF SITE RENT by Land-Value Taxation, Land-Value Rating, or as Land Rentals from Publicly Owned Leasehold Properties ($ Million)			
State or Territory	Land Value Taxes	Land Value Rates	Land Lease Rents	Totals
New South Wales	111.638	667.825	20.157	799.620
Victoria	59.804	293.065	16.904	369.773
Queensland	12.764	181.726	10.594	205.084
South Australia	18.348	71.748	3.200	93.296
Western Australia	13.930	75.249	5.700	94.879
Tasmania	3.373	13.874	0.500	17.747
Aust. Capital Territory	-	12.098	3.500	15.598
Northern Territory	-	3.405	1.000	4.405
Totals	219.857	1,318.990	61.555	1,600.402

Hutchinson also made a comparison of site revenue collections with total taxation of the $24,824 millions ($24 billion, 824 million) in revenue for all Australian public authorities; $2,676 millions were estimated to be actually site rental in its nature, as follows:

(1) $220 millions as land-value taxes levied by state governments; (2) $1,319 millions as land-value rates paid to local government councils or to water and sewerage corporations within the states; and (3) $1,137 millions as crude oil levy and other mineral levies collected by the federal government from local producers and recorded under excise revenue, but which really equate with royalties on state-owned minerals.

Table 4

APPARENT SITE RENT COLLECTED COMPARED TO TOTAL (Dollar amounts in millions)				
State or Territory (1)	Portion publicly collected (2)	Portion not yet publicly collected (3)	Total site rent (4)	Publicly collected as % of total (5)
Land-Value Rating States				
New South Wales	799.620	1697.050	2,496.670	32.02
Queensland	205.084	365.725	570.809	35.93
Western Australia	94.879	183.800	278.679	34.05
Improvement Rating States				
Victoria	369.773	1,519.945	1,889.718	19.57
South Australia	93.296	340.525	433.821	21.51
Tasmania	17.747	61.880	79.627	22.29
The Territories				
Aus. Capital Territory	15.598	46.275	61.873	25.21
Northern Territory	4.405	12.000	16.405	26.85
TOTALS	1,600.402	4,227.200	5,827.602	27.46

Hutchinson also estimated the apparent site rent collected as a proportion of the total; he used the term "apparent" partly because official figures tend to lag behind actual market values. Table 4 highlights the fact that in three of the states there is a predominance of land-value rating for municipal purposes—indeed in New South Wales and Queensland this is nominally universal, while in the other three states net annual value rating prevails, though there are significant site-value rating areas in Victoria and South Australia.

IV

A Cautionary Note

ON THIS BASIS, site-value revenue amounted to 10.85 percent of total revenue. However, in an article in *Progress*, October, 1995, Alderman David Brooks[6] gave some disturbing information about his own council, viz. Hervey Bay, Queensland. This showed that of its total income of $49,807,736, only $10,604,572 came from site-values—other sources being specific (sewage, water, garbage) fees and charges, and grants and subsidies from state and federal governments. Here is indicated a disturbing trend away from site-value revenue, which is also observable in other states, though very difficult to quantify. In general, it is believed that only about 50 percent of municipal revenue is derived from property rates, although (as shown in Table 3) land-value capture is greatest at this level.

V

The Herps Estimate

AT THE INTERNATIONAL Georgist Conference held in Melbourne, September/October 1993, Douglas Herps, a senior valuer and consultant to the Commonwealth Grants Commission during 1978–91 advising on land valuation law and land tax capacity of various Australian states, stated that "the magnitude of Australia's economic rent is such that it could provide at least 50 percent of all the country's present inflated taxation." It is important to recognize that land values at present include not only genuine site rent but also speculative rent which would dissipate under a Georgist economy. Hence, the site rent available for community purposes would initially tend to be less than Herps' estimate. However, as a Georgist economy got under way, this would change.

VI

The Victorian Review

IN 1991, THE Victorian Government instituted a review of state land tax.[7] Its report, issued in August of that year gave the following data relating to 1989–90:

Table 5

STATE LAND TAX		
State	Land Tax ($M)	Land Tax Per Capita ($)
New South Wales	627	108.15
Victoria	307	70.57
Queensland	137	47.70
South Australia	72	50.28
Western Australia	91	56.33
Tasmania	21	46.37
Total	1,255	

Not only do the states vary considerably in the quantity of land tax collected, but also in the manner of implementation in terms of exemptions, valuation cycles, and related matters.

One other item of interest is the following table showing the increase in land tax revenue in the later eighties in the two most populous states:

Table 6

VICTORIA AND NSW—LAND TAX PER CAPITA 1984–85 TO 1989–90				
Year	Land Tax Revenue ($M) Vic.	NSW	Land Tax Per Capita ($) Vic.	NSW
1984–85	153.3	225.6	37.41	41.51
1985–86	183.3	295.9	44.20	53.82
1986–87	195.3	345.6	46.68	62.03
1987–88	209.5	412.8	49.46	72.94
1988–89	230.2	497.0	53.60	86.53
1989–90	307.0	627.0	70.57	108.15
Even allowing for inflation (approx. 20 percent for the period involved), there are significant increases here.				

VII

Philip Day's Estimate

IN A THOUGHTFUL and well-written book published in 1995, Philip Day, an academic town planner, estimated the capital value of all land in Australia to be about $450 billion. "Depending on the capitalization rate used, this suggests that the present uncollected annual rental revenue in Australia could be something approaching $40 billion; this is to be compared with the total revenue raised in Australia by all levels of government in 1993–94 being of the order of $148 billion."[8]

VIII

Total Tax Revenue

THE LATEST AUSTRALIAN Bureau of Statistics publication (1994–95) for taxation revenue shows a total government revenue (all levels) of $138.526 billion. For state land taxes for 1994–95, the total is $1.373 billion. However, for 1989–90, the figure quoted is $1.295 billion. (Cf. $1.255 billion in the Victorian survey cited on p. 279. The present writer is not able to explain this discrepancy.)

The figure for municipal rates throughout Australia for 1994–95 is shown as $4.966 billion. Unfortunately, the differentiation between site-value revenue and revenue from improvements is now no longer readily available—if at all. In view of all the uncertainties involved, it seems scarcely worth the effort to try to ascertain whether from many hours of searching that differentiation could be realized.

There are also other categories of local government levies on property, but these are small by comparison with rates, and would be largely on the basis of improvements. As already indicated, even where municipal rates are nominally on the unimproved or site-value basis, there is an increasing tendency to rely on fixed charges for specific purposes, or in some cases, a minimum rate for all properties, as well as the levy directly related to the site-value.

It is sometimes asserted that taxes on income include some site revenue. This is undoubtedly true, but the percentage would be small, and very uncertain to estimate. What percentage of the municipal rate revenue of $4.966 billion can be regarded as site-value? In Hutchinson's 1976–77 study, the figure was 77.3 percent (table not included here). If we assume a figure of 75 percent, this would in round figures, be $3.700 billion. The fact that this is almost certainly an overestimate might be compensated to some extent by the indirect collection of site revenue from income taxes, etc.

If we add the state land tax figure of $1.373 billion to the municipal figure of $3.700 billion, we obtain $5.073 billion or 3.7 percent of total government revenue at all levels. However, as calculated by Hutchinson (Table 4) there are also the crude oil levy and other mineral levies which amounted to 42 percent of his estimate of site-revenue.

The present writer has been unable to locate more up-to-date comparable figures. (In mid-November, 2000, the Australian dollar exchanged for just under US$ 0.52. Ed.)

When this component is taken from Hutchinson's percentage (Table 4), we are left with 6.3 percent. This should mean a drop from 6.3 percent to 3.7 percent over the last two decades, and while open to dispute as to precise figures, would undoubtedly reflect, unfortunately, a clear quantitative trend. Conversely, if an equivalent amount of resource rent revenue were being collected now, the 3.7 percent figure would be raised to 6.4 percent, in comparison with the previous 10.8 percent.

IX

Two Public Inquiries

TWO PUBLIC INQUIRIES merit comment. In New South Wales in 1967, a very comprehensive report was presented by a three-member Royal Commission on Rating, Valuation, and Local Government Finance under the Hon. Mr. Justice R. Else-Mitchell.[9] Of the seven questions in the terms of reference, the main findings on the ones especially concerned with the rating system were: "A rate on land is the most appropriate method of financing the services which councils are authorized to provide under the Local Government Act . . . The claim that 'rates have reached saturation point' is not established . . . On the question whether the rate should be on the unimproved, improved, or assessed annual value, the findings were that there should be complete local option within the municipal council areas on choice of system. This choice should be available for councils which now rate on the unimproved capital value basis, and the three water and sewerage corporations, now restricted to rating the improved value, should also be given powers to use the unimproved value if desired."

However, it was made clear in the report that this preference for local option, as opposed to a mandatory system, was simply because the commission favored the general principle of free choice and not because of any evidence of desire on the part of local government or other bodies to depart from the site-value basis. The vast majority of organizations making submissions to this Commission supported site-value rating.

In 1989, the Brisbane City Council held an inquiry into valuation and rating; an exhaustive two-volume report appeared in September 1989.[10] The Committee evaluated, against its chosen criteria, poll taxes, taxes on income and on sales, taxes on land value and on improved property value, and license fees (in addition to the scope for local government trading enterprises and joint ventures). It arrived at the unanimous conclusion that rating on the unimproved value of land was the most efficient and equitable general revenue base for Brisbane, and significantly expressed the view that "in principle, the unimproved value of land is a logical and appropriate basis for revenue raising *irrespective of the level of government.*" (Emphasis added.)

In reaching this conclusion, the committee noted, amongst other advantages, that a tax on land value was virtually impossible to evade; that it represented a contribution by every member of the community either directly as a property owner or indirectly by way of rent or board; that its administration was simple and inexpensive; and that its compliance costs for citizens were minimal. It also noted that a land-value tax was an effective mechanism for achieving a city's town planning objective since it encouraged the development of land for its best and most intensive permissible use.

A useful qualitative table, Table 7, prepared by the late Noel Wigmore, a professional valuer, is worth pondering at this stage:

Table 7

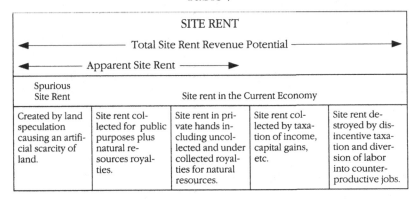

SITE RENT				
◄——————— Total Site Rent Revenue Potential ———————►				
◄————— Apparent Site Rent —————►				
Spurious Site Rent	Site rent in the Current Economy			
Created by land speculation causing an artificial scarcity of land.	Site rent collected for public purposes plus natural resources royalties.	Site rent in private hands including uncollected and under collected royalties for natural resources.	Site rent collected by taxation of income, capital gains, etc.	Site rent destroyed by disincentive taxation and diversion of labor into counterproductive jobs.

X

Recent Study

IT IS ALSO worth making reference to a recent Land-Values Research Group study.[11] This shows that the extent of investment in land in Australia has in fact been documented and therefore can be assessed. Statistics compiled show that rising from $42.308 billion in 1986, the total value of real estate sales in Australia (buildings and land) doubled to $87.709 billion at the peak of the real estate boom in 1989. Of this total value of sales, the estimated land value component was $61.4 billion, or approximately 70 percent. In fact, the land value component was equivalent to more than 22 percent of national income in 1989.

That this huge investment in property and land was not sustainable is indicated by the writing down of property values when the boom collapsed, resulting in higher unemployment and economic dislocation generally. By June 1992, the LVRG's data show that some $306 billion (equivalent to one year's national income) had been written off the value of Australian property—mainly in written down land or site-value.

XI

General Remarks

IN CONCLUSION, QUANTIFICATION is beset with so many uncertainties that most figures should be treated with caution. Hence, it has been felt that further exertion in collecting more statistics is not warranted.

What is clear, however, is that revenue from site rents as a percentage of total revenue has been falling. What is also clear is that site revenue stimulates building activity (and hence employment activities), as numerous studies have shown.[12] A typical example is that of Seymour Shire in rural Victoria, which changed from net annual-value rating to site-value rating in 1982. Comparing the three years after the change with the three previous years, the number of dwelling permits increased by 225 percent, the value of dwelling permits increased by 264 percent, and the value of all new building permits increased by 285 percent.

It is also clear of course, that most estimates of site revenue fall short of current levels of revenue. But this need not be a cause of alarm. One would be hard put to argue with the contention that, under a Georgist economy, the need for so much revenue would be considerably reduced (e.g., welfare payments). Further, as Hutchinson's earlier study demonstrated, under even a greatly diluted approach to such an economy, the production of goods and services is stimulated, and living standards raised. This results in increasing site rent, both absolutely and relatively.

In any case, the proposal advanced by Ronald Burgess,[13] as well as others, that governments should operate only within a budget limited by site revenue plus perhaps specific charges for certain purposes, (e.g., a drug tax for treating drug addiction) is an option worth considering.

Finally, while in Australia there is a significant measure of site revenue and also a sound basis for its implementation (i.e., competent valuation, etc.), the old adage about the price of liberty being eternal vigilance is as apposite as ever. The retention of past achievements and the achievement of further extensions unfortunately require hard effort, as the forces opposing socio-economic justice are far from inactive. Nevertheless, the numerous studies (mainly in Victoria) in local government areas give empirical vindication of the economic and ethical soundness of the site-value approach.

Notes

1. Yu-Hung Hong, "Myths and Realities of Public Land Leasing: Canberra and Hong Kong," *Land Lines*, Vol. 11, No. 2 (March, 1999), p. 2.

2. Frank Brennan, *Canberra in Crisis* (Canberra: Dalton Publishing Company, 1971).

3. A. R. Hutchinson, *Public Charges Upon Land-Values* (1960; Melbourne: Land-Values Research Group, rpt. 1963).

4. Kenneth M. Lusht, "The Site Value Tax and Development Patterns: Evidence from Melbourne, Australia." Working paper issued by the Lincoln Institute of Land Policy, Cambridge, MA, 1992.

5. A. R. Hutchinson, *Natural Resources Rental Taxation in Australia* (Melbourne: Land-Values Research Group, circa 1978).

6. David Brooks, "Beautiful One Day!" *Progress*, No. 1011, October 1995, pp. 6–7.

7. Report of the *Land Tax Review*, Victoria, 1991, p. 209.

8. Philip Day, Land: *The Elusive Quest for Social Justice, Taxation Reform and Sustainable Planetary Environment* (Brisbane: Australian Academic Press, 1995), p. 120.

9. Royal Commission on Rating, *Valuation and Local Government Finance*, Sydney, NSW 1967.

10. Lord Mayor's Committee of Inquiry into Valuation and Rating, Brisbane, September, 1989.

11. Bryan Kavanagh, *Anatomy of a Depression* (Melbourne: Land-Values Research Group, September, 1993).

12. Lusht's study of the Melbourne Metropolitan Statistical District was mentioned earlier in this chapter. Other examples showing similar clear-cut results include South Melbourne, Vic., see *Progress*, No. 756 (Sept., 1972), p. 5; Perth, W.A., see *Progress*, No. 813 (Nov., 1977), p. 10; and Wonthaggi, Vic., see *Progress*, No. 910 (Oct., 1985), p. 3.

13. Ronald Burgess, *Public Revenue Without Taxation*, (London: Shepheard-Walwyn, 1993), p. 120.

Located in the suburbs of Melbourne, Australia, this poorly improved industrial (wool trading) property is "encouraged" by the capital improvement rating (inputs/site ratio, 1.55).

Also located in the suburbs of Melbourne, Australia, this well developed industrial property would be encouraged by the adoption of site value rating (Inputs/site ratio, 21.2).

Chapter 26

New Zealand

By ROBERT D. KEALL*

NEW ZEALAND IS a "small country at the world's end,"[1] its closest significant neighbor being Australia, more than a thousand miles distant. Its population of over 3.5 million mainly occupies two narrow islands with a combined area somewhat larger than Great Britain, lying diagonally in the South Pacific roughly midway between the Tropic of Capricorn and the Antarctic Circle.

For scenic beauty and variety, the nation has few if any rivals. In the north, lush, semi-tropical vegetation and thermal geysers may be found; in the south, alps, glaciers, fjords, lakes, forests, and rolling heathland; while attractive cities grace both islands. Because they are narrow, the sea is never far away.

Its fertile soil and temperate climate make the land eminently suitable for agricultural and pastoral pursuits, but, although the chief source of export earnings, they employ only about ten percent of the workforce; this may be attributed both to advanced technology (including mechanization) and to the fact that pastoral production, by its very nature, has never been labor-intensive.

Most New Zealanders are descended from settlers from the British Isles who came after 1850, seeking greater opportunity. Between 10 and 12 percent are of Maori extraction. The Maoris are a Polynesian people who arrived a few centuries before the Europeans. Never conquered, in 1840 their chiefs signed the Treaty of Waitangi, acknowledging Queen Victoria as ruler. New Zealand

---

*Robert D. Keall was a finance company executive and investment broker. He has been honorary treasurer since 1956 and honorary secretary since 1959 of the New Zealand Land Value Rating Association, and founded the Resource Rentals for Revenue Association (International) in 1994. He is author of several submissions to the New Zealand Parliament, as well as tracts on such topics as inflation, unemployment, rating systems, and funding for local government.

became a self-governing colony of Britain in 1852, and was granted dominion status within the empire in 1907. It is now an independent Commonwealth nation, recognizing the British monarch, represented by a governor general, as chief of state. It has a unicameral parliamentary government, headed by a prime minister.

Historically, New Zealand was long known for its advanced social legislation. It pioneered female suffrage, and was among the first countries to adopt social security, old age pensions, and universal health care. A measure of land-value taxation was introduced even before the publication of Henry George's *Progress and Poverty* in 1879.

As has been noted, New Zealand's export production provides jobs for only about 10 percent of its workforce, yet full employment has long been an overriding political goal. In seeking to achieve this goal, successive governments up until the mid-1980s subsidized inefficient industries, restricted imports, and maintained a vast corps of public servants. They also progressively increased expenditure on welfare. These policies, together with compulsory union membership and mandatory arbitration of labor-management disputes, helped to insulate the economy from market discipline, and kept wages artificially high. All this was accompanied by a degree of state regulation "unparalleled in most other Western economies."[2] The mix of inefficient subsidized enterprises, non-market-oriented capital investment, union monopoly, cumbersome over-regulation, and a "safety net" so high as to discourage initiative for work and training, helped to produce an ill-prepared, poorly motivated labor force and a low rate of per capita economic output.[3]

For some three decades after World War II, this program, initiated by Labour but continued and expanded by the National (Conservative) Muldoon government, seemed to work: New Zealand enjoyed one of the highest living standards on earth. As long as tax revenue from exports fueled government spending, the illusion of prosperity could be sustained. But eventually, with the development of synthetic fibers to compete with wool, the rise of West Germany and Japan as economic superpowers, the erection of European Common Market barriers against New

Zealand exports followed by Britain's decision to join the Common Market, the oil shocks of 1973 and 1979, etc., the terms of trade turned against New Zealand. For a while, the government was able to stave off the inevitable by overseas borrowing, but only for a while. "From having been one of the three or four richest countries in the world in the early 1950s, New Zealand moved to about 20th in international rankings by the end of the 1970s."[4] Moreover, by 1981, inflation had reached 17 percent.

Land-value taxation, in the form of rating at the local government level, counteracted these tendencies to a minor extent, providing a degree of stimulation especially in the building industry. But although successful as far as it went, it did not collect enough of the economic rent or account for a large enough share of the total budget to constitute anything like a decisive factor in the economy. Furthermore, it is doubtful that even full rating of land values, coupled with the complete lifting of rating on improvements, could have in themselves prevailed against such massive forces for stagnation.

"By the time of Labour's victory in the 1984 election, the economy was seen to be on the brink of collapse, with the old-style interventionist policies of the Muldoon era clearly indicted as failures."[5] The new government faced a crisis situation, driven by a severe depletion of foreign exchange reserves. It was Roger Douglas, the incoming Labour minister of finance, who had mapped out a program of radical reform, and was able to push it through. Douglas, grandson of a member of the first Labour administration, had himself been minister for housing in the third Labour government, and spent many years in Parliament. At first, he had embraced the traditional interventionist position of his family and party, but gradually became convinced that instead of helping the less fortunate it actually made their position worse.[6] Through participation in a discussion group made up partly of academic friends, he became familiar with theoretical economics of the neo-classical and public choice schools, and arrived at the strongly free market views expressed in his 1980 book, *There's got to be a better way*. The sweeping turnaround he engineered set New Zealand on a course of economic expansion, international competitiveness, and negligible inflation which continued under succeeding National Party (solely or in coalition) governments that maintained much the same policy direction until it was repudiated by the electorate in November, 1999.

By this time, Douglas had left Labour to form a party of his own. Disillusionment with his program had set in, engendered by the feeling that the price for its successes was too high. For all is not well in Kiwiland. Wholesale privatization led to the selling off (frequently to foreign investors at bargain basement prices) of much publicly funded infrastructure that, from the standpoint of long-term social benefit, might better have been turned over to private operation rather than ownership. Although inflation was reversed, the national debt greatly increased, as did unemployment. As might be expected, some segments of the population found it difficult to cope with cutbacks (engendered by the unaccustomed regime of austerity) to entitlements and other public services. Finally, at Douglas' initiative, the reforming Labour government of the 1980s had turned against land-value taxation, and managed partly to dismantle it.

This will be discussed in greater detail later. The editor has hazarded the suggestion (admittedly conjectural) that Douglas, who had once been a member of the New Zealand Land-Value Rating Association, came, perhaps unconsciously, to associate land-value taxation with the discredited Labour Party socialism of his earlier years. If so, this was a tragic and unwarranted mistake. Although land-value taxation had traditionally had the support of Labour, its history in New Zealand long antedates that party, and it is conceptually distinct from (and, in its full Georgist form, antithetical to) socialism and the welfare state.

For over 150 years, land values in New Zealand have been collected for public purposes in three main ways: (1) by the sale and lease of Crown land, (2) from a national land tax, and (3) from land-value rates for local government. This record shows that the tax technique, however commendable in many ways, has significant practical limitations as well as being susceptible locally to administrative problems that, if not successfully addressed, are eagerly used against it; and that the principle and technique of institutionalized leases may be extended to include infrastructural monopolies, and thence more widely to land itself.

From 1896 until recently, a government Valuation Department independently recorded the market values of the land, the improvements, and the composite or capital value. In 1999, the role of its successor agency was reduced to monitoring valuations done by private valuers under contract to local authorities, and to competing with private valuers for such contracts.

I

Crown Leases

UNDER THE TREATY of Waitangi, only the government could buy land from the Maoris. Some of this land the government then resold in order to finance immigration, some it disposed of as grants to individuals in return for services, and some it retained on a perpetual leasehold basis. As local government evolved, some allocations were made on a leasehold basis to statutory bodies such as hospital and education boards to finance their statutory functions. Some coastal cities and harbor boards reclaimed land from the sea and leased it.

The operation of these leases was eventually regulated in the Public Bodies Leases Act of 1908; amended in January 1970. The act specifies the ways in which leases may be applied for, tendered for, or auctioned. It covers rent reviews, compensation for improvements on surrender or forfeiture, covenants and conditions, etc. The Act dismisses the fears of those who contend that state leases lead to bureaucratic nightmares. The leases are popular with the lessees who then put more into improvements instead of land price. Because the rentals tend to be low and too infrequently reviewed, the leases are often traded as freehold. Such a shortcoming does not condemn leasehold tenure, but indicates the need for regular adjustment in favor of the community at large. The lease mechanism provides the ideal means of applying environmental constraints as covenants in the agreement covering the interests of both parties.

The traditional government agency administering its leases was the Department of Lands and Survey, later known as the Department of Survey and Land Information (DOSLI). As from 1 July,

1999, it has again changed its name, and is now Land Information New Zealand (LINZ). Its specified purposes are to provide certain essential information, and to effectuate "the transfer of all Crown lands to the private sector, to Maori, Local Authorities or the Conservation Estate."[7]

In addition to LINZ, the government established Land Corporation Ltd. to manage and sell, in an orderly way, certain government-owned leases, property, and livestock. Its subsidiary, Landcorp Investments Ltd., "has continued its successful programs to encourage lease freeholdings, early loan repayments, and the sale of freehold land, . . . and to realize the remaining land and loan assets. . . ."[8]

Settlement of Maori land claims under the Waitangi Tribunal to redress historic wrongs seems directed at entrenching the principle of freehold as the only means of tenure.

Significantly, some tribes having secured their claims now propose to lease them.

II

The National Land Tax

IN 1853, GOVERNOR Sir George Grey, instructed by the Crown "to form Regulations for the sale and disposal of Crown Lands," gazetted regulations in which "he intended to impose a Land Tax, to prevent the acquisition of large areas of unoccupied land."[9] This plan was frustrated.

In 1868–69 on a visit to Britain, Grey discussed with John Stuart Mill the theory of taxing the unearned increment of land.[10] (In 1871, Henry George published his booklet, *Our Land and Land Policy*, anticipating the theme of *Progress and Poverty*, which followed in 1879). Finally, in 1878, as premier now, Grey with his treasurer, John Ballance, actually introduced a land tax.[11] Subsequently converted to a property tax, it was finally confirmed as a land tax in 1891 by Grey's successors[12] both for the revenue and to break up large estates. Correspondence[13] between Henry George and Sir George Grey and Representative P.J. O'Regan from 1880 to 1893 indicates Henry George's influence in this and later measures. By 1922, the land tax yielded about 10 percent of the Budget. As overseas trade developed and inflation became the accepted means of financing wars or social policy, so land values grew and were protected from any land tax by governments elected to do just that at all costs. Thus by 1989, or 98 years after its confirmation, the land tax yielded only 0.4 percent of the budget and was commonly regarded as an antiquated irritant.

Rural land was already exempt (see below).

During 1989, there developed a justifiable concern about the tax because:[14]

a. Commercial land values in Wellington and Auckland mainly, rose sharply but soon after fell just as sharply.

b. The land values had been assessed, in the normal course, at or near the peak, but the tax was collected a year later in the circumstances precipitating the fall in values.

c. In these peculiar circumstances, this caused real hardship. Where the site was underdeveloped (partly because of the insignificant level of the land tax hitherto) there were too few occupiers to absorb the tax, directly or indirectly.

d. Just prior to the collapse of the land values, the Labour government of the day with Roger Douglas as minister of finance, moved to lower the rate of the tax and also the threshold at which it was payable. This would have increased the tax-take to 0.5 percent of the Budget and as a prelude to widening the tax base was generally accepted. The collapse in land values changed all that.

The tax became a political football. So to pre-empt a Conservative National Opposition promise to abolish the tax, the Labour government did just that. The previous National Party government under Muldoon had already abolished the land tax on rural land (so benefiting 1,300 of the richest people in New Zealand and those most able to pay) but had increased it on commercial land. In context it now seems that as a matter of political expediency, the Labour government, having adopted policies of the "New Right," used the opportunity to progress its agenda of shifting all charges off land values onto goods, services, and users.

In 1990–91, the New Labour Party (NLP), as a splinter group from the now rightward-leaning Labour Party, in its Alternative Budget proposed to re-instate and increase the land tax eightfold, levied at up to 4.5 percent of land value, but exempting home owners and small farmers on land values of less than $100,000. It would yield about 5.0 percent of the Budget and was the one ingredient that would make all other objectives attainable.

To generate some political clout, the NLP formed the Alliance with numerous small parties. The results of the general election of November, 1999, reflected widespread disenchantment with fifteen years of New Right policies, and represented a swing to the Center-Left. The new government is a Labour-Alliance coalition. The Alliance, headed by Jim Anderton, now deputy prime minister, is pledged to push land as a source of public revenue.

III

Local Authority Rates

THESE ARE THE property taxes levied to pay for certain local amenities. In New Zealand, police, education, social welfare, and such, are the responsibility of the central government.

A. Terms

Uniform Annual Charge is a flat charge applied to each rating assessment for a specific purpose, i.e., administration, water, sewerage, refuse, etc. There may be several such charges, but in total, they may not exceed 30 percent of the total rates. They tend to increase the rates on the lower valued properties and reduce the rates on the higher, even above or below the 30 percent limit in total.

Land-Value Rating means that local government rates are levied on the government valuation of the market value of the land alone, exempting the improvements.

Capital Value Rating means that the rates are levied on the government valuation of the composite market value of the land and the improvements. Improving the property thus leads to higher rates. The improver pays while the land speculator wins.

Annual Rental Value Rating means the rates are levied on the value a property is rented for or would rent for, or five percent of the fee simple as assessed by the city council.

B. History

In 1849, in Wellington and Marlborough,[15] ordinances allowed rates to be levied on an estimate of the value of the land alone, excluding houses or buildings. This was confirmed in 1854 and 1855 respectively. To what extent these early colonial initiatives were inspired by John Stuart Mill and his contemporaries may never be known precisely. Henry George would have been sixteen at that time.

Auckland city is the last remaining instance of annual rental value rating—a relic from the nineteenth century. The original provinces of New Zealand drew their revenues from the sale and lease of land.[16] When the provinces were replaced by local government in 1876, rates were based on the annual rental value, as in England. Within six years it became apparent that with most properties being sold rather than rented, the capital value was a more realistic base. Accordingly, councils were permitted to switch to or from capital or rental value by resolution.

About this time, the writings of John Stuart Mill, Henry George, and others drew attention to the unearned increase in land values generated by growing communities whether derived from pressure of population or from public works. As a result, Grey's successors not only introduced the land tax in 1891, but also in 1893 a measure allowing local rates to be collected from land values alone if a poll of rate payers required it. The measure was blocked by the Upper House for three years, but in 1896, it became possible for 15 percent of ratepayers to demand that a poll be held to decide whether the rates should be collected from the unimproved value only, i.e., the land value exempting the improvements.[17] Under this dispensation, hundreds of rating polls were held so that by 1982, just 86 years later, 90 percent of all municipalities had by poll adopted land-value rating, which accounted for 80 percent of local government revenue.[18] The main dissident ones were remote, thinly-populated rural areas; a few counties with a large dairy factory carrying a big proportion of the rates; the old boroughs on the Auckland isthmus largely parasitic on Auckland City; Lower Hutt, then a dormitory suburb of Wellington with extensive state rental housing but without its own hard core of land values; and Queenstown—a speculator's paradise.

On the strength of this overwhelming democratic endorsement of land-value rating, the New Zealand Land-Value Rating Association in 1985 repeated its representations to the new 1984 Labour Government that land-value rating be made mandatory and that the land tax be allocated to regional councils for major works and disaster relief. This would have given regional councils a vested interest in the land tax and entrenched it. The Association recommended too that homeowners' land-value rates be made income tax-deductible. It recommended stronger local units of government, and cited land-value rating as the proven catalyst for voluntary amalgamations.[19] Devolution of function from central government to the stronger local units would have involved an intensification of the land value charges at the expense of income taxes—a bloodless revolution!

Notwithstanding the Association's reference to the Labour Party's affirmation of land-value rating in 1948, it seems that during 1987, Labour (now in government) let it be known that it favored capital value rating. Accordingly, in 1988 devious reversions to capital value began. Christchurch moved from partial land value back to capital value by council resolution, when a poll should have been held. Dunedin fragmented its general rate into separate and special rates so they could then be changed by council resolution without recourse to the ratepayers and despite the ratepayers' vociferous protest march. The mayor threatened to take his council to court. The council action was not in fact illegal, but clearly a misuse of its powers. In 1953, the Dunedin ratepayers had voted for land-value rating, with an increase in building permits as a consequence. In Wellington, a year-long Rates Review Committee came down firmly in favor of retaining land value with an adjustment to the differentials between city center and suburbs. Nevertheless, the mayor contrived to have capital value narrowly adopted but needed a government Order in Council to validate his procedures, which an eminent lawyer and the local press regarded as illegal (*Dominion*, April 19, 1988). In the Rating Powers Act of 1988–89, the government withdrew the traditional right to demand a poll, at the same time as it propounded the merits of "local decisions locally made"! The right to demand a poll on a council loan still applies, but not to change the rating system.

In 1990, local government was restructured on the basis of topographical unity and presumed community of interest. In many ways, some such reform was long overdue after the demographic changes of 100 years—erstwhile towns no longer existed. The restructuring reduced 231 local units to 73. It also reduced proportionally the number of municipalities which by poll had adopted land-value rating from 90 percent to 73 percent, with little change since.

It must be pointed out that wherever land-value rating applies, it has been adopted by a poll of ratepayers representing a great amount of work and profound social concern. Wherever capital or annual value rating applies, it has been imposed by government or local councils, contrary to the express wish of the ratepayers in almost every case.

In 1990, the finance minister introduced a measure that would abolish annual rental value rating and would make capital value rating irreversible wherever it was in place or might be adopted subsequently. The move failed and the government changed at the end of that year.

Since then, several moves by councils to revert to capital value have been successfully opposed by ratepayers, even without the right to demand a poll. One or two moves have succeeded but later have been reversed. One or two changes have stuck—uncomfortably.

A valid confusing consideration in the moves to revert to capital value as the only legal alternative arises from the amalgamation of urban with rural areas, which previously raised and spent their own rates. Amalgamation can mean that a highly valued rural property pays for urban facilities. The land value of the rural property is determined far more by overseas prices and exchange rates than by council expenditure. Even the advantage of a nearby town comes from investment by the private sector, not by the council. Urban amenities provided by the council are little used by the remote farmer. This does not deny the validity of a national land tax for its own sake, but does introduce a cost/benefit issue in respect of local rates. The solution is not to revert to capital value rating, but to apply a differential land-value rate that relates public income to expenditure in both town and country so that each enjoys the advantages of land-value rating but not at the expense of the other. Any capital gains for the rural property derived from the rates relief afforded by the differentials are not the concern of the council, however important they may be as objectives of social reform through central government. A precedent for this sort of dispensation occurs in the Urban Farmland Rating Act of 1932 and with Special Ratable Values.[20] So long as the functions of local government are relatively limited, funding for those purposes will be restricted and must be related. Failure to recognize this invites having the principle dismissed as irrelevant by those eager to propose any alternative. In the urban/rural amalgamation, the farmer tends to be under-represented on council because of occupational commitments. Frequent, inconvenient committee meetings to solve urban problems preclude election to office.

The practical consensus now seems to be a basic land-value rate with differentials to distinguish between residential, rural, and commercial zones and to offset the advantages of tax-deductibility enjoyed by some, supplemented by uniform annual charges. Some councils have settled for a mix of land value and capital value as a placatory gesture devoid of any apparent reason. (NB: The differentials should not be extended to allow a hodgepodge of inner-city zoning dispensations.)

Any increase in rates to meet the widening costs of regional government due to devolution from central government should be accompanied by income tax-deductibility for the homeowner also—revenue sharing, they call it.

C. Endorsements

Land-value rating has been endorsed by:

1. The Royal Commission on Local Government Finance, 1958.

2. The Wellington City Committee, 1989.

3. The Internal Affairs Department Coordinating Committee, 1989, which concluded "that there should be a nationwide uniform base for rating," and "that undifferentialled land-value rating is the only rating system fully consistent with efficient resource

allocation. It encourages an optimal use of high-value sites because rates based on land value penalize inefficient usage of the site [since] a landowner is nonetheless required to contribute financially to the community on the basis of that property's potential."

4. The 90 percent of municipalities in New Zealand that by poll adopted it and likewise could have rejected it.

5. All the newer areas of Auckland-North, South, East, and West that have long enjoyed it and clearly intend to retain it.

6. The cities and districts of Palmerston North, Waitakere, New Plymouth, Horowhenua, Kaipara, Tararua, Waimakariri, and Franklin, where proposed reversions to capital value were rejected, most of them heavily, by as much as eight to one.

The above-cited entities are in general agreement that land-value rating has the following merits:

1. It usually means lower rates for the majority of ratepayers. The common ratio of improvements to land value is three to one. Properties developed above that (usually homesteads) get a rate reduction at the expense of those with a lower ratio—usually underdeveloped or vacant sites held for speculation, and poorer commercial properties.

2. It promotes employment because:

a. It reduces the price of land, which means a lower outlay and greater accessibility for home-builders, farmers, developers, and property improvers of any sort.

b. It deters the speculator and under-user of land, with a constant stimulus for improvement and better land use.

c. It ensures the optimum use of land free of further penalty—truly an incentive tax, both stick and carrot. Thus, it tends to bed in and become accepted. It generates steady urban renewal, as in Sydney, Australia, and hitherto in Wellington, rather than deferred boom and bust as in parts of Auckland. Renewal in Wellington has slowed noticeably since reverting to capital value rating.

d. Given these incentives, every person who gains employment in primary industry or property improvement of any sort generates four more job opportunities downstream in secondary and tertiary industries. If another 10 percent of our primary work force, i.e., 25,000, were employed in housing, farming, fishing, and transport, another 100,000 would find work (see the Auckland *Star*, May 1, 1988). In these ways, land-value rating reduces the disparity between the easy rich and the unemployed. Any other form of rating does exactly the opposite—fourfold, as shown above.

3. It is environmentally friendly. By optimizing land use, it maximizes the natural, undisturbed environment.

4. It recovers some of the community-created land value for community purposes. Indeed, land price only arises because the community fails to collect its just dues. Insofar as it does collect them, so land prices diminish. There is thus a unique, important, moral imperative in land-value rating which is entirely consistent with its other virtues.

D. User Pays and/or Cost/Benefit

Court actions against councils have recently been brought on the ground that there was no equitable relationship between the rates paid and the benefits enjoyed. These actions, until recently (see below), had only ever been taken in areas rating on the capital value—quite rightly. There is no connection between the private investment of capital and council services. Reticulation of any sort is better used by high-rise improvement than extended for miles. Community services are more accurately reflected in site values than in capital values. Moreover, land value is itself a cost/benefit measurement. As a land-value rate reduces the price by the amount of the charge capitalized, the site user either pays initially to a vendor or progressively, to a small degree, to the council. The principle of User Pays is eagerly directed at as many council services as possible by those who seek to relieve property of rates, thereby increasing the land values. However, the principle of User Pays applies logically first and foremost to the user of the site (and other natural resources) either as purchase price, or progressively in the form of rates that recover for the rest of the community the community-created land value so that it can be used to pay for public services available to all. Land value rating to fund local government is a significant step along that road.

In fairness, though, the rate-payers' land value rates must then be made set off against income tax as deductions or rebates. In this way, the costs as well as the benefits of community services are equitably spread without an impossible statistical analysis.

Unprecedented litigation, outside the provisions of the rating legislation, has established that (a) a minute cost/benefit analysis with apportionment accordingly is not the intention, and (b) a council has to use the dispensations available to achieve a reasonable cost/benefit relationship.[21]

E. Rating Summary

By 1982, land-value rates comprised about 80 percent of local government revenue and were a significant factor in deciding site usage. Since then, the reversions in Wellington, Christchurch, and Dunedin, the spread of mixed systems, and the greater use of differentials with direct user charges have reduced their proportion of local government revenue to an estimated 40 percent. Draft legislation extends the use of direct charges to further reduce the rates. Since the restructuring in 1989, the collection of statistics has also changed without the detail previously available. The lower level has also lowered the level of economic impact and made the issue less critical for the majority of taxpayers. Macro-economic forces influence changes far more than the rating system. Nevertheless, at the ratepayer level, the preference to have improvements excluded from rates seems firmly entrenched.

Rating System Chart

RATING SYSTEMS IN NEW ZEALAND 1 July, 1999				
	L.V.	**C.V.**	**A.V.**	**Total**
Cities	9 60%	5 33%	1 7%	15
Districts	41 71%	17 29%		58
Total	50 69%	22 30%	1 1%	73

L.V. – Land Value   C.V. – Capital Value   A.V. – Annual Rental Value

Note: Since the restructuring of 1990, local government in New Zealand has been divided into cities and districts respectively. Both are accorded the same funding options by the central government, from which their authority is derived. There are no intermediate jurisdictions between central and local government.

IV

Recent Developments

DEMOLITION OF THE welfare state has seen the sale of many community facilities without distinguishing the operations from the assets. One-time local power boards retailing electricity have been privatized. The new shares issued free to consumers have rapidly devolved into a few hands, with mergers, buy-outs, and overseas minority holdings inflating the price. "This has released over a billion dollars worth of shares into the community" (*NZ Herald*, September 13, 1995). Even state-owned generators, hydro and coal, have now been sold. There is still some publicly-owned radio and television. Some water and sewage facilities have been corporatized, under vigorous protest and dissatisfaction with the charges. A new statutory obligation to provide for depreciation long deferred, inspires councils to try to distance themselves from the problem, to avoid the rate increases and to apply the User Pays principle. In various other ways, central government directly and indirectly requires or encourages local governments to off-load their operations, to "externalize" their costs, and to reduce their rates (predominantly on land values), with no apparent hesitation about turning monopoly rights over to private interests. Roads are talked about only, yet. The right to pollute is recognized. The government has also sold fishing rights (under a quota system), which it must now buy back when it wants to reduce the quota for conservation reasons.

In contrast, the Auckland Regional Services Trust, resisting pressure to privatize, has demonstrated the high profitability of retaining public utilities when run on a corporatized or accountable basis.

In 1996, over half the Reserve Bank's recent breach of its underlying inflation target was due to house-price inflation (up to 36 percent in two years in Auckland) and inflation in the nonproducing property sector (up to 84 percent in other areas) despite balanced, even surplus, budgets. "The Bank's failure has cast into doubt the monetarist framework that has underpinned the government's economic policy" (*Sunday Star-Times*, June 30, 1996).

V

Summary and Conclusions

OVER NEARLY 150 years until the late 1980s, land-value taxation in all its forms had become increasingly accepted, even popular, in New Zealand. It was reckoned then that without it, land prices would have been half as high again. Since 1989, the public appropriation of land (resource) values has significantly diminished, due to:

a. abolition of the land tax.

b. the lower level of land-value rates, even where it is the main system; the reversion to capital value rating in Wellington, Christchurch, and Dunedin, plus some rural areas; the increase of a mix of land and capital value rates; and the maximum use of direct charges, whether as rates or fees.

c. the limited scope for increasing land value charges of any sort for local government without making other provisions, such as tax-deductibility.

d. the progressive alienation of Crown land.

f. the privatization of state assets, natural monopolies and public utilities.

Regarding the land tax, Reece[22] explains that "New Zealand's abolition of land taxation in 1991 is atypical because of the rare combination of influences involved . . . not likely to be repeated elsewhere." The system may even be revived here by those who had to forsake it as a political expedient—when those influences change, as the necessity for it becomes clearer again, and when it is supported by other moves in the same direction (see below).

The tax-deductibility of homeowners' rates (essential to any intensification at the local level) was debated in Parliament about twenty years ago and was defeated for no other reason than that the two major parties joined to oppose it in order to denigrate the rising third party introducing it.

The sale of Crown leases is less in the public eye and has been carried out almost clandestinely, but is now being monitored and has slowed.

The sale of other strategic community assets in communications, transport, and power, etc., especially to foreign control, is of growing concern and was an issue in the last general election. Over 50 percent of the New Zealand share market is owned abroad.

A proposal not long ago to regulate the privatized power companies was an admission of the inherent impossibility of natural monopolies being controlled by a free market. Telecom's misuse of its monopoly position to obstruct competition is constantly in the news, and its profits remitted abroad are a major cause and indicator of New Zealand's growing overseas debt. Tranzrail's lease of the nation's railways for a dollar a year enables it to hold the Greater Auckland area at ransom in resolving a desperately urgent public transport bind.

These policies were pursued (often in contradiction to election manifestos) by a coalition government stitched together on the basis of unrelated political issues and through the mechanism of an ill-contrived form of preferential party representation. The Asia-Pacific Economic Cooperation Group (APEC) conference held in New Zealand in the Fall of 1999, expressly designed to extend "trade liberalization," brought that approach under close scrutiny and adverse comment from, among others, a former governor general and a former prime minister. The underlying cause of concern is the failure to distinguish between free trade in produced goods and services, and treating the nation's patrimony of natural resources as a mere commodity to be bartered away to foreign interests instead of serving as a continuing source of opportunity for its citizens and revenue for its public services.

This diminished level of economic rent appropriation for community purposes has had the results that should have been expected. While glowing reports go 'round the world extolling the recent growth of the economy (which is fine for those who own "the economy"), wages fail to keep pace with even relatively low overall inflation and are inadequate to meet the new demands of individual responsibility. The benefits of deregulation have not trickled down. The rich have got richer, and the poor, poorer. State assets have been sold cheaply, ostensibly to repay debt. But the national debt and current account deficits have risen alarmingly. All basic government services are run down—health, education, police, etc., to meet tax cuts directed at the top end. Poverty and violence have attracted unprecedented comment by the judiciary. All these factors and more were issues in the 1999 election that resulted in the present government. The question now is whether New Zealand's repudiation of the failed program of the New Right presages a return to the failed program of the Old Left. *There's got to be a better way* than either. That way is sketched in the final paragraphs of this chapter.

New Zealand's experience of having practiced land-value taxation in several ways over 150 years; the demonstrated bankruptcy of other approaches at both ends of the political spectrum; the paucity of viable fresh alternatives on offer at the recent election; the liberal attitude of the media and the hunger for change of freelance journalists; in short, the crossroads the country is now at, make it a crucible for the resolution of these historic issues.

The current confluence here of the related critical issues (alluded to under Recent Developments and more immediately above) presents an unexpected opportunity to promote new ways to collect economic rent, and to secure the community's interest in natural monopolies, akin to the rating legislation of a century ago. Addressing this opportunity requires an approach (including appropriate terminology) that: (1) commends itself to the electorate; (2) is mutually exclusive of other taxes;[23] and (3) institutionalizes the principle so it is less vulnerable to political interference and to every tax collector, at every level, every year. To this end, a market "resource rental" is now more appropriate than a land tax in relation to the significant infrastructural industries currently the cause of concern. The term is already used by government and political aspirants. It inferentially distinguishes the operation from the ownership of the asset—one need not own it to use it. Private enterprise must not include private ownership of the natural elements of life. When the objective is recognized, a wide variety of well known techniques may be used as transitional or enduring means of achieving it. In some cases, a capital investment by the state may be necessary to manage the resource and to recover the rent.

Because land (and thus land value) is perceived as sacrosanct private property, land value charges are too often seen as an invasion of private property, whereas infrastructural assets built up over time out of taxes are seen as public property and therefore eligible for public participation. Once adopted here, extending the principle to land would be a logical step.

In addition to the radically more equitable distribution of wealth and all the other merits of land value charges documented earlier in this chapter and elsewhere, the collection of market Resource Rentals for Revenue in lieu of other taxes has these advantages: (1) it resolves the inflation concern in that the rental destroys the inflationary tradable price by commuting it to essential social income; (2) it eliminates natural resources and natural monopolies as a form of investment or ownership, by whomsoever; and (3) it allows competition in the operation (under license), which is not possible when the resource is privately and exclusively owned. Any rental paid must of course be set off against any income tax payable, or vice versa, i.e., the charges must be mutually exclusive, which avoids the obligation to first re-purchase the resource. Who can quibble over a re-incidence of the charges?

Above all, set-off makes it immediately clear to the individual that the resource rental is not just another tax. Instead, it is the alternative to taxes on endeavor. Widespread understanding of this crucial point provides the political dynamic essential for the ultimate adoption of a thoroughgoing resource rental system of public revenue.

Notes

1. Rolland O'Regan, "New Zealand" in H.G. Brown et al., eds., *Land-Value Taxation Around the World* (1st edition; New York: Robert Schalkenbach Foundation, 1955), p. 27.

2. Patrick Massey, *New Zealand: Market Liberalization in a Developed Economy* (New York: St. Martin's Press, 1995), p. 7.

3. Ibid., chapter i, pp. 10, 29, and passim.

4. Organization for Economic Cooperation and Development (OECD), *OECD Economic Survey: New Zealand* (Paris: OECD, 1989), p. 89.

5. Massey, op. cit., p. 70.

6. Roger O. Douglas, *Unfinished Business* (Auckland: Random House, 1993), p. 10.

7. Department of Survey and Land Information (DOSLI), *Annual Report*, June 30, 1998.

8. Land Corporation Limited (LANDCORP), *Annual Report*, June 8, 1999.

9. W. L. and L. Rees, *The Life and Times of Sir George Grey, K.C.B.* (Auckland: H. Brett, 1892) p. 134; J. B. Condliffe, *New Zealand In The Making* (London: George Allen & Unwin Ltd., 1930) p. 100.

10. J. Rutherford, *The Life and Times of Sir George Grey, K.C.B., 1812–1898* (London: Cassell, 1961) p. 584.

11. Condliffe, op. cit., p. 107; Rees, op. cit., p.419; Rutherford, op. cit., p. 612.

12. Condliffe, op. cit., pp. 178–185.

13. G. M. Fowlds, ed., *An Interesting Correspondence. Sir George Grey and Henry George.* (Auckland, Auckland Public Library, 1950). It also records their meeting in Auckland, New Zealand, on March 1, 1890. A letter from Henry George to P. J. O'Regan, November 11, 1893 (NZ Land-Value Rating Association). P. J. O'Regan was MP for Inangahua from 1893–1896 and for Buller 1897–1899. The rating on the Unimproved Value Act is believed to have been introduced under his auspices.

14. Barry F. Reece, "The Abolition of Land Tax in New Zealand: Searching for Causes and Policy Lessons," *Australian Tax Forum*, Vol. 10, No. 2 (Spring 1993), pp. 223–244. An invaluable evaluation of the facts and conjectures regarding the abolition.

15. J. S. H. Robertson, *Local Rating in New Zealand, a Study of its Development* (Wellington, NZ: Valuation Department Research Paper 663, May, 1966). Rolland O'Regan, *Rating in New Zealand*, 2nd ed., (Petone, NZ, Baranduin Publishers, Ltd., 1985), p. 23.

16. Condliffe, op. cit., pp., 98–104.

17. R. O'Regan, op. cit., pp. 27–28.

18. Ibid, pp. 31–32.

19. Ibid, pp. 53–59, etc.

20. Ibid, pp. 112–125.

21. Ibid, pp. 123–124.

22. Reece, op. cit.

23. Condliffe, op. cit., p. 180.

Contributors

Fuller biographical information (including degrees and publications) on each contributor to the main body of the text may be found at the foot of the first page of his or her respective chapter(s). Inasmuch as this has not been done in connection with the front matter, a similar biographical sketch of the author of the Foreword, Professor Samuels, appears below. We regret that, in some cases, photographs could not be obtained in time for inclusion.

Professor Ahene (economics, Lafayette College) is also a staff consultant for the World Bank and the governments of Malawi and Uganda. He is the author of Chapter 16, "Nations of Eastern Africa" (pp. 273–298).

Rexford A. Ahene

Robert V. Andelson

Professor Andelson (philosophy, Auburn University) is president of the International Union for Land-Value Taxation and Free Trade, and vice-president of the Robert Schalkenbach Foundation. In addition to serving as the editor, he is author of the Introduction (pp. xix–xlii), of Chapter 18, "Abu Dhabi" (pp. 315–326), and co-author (with Prof. Yamasaki) of Chapter 21, "Japan" (pp. 353–363).

Jürgen G. Backhaus

Professor Backhaus (public economics, Maastricht University) has published copiously in his discipline. He is co-founder and managing editor of *The European Journal of Law and Economics*. He wrote Chapter 13, "Germany" (pp. 221–237).

Owen Connellan is a chartered surveyor and valuer who is currently a research fellow at Kingston University near London, where he formerly headed the School of Surveying. He is co-author of Chapter 14, "Great Britain" (pp. 239–257).

John M. Copes, an eminent Australian valuer, served as commissioner of valuations of Jamaica from 1957 to 1962. He died some two months after completing the chapter on "Jamaica and Other Caribbean States" for the second edition of *Land-Value Taxation Around the World*. It has been updated (by Walter Rybeck) as Chapter 7 (pp. 111–127) of the present edition.

Mr. Dunkley, formerly national president of the South African Institute of Certified Mechanical and Electrical Engineers, is immediate past president of the International Union for Land-Value Taxation and Free Trade. He contributed Chapter 17, "South Africa" (pp. 299–311).

Godfrey R. A. Dunkley

Geoffrey A. Forster

Mr. Forster's professional career has been largely spent as managing editor of scientific research journals, including *The Australian Journal of Agricultural Research*. He is author of Chapter 25, "Australia" (pp. 399–416).

Dr. Furtado, whose background is in architecture and urban planning, is a fellow and faculty member of the Lincoln Institute of Land Policy. She contributed Chapter 6, "Columbia" (pp. 97–110).

Fernanda Furtado

The late **Professor Tseng Hsiao**, a founder of the department of land administration at Chengchi University, also founded the Chinese Research Institute of Land Economics and the China Land Reform Association. His contribution to Chapter 22, "Kiao-chau" (pp. 365–369), is excerpted from a monograph published by the Lincoln Institute of Land Policy in 1977.

Michael Hudson

Dr. Hudson is president of the Institute for the Study of Long-Term Economic Trends (ISLET), and co-chairman of the International Scholars Conference on Ancient Economics. He wrote Chapter 1, "Mesopotamia and Classical Antiquity" (pp. 3–25).

Kenneth Jupp

Sir Kenneth was a justice of the British High Court for 15 years until his retirement in 1990. He is the author of Chapter 2, "European Feudalism from its Emergence through its Decline" (pp. 27–45).

Robert D. Keall

Mr. Keall was a finance company executive and investment broker. He held various offices for many years in the New Zealand Land-Value Rating Association, and in 1994 founded the Resource Rentals for Revenue Association (International). He contributed Chapter 26, "New Zealand" (pp. 417–438).

Dr. Kónya served as a department head at the Hungarian Chamber of Commerce, and then as a special researcher at the Scientific Institute of the Hungarian Planning Office. He is the author of Chapter 15, "Hungary" (pp. 259–270).

Balázs Kónya

Alven H. S. Lam, a specialist in urban and regional design, is advisor to the US-China Housing Initiative, Office of Policy Development and Research, US Department of Housing and Urban Development, and has been dean of the Land Reform Training Institute, Taiwan. He contributed Chapter 19, "Republic of China (Taiwan)" (pp. 327–336).

Karsten K. Larsen is a section head at the Danish Statistical Office. He contributed to Chapter 10, "Denmark" (pp. 185–204).

Tae-Il Lee

Dr. Lee is the director of the Chungbok Development Institute in Korea. He served for 15 years as a senior Research fellow and director of the Land Policy Research Division, Korea Research Institute for Human Settlements. He is the author of Chapter 23, "Republic of Korea (South Korea)" (pp. 371–383).

Mr. Lefmann, deputy president of the International Union for Land-Value Taxation and Free Trade, recently retired from the insurance business. For eight years, he served on the Assessment Committee of the Borough of Copenhagen. He is co-author (with Mr. Larsen) of Chapter 10, "Denmark" (pp. 185–204).

Ole Lefmann

Nathaniel Lichfield

Professor Lichfield (environmental planning economics, University of London) has been chair of the program there since 1966. He is also a principal in a consulting firm, and has served as president of the Royal Town Planning Institute of Britain. He is co-author (with Mr. Connellan) of Chapter 14, "Great Britain" (pp. 239–257).

H. J. Manning, a fellow and medallist of the Australian Institute of Valuers, has held a number of high appointments in his profession, including that of chief valuer and assessor of Singapore. In 1970, his paper won first prize in the Donahoo Essay Contest of the International Association of Assessing Officers. He is co-author (with Prof. O'Faircheallaigh) of Chapter 24, "Papua New Guinea" (pp. 385–395).

Mr. Nixon, head of a tax consulting firm with offices in Vancouver, BC, and Cork, Ireland, has been a community newspaper publisher and dean of arts at Columbia College, Vancouver. He contributed Chapter 4, "Canada" (pp. 65–84).

Garry B. Nixon

Professor Ciaran O'Faircheallaigh (politics and public policy, Griffith University) has worked as a consultant for numerous organizations in both public and private sectors. He contributed the section on mineral taxation to Chapter 24, "Papua New Guinea" (pp. 385–395).

Dr. Manuel Perló Cohen is a tenured researcher at the Institute of Social Investigation, National Autonomous University of Mexico. Dr. Perló is the author of Chapter 8, "Mexico" (pp. 129–136).

V. G. Peterson

Miss Peterson was executive secretary of the Robert Schalkenbach Foundation. Upon her retirement, she was elected to the board of the Foundation, and served in that capacity until her death. Her chapter on "Kiao-chau" in the first edition of *Land-Value Taxation Around the World* has been supplemented from other sources to form Chapter 22 (pp. 365–369) of the present volume.

Professor Phang (economics, Singapore Management University) has been a board member of Singapore's Urban Development Authority and Land Transit Authority. She is the author of Chapter 20, "Hong Kong and Singapore" (pp. 337–352).

Sock-Yong Phang

Walter Rybeck

Mr. Rybeck, director of the Center for Public Dialogue, has been Washington, DC, bureau chief for the Cox newspaper chain, assistant director of the National Commission on Urban Problems, and editorial director of the Urban Institute. He is the author of Chapter 9, "The United States" (pp. 137–182), and co-author of Chapter 7, "Jamaica and Other Caribbean States" (pp. 114–127).

Professor Samuels (economics, Michigan State University) recently accepted emeritus status, having taught at Michigan State since 1968. His Ph.D. was earned at the University of Wisconsin. He is a past president of the History of Economics Society and of the Association for Social Economics, and a distinguished fellow of the former. His awards include the Veblen-Commons Award from the Association of Evolutionary Economics, the Thomas Divine Award from the Association for Social Economics, and the Distinguished Faculty Award from Michigan State University. Among his many books are *The Classical Theory of Economic Policy* (1966), *Pareto on Policy* (1974), and, with S. G. Medema and A. A. Schmid, *The Economy as a Process of Valuation* (1997). A five-volume collection of his work was published by Macmillan and New York University Press (1992). He wrote the Foreword to the present book.

Warren J. Samuels

Fernando Scornik Gerstein

Mr. Scornik was advisor consecutively for many years to several important bodies in his native country—the Argentinean Agrarian Cooperatives, the Ministry of Economics, and the Ministry of Agriculture. In 1975, he chaired the Special Commission on Land Taxation set up by the latter. Anticipating the military coup of 1976, he moved to Spain, where he now heads a law firm. He is the author of Chapter 3, "Argentina" (pp. 49–63).

Professor John Strasma (agriculture and applied economics, University of Wisconsin-Madison) is also director of the Center for Development there—a training program in economics for civil servants from around the world. Except for periods with the United Nations Secretariat, the Brookings Institute, etc., he taught at the University of Chile from 1960 to 1972. He contributed Chapter 5, "Chile" (pp. 86–96).

Aivar Tomson is vice-director of Kinnisvarackpert Ltd., a valuation and market research firm. He headed a country-wide mass valuation project for the Estonian National Land Board, developing a cadastral Register and mass valuation system. He contributed Chapter 11, "Estonia" (pp. 205–210).

Pekka V. Virtanen

Professor Virtanen (urban and regional planning, Helsinki University of Technology) began his career as a surveyor, and served as a regional planning director for 11 years before entering the professoriate. He is the author of Chapter 12, "Finland" (pp. 211–220).

Professor Yamasaki (social policy, Kōbe University) is the leading Japanese authority on Henry George's theory of land reform. He is co-author (with Prof. Andelson) of Chapter 21, "Japan" (pp. 353–363).

Yoshisaburo Yamasaki

Index

A

Aaron of Lincoln, 39
Abatements, 21, 158–160
Abatements, property tax. See also tax exemption
Ability to pay, mainstream view of tax equity as, 223
Abu Dhabi (city), 316, 319, 321, 325
Abu Dhabi (emirate), 315–326
  oil and gas revenue of, 317
  population imbalance in, 322
  "single-tax limited" in, 317–320
Adams y Michelina, Federico, 53
Ager publicus, 28, 29, 34
Agricultural cooperatives, Denmark, 187
Agricultural policy
  ancient Babylonia, 8–12
  Chile, 90, 91
  in Argentina, 56, 57
Agricultural property, taxation of
  Belize, 121–123
  Chile, 90, 91
  in Argentina, 59
Agriculture
  impact of land-value rating and improved value rating
    mentioned, 120
Agüero, Julián S. de (quoted), 51
Ahene, Rexford A., 439
Airwaves (broadcast spectrum), 78
Al Ain, Abu Dhabi, 319
Alaska, 174–176
Alberta, 69–71
Albertslund, Denmark, 192
Alessandri Rodriguez, Jorge, 85, 86
Alfonsin, Raúl, 61
Aliquippa, Pennsylvania, 169

Allende, Dr. Salvador, 86
Allentown, Pennsylvania, 169, 170
Alliance Party, New Zealand, 424
Amargi, 14
Amin, Idi, 283
Ammisaduqa, Edict of, 15
Amos, Book of, xli
Amsterdam, New York, 181
Anchorage, Alaska, 175
Ancient fiscal systems, 20–24
Andelson, Robert V. ("the editor"), xii, xix, 315, 353, 439
Anderton, Jim, 424
Andreades, A.M. (quoted), 13
Andurarum, 14
Annual value rating, 401, 402, 404, 407, 427
Antall, József, 266
Antidosis, 13
Apartheid, 300, 305, 310
APEC (Asia Pacific Economic Cooperation), 434
Appalachia, 175
Arad, Hungary, 260, 261
Aramburu, Gen. Pedro Eugenio, 57, 58
Arden, Delaware, 151–153
Ardencroft, Delaware, 151
Ardentown, Delaware, 151
Argentina, 49–64
    approaches to land-value taxation in, 57, 58
    Law No. 18.033 (ITAEA), 59, 60
    public leasehold rent in, 49–52
Arlington, Virginia, 161, 162
Asbestos, 82
Assessed value of land and buildings in the US, 142
Assessment
    in Canada, 65, 68
    in Chile, 89, 90
    in Denmark, 200–202
    in Finland, 217, 218
    in Hong Kong, 339–344

in Jamaica, 113
in Singapore, 344–350
in South Korea, 376, 377
in Taiwan, 330–332
in Tanzania, 280–282
in US, 161–164
in Zimbabwe, 287–290
Assur, Assyria, 10
Auckland, New Zealand, 423, 425, 429, 430, 434
Auckland Regional Services Trust, 433
Augustus (Roman emperor), 29, 30
Austin, Francis, 161
Austin, M.M., and Vidal-Naquet, P.
   (quoted), 5, 12
Australia, 399–416
   advance and set-backs of land-value taxation in, 400, 401
   federal land tax in, 399, 400
   local land tax in, 401
   mineral taxation in, 407
   property taxation in Papua New Guinea reflects influence of,
      391–395
   property taxation of improved value in, 399, 400
   property taxation of land value only in, 403
   state land tax in,409–411
   total tax revenue in, 410, 411
   use-value of land exceeds former speculative value in, 408
Austro-Hungarian empire, 259, 264
Automobile taxation. See Motor vehicle taxation

B

Babbitt, Bruce, 83
Babylon, city of, xxiv, 10
Babylonia
   edict of Ammisaduqa, 15
   laws of Hammurapi, 9, 15, 16
Backhaus, J. G., 440
Bacon, John L., 163

Bacon, John L. (quoted), 163
Bailey, William Warren, xxi
Baja California, Mexico, 130, 134
Baja California Sur, Mexico, 130, 134
Baldwin County, Alabama, 149
Ballance, John, 422
BANOBRAS (*Banco Nacional de Obras Servicios*), Mexico, 131
"Bantustans" (black homelands), 304
Barbados, 121, 122
Barr, Joseph M. (quoted), 168
Bauxite, 112, 115
BC Gas Corporation, 71
Belgrano, Gen. Manuel, 49
Belize, 121–123
Bellamy, Edward, xi
Bellangee, James, 148
Beneficium, 32
Benefit assessment districts, 142
Betterment levies, Great Britain, xiii
BHP Ltd., 393
Birabent, Mauricio, 56, 57, (quoted) 63 n. 12, 13
Birmingham, Alabama, 159
Bishop Estate (Hawaii), 172
Black Death, 40
Blantyre, Malawi, 273, 285, 286
Bloomberg Commission (Jamaica), 113
Blundell, V.H. (cited), 251
Bodenreform, 224, 260, 367, 368
Bogotá, Colombia, 101
Bonaparte, Napoleon, 223
Boston, Massachusetts, 148, 150, 159
Bosworth Field, Battle of, 40
Bougainville Copper Limited (BCL), 391
Bougainville Island, Papua New Guinea, 386, 391, 392
"Boundary plants," 112
Braun, Robert, 259, 260
Brennan, Frank (cited), 401
Brisbane, Australia, 412

British Columbia
  mentioned, 66
  property taxes in, 66
British East Africa, 275
  Crown Land Bill, 275, 276
  Crown Land Ordinance, 276
British East India Company, 345
British India, 207
Broadcast spectrum. See Airwaves (broadcast spectrum)
Brondby, Denmark, 191, 192
Brooks, David, 408
Brown, Harry Gunnison, xvi
Bryant, Lyle C., 161, 164
Bryan, William Jennings, xl
Brycg bot, 33
Budapest, Hungary, 260–262
Buenos Aires (city), Argentina, 49, 50, 53, 55
Buenos Aires (province), Argentina, 54
Buganda, kingdom of, 274, 282
Building ordinance, Hong Kong, 341
Bulewayo, Zimbabwe, 288, 289
Burgess, Ronald, 414
Buttenheim, Harold S., xv, 161
Byrh bot, 33

C

Cahill, Joan (quoted), 176
California
  Central Valley Irrigation Project, 156
  Irrigation District Act (Wright Act), 154–156
  Proposition 13, 181
      mentioned, 154–156, 177
Cámpora, Hector, 59
Canada, 65–84
  Indian land claims in, 69, 75, 76
  property taxation in, 65–68

public resource rents in, 72–74
railroad givaways in, 76, 77
Canadian Pacific Railroad (CPR), 76
Cansino, Armin (cited), 123
Canton, China, 368
Cape Town, South Africa, xiv, 302, 304, 307–309
Capital gains taxes, Great Britain, 249, 252
Capital Territory, Australia, 399, 401, 406, 407
Capital value rating, New Zealand, xxxvi, 429, 426, 427, 429, 433
Caribbean Community Secretariat (quoted), 124
Caribbean states, 111–128
Castellanos Gout, Milton, 131–133, 135
Castells, M. (cited), 344
Catholic Church, 57, 58
Chamber of Mines, South Africa, 309
Chan, Sir Julius, 387
Charles II, King of England, 245
"Charter of the Forests," 38
Chelliah Commission, Zimbabwe, 289
Chen Shui-bien, 336
Chiang Kai-shek, 328, 335
Chile, 85–96
    assessment of land value in, 89, 90
    land policy in, 87
    mineral taxation in, 94, 95
    property taxation in, 87, 88
    unit value methodology in, 90, 91
China, ancient, 332, 339
Choregia, 13
Christchurch, New Zealand, xxxvi, 426, 431, 433
Churchill Falls Hydro Project, 74
Ciskei, 305
Clairton, Pennsylvania, 166, 169
Clarkson, S. James (quoted), 163
Classification of land, xxix, 92, 213, 214, 283, 291, 378
Clean Slates, 7, 13, 15, 16
Clinton, Bill, 84
Clunies Ross, Anthony, 392

Coal, 69, 71, 73, 176, 226, 239
Coatesville, Pennsylvania, 169
Colombia, 97–110
  Conatribución de Valorización (CV), 97–99, 101–105, 107, 108
  Impuesto de Valorización, 101
  Participación en Plusvalias (PP), 98, 105–107
Columbia River, 73, 74
Commendatio, 31
Common Market, European, 418, 419
Communist Party, Hungary, 265
Community Land Scheme, Great Britain, 249–251
Community Land Tax Act of 1975, Great Britain, 249
Community Land Tax Act of 1976, Great Britain, 249
Competitive bidding, exemption of US radio and TV, 165
Confiscation, 15, 155, 300
Connellan, Owen, 440
Conservative Government, Great Britain, 247, 249
Conservative (National) Party, New Zealand, 420, 423
Conservative Party
  Argentina, 55
  Great Britain, 249
  Hungary, 266
Constantine (Roman emperor), 31
Contribución de Valorización (CV), Colombia, 97–99, 101–105,
    107, 108
Control of Rent Act, Singapore, 347
Copello, António César, 62
Copes, John M. ("one of the two authors of this chapter"), 111, 440
Copper, 391
Copyholders, 37
Coquitlam, British Columbia, 82
Cornick, Philip H., xvi, 236
Corn Laws, Great Britain, xii
Coyne, William J., 169
Cradock, Sir John, 300
Crown lands, 276, 400, 422
Crown leases, 340, 341, 421, 434

Cruden, Gordon N. (cited), 341
Curtis, Mike, 153

D

Damaschke, Adolf, 225
Dandamayev, Mohammed and Lukonin, Vladimir G. (quoted), 11
Danegeld, 33, 36, 241
Danelaw, 33, 35
Dar es Salaam, Tanzania, 273, 280, 281
Darius I (Persian emperor), 11
Day, Philip (quoted), 410
Dayton, Ohio, 153, 154, 170
Debrecen, Hungary, 261
Denmark, 185–204
    advance and setbacks of land-value taxation in, 193–195
    agricultural cooperatives in, 187
    estimated economic rent in, 188
    Ground Duty Government in, 188, 193–195
    Hartkorn Tax, 186, 1
    Justice Party in, xxxiii, 187, 193, 195–197, 200
    land bills of, 197, 198
    land-value increment taxation in, 190, 191, 196, 198, 199
    system of state rental smallholdings in, 189, 190
    taxes and land values (1950–95), 188
Detroit, Michigan, 160, 162, 170
Development value capture, Great Britain, 239, 244
Diamond, Walter H. and Dorothy B. See *Tax Havens of the World.*
Diederichs, Admiral Otto von, 366, 368
Diocletian (Roman emperor), 30
District of Columbia, 177
Dixon, Norma E. (quoted), 118
Dobbert, F., 224
Doman Industries, 76
Domesday Book, the, 33–35
Domínguez, Carlos Villalobos, 54
Don Pedro Dam, California, 155
Dore, R.P. (quoted), 356

DOSLI, 421
Douglas, Sir Roger O., 419, 423
DuBois, Pennsylvania, 169
Due, John F., 274
Dunedin, Lord (quoted), 114
Dunedin, New Zealand, xxxvi, 426, 431, 433
Dunkley, Godfrey R. A. ("the present author"), 299, 441
Duquesne, Pennsylvania, 166, 169

E

E&N Railway, 82
Earmarked revenues, 6, 9, 88
East Africa, British, 275
   Crown Land Bill (1908), 275, 276
   Crown Land Ordinance (1915), 276
   Hut Tax Regulation (1901), 275
East London, South Africa, 305
Eastern Africa, nations of, 273–298. See also Kenya, Malawi,
   Tanzania, Uganda, Zambia, and Zimbabwe
   land taxation mostly urban in, 274
Ecker-Racz, L. L., 161
Economic Development Board, Singapore, 349
Ecuador, xv
Edward I (King of England), 39
Eisphora, 6
Elgin, Lord, 292
Elourdy, Eugenio, 133, 135
Else-Mitchell Commission, New South Wales, 411
Emery, Carlos, 60
Emphyteusis, Law of, 49–53
Enclosures, 41, 43, 44, 76
England. See also Great Britain
   Property Acts of 1925, 43
   rating system in, 242
   social classes in medieval, 40
   Statute of Tenures (1660), 43
   Tudor, 40–42

urban land tax free in medieval, 30
vacant land tax-free in, 241
Entebbe, Uganda, 273, 282
Enterprise zones, 159
Equity, tax, xii, xxiv, xxxi, 94, 132, 135, 208, 222, 223, 229, 291, 309
Estate taxes, 148
Estonia, 205–210
Ethiopia, 292
Evans, E. Howard, 161
Excise duties, 6
Exemption, tax. See Tax exemption
Extractive resources, severance taxes on. See also Mineral
    deposits; Mining

F

Fairbanks, Alaska, 174, 175
Fairhope, Alabama, xxxiii, 148–151
    public leasehold rent in, 149
Fairhope Single Tax Corporation, 149
FSTC, 149–151
Falklands War, 60
False Creek, Vancouver, British Columbia, 76, 77
Feather River (California) Irrigation Project, 156
Federal lands, uncollected rent of US, 165
Federales (political faction), Argentina, 51
Federation of Rhodesia and Nyasaland, 285
Fels, Joseph, 148, 151, 187
Feorm, 33
Feudalism, European, 27–46
"Fifteenths and tenths," 38
Fiji, 326, 395
Finance Act of 1909–10 (Lloyd George), Great Britain, 242
Finance Act of 1931 (Snowden), Great Britain, 242
Finland, 211–220
    assessment in, 217, 218
    breakdown of 1993 national tax revenue in, 212
    municipal tax on real property in, 216, 217

national "capital" taxation in, 215, 216
national forest taxation in, 212–214
national inheritance and gift taxes in, 218
national land transfer tax in, 218, 219
taxation of sales in, 215, 216
two-rate property taxes in, 216, 217
Finkelstein, Philip (quoted), 127
Finley, Moses (quoted), 11
Fishing rights, 433
Flat rating130, 299, 302–304, 307
Flood control, 74, 153, 154
Flores, Peña, Sergio, 132, 135
Flürscheim, Michael, 225
Folk Schools, Danish, 186
Forest laws, medieval English, 37, 38
Forest taxation, 212
Forster, Geoffrey A, 441
Fort Jackson, South Africa, 305
France, 17, 36, 37, 42
Frankfurt-am-Main, 225, 367
Frankish kingdom, 31
Franklin, New Zealand, 429
Frederick VI, King of Denmark, 186
Freemasons, Hungarian, 260, 261
Frei Montalvo, Eduardo, 86
French Canadians, 83
Frontier, the US, 144, 164
Furtado, Fernanda, 442
Fyrd, 33

G

Gaffney, Mason, 361, (quoted) 363 n. 13
Galilei Circle, 259
Gallup Market Analysis Institute, Copenhagen, 196, 198
Garnaut, Ross, 392
Garrison, William Lloyd, III, 323
Garst, Charles E., 359

Gaston, E.B., 148, 149
Gatooma, Zimbabwe, 288
Gemara, xli
General Confederation of Labor, Argentina, 56
George, Henry, xi, xv, xix, xxi, xxii, (quoted) xxvi, xxxvii, xxxix,
    (quoted) xl, 53, 145, 151, 153, 186, 212, 221–225, (quoted) 224,
    232, 241, 243, 244, 259, 266, 267, 323, 324, 327, 328, 338, 347,
    359, 361, 368, 373, 400, 418, 422, 425
  influence of in Argentina, 53
  influence of in British East Africa, 292
  influence of in China, 327
  influence of in Germany, 221
  influence of in Hong Kong, 338
  influence of in Hungary, 259
  influence of in Japan, 359
  influence of in Kiao-chau, 368
  influence of in Korea, 372
  influence of in New Zealand, 418
  influence of in Singapore, 347
  influence of in US, 149
  views and arguments of, xix–xxxvii
Georgist theory
  adequacy of land-value taxation, xi
  economic efficiency of land-value taxation, xix
  moral case for land-value taxation, xxvi
  on concept of land, xix
  tax equity, xix
Georgists
  in Argentina, 54
  in Denmark, 191
  in Hungary, 259
  in Japan, 359
  mentioned, xxii
Germany, 221–238
  general characteristics of land taxation in, 227–229
  narrow concept of land held by reformers in, 222
  property tax yield as percentage of total tax revene, 229

quasi-Georgist nature of income tax in, 222
tax categories of real estate in, 228
Gerstein, Fernando Scornik. See Scornik Gerstein
Ghettos, Jewish, 11
Gilgamesh Epic, 10
Giroward, Sir Percy, 292
Goh, L. (cited), 344
Gold, 16, 31, 39, 154, 155, 174, 387, 391, 393
Goroka, Papua New Guinea, 388
Gorton, John, 401
Gosnell, Fred A., Sr., 162
Graded tax. See also Two-rate tax
Graham, Rev. Billy, xxiv
Grand Trunk Pacific Railroad, 82
Grazing rights, xxxv, 12, 28, 53, 78, 165, 300
Great Britain, 239–258
  betterment levies in, xiv
  Community Land Scheme, 249–251
  Community Land Tax Act of 1975, 249
  Community Land Tax Act of 1976, 251
  Conservative Government, 247, 248
  development value capture, 239, 244
  Finance Act of 1909–10 (Lloyd George), 242
  Finance Act of 1931 (Snowden), 242
  Finance Act of 1967, 249
  Finance Act of 1974, 249
  Labour Government, 245, 248, 249, 252
  Land Commission Act of 1967, 248, 249
  Land Drainage Act of 1930, 244
  recoupment of infrastructure costs, 252–254
  Sewer Acts of 1427 and 1531, 244, 245
  Town and Country Planning Acts of 1909–32, 245, 246
  Town and Country Planning Act of 1947, 245–247
  Town and Country Planning Acts of 1953, 1954, and 1959, 247, 248
  Uthwatt Committee, 242
  vacant land entirely tax-free in, 241

Wales, Land Authority for, 251
Welsh Development Agency, 251
Great Northern War, 205
Great Trek, 300
Greater Cape Metropolitan Area, South Africa, 307
Greece, xv
Grey, Sir George, 422
Griffin, Walter Burley, 401
Ground Duty (Grundskyld). 191
Ground Duty Government, Denmark, 188, 193–195
Grundtvig, Bishop Severin, 186
Gütschow, C.D.F., 235
Gwartney, Ted, 162, 163
Gwelo, Zimbabwe, 288

H

Halidon, Maine, 148
Hall, Bolton, 148
Hammurapi, Laws of, 9, 15, 16
Harare (formerly Salisbury), Zimbabwe, 288, 289
Harcourt, Lord (quoted), 292 n. 7
Harcourt, Mike (quoted), 83 n. 41
Hardship cases (Jamaica), 115, 116
Harran, Assyria, 10
Harrisburg, Pennsylvania, 168, 171, 172
Harrison, Fred (quoted), 355, 357, 359
Hartkorn Tax, Denmark, 186, 191
Hat Creek coal fields, British Columbia, 82
Hawaii, 172, 173
Hazeltown, Pennsylvania, 169
Heard-Bey, Frauke (quoted), 320
Helsinki, Finland, 212
Henry George, xi, xv, xix, xxi, xxxvii, xxxix, xl, 53, 145, 151, 153,
    186, 212, 221–225, 232, 241, 243, 244, 259, 266, 267, 323, 324,
    327, 328, 338, 347, 359, 361, 368, 373, 400, 418, 422, 425
Henry George Foundation, Great Britain, 244
Henry George Society of Hungary, 267, 268

Henry VIII (King of England), 41
Heritage Fund, Alberta, 81
Hermosillo, Victor, 133, 135
Herps, Douglas (quoted), 408
Hervey Bay, Queensland, 408
Hidage, 33, 36
Hirōta cabinet, Japan (1936), 359
Hirsch, Max, 400
Holdsworth, Sir William (quoted), 32
Homelands, Black. See Bantustans
Homestead Act (1862), US, 140
Hong Kong, 337–344
    economic development in, 343, 344
    Hong Kong Island, 339, 340
    Kowloon Peninsula, 339, 340
    Land Commission, 342
    New Territories, 339, 340
    public leasehold rent in, 342
    similarities between Singapore and, 337–339
    Sino-British Joint Declaration on, 339
    subsidized housing in, 344
    Town Planning Ordinance, 341
Hong, Yu-hung (quoted), 350, 414
Honolulu, 173
Hoover, Glenn E., xv, 236
Ho, P. Sai-wing (cited), 351
Horn, Gyula, 267
Horne, Bernardino, 57
Horowhenua, New Zealand, 429
Horthy, Admiral Nicholas, 261
House tax, Taiwan, 332
Houston, Texas, 163
Hoyt, Homer, 161
Hsiao, Tseng, 442
Hudson, Michael, 3, 442
Hulton, John (quoted), 44
Hungarian Academy of Sciences, 268
Hungarian Henry George Society, 266, 267

Hungary, 259–270
  agricultural mainstay of Austro-Hungarian Empire, 259, 264
  influence of Henry George in, 259, 266–268
  land policies under Communist regimes in, 265
  land reform of 1945 in, 262
  land taxes 1917-21 in, 260–262
  "old cadastre system" in, 269
  post-Communist land programs in, 265–267
Hut tax, 275
Hutchinson, A.R., xxxiv, xxxv, 402, 406, 407, 411, 414
Hwange, Zimbabwe, 288
Hydro power, 69, 73–75
Hydro Quebec, 74

I

Ilia, Arturo, 58
IMF (International Monetary Fund), xiv
Immigration
  effect on Canadian land prices of, 77, 78
  Henry George on, xxxiv
  problem of, in Abu Dhabi, 323
Improvement, exemption from taxation of. See Abatements; Tax
    exemption
Impuesto a la plusvaliá, Mexico, 129
Impuesto de radicación, Mexico, 129
Impuesto de Valorización, Colombia, 101
Income taxes
  Denmark, 186, 191, 195
  Germany, 222, 229
  Singapore, 348
  US, 144, 171
Indian land claims in Canada, 75, 76
Inland Revenue Department, Jamaica, 117
Instituto de Capacitacion Economica (ICE), 58
Internal Affairs Department Coordinating Committee, 428
International Bank for Reconstruction and Development, 113

International Union for Land-Value Taxation and Free Trade, 203, 270, 306
Iraq, xv
Ireland, 28
Irigoyen, Hipólito, 55
Irrigation Districts Act (Wright Act), California, 154–156
Israel, xxxv, xxxvi
ITAEA, Argentina, 59, 60

J

Jacques, Michael, 309
Jamaica, 111–120
   Inland Revenue Department, 117
   introduction of land value taxation in, 113, 114
   Land Valuation Law (1957), 113–116
   schedule of land-value tax rates (1977) in, 118
   yield of land-value as compared to other taxes in, 117
Japan, 353–364
   Agricultural Land Adjustment Law (1938), 357, 358
   Agricultural Land Law (1952), 358
   brings land-value taxation to Korea, 371
   land reform under Allied Occupation in, 357–359
   land speculation in, 356, 359, 360
   Land Tax Law (1931), 356
   Land Tax Revision Act (1873), 354–356
   Meiji land tax in, 354–357
   national land value tax (1992) in, 361
   recession beginning 1990 in, 360, 361
   Second Agricultural Land Reform (1946), 358
   Tokugawa land tax in, 353–356
Jarach, Dino, 58
Jefferson, Thomas, 139, (quoted) 164
Jenson, Jens P. (quoted), 141
Jepsen, Gunnar Thorlund, 198
Jews in medieval England, 38, 39
Jinja, Uganda, 282
Jo, Sentaro, 359

Johannesburg, South Africa, 301, 302, 308, 310
John (king of England), 37
John Paul II, Pope, xxiv
Jones, A.H.M. (quoted), 30
Joshua, Book of (Josh.), xxiv
Joseph II (Hapsburg emperor), 268
Jubilee
    2000, xxiii
    Biblical, xxiv, xxv, 14, 19
Jupp, Kenneth, 443
Jurong Town Corporation, Singapore, 349
Justice Party, Denmark, xxxiii, 187, 193, 195–197, 200
Justicialist (Peronist) Party, Argentina, 58, 59, 61

K

Kádár, Janos, 263–265, 267
Kaipara, New Zealand, 429
Kampala, Uganda, 273, 282
Kaposvar, Hungary, 261
Katz Commission, Third Interim Report (quoted), 306
Katz Tax Commission, South Africa, 308
Kauai (county), Hawaii, 173
Keall, Robert D., 443
Keller, Helen (quoted), xxxix
Kelly, John L. (quoted), 159
Kenya, 277–280
Khalifa, Ali Mohammed (quoted), 321
Kiao-chau, 365–370
Kiap system, 388
Kidinnu stones, 10
Kidwell, Jon (quoted), xxxi
Kigezi District, Uganda, 283
Kinch, B.O. (quoted), 121
Knowland, William F. (quoted), 155
Konoye, Prince Fumimaro, 357
Kónya, Balázs, 444
Korea, 371–384

Korea, South, 371–384
  Comprehensive Landholding Tax (1988), 374–376
  Compulsory Property Registration Act (1990), 380
  land assessment in, 372, 373
  land ownership distribution in, 371, 372
  land reform ("Public Concept in Land") in, 373–380
  land value taxation in, 372, 373
  land-value increment taxation in, 377, 378
  table of land taxes in, 372
  taxation of capital gains in, 372
Kowloon Peninsula, Hong Kong, 339, 340
Kristensen, K.J., 203
Kugler, Walter, 58
Kuomintang, 335
Kwekwe, Zimbabwe, 288
Kwok, R.Y.W. (cited), 344

L

Labour Government, Great Britain, xiii, 245, 248, 249, 252
Labour Party
  Great Britain, 242
  New Zealand, 420, 423, 426
  South Africa, 301
Ladejinsky, Wolf, 359
Lae, Papua New Guinea, 388
Lam, Alven H. S., 444
Lamas, Andres, 53
Land
  availability of, 90
  basic to development of US, 137, 138
  defined, xix
  narrow concept of, held by German reformers, 224
  paid virtually all costs of government from fall of, 27
  supported ancient public services at institutions, xxvi, xxix
  under urban buildings not taxed in medieval England, 40
Land Acquisition Act of 1966, Singapore, 346
Land and Liberty, 244

Land classification, xxix, 92, 213, 214, 283, 291, 378
Land Commission Act of 1967, Great Britain, 248, 249
Land Commission, Hong Kong, 342
Land Drainage Act of 1930, Great Britain, 244
Land Policy Council, Great Britain, 244
Land reform
  in Chile, 85–87
  in Hungary, 262, 263
  in Singapore, 345
  in Taiwan, 328, 334, 335
Land rent
  conversion of, into mortgage interest, 23
  imputed, 58, 59, 61, 62, 222, 278
Land speculation
  in Australia, 413
  in California Irrigation Districts, 156
  in Canada, 66, 67, 72
  in Japan, 356, 359, 360
  in Korea, 373
  in Montserrat, 124
  in New Zealand, 429
  in Surrey, British Columbia, 67
  in Taiwan, 328, 331, 334
  in Tudor England, 40
  in US, 139, 156, 168
  discouraged by land-value taxation, 194
Land taxes, urban, 30, 91, 104, 108, 274, 305
Land tenure
  in Africa, 274, 281, 283, 290
  in Belize, 122
  in England, 28
  in Fiji, 394
  in Hungary, 262
  in Jamaica, 122
  in Malawi, 285
  in Papua New Guinea, 389
  in South Africa, 305

in Uganda, 280
early Teutonic and Celtic, x, xxiv, 34, 40
Land value, defined, xix
Land Values Research Group, Australia, xxxiv
Land-value increment taxation
    advocated by List for Kingdom of Hungary, 223
    advocated by Vickrey to pay for public infrastructure, xxvii
    criticized as half-way measure by Pikler, 260–262
    in Denmark, 190
    in Germany, 222
    in Kiao-chau, 367
    in South Korea, 372
    in Taiwan, 332–335
Land-value taxation. See also individual countries
    a "super user charge" rather than a true tax, xxiii
    economic efficiency of, xxviii
    empirical evidence for, evaluated, xxxiii
    endorsements of, 426
    fiscal case for, xix, xxviii
    incidence of, 53, 190, 304
    moral case for, xxvi–xxviii
    scope of term as used in this book, xix
    supported by small farmers in Denmark, 186
    supported by small farmers in Hungary, 261
Land-Value Taxation Around the World, first edition, xix, 62, 80,
    178, 179, 203, 269, 294, 302, 437
Land Value Taxation Campaign, Great Britain, 244
Landcorp, 422
Lange, Jakob E., 187
Lanusse, Gen. Alejandro, 59
Larsen, Karsten K., 444
Latimer, Hugh (quoted), 41
Laurion silver mines, 12
Lawrence, David (quoted), 168
Laws, The, Plato, xl
Lea, David(quoted), 326 n. 10
Leasehold rent, public
    in Abu Dhabi, 321

in Alaska, 174
in Alberta, 70
in Argentina, 49
in Australia, 401
in British Columbia, 66
in Canada, 66, 70
in Denmark, 201
in Fairhope, Alabama, 148–151
in Hong Kong, 339
in Israel, xxxv
in New Zealand, 421
in Quebec, 72
in Rhodesia, 285
in Saskatchewan, 72
in Singapore, 342
in Single Tax enclaves, 147–153
in the Ardens, Delaware, 151–153
in US, 147–153
Leasing of public assets, 21
Lee, Tae-Il, 444
Lefmann, Ole, 185, 195, 445
Leiturgoi, 6
Lent, George E., xv
Levesque, René, 74
Levi, Tribe of, xxiv, xxv
Leviticus, Book of (Lev.), xxiv
Li Ka-shing, 77
Liberal Party
  British Columbia, 80
  Denmark, 186, 193
  Hungary, 265, 267
Lichfield, Nathaniel, 445
Lilongwe, Malawi, 285
Lincoln, Abraham, 140
Lincoln Institute of Land Policy, xiii, 361
LINZ (Land Information New Zealand), 422
Lissner, Will and Dorothy Burnham (quoted), xxxii
List, Friedrich (quoted), 223

Livy, 17
Lloyd George, David, 242
Lock Haven, Pennsylvania, 169
Logsdon, Chuck (quoted), 175
London Naval Conference (1930), 356
Lorince, Terry (quoted), 173
Lower Hutt, New Zealand, 425
Lucas, Frank A. W., 301
Lukonin, Vladimir G., and Dandamayev, Mohammed (quoted), 11
Lusaka, Zambia, 273, 289
Lusht, Kenneth M. (quoted), 405
Luther, Martin, 43

M

MacArthur, Gen. Douglas, 358
MacMillan Bloedel company, 82
Madang, Papua New Guinea, 388
Madison, James, 139
Magna Carta, 37
Mailo tenure, 282, 283
Maipo River Valley, Chile, 86
Malawi, 284–287
Malaysia, 345, 346
Malthus, Thomas Robert, xii
Manishtushu, Stele of, 10
Manitoba, 66, 72
Manley, Norman (quoted), 114
Manning, H. J. ("the present writer"), 385, 445
Manor, the, 33
Mao Tse-tung, 328
Maoris, 417, 421
Marchionatto, Juan Maria, 62
Marlborough, New Zealand, 425
Marosvásárhely, Hungary, 261
Martin, Paul A. (quoted), xiv, xvii
Martínez, Saúl P., 61, 62
Maryland, 170, 177

Masaka, Uganda, 282
Mason, J. Rupert (quoted), 155
Massey, Patrick(quoted), 418, 419
Mataquali lands, Fiji, 326
Maui (county), Hawaii, 173
Mazari, Darlene, 77
Mbale, Uganda, 282
McKeesport, Pennsylvania, 166, 168
Meakin, Peter, 309
Medellín, Colombia, 101, 102, 104
Meiji (Japanese emperor), 354
Meiji land tax, 354–357
Meiji Restoration, 354, 362
Melbourne, Australia, 402, 405, 408
Melbourne Statistical District, 405
Menem, Carlos Saúl, 58, 61
Mera, Koichi, 361, (quoted) 363 n. 18
Metoikion, 5
Mexicali, Mexico, 130–135
Mexico, 126–136
    Impuesto a la plusvaliá, 129
    Impuesto de radicación, 129
Miami Conservancy, Ohio, 153
Mill, John Stuart, 223, 224, 241
Mineral deposits. See Extractive resources, severance taxes on. See
    also Mineral deposits
  public revenue treatment of, 94, 115
Mineral deposits, public revenue treatment of
    in Abu Dhabi, 317–320
    in Alaska, 174–176
    in Australia, 407
    in Canada, 72, 73
    in Chile, 94, 95
    in Jamaica, 115
    in Latin America, 94, 95
    in Papua New Guinea, 391–394
Mining. See specific minerals
Minnesota, 177

Misharum, 14
Missouri, 159, 177
Mitchell Commission, New South Wales, 411
Modesto Irrigation District, California, 155
Molinari, Antonio Manuel, 556, 57
Mombasa, Kenya, 277
Montoneros, the, 58
Montserrat, 124–126
Moody, Harris L., 163
More, Sir Thomas, 40
Morgan, Arthur E., 153
Mortgage banking, 19
Mortgage interest, conversion of rent into, 23
Mosaic Law, xxv, 14
Motor vehicle taxation, Singapore, 348
Mueller, Walt (quoted), 159
Mulanje District, Malawi, 287
Muldoon, Sir Robert, 418, 419, 423
Muleta, Bekale (quoted), 292 n. 3
Murray, J.F.N., 113
Mussolini, Benito, 56
Mutsuhito. See Meiji (Japanese emperor)
Mzuzu, Malawi, 285

N

Nagy, Ferenc, 263
Nagy, Imre, 263
Nairobi, Kenya, 273, 277–280
National (Conservative) Party, New Zealand, 420, 423
Natural gas, 69, 71
Natural Resources Rental Taxation in Australia, 415
Net product taxes, xli
New Castle, Pennsylvania, 152, 168
New Guinea Australia Administrative Unit, 388
New Guinea, German Territory of, 387
New Hampshire, 177
New Labour Party, New Zealand, 423

New Plymouth, New Zealand, 429
New South Wales, 114, 399–404, 406, 407, 409, 411
New Territories, Hong Kong, 339, 340
New Westminster, British Columbia, 67
New York (city), 127, 152, 156, 158, 159
New York (state), 74, 177
New Zealand, 417–438
    advance of land-value taxation up to 1988 in, 425–428
    annual rental value rating in, 424
    capital value rating in, 424
    endorsements of land-value rating in, 428–430
    land the source of public revenue in original province, 425
    land-value taxation partly dismantled in, 420
    local jurisdictions rejecting proposed reversions, 429
    local property taxes (rates), 424–432
    national land tax in, 422–424
    Public Bodies Leases Act (1908), 421
    public land leases in, 421, 422
    rating polls in, 425
    Rating Powers Act (1988–89), 426
    Urban Farmland Rating Act (1932), 428
    user charges in, 431
New Zealand Land Value Rating Association, xxxvi
Newfoundland, 74
Nexum, 29
Nicaragua, xiii, xiv
Nippur, Babylonia, 10
Nixon, Garry B., 446
Noel, Carlos S., 55
Norman Conquest, 36, 37
Northern Rhodesia. See also Zambia
Northern Territory, Australia, 399, 406, 407
Nova Scotia, 79
Numbers, Book of (Num.), xxiv
Nuñez, Ignacio, 50
Nystad, Treaty of, 205

O

Oahu Island, Hawaii, 172
OECD (Organization for Economic Cooperation and
    Development), 208
O'Faircheallaigh, Claran, 385, 446
Oganization for Economic Coorperation and Development, 208
Ohio, 153, 154
Oil City, Pennsylvania, 169
Oil reserves, United Arab Emirates, 324
Oil revenues
    Abu Dhabi, 319
    Alaska, 174, 175, 176
    Alberta, 81
    Canada, 69, 70
Oil, severance taxes on, xx, 174, 175
OK Tedi mine, 393
"Old cadastre system," Hungary, 269
Onganía, Gen. Juan, 58
Ontario, 69
Ontario Hydro, 82
Oppenheim, Leo (quoted), 10
Orange Free State, 300
Orban, Viktor (quoted), 267
O'Regan, Dr. Rolland, 122, (quoted) 285
O'Regan, P.J., 422
Ottawa-Carleton, Ontario, 80
Our Land and Land Policy, 422
Owens, Herbert T. (quoted), 66, 67, 80 n. 13

P

Pacific Rim, xxxiii
Paine, Thomas, 139
Palacios, Alfredo, 56
Palmerston North, New Zealand, 429
Papua New Guinea, 385–396
    local property taxation in, 389–391

mineral taxation in, 391–394
Prescribed Infrastructure Development in, 394
Papua, Territory of, 387
Paraguay, xv, 57
Participación en Plusvaliás (PP), Colombia, 98, 105–107
Partido de Acción Nacional (PAN), Mexico, 133
Partido Liberal Georgista, Argentina, 54
Partido Revolucionario Institucional (PRI), Mexico, 133
Pastoriza, J. J., 163
Peasant propriator, Roman, 28
Peasants' War in Germany, 42, 43
Peddle, Francis K. (quoted), 65, 80 n., 84 n.
Pennsylvania, xxi, xxiv, 166, 167, 171, 177
   Aliquippa, 169
   Aliquippa School District, 180 n. 42
   Allentown, 169, 170
   Clairton, 166, 169
   Coatesville, 169
   DuBois, 169
   Duquesne, 166, 169
   Ebensburg, 169
   Harrisburg, 168, 171, 172
   Hazleton, 169
   Local Economic Revitalization Tax Act (LERTA), 167
   Lock Haven, 169
   McKeesport, 166, 168
   New Castle, 168, 169
   Oil City, 169
   Pittsburgh, 168–170, 172, 173, 177
   Pittsburgh Improvement District, 180 n. 42
   Scranton, 168, 169, 177
   Steelton, 169
   Titusville, 169
   Uniontown, 169
   Washington, 169
People's Action Party, Singapore, 345
Peoria, Illinois, 159
Pérez, Tejada, Francisco, 133, 135

Phang, Sok-Yong, 445
Perló Cohen, Manuel, 446
Permanent Fund, Alaska, 174–176
Perón, Eva ("Evita") Duarte de, 63
Perón, Juan Domíngo, 56, 57
Persian empire, 11
Personal property taxes, 178
Peru, xv
Peterson, V. G., 446
Phang, Sock-Yong, 447
PHARE (*Pologne-Hongrie: assistance à la restructuration des economies*), 208
Philadelphia, Pennsylvania, 151–153, 159
Phillips Petroleum Company, 81
Physiocracy, 49
Pikler, Dr. Julius J., 260–262
Pinochet, Gen. Augusto, 86, 87
Pittsburgh, Pennsylvania
    federal urban renewal program inspired by, 168, 180
    "Golden Triangle," 168
    Improvement District, 173, 180 n. 42
    two-rate property tax in, 168
Plato, xl, 40
Plymouth, Montserrat, 124
Poole, Austin Lane (quoted), 39
Poor Relief, 41, 120
Popitz, Johannes, 227
Port Elizabeth, South Africa, 302, 304, 308
Port Moresby, Papua New Guinea, 386, 388
Potash, 72, 73
Prentice, P.I., xxviii
Prescribed Infrastructure Development, 394
Prest, A.R. (quoted), 252
Pretoria, South Africa, 293, 308
Price, George, 123
Price, Will, 151
Pringles District, Argentina, 54

Privatization, xxxvii, 7, 10, 15, 17, 20, 60, 61, 68, 206, 209, 265, 266, 277, 285, 420, 434
Progress and Poverty, xix, 53, 145, 187, 223–225, 259, 260, 338, 418, 422
Property taxation. See individual countries
Proposition 13, California, 181
Public Charges Upon Land Values, xxiii, xxxiv
Public debt, 6, 7, 14, 16–18, 21, 22
Public domain
  ancient, 12
  feudal, 28
  in Argentina, 49
  in Denmark, 192
  in Fiji, 326
  in Finland, 2212
  in Hong Kong, 346
  in Hungary, 260
  in Israel, xxxv
  in Kiao-chau, 367
  in New Zealand, 433
  in Singapore, 346
  in Tanzania, 280–282
  in US, 139, 140, 164, 165
Puig, Magin, 53
Punic War, Second, 17

Q

Quebec (province), 69, 72, 74
Queen Anne's Bounty, 241
Queensland, 399, 401–409
Queenstown, New Zealand, 426

R

Rabaul, Papua New Guinea, 388
Recca, Lucio, 51
Radical Civic Union, Argentina, 55. 58

Radical Liberal Party, Denmark, 193
Raffles, Sir Stamford, 344, 345
Railroads, 76, 154, 165, 226, 366
Ralston, Jackson H., xxxvii
Ramsey, Peter (quoted), 41
Rating. See individual countries: listed also under local land tax.
Ravignani, Emilio, 55
Rawson, Mary (quoted), 65
Reagan Tax Reform Act, US (1986), 81
Real estate, tax categories of, in Germany, 228
Recoupment of infrastructure costs, 239, 252, 253
Reece, Barry F. (quoted), 434
Reed, Stephen R.(quoted), 172
Rees, W.L. and L., 437
Rent
    defined, ix
    converted into mortgage interest, 18
    non-speculative, may be borne by sites without sale value, xxii
"Rental," xxii
Republic, The, Plato, xl, 40
Reserve Bank, New Zealand, 433
Resource Rentals for Revenue, xxxvii, 436
Reventlow, Count Christian Detlev, 186
Rhodesia and Nyasaland, Federation of, 285
Rhodesia Municipal Ordinance (1914), 285, 288
Ricardian rent theory, ix–xi
Ricardo, David, ix–xi, 241
Richard I, the Lionhearted (king of England), 37
Riebeeck, Jan van, 300
Rivadavia, Bernardino, 49–51, 53
Robertson, Rev. Pat, xxiv
Robin Hood, 38
Roman empire, 221, 24, 27, 29–31, 33, 240, 241
Roman land tax (tributum), 30
Roman republic, 28
Rosas, Gen. Juan Manuel de, 52
Rosslyn, Virginia, 160–162
Royal Commission on Local Government Finance, New, 428

Rural land taxation
  in Africa, 291
  in Caribbean, 117
  in feudal England, 32–36
  in Nicaragua, xiv
Russia, xxxiii, xxxv, 174
Russian Cities, Union of, xxxiii
Rybeck, Walter, xv–xvii, (quoted) xxiii, 111, 137, 447
Ryot tax, 207

S

Saenz Peña, Roque, 54
"Sagebrush revolution," 165
Saladin Tithe, 37
Salem, Montserrat, 124
Sales taxes, 6, 7, 24, 31, 144, 171
Salinas de Gortari, Carlos, 131
Salisbury, Southern Rhodesia (now Harare, Zimbabwe), 288
Samuels, Warren J., 448
Smallholders Party, Hungary, 263, 265, 267
San Diego, California, 163
Sandler, Hector Raúl, 58, 60, 62
Santiago, Chile, 91
Saskatchewan, 66, 72
Saxons, 32, 33
Schrameier, Ludwig W., 368
Schumpeter, Joseph A. (quoted), 222
Scornik Gerstein, Fernando ("the present writer"), 49, 448
Scottish Ogilvie Council, 244
Scranton, Pennsylvania, 168, 169, 177
Scutage, 36, 38
"Second Land Reform," Taiwan, 335, 336
Sehested, Hannibal, 186
Seisachtheia, 14
Seligman, Edwin R. A. (quoted), 140
Senegal, xv
Serf, 14, 34, 42

Severance taxes. See also specific extractive resources; Mineral deposits: public revenue treatment of; Mining
Servicio de Impuest Internos (SII), Chile, 88, 89, 92
Seward, William H., 174
Sewer Acts of 1427 and 1531, Great Britain, 244
Seymour Shire, Victoria, 414
Shakerton, Massachusetts, 148
Shakhbut, Sheikh (emir of Abu Dhabi), 324
Shantung Peninsula, China, 365
Shaw, George Bernard, 241
Shearman, Thomas G. (quoted), xxxi, 319
Silagi, Michael (quoted), 366
Simes Committee, Great Britain, 242, 243
Singapore, 344–350
    and Hong Kong, similarities between, 337–339
    capital gains taxation in, 346
    Control of Rent Act, 347
    Economic Development Board, 349
    economic development in, 348–350
    Land Acquisition Act of 1966, 346
    motor vehicle taxation in, 348
    public leasehold rent in, 346
    subsidized housing in, 351
    Urban Redevelopment Authority, 349
Single Tax, xi, xxx, xxxviii, 67, 197, 223, 225, 242
Single tax enclaves, US, 147–153
    Fairhope, Alabama, 148–151
    Free Acres, New Jersey, 148
    Halidon, Maine, 148
    Shakerton, Massachusetts, 148
    Tahanto, Massachusetts, 148
    the Ardens, Delaware, 151–153
    Trapelo, Massachusetts, 148
"Single tax limited," Abu Dhabi, 317–320
Sino-British Joint Declaration, 1984, 339
Sippar, Babylonia, 10
Site value. See also Land value

Site value rating. See Land-value taxation: listed both separately
    and under individual countries
Skate, Bill, 387
Slavery, 29, 144
Smith, Adam, 18
Snowden, Philip, 242
Socage tenure, 43
Social Agrarian Party, Argentina, 57
Social classes in medieval England. See England: social classes in
    medieval
Social Credit, 53
Social Democratic Party, Denmark, 193
Social Science Society, Hungary, 260
Social Security, 7, 21, 22, 318, 418
Socialist government, British Columbia, 71
Socialist Party, Argentina, 55
Socialist Party, Hungary, 265
Sokeman, 35
Solon, 5, 13, 14
Somers system, 178
Sopron, Hungary, 261
South Africa, 299–312
    land taxation mostly urban in, 300
    land-value taxation as percentage of total municipality, 301
    recent extension of land-value taxation in, 304–310
    rental value of land in, 311
South African Agricultural Union, 309
South Australia, 399–408
South Melbourne, Australia, 415
South Moresby Island, British Columbia, 75
Southern Rhodesia, 288
Southfield, Michigan, 160, 162, 163
Späth, Lothar, 233
Speculation, land. See Land speculation
St. Albans, Suzanne (quoted), 319
Starke, Dr. Viggo (quoted), 193–195
Stavad, Ole, 201
Stenton (quoted), 36

Stephen I (St. Stephen), King of Hungary, 268
Stephens, Donald (quoted), 151
Stephens, Frank, 151
Stibbe, W., 307
Strasma, John, 449
Subsidized housing: in
  Abu Dhabi, 318
  Hong Kong, 344
  Singapore, 351
  US, 158
Sumer, 5, 10, 14, 19
Sun Yat-sen, Dr. (quoted), 327–328, 368
Supreme Court, US, 154, 155
Surrey, British Columbia, 67
Sven Forkbeard, King of Denmark, 185
"Swamp decree," 223
Sydney, Australia, 429
Szeged, Hungary, 261

T

Tahanto, Massachusetts, 148
Taiwan, 327–336
  house tax in, 332
  land speculation in, 334
  Land Tax Law (1977), 328
  land-value increment tax in, 331
  land-value tax in, 330
  local tax jurisdictions in, 328, 329
  real property assessment in, 330–332
  Statute for Equalization of Urban Land Rights, 328
Tallage, 39
Tallinn, Estonia, 205, 207, 209
Talmudic commentary, xxv
T'ang dynasty, 332
Tanzania, 280–282
  Land (Rents and Service Charge) Act (1974), 293
  Local Government (District Authorities) Act (1982), 293

Rent Restriction Act (1962), 281
Rent Restriction Act (1984), 293
Urban Authorities (Rating) Act (1983), 281
Tartu, Estonia, 207
Tasmania, 399–407, 409
Taxation. See also specific taxes listed both separately and under
    individual countries.
  as military tribute, 10–12
  considered degrading by ancients if regular and direct
  defined, ix
  evolution of, in Sumer and Babylonia, 4–7
  of Jewish ghettos in Spain, 11
Tax equity, 208, 291
Tax exemption. See also Abatements
"Tax Freedom Day," 44
Tax Havens, 21, 126, 127
Tax Havens of the World, by W.H. and D.B. Diamond (cited), 122
Taylor, L.D. "Single Tax," 67
Technocracy, xl
Teisaire, Rear Admiral Alberto, 57
Teutonic Knights, 205
Thatcher, Margaret, 68, 73, 251
Three Kingdom Period, Korea, 371
"Three Principles of the People" (Sun Yat-sen), 327, 335
Tideman, Nicolaus, xvii, xxix, (quoted) 218
Tildy, Zoltan, 263
Tirpitz, Admiral Alfred von, 366, 368
Tithe, Old Testament, x, xi, xxv, 9, 37, 300
Titusville, Pennsylvania, 169
Tocqueville, Alexis de (quoted), 42
Tokugawa land tax, 355, 356
Tokugawa shogunate, 354
Tomson, Aivar, 449
Toronto, Ontario, 67, 77
Town and Country Planning Acts of 1909–32, Great Britain, 245
Town and Country Planning Act of 1947, Great Britain, 245
Town and Country Planning Acts of 1953, 1954, and 1959, Great
    Britain, 247, 248

Town Planning Ordinance, Hong Kong, 341
Townsend Plan, xl, 53
Toynbee, Arnold, 17
Tradable licenses, 83
TransAlaskan Pipeline, 174
Transvaal, 300–303
Transvaal Provincial Ordinance No. 1 (1916), 301
Tranzrail, New Zealand, 434
Trapelo, Massachusetts, 148
Trevelyan, G.M. (quoted), 35
Trobriand Islands, 387
Trott, Harlan, 155
Trudeau, Pierre E., 70
Tsinan, China, 366
Tsingtao, China, 226, 365, 366
Tudor England, 40–42
Turkey, xv
Turlock Irrigation District, California, 155
Turner, Frederick Jackson, 178
Tutu, Archbishop Desmond, xxiv
Two-rate property taxation, xvi, 164, 166–172, 177, 187, 399
    in Australia, 399
    in Denmark, 187
    in US, 164, 166–172, 177

U

UAE, 316–318, 321, 323, 324
Uganda, 274–276, 280, 282–284, 290
    Land Reform Act (1975), 283
Ujpest, Hungary, 261
Ullman, Viggo, 187
Union of Argentine People (UDELPA), 57
Uniontown, Pennsylvania, 169
Unit value methodology, 90
Unitarios (political faction), Argentina, 51
United Arab Emirates ("the Federation"), 316–318, 321, 323, 324

United Committee for the Taxation of Land Values, Great Britain, 243
United Nations, 113, 123, 268, 388
United Nations Declaration of Human Rights, 268
United States, 137–182
    assessed value of lands and buildings in, 140–142
    benefit assessment districts in, 142
    estimated proportion of property taxes represented, 141
    Homestead Act (1862), 140
    International Rivers Treaty (1911), 73
    local land-value taxation in, 142, 143
    personal property taxes in, 141
    public lands in, 164–166
    real property taxes at all levels of government in, 173
    Revenue Act (1916), xxi
    single tax enclaves in, 147–152
    the frontier in, 144
    two-rate property taxes in, 164, 166–172, 177
Urban Land Institute, 161
Urban land taxes, 170
Urban Redevelopment Authority, Singapore, 349
Urban renewal, 158, 429
User charges
    in Australia, 400
    New Zealand, 431
    South Africa, 299
    taxes on land-values defined as, xxiii
Usufruct, 3, 5, 7, 9
Uthwatt Committee, Great Britain, 242

V

Valdemar the Great, King of Denmark, 185
Vancouver, British Columbia, 65, 67, 68, 76, 77
Versailles, Treaty of, 229
Vestry system, 120
Vickrey, William S., xxvii
Victoria (Australia), 399, 401–410, 414, 415

Vidal-Naquet, P., and Austin, M.M. (quoted), 5, 12
Villalobos-Dominquez, Carlos, 54
Virginia. See also Rosslyn, Virginia
Virtanen, Pekka V., 449

W

Wagner, Adolf, 223, 225
Waimakariri, New Zealand, 429
Waitakere, New Zealand, 429
Waitangi, Treaty of, 417, 421
Waitangi Tribunal, 422
Wales, Land Authority for, 251
Warren, Fiske, 148, 151
Wars of the Roses, 40
Washington (state), 82
Washington, George, 139
Washington, Pennsylvania, 162, 169
Wasserman, Louis, 197, (quoted) 203 n. 8
Water, xxviii, xxxv, 72, 75, 78, 90, 142, 152, 154–156, 165, 223, 224,
    299, 322, 391, 407, 408, 412, 424, 432
Water rights, 78
Webb, Beatrice, 241
Webb, Sidney, 241
Wehrly, Max, 161
Wellington, New Zealand, xxxvi, 423, 425, 426, 428, 429, 431, 433
Wellington Rates Review Committee, New Zealand, 426
Wells, H.G., 241
Welsh Development Agency, 251
Wergild, 33
Wessex, 332, 33
West Virginia, 177
Western Australia, 399, 401, 402, 406, 407, 409
Wigmore, Noel, 413
Wilks, H.M. (cited), 241, 243
William I, the Conqueror (King of England), 35, 36
Winnipeg, Manitoba, 67
Wisconsin, 86, 177

Wolsey, Thomas Cardinal, 41
Wonthaggi, Australia, 415
World Bank, xiv, 94, 279, 283, 286, 290
"World territorial rent," 321–323
Wright Act (Irrigation District Act), California, 154–156
Wright, C.C., 154

Y

Yamasaki, Yoshisaburo, 450
Yardland, 34
Young Democrats Party, Hungary, 266

Z

Zambia, 274, 276, 284, 285, 287–290
Zayed, Sheikh (emir of Abu Dhabi), 316, (quoted) 322, 324, 325
Zimbabwe, 274, 276, 284, 287–291
Zomba, Malawi, 285